THE
EUROPEAN PAYMENTS UNION

THE EUROPEAN PAYMENTS UNION

Financial Diplomacy in the 1950s

by

JACOB J. KAPLAN

and

GÜNTHER SCHLEIMINGER

CLARENDON PRESS · OXFORD

1989

Oxford University Press, Walton Street, Oxford OX2 6DP

Oxford New York Toronto
Delhi Bombay Calcutta Madras Karachi
Petaling Jaya Singapore Hong Kong Tokyo
Nairobi Dar es Salaam Cape Town
Melbourne Auckland

and associated companies in
Berlin Ibadan

Oxford is a trade mark of Oxford University Press

Published in the United States
by Oxford University Press, New York

British Library Cataloguing in Publication Data
Kaplan, Jacob J.
The European Payments Union: financial diplomacy in
the 1950s
1. European Payments Union, history
I. Title II. Schleiminger, Günther
332.1′55′094
ISBN 0-19-828675-9

Library of Congress Cataloging in Publication Data
Kaplan, Jacob J. (Jacob Julius), 1920-
The European Payments Union: financial diplomacy in the 1950s
by Jacob J. Kaplan and Günther Schleiminger.
Bibliography: Includes index.
1. European Payments Union—History. 2. International finance-
-History. I. Schleiminger, Günther. II. Title.
HG3881.K28 1989 341.7′54—dc20 89-33657
ISBN 0-19-828675-9

Text processed by Oxford Text System
Printed in Great Britain
by Biddles Ltd.
Guildford and King's Lynn

To
Hans Karl von Mangoldt
1896-1972

Foreword

by
Alexandre Lamfalussy
General Manager, Bank for International Settlements

THE creation and operation of the European Payments Union constitute an important chapter in the economic history of western Europe since the Second World War. Set up in 1950 within the framework of the Organisation for European Economic Co-operation and supported at its outset by the Marshall Plan, the EPU was the institution through which the countries of western Europe freed their mutual trade and payments relations from the post-war straitjacket of bilateralism and import restrictions. Moreover, contrary to the expectations of some observers, the liberalization of intra-European trade during the EPU years was accompanied by a substantial, although less comprehensive, reduction of quota restrictions on European imports from the dollar area. These developments paved the way for restoring the external convertibility of EPU countries' currencies at the end of 1958. In short, the EPU was a successful pioneering effort in economic and monetary co-operation. The authors of this book, one American and the other European, both represented their countries on the board that managed the Union's affairs. Their account of the Union's origins, its workings, its achievements, and the difficulties it encountered during the eight and a half years of its existence has therefore been written with the benefit of inside knowledge.

The BIS, which has sponsored the production of this book, has a twofold interest in the history of the EPU. Firstly, the Bank was the Union's agent responsible for operating its monthly compensation and settlements system. Secondly, the BIS is, as the EPU was, an institution whose *raison d'être* is to promote international co-operation. During the 1950s, central bank co-operation at the BIS was taking place in parallel with the work of the EPU. The most important members of the Union were those countries whose central bank Governors were meeting every month in Basle. This meant that the economic and monetary problems which EPU countries faced were discussed both in Paris, at EPU meetings, and in Basle. It hardly needs to be added that the interest of the BIS in international co-operation is still very much alive today.

A number of factors combined to account for the success of the EPU. Some of these are to be found in the political and economic circumstances of that time and others in the mechanism of the system itself and the way in which it was jointly operated.

One external factor which both favoured the launching of the EPU experiment and contributed to its success was the political climate at the end of the 1940s. The experience of two world wars and the great depression, within a time span of no more than thirty years, had produced a deep-seated desire for a better world, both politically and economically, and a widespread belief in the need for international co-operation in place of the conflicts of the past.

Before the Second World War had ended, that belief had already led, in the political field, to the creation of the United Nations Organisation and, in the economic and monetary field, to the setting up of the International Monetary Fund and the World Bank. Then, in 1948, when the post-war economic situation of western Europe proved to be more serious than had been foreseen, the United States launched the Marshall Plan for European economic recovery. Seventeen western European countries which, with the exception of Switzerland, were recipients of Marshall Aid responded by creating the OEEC as a permanent institution for European economic co-operation. Public and political sentiment in favour of international co-operation was reinforced by the challenges presented by the outbreak of the cold war. In addition, with the economic sovereignty of European countries being severely limited by their dependence on Marshall Aid, the United States was able to use the influence conferred on it by its predominant position in the world at that time to give strong support, with both ideas and money, to the launching and operation of the EPU.

Economic factors, too, were favourable to the EPU initiative. One of these was a widespread recognition that the conduct of intra-European trade and payments on a bilateral basis was a major obstacle to achieving the aims of the European recovery programme and the OEEC. Another was the fact that the EPU existed during a period of fixed exchange rates, when the Bretton Woods par value system was in operation. By the early 1950s all EPU countries, except Portugal and Switzerland, were members of the IMF and most of them had declared par values to the Fund that could only be changed in situations of 'fundamental disequilibrium'. Fixed exchange rates, plus the absence at that time of well-developed international financial markets in which countries could borrow to supplement their monetary reserves, thus provided a strong element of balance-of-payments discipline for EPU countries.

The main factors internal to the EPU system which contributed to its success were three in number: the legal framework of the EPU Agreement itself; the balance between financing and adjustment of payments surpluses and deficits that was built into the Union's settlement mechanism; and the way in which payments crises in member countries came to be handled cooperatively between the individual countries concerned and the Union's Managing Board at the centre of the system.

The importance of the legal framework within which the EPU operated can hardly be overstated. The EPU Agreement was a treaty between the seventeen member countries, who thereby agreed to observe the rules of the system and the balance-of-payments and policy constraints it contained. Without the willing co-operation of member countries' governments and their central banks the achievements of the EPU would have been impossible.

No less important was the balance between the financing and adjustment of intra-European payments disequilibrium that was built into the system. On the financing side EPU members were able to economize in two ways on the use of their scarce monetary reserves in settling their payments imbalances. In the first place, there was the offsetting of countries' monthly bilateral surpluses and deficits with each other, which left each member to settle only its net surplus or deficit with the rest of the membership taken together. In effect, the EPU system made member countries' currencies freely transferable between one another, in so far as those currencies were held on accounts at central banks. Secondly, the monthly settlements of each country's net position *vis-à-vis* the rest of the Union's membership were made partly through the giving and taking of credit. This both supplemented countries' monetary reserves and supported the process of liberalizing intra-European trade.

At the same time the EPU system promoted balance-of-payments adjustment in two ways: by setting quota limits for each country, beyond which it could no longer automatically run further surpluses or deficits in the system; and through the cash element in the monthly settlements, which during the early years of the Union's existence progressively increased as deficit countries made cumulative use of their quota facilities.

The third main ingredient in the EPU's success was the development of a system for joint handling, by the Managing Board and the countries concerned, of the payments difficulties that members experienced during the life of the Union. Such difficulties threatened to, and in some cases actually did, exhaust countries' quota limits for automatic settlements of their deficits in the system, as well as endangering these countries' progress towards liberalizing their intra-European trade. When such situations arose, the Managing Board was empowered to propose policy changes to the governments concerned and to offer them, if necessary, temporary special assistance. In some instances, the Managing Board in effect provided conditional balance-of-payments finance for deficit countries, of a kind essentially similar to that which is available at the International Monetary Fund. In addition the Board urged structural surplus countries to take action to limit their surpluses, notably through further liberalization of imports. In these ways, the EPU developed a co-operative approach to countries' trade and payments problems.

While the history of the EPU is important in its own right, its influence did not cease with the liquidation of the Union at the end of 1958. Moreover, problems of the sort that arose during the EPU years have been encountered again, albeit in different circumstances, both in Europe and elsewhere during the thirty years that have elapsed since the Union was liquidated. It is therefore pertinent to look briefly at what the legacy of the EPU was in Europe and at whether the experience of those years may be of any relevance for those countries which, whether in Europe or in a wider than European context, are today attempting to bring about co-ordination of their economic and monetary policies.

By demonstrating the benefits that western European countries could derive from policies of economic integration and from practising a co-operative approach to their trade and payments problems, the EPU pointed the way to the further progress in those areas that has since been made by the countries of the European Community. Moreover, the experience of the European Monetary System has confirmed the importance of certain salient features of the EPU in promoting international policy co-ordination.

Like the EPU, the EMS is a system in which the member countries have accepted certain obligations, embodied in an international agreement, with the governments and central banks of the member countries having joint responsibility for the workings of the system. The principal constraint in the system on countries' policies is provided—but only for those EMS countries which belong to it—by the exchange rate mechanism. This regime of fixed but adjustable exchange rates, of the kind that existed under the old Bretton Woods system, has contributed to a marked convergence of member countries' economic performances and their economic policies. In particular, the setting of rather narrow limits to the permitted movements of nominal exchange rates has contributed to the reduction of inflation differentials between countries that are members of the exchange rate mechanism, through the discipline it has exerted on both their policies and their wage developments. At the same time periodical adjustments of exchange rates have given the system sufficient flexibility to avoid major and sustained departures from purchasing power parities of the kind that have repeatedly affected the main floating currencies since the end of the Bretton Woods par value system in March 1973. The fact that these adjustments have remained small has meant that the exchange rate constraint retained its ability to shape the behaviour of both governments and labour market participants and has led to a gradual but decisive stabilization of exchange rate expectations.

It is, of course, true that certain external circumstances have contributed to the success of the EMS, as they did to that of the EPU. Firstly, the convergence of the EMS countries' inflation rates was helped by the widespread adoption of firm anti-inflationary policies in the industrial world at the end of the 1970s. Secondly, the appreciation of the dollar during the first half of the 1980s helped to limit upward pressures on the Deutsche Mark at a time when inflation differentials between EMS countries were still rather wide. Thirdly, since the dollar began to depreciate in 1985 the EMS has been helped by the favourable effect on member countries' balances of payments of the major decline in oil prices. However, the key to the success of the EMS has been the exchange rate mechanism.

Turning from the European context to the wider one of the international monetary system as a whole, does the experience of the EPU years suggest any lessons for the international policy co-ordination efforts that the leading industrial countries have been making since 1985? There are, of course, some similarities between these efforts and the workings of the EPU or, for that matter, the EMS. There is joint surveillance by the participants of their economic policies and performances; there are policy commitments undertaken by participants and published in the communiqués that customarily follow their meetings; and there are exchange rate targets, although these are not published. However, the differences between this type of co-ordination and that practised in the EPU are greater than the similarities. Firstly, it is not placed within the framework of an international treaty, which formally imposes on the participants obligations to co-operate with one another. This means that the exchange rate and other policy undertakings of participants do not have the same binding quality as those which were contained in the EPU, or which are present in the EMS. Secondly, the fact that the exchange rate undertakings are in the form of target zones for participants' exchange rates *vis-à-vis* one another, and that these targets are not published, means that they do not stabilize market expectations about the future course of exchange rates in the same way as a system of fixed but adjustable rates can do.

These co-ordination efforts certainly have some successes to their credit. Examples are the Plaza Agreement of 1985, and the central banks' joint response to the 1987 stock market crash and their co-ordinated attempts during the past year to ward off a resurgence of inflationary expectations. However, such actions have occurred only at times when the participants were able to agree both that a problem existed and on joint action to deal with it. Moreover, they have mostly been limited to central bank intervention in the exchange markets and/or monetary policy measures. Fiscal policy measures, with the exception of Japan's expansionary budget package in the spring of 1987, have been less convincing. In addition, when the preconditions for joint action were not present the co-ordination process has at times appeared to falter, with policy-makers in different countries giving conflicting signals to the markets.

What conclusions does this experience with pragmatic, case-by-case co-ordination of policies suggest? Is it that joint crisis management, while welcome, is not enough? Do these efforts need to be made systematic in character, as they were in the EPU, and, in particular, to include some sort of explicit exchange rate commitments, to provide both a formal constraint on the behaviour of policy-makers and economic agents and an anchor for market expectations about the future course of exchange rates?

There is no simple answer. Powerful arguments can be advanced in favour of the view that the introduction of formal exchange rate commitments is simply not feasible. In the first place, the present situation is far from being an ideal one in which to introduce them. There are still very large payments imbalances in a number of the largest industrial countries. It is hard to guess what would be a sustainable pattern of current-account balances, and it would be even harder to estimate the exchange rates that would be compatible with such a pattern. Secondly, because of these imbalances, and despite the progress made since the Plaza meeting in correcting earlier exchange rate misalignments and reducing short-term volatility of exchange rates, market expectations about the future course of the main floating currencies are far from stable, not least because of the long experience of exchange rate misalignments and volatility since the breakdown of the Bretton Woods par value system. Thirdly, the leap that would be involved in moving from the present sort of pragmatic, case-by-case policy co-ordination to a world-wide system of formal exchange rate commitments would require tough negotiations. Reaching an agreement could turn out to be a much more demanding task in the present multi-polar world economic power structure than it was in the immediate post-war years characterized by the unquestioned domination of the United States. And, as is well shown in this book, even in those circumstances the negotiations leading to the EPU agreement were far from easy. In other words, circumstances are not as favourable to the institution of a more formalized system of policy co-ordination as they were in the very different situation, both political and economic, that existed when the EPU was established.

These are weighty objections, but we should at the same time be aware of the costs involved in exchange rate volatility, major exchange rate misalignments, and the associated large and sticky current-account imbalances. These engender a climate of uncertainty which is the worst enemy of investment. They are detrimental to financial stability. They induce a misallocation of resources. All these are obvious costs, even though difficult to measure. But in addition I see a great risk that exchange rate misalignments may lead to the re-emergence of both trade and financial protectionism which could result in a major set-back in the process of economic and financial integration.

The experience of the EPU took place in a world that was very different from that which faces policy-makers today. At that time the goal was to achieve greater economic and financial integration. Today's challenge is to preserve the progress that has been made in these areas and the benefits that have flowed from it. The EPU system was a creature of its time, many of whose features could have no application today. Nevertheless, the experience of the EPU suggests to me the desirability, in dealing with current international payments problems, of seeking to extend the scope of international policy co-ordination beyond crisis management, in which it has repeatedly proved its worth, to more ambitious goals.

Basle
February 1989

Preface

ENCOURAGEMENT to write this book came from many quarters, both public and private. The authors are grateful to all who gave the project material and moral support. Their work depended on assistance from international economic and financial institutions and from national agencies. Last, but not least, was the contribution of individuals who were among the key players on the stage of international finance during the 1950s.

The preparation of the book was sponsored by the Bank for International Settlements and several European central banks. The Organisation for Economic Co-operation and Development provided the authors with relevant original documentation, as did the International Monetary Fund. Additional documents were obtained from national archives and from central banks. Curators, historians, and librarians of these institutions were of great help in identifying and assembling relevant materials.

The authors are particularly indebted to Harry Travers, a former staff member of the OECD, for performing much of the preliminary work — the extraction and organization of documents from the files of the OECD and of several national agencies.

Interpretations of the documents derive, in large part, from the authors' personal involvement in many of the events. A number of other participants graciously agreed to be interviewed and to review drafts. They corrected, supplemented, and corroborated the account.

For perceptive suggestions after reviewing draft manuscripts, the authors are especially indebted to Gérard Bauer, Willy Bruppacher, Pierre Calvet, Theodore Geiger, Guillaume Guindey, Alexandre Hay, Otto Pfleiderer, F. J. Portsmore, Sir Denis Rickett, Frank Southard, and Baron Cecil de Strycker. Michael Dealtry, Rolf Gocht, and Edgar Paltzer also read the manuscript and commented extensively as interested observers of the events at that time.

The authors, of course, accept full responsibility for the contents of the book. It is not an official history, nor has the final manuscript been reviewed by any of the sponsors or readers, or by any of the international or national institutions that appear in its pages.

Roberta Kaplan at first undertook to harmonize the writing styles of two different authors. Ultimately she carefully edited the entire manuscript, with particular attention to its readability. She contributed substantially to the authors' efforts to make the book comprehensible to an audience without great proficiency in the technical intricacies of international finance.

Ruth Keller carefully transcribed the authors' drafts and numerous revisions, as well as performing a variety of administrative chores. At a later stage, Arlette Erbland took over these responsibilities and completed the manuscript.

Throughout the project, the BIS provided efficient and essential support. Under the leadership of Alexandre Lamfalussy, General Manager, a large number of its staff contributed an invaluable array of substantive, technical, and administrative assistance.

J.J.K. and G.S.

Basle, Switzerland
November 1988

Contents

List of Tables

Abbreviations

Amb.	Ambassador
APU	Atlantic Payments Union
Benelux	Belgium, Netherlands, Luxembourg customs union
BIS	Bank for International Settlements
CEEC	Committee for European Economic Co-operation
Com.	Committee
del.	delegation
DM	Deutsche Mark
ECA	US Economic Cooperation Administration
EDC	European Defence Community
EMA	European Monetary Agreement
EPU	European Payments Union
ERP	US European Recovery Program (Marshall Plan)
Euratom	European Atomic Energy Community
Exec.	Executive
Finebel	Proposed economic grouping of France, Italy, and Benelux
FOA	US Foreign Operations Administration
FY	Financial Year
GATT	General Agreement on Tariffs and Trade
IBRD	International Bank for Reconstruction and Development (World Bank)
IEPS	Intra-European Payments and Compensations Scheme
IMF	International Monetary Fund
Min.	Minister or Ministerial
MSA	US Mutual Security Administration
NAC	US National Advisory Council on International Monetary and Financial Problems
NATO	North Atlantic Treaty Organisation
OECD	Organisation for Economic Co-operation and Development
OEEC	Organisation for European Economic Co-operation

PRO	Public Records Office of the United Kingdom
Rep.	Representative
Sec.	Secretary
T	Treasury
tel.	telegram
UK	United Kingdom (Great Britain)
UN	United Nations
Uniscan	United Kingdom and Scandinavia economic group
UNRRA	United Nations Relief and Rehabilitation Administration
US	United States of America

Introduction: What was the EPU?

The European Payments Union was conceived during the last weeks of 1949 and liquidated during the last days of 1958. Having completed its work and fulfilled its purpose, it was dissolved.

It was probably the only multilateral institution created after World War II whose claim to unmitigated success has gone unchallenged. Yet, despite its singular and successful record, it is almost unknown today. Its name is rarely recognized outside the declining community involved in international monetary policy at the time. Otherwise, only chroniclers of European economic history of the 1950s can recall its existence. Histories of twentieth-century Europe and modern textbooks on international finance seldom list the EPU in their indices. Not many contemporary experts in these fields can give a reasonably accurate explanation of what it was or what it did—let alone how it operated.

A creature and component of the Organisation for European Economic Co-operation, the EPU was both an instrument of Europe's economic integration and a half-way house in its transition from bilateralism to currency convertibility. It made all the currencies of western Europe transferable into one another, making it possible to free intra-European trade from quantitative restrictions and discriminatory regulations. Its Managing Board became the principal forum for multilateral negotiations about European financial policies.

Subsequent literary neglect probably stems from emphasis during its lifetime on the EPU payments mechanism and the associated trade rules, matters of limited contemporary relevance. Information about these features of the EPU system was reported and widely discussed at the time. Information about the negotiations within the Managing Board and its creative influence on policy-making was less readily accessible, though both were critical to the EPU's survival and achievements. Unprecedented in its intensity and character, EPU diplomacy produced decisions and agreements of contemporary significance and lasting importance. In the 1950s, the European Payments Union sponsored policies to correct European payments imbalances and negotiated a joint European approach to currency convertibility. The International Monetary Fund, one of its severest early critics, has noted its significance. The official history of the IMF comments that '. . . to many observers, for some years following the establishment of the EPU, the focal point of important monetary decisions was that organisation rather than the Fund.'[1]

Major attention is given in this book to the financial diplomacy that enveloped the EPU and dominated the work of its Managing Board. The results of that diplomacy and the achievements of the system deserve greater recognition than they have received. In its day, the EPU managed the settlement of two-thirds of all the world's international economic transactions. Of even more significance, it was a necessary condition for the most important efforts in this century to promote economic welfare in Europe. They were:

1. the modernization and industrialization of the economy of western Europe;

2. the freeing of international trade and payments from a variety of nationalistic, autarchic restrictions—making possible an enormous increase in economic efficiency and international specialization on a global scale;

3. the integration of the economies of western Europe into a single market, providing consumers and business enterprises with relatively free access to the output of farms and factories situated in other countries;

4. the adjustment of economic policies to control foreign exchange imbalances, an essential factor in the successful functioning of the EPU.

All four of these developments have been part of a historical process that has yet to run its full course. Once again, further progress in each seems beset by extraordinary obstacles. At the beginning of 1950, however, the process was stymied by even more difficult—some thought insurmountable—barriers. Indeed, it had then been blocked for more than thirty years, since the outbreak of the First World War.

The EPU provided the environment and the impetus for getting the process going and surmounting the hurdles of the time. The results have been striking. By a variety of measures, the growth in economic welfare during the past 35 years has been without historical precedent.

Perhaps this would have happened anyway. Perhaps the forces that brought the EPU into being and made it work were so powerful that the obstacles would have been overcome by some other means. Other means might have been even more effective. Perhaps! But in 1950, the obstacles seemed even more formidable than those that now seem to impede further economic progress on a global scale. Moreover, they had not been overcome—except for a limited time and in limited areas—for several decades.

For half a century, academic experts and policy-makers have pondered numerous designs for an international monetary system that would accommodate unexpected major events that are both inevitable and

---

[1] de Vries, Horsefield, et al. (1969), ii. 317.

inevitably seem to threaten the survival of any existing system. The EPU passed such tests. For its members, it proved flexible enough to survive the economic and financial consequences of the Korean War, the Suez crisis of 1956, hostilities in South East Asia and North Africa, the demise of the French Fourth Republic, extensive decolonization, and major defence efforts. None of these sources of strain had been anticipated. Yet the system was able to function while the member economies prospered.

In the 1980s, the huge US balance-of-payments deficit and German and Japanese surpluses rank high on the international agenda. Quantitative restrictions and other non-tariff trade barriers have reappeared to menace the growth of world trade. The EPU was created to cope with just such problems. It maintained a tight link between liberalizing trade and freeing payments from restrictions.

Today's burden of international debts incurred by developing countries may seem overwhelming. In its last days, the EPU organized one of the first and most successful multilateral debt consolidation efforts. All the debts involved were paid off.

To be sure, the circumstances of the present and the particulars of its problems are different. Specific solutions and approaches will undoubtedly have to be different as well. Nonetheless, successful experience—even three decades old—should help us understand the contemporary aspects of these persistent issues.

Part One

Birth of the European Payments Union
1945-1950

1 The Age in which the EPU was Conceived

Western newspapers in the 1980s are full of stories about the weak dollar and the globalization of financial markets. Familiar with such conditions, their readers may have trouble envisaging the economic world in which the European Payments Union was conceived. That was barely forty years ago; yet the circumstances were radically different.

The European market in the late 1940s was neither Common, nor free, nor unsegmented. Some 200 bilateral trade agreements had been negotiated between the governments of continental Europe. Each of them limited the quantities of goods that citizens could purchase from the bilateral partner, resulting in a kind of barter trade. Each government used exchange controls and import restrictions to balance its exports and imports from every other country, because any deficit would have to be paid in dollars or gold, both desperately scarce. For a full decade after the end of World War II, the US dollar—not the Japanese yen or the Deutsche Mark—was in extremely short supply. It was the heyday of the 'almighty dollar'.

An international money market did not exist, and transfers of capital from one country to another were permitted only in exceptional circumstances. Maintaining a legal bank account in a foreign country or a foreign currency was out of the question. Living standards in Europe were low, perhaps at best half that in the United States.

The maze of restrictions on international trade and payments reduced the benefits that normally accrue from exchanging goods and services across national borders. Neither individuals nor businesses could meet their needs by buying better quality or lower priced products from other countries. All European countries needed to increase production levels, investments, and the competitiveness of their products; all such efforts were critically hampered by the lack of foreign exchange.

Only a small part of this state of affairs can be attributed to war damage, severe as it was. As early as 1948, industrial production on the Continent approached or exceeded that of 1937, the best prewar year.[1] In all of western Europe, only Germany was still producing well below its prewar level. However, North American industrial production was

[1] BIS, *Nineteenth Annual Report, 1948–49*, 57.

then 70 per cent higher than before the war. Competing with that modernized giant seemed an awesome task for European industrialists. Even those who might have had a reasonable chance of succeeding were reluctant to take the risk. Another decade would elapse before European manufacturers would begin to penetrate the US market on a significant scale.

The economic disruption that followed the war was much harder to rectify than the physical damage. The Soviet Union moved the boundaries of eastern Europe westward and diverted to its own purposes the supplies of food and raw materials that were previously exported to western Europe. By war's end, western Europe had sacrificed many of its prewar sources of foreign exchange. Overseas investments were liquidated to finance wartime requirements. European merchant fleets were decimated, and foreign exchange reserves were depleted during the war and the first postwar years. France, Greece, the Netherlands, Italy, Norway, and especially Great Britain were hard hit by these losses. In short, the sources of financing Europe's imports in prewar times were severely diminished. Furthermore, new sources of supply and new markets had to be developed to replace the ones in eastern Europe.

Damage from the war and subsequent dislocation were added to an unhappy heritage from the thirty years that had passed since the outbreak of the First World War. Nationalist excess had borne bitter fruit as it dominated that era of peacemaking, postwar reconstruction, and Depression. By 1948, production was approaching the level of the best prewar year; yet it was not enough to stabilize the political or the economic situation in Europe. The people of the Allied countries in World War II had high expectations of a better life in the postwar world.

Over-optimistic and misguided government policies were partly responsible for the shortages. However, those policies were carried out by democratically elected governments who thought they were responding to the felt needs of their constituencies. Not many constituencies looked back fondly on the interwar period.

THE INTERWAR PERIOD: A STORY OF FAILURE

Before World War I, the international economy was flourishing, despite sizeable cyclical swings. Increasing trade and investment were leading to more specialization in production and more efficient use of resources. The war brought this process to a halt; it had not regained its momentum when the next war broke out.

The interwar era was one of unalloyed nationalism, the glorification of the nation state. The peace treaties created on the continent of Europe new nation states, whose economic prospects were jeopardized by the trade barriers surrounding their traditional markets. Mercantilist thinking dominated international economic policy. Every country sought to promote its own economic interests, with little regard for the effect on others.

Central bank co-operation was initiated, but left much to be desired. The occasional international economic and monetary conferences yielded little in constructive results. Governments were particularly concerned that there be no 'interference' by other countries in their internal affairs. No internal affair seemed more important than economic policies, which were beyond the pale of discussion with other governments. Neither international organizations nor rules of conduct for international economic behaviour received serious recognition. Even the collection of statistics by international institutions was suspect. The League of Nations proved to be impotent.

In this climate, international trade was buffeted from every side. Attempts at stabilizing economies, after the inflationary abuses of World War I, had been uncoordinated. Both the British pound and the French franc were allowed to float in 1919 and depreciated sharply.[2] The French franc was stabilized against gold first in 1924 and again in 1926, but it was seriously undervalued. Reinforced by high tariff walls, the undervaluation resulted in large French accumulations of gold and foreign exchange. Britain stabilized against gold in 1925 at a rate that overvalued sterling and gravely damaged its export industries. These misguided attempts to re-establish the gold standard on the basis of old par values destroyed any possibility of maintaining a stable international monetary system or promoting a global free-trading system.

The Great Depression was spread from country to country, in part by rapid and unpredictable movements of capital by worried banks and investors. Thereafter, trade barriers of every variety swelled in size and number. Britain and the US devalued their currencies; but Belgium, France, Germany, Italy, Luxembourg, and the Netherlands refused to follow suit. Britain imposed a tariff, exempting imports from the Empire. These tariff preferences and the overvaluation of currencies in the western part of continental Europe led to a proliferation of trade restrictions. In 1930, France introduced quantitative restrictions to protect its agriculture from import competition. Thereafter, other countries began imposing quotas on imported goods to deal with shortages of foreign exchange. Quantitative restrictions soon became the principal trade barrier, prompting bilateral trade and clearing agreements to spread throughout Europe.[3]

The United States erected the infamous Smoot-Hawley tariff; the

---

[2] Kindleberger (1984), 391–2.
[3] Pollard (1981), ch. v.

United Kingdom reinforced the sterling area and the system of Imperial Preference. Japan sought an Asian Co-Prosperity sphere, and Schachtian Germany organized half of its foreign trade on the basis of bilateral clearing agreements. Despite universal import barriers, the European victors in World War I wanted reparations to be paid, and the United States insisted that its wartime loans to Allies be serviced.

Not surprisingly, the international economy and economic welfare were the principal victims of these autarchic policies. Individual countries enjoyed brief periods of economic resurgence at one time or another, but the Great Depression overwhelmed whatever gains had been realized. It is easy to conclude that economic nationalism sowed the seeds of World War II; some have argued that the war was its logical outcome.

The industrialization of Europe had been brought to a sharp halt by the First World War, and the subsequent recovery was very slow. The short-lived boom of 1925-9 was followed by the Depression, and the resumption of growth was again short-circuited by the Second World War. One historian concluded that there had been no net increase in the total real wealth of the United Kingdom between 1913 and 1951.[4]

Meanwhile, overseas competitors—especially the United States—greatly expanded and modernized their industrial plant, as well as their agricultural capacity, during both world wars and the 1920s. At the end of World War II, much of Europe's industrial capacity was old and its technology antiquated, not to mention damaged.

Even if post-World War II Europe had been able to divert production into exports, it would have had great difficulty in meeting the competitive pressure of US industrial and agricultural capacity. It now needed to export even more overseas than before the war to replace lost income from investments, shipping, and other services. Yet both competitiveness and capacity were lacking. Moreover, widespread social unrest and rising expectations made it difficult for the governments of liberated countries to restrain the expansion of money income and government services. Diverting production to export markets was thus doubly difficult—the home market wanted more goods, and European output was not competitive in export markets. Another two decades of heavy investment and rapid economic growth would be needed before the European economy could fully meet US competitive pressures.

In retrospect, it seems these problems could have been anticipated. They should have been readily apparent to those who laid plans for rebuilding the postwar international economy. Hindsight is, however, a poor basis for passing judgement. The fact is that the early planners grossly underestimated the problems.

[4] Matthews *et al.* (1982), quoted in Cairncross (1985), 8.

UNIVERSALIST PLANS FOR THE POSTWAR ECONOMY

After World War I, the populations of the victor countries had voiced an overwhelming urge for a return to 'normal'. Responsive governments had sought to restore prewar conditions. The same urge for normalcy was present after World War II, but this time it was associated with aspirations for something more. People wanted a better life than the prewar period had provided—more goods, more economic opportunity, more stability, and more security. They wanted to build a better international order—one that would be more durable and not break down into another global conflict, whether economic or military. British Prime Minister Winston Churchill and US President Franklin D. Roosevelt provided strong leadership for such aspirations. Indeed, they made them an integral part of their war effort and war aims.

On both sides of the Atlantic, planning for the postwar era began very early. John Maynard Keynes had achieved international recognition in 1919 for his book, *The Economic Consequences of the Peace*. It was a perceptive and forceful essay attacking the economic blinders of the policy-makers at the Versailles Peace Conference. To forestall a repetition of earlier mistakes, Keynes circulated in September 1941 a first draft of his proposal for a new international monetary system. A fifth draft was handed to Harry White, US Assistant Secretary of the Treasury, in August 1942. White and his staff prepared their alternative views. Within the year, Roosevelt and Churchill announced the Atlantic Charter. Features of both the British and US drafts were reflected in the Bretton Woods agreements of 1944, which created an International Monetary Fund (IMF) and an International Bank for Reconstruction and Development (IBRD), commonly called the World Bank. In 1946, the United Nations Organization was brought to life. A proposal for an International Trade Organization followed, although it was rebuffed by the US Congress.

The postwar planners were visionary and idealistic. As one author was later to characterize their efforts, they 'worked under the influence of their experience and their memories. . . . Deeply conscious of the errors committed between the two wars, they sought to avoid a repetition.'[5] Some have termed them 'universalists', and indeed their plans were intended to apply with equal force to every corner of the globe. However, like the proverbial generals who always plan to fight the last war, they conceived an international order designed primarily to redress the self-defeating policies and behaviour of the interwar period.

The universalists were perceptive about the problems of the past, correctly foresaw that the issues would survive the end of the war, and tried to address them. They expected the United Nations to become the

[5] Guindey (1977), 5.

forum for resolving international disputes peacefully and without resort to force. The economic organizations would finance reconstruction, oversee changes in exchange rates, and eliminate barriers to the free flow of goods and currencies across national borders. Free market access to raw materials would be assured to victors and vanquished alike. The victors would be more circumspect about reparations this time. The new economic order would incorporate all nations, including the colonial states as they gained independence.

The wartime planners did recognize that new difficulties would arise after the war and anticipated the need for a transition to the new international economic order. The US military prepared for and delivered relief supplies to the populations of both liberated and occupied territories, as they advanced across the Continent. A relief organization, the United Nations Relief and Rehabilitation Administration (UNRRA), was created to provide food, clothing, and medical supplies in the transitional period. The Bretton Woods agreements contained an obligation to establish fixed exchange rates and to remove quantitative restrictions on trade, as well as controls over foreign exchange payments. But this obligation was to be allowed a respite of five years while economic life returned progressively to normal.

The 'transition' apparently was expected to last only long enough to restore the European economy to its prewar status. At least that seems to have been the American, British, and Canadian conception. Other governments were preoccupied with re-establishing political stability within their own borders when they returned to the Continent. They could not pay much heed to planning for a better international economic order.

DIFFICULTIES OF TRANSITION

Postwar problems proved more difficult than the planners had foreseen, in Britain and on the Continent. The British expected to maintain their traditional role as a major world power alongside the United States, to strengthen their leadership of the Empire, maintain the sterling area, and re-establish the role of sterling as both a major reserve and trading currency. To these ends, they chose to be a major contributor to UNRRA and other UN bodies, to maintain a large and active overseas military establishment, to finance relief supplies in the zones they occupied in Austria and Germany, and to permit countries in the sterling area free access to the London capital market.

As the British government's principal economic adviser, Keynes estimated in August 1945 that the British cumulative deficit over the postwar transition period would be about $7 billion.[6] By the time he began negotiations with the United States for a settlement of lend-lease obligations and a transition loan, he had pared his estimate to $5 billion for a period that would end with the year 1948. He regarded $5 billion as 'probably the minimum required to permit a full multilateralisation of trade and payments from the start'.[7] Canada and the United States together provided $5 billion in credits, but with stringent conditions. Within one year Britain was to make the pound sterling convertible on current account for all non-residents of the sterling area, without discrimination as to where such sterling could be spent. Sterling balances held by other countries were to be released or funded. Such releases, as well as all new earnings of sterling by any country, were to be allowed to be spent freely in the United States and elsewhere.

Long aggrieved by the Imperial Preference system, the United States wanted access to sterling area markets on equal terms. Keynes had expected convertibility and non-discrimination to apply only to members of the sterling area. The United States and Canada insisted, however, on their being extended to any country earning sterling from current sales of goods and services. Even that issue did not become a serious sticking point in the negotiations. Succeeding events demonstrated that the North Americans were as unwise to impose such stringent conditions as the British were to accept them. Both parties apparently were blinded by their impatience to establish the new system they had conceived at Bretton Woods.

When, in 1947, the United Kingdom attempted to implement its convertibility commitment, the worldwide shortage of goods and dollars with which to purchase them engulfed the effort. Countries on the Continent joined the rush to acquire sterling balances and convert them into dollars. For example, in the first five months of 1947, Belgium 'accepted from other European governments in settlement of debts nearly 13 million pounds sterling [over $50 million] which was promptly sold for dollars . . . by the end of the year she had drawn $208 million'.[8]

The convertibility experiment lasted only six weeks before it had to be suspended. That suspension eliminated any realistic prospect of a global system of non-discriminatory trade and payments within any brief period. However, the hopes of many of the universalist economists were not yet extinguished.

The failure of the convertibility experiment sharply underscored the problems of restoring a 'normal' international economy—a standard that had not been realized for over three decades. The new norm could hardly

[6] Cairncross (1985), 79.
[7] Cairncross (1985), 92.
[8] Cairncross (1985), 128.

be the same as that of 1913, and it would have to operate under very different conditions than the proverbial 'prewar'. For years, Europe had run trade deficits with the western hemisphere, financing them with earnings from investments, other services, and the trade surpluses of its colonial territories. In the immediate postwar period, the trade deficit with the western hemisphere was much larger, and the earlier means of financing had vanished.

The desperate shortage of dollars had many facets and deep-rooted causes. One hesitates to use the much abused word 'structural', but the causes of the dollar shortage would not be readily overcome. A simple list should suffice to explain why it would be ten more years before Europe would participate fully in a relatively free and non-discriminatory trade and payments system on a global basis. Each of the items on the following list were both identifiable and identified in the early postwar years. In retrospect, the implications should have been readily apparent, given their number and nature. Yet they were neglected by policy-makers who were, understandably, eager to get things back to normal and impatient to inaugurate their new international economic system, free of the sins of the interwar order.

Many of the following items have already been mentioned: (1) destruction from the war; (2) loss of shipping and investment income from overseas; (3) an economically prostrate Germany, unable to provide its traditional industrial exports from redefined borders and preoccupied with absorbing a flood of refugees; (4) the loss of food and raw materials previously exported to western Europe from the eastern lands occupied by the Soviet armies; (5) continued fighting in Greece, Soviet threats to Turkey, and a divided Austria; (6) liquidation of gold stocks, dollar balances, and other external assets, reducing Europe's hard currency reserves by $4.5 billion in 1947 alone to grossly inadequate levels in almost every country; (7) rapid use of early credits from the World Bank and the International Monetary Fund and the virtual cessation of new credits to Europe from these international agencies; (8) demands from overseas creditors who had accumulated European currencies during the war and afterwards wanted to spend them on imported goods; (9) popular demands in the western democracies for something better than a return to the prewar situation, leading to an early postwar election of labour and socialist coalition governments in Belgium, France, the Netherlands, Scandinavia, and the United Kingdom; (10) increased power of trade unions and government commitments to full employment policies; (11) nationalization of private companies, government-financed investment, and government-sponsored housing programmes that created inflationary pressures that were difficult to control; (12) intra-European trade rebuilt on a weak foundation of bilateral trade and payments agreements that discouraged the efficient use of Europe's productive capabilities.

An extremely harsh winter early in 1947 generated a coal crisis. A terrible harvest exacerbated and dramatized food shortages that were already being controlled through rationing, allocations, and price controls. Those who experienced life in western Europe in 1947 know that it was bitter. Had the flow of exports from North America been cut off at that point, life could only have become much harsher.

John H. Williams, professor of economics at Harvard University and a key adviser on international finance to the Federal Reserve Bank of New York, was a lone voice crying vainly in the wilderness in the mid-1940s.[9] He called for postponing the creation of the IMF until the more serious problems of the transition could be resolved. Williams advocated that exchange stability be approached one currency at a time, beginning with sterling. Ignored by the participants at Bretton Woods, he turned to European integration as the principal hope for the increased productivity that would 'overcome the disequilibrating effects of American predominance'.[10]

THE MARSHALL PLAN

Only a small minority in the US Department of State felt a primary responsibility for the new universalist system. Though all supported it as established US policy, the leadership and most of the staff were occupied with political developments and pressing economic problems. Their immediate priorities were the problems of Europe as a region, not the global trade and payments system. From the beginning of 1947, two points became increasingly clear to them: (1) European economic recovery was proceeding at a dangerously slow pace and (2) the Congress was unlikely to vote more funds for European relief and reconstruction.

A very discouraged Secretary of State, George C. Marshall, returned from Moscow early in 1947. It was clear that Soviet Premier Joseph Stalin had no intention of relinquishing his political control of the territories still occupied by Soviet armies. Nor would he stop commandeering their resources. Regardless of Soviet behaviour to their east, economic hardship seemed to strengthen the appeal of western European Communist parties, particularly in France and Italy. Thus a westward expansion of Soviet hegemony appeared within the realm of the possible.

[9] Williams, J. H. (1945).
[10] Williams, J. H. (1952), (1953).

In these circumstances, a new approach to European economic reconstruction and a different appeal to the American public seemed to be required.

Early in June 1947, Marshall took advantage of an invitation to address the Harvard Alumni Association to unveil his historic initiative.[11] He stated the obvious and unpleasant fact that Europe's need for essential goods from America over the next three or four years was substantially in excess of Europe's ability to pay for them. Without substantial additional aid, Europe would be exposed to economic, political, and social dislocations. Yet a unilateral aid programme devised by the United States was unlikely to succeed. The initiative for developing a programme of economic recovery must come from Europe. The appropriate role for the United States was to support and contribute to a programme devised and agreed to by the governments of Europe.

Eleven days later, the British and French Foreign Ministers—Ernest Bevin and Georges Bidault—invited their Soviet counterpart to join them in preparing a response to Secretary Marshall. Ten days later, the Soviet Foreign Minister, V. M. Molotov, demonstrated that he was only interested in preparing a list of goods that the US government should finance. By 12 July 1947, a Conference on European Economic Co-operation had been assembled in Paris, though the Soviet Union and the countries it occupied ignored their invitation to attend. By October, the CEEC— a formal committee of the western European governments—had met, prepared and agreed on a four-year programme, and sent a delegation to present it to the government of the United States.

The effort to gain public support in the United States was equally vigorous. The Council of Economic Advisors and a committee headed by the Secretary of the Interior prepared formal reports on America's ability to finance and supply the needed exports. Averell Harriman, then Secretary of Commerce, chaired a committee of private citizens, and Christian Herter, a Congressman from Massachusetts, chaired a joint Congressional committee, both of which examined the CEEC report and offered their recommendations. Private citizens groups organized meetings, provided speakers, and sought to educate the public concerning the need and the opportunity.

Before the end of the year, the Department of State was ready to submit enabling legislation to the Congress for a European Recovery Program. It forwarded an elaborate explanation and detailed documentation of its programme, as well as proposed arrangements for the administration of US assistance. By the following April, both authorization and

---

[11] For further accounts of the Marshall Plan, see Jones (1955); Lord Franks, 'Lessons of the Marshall Plan Experience', in OECD (1978); Wexler (1983); Hogan (1987).

appropriations legislation had been passed by the Congress, key officials of the newly established Economic Cooperation Administration (ECA) had been appointed, and the first procurement for Europe had been authorized.

Marshall's speech and the European response had challenged both America's constructive instincts and its organizational capabilities. The Congress, as well as the Executive Branch, accepted the challenge, with broad support from the public. The new ECA was able to recruit a select staff of exceptional analytical and administrative talent from all walks of American life. It was led by Paul Hoffman, president of a then newly successful Studebaker Corporation and an acknowledged leader in the postwar US business community. An equally innovative and competent staff, headed by Averell Harriman, was recruited for service in Europe. As the US Special Representative in Europe, Harriman supervised ECA resident missions sent to each participating European country. Later, he served as the chief representative of the United States to the CEEC's permanent successor organization.

The ECA archives reveal a great deal of creative and high-minded activity. Controversial ideas and policies were formulated and debated, though they were not necessarily advocated to European governments. Ultimately it was the ECA's official behaviour *vis-à-vis* those governments that counted. That behaviour was more circumspect than the ideas that circulated within US circles. On the whole, it reveals more of an effort to resolve conflicts and ease problems than to promote ECA views. Ideas were advanced, but seldom pressed in the face of firm European opposition. When the Europeans were agreed among themselves, their resistance was invariably successful. Compromise and the search for agreement controlled the operation of the Marshall Plan.

It was not a Pax Americana, accepted and acquiesced in by a docile Europe forced to act against its own perceived interests as the price for urgently needed resources.[12] ECA generally decided to leave the detailed administration of the programme in the hands of the European authorities. Country programmes were established on the basis of European proposals. Thereafter, ECA issued procurement authorizations to individual governments for specific purchases, up to the dollar amount of each country programme. Procurement was not restricted to the United States but was permitted offshore. Such purchases in Europe broke up a logjam in intra-European trade at an early date.

ECA-financed imports were sold on European markets for local currency, called counterpart funds. Five per cent of a country's counterpart was allocated to ECA to meet administrative and other expenses. The country

---

[12] Marjolin (1986), 211-12, provides eloquent and authoritative firsthand testimony.

could use the remaining 95 per cent for its own economic purposes as agreed jointly between its government and ECA. Some of the counterpart was frozen to limit inflationary pressures; the rest was available to meet the needs of European governments and used primarily for domestic investments. Hoffman liked to refer to Congressional appropriations as 'double-duty dollars'—used to pay for imports and to generate counterpart for local purposes.

THE OEEC

The original CEEC was converted into a formal international body by virtue of a Convention signed on 16 April 1948.[13] The new Organisation for European Economic Co-operation (OEEC) had resident national delegations and an international secretariat, headed by Robert Marjolin. A French economist still in his thirties, Marjolin had a talent for both leadership and diplomacy. The heads of delegations were plenipotentiaries who met formally and regularly as the permanent OEEC Council. The Council also met periodically at ministerial level. On these occasions, countries were usually represented by their foreign or finance ministers or other cabinet-level officers.

The Convention responded fully to Marshall's call for a co-operative European programme, a call that was emphasized vigorously in all the US committee reports. The contracting parties agreed to elaborate and execute a joint recovery programme. It was designed to achieve a satisfactory level of economic activity without further dollar aid and to develop exports to the rest of the world. They also agreed to achieve 'as soon as possible a multilateral system of payments among themselves and . . . [to] co-operate in relaxing restrictions on trade and payments between one another'. They further agreed to 'continue the study of Customs Unions or analogous arrangements such as free trade areas' as well as to reduce 'tariff and other barriers to the expansion of trade, with a view to achieving a sound and balanced multilateral trading system'. Each contracting party agreed to 'achieve or maintain the stability of its currency and of its internal financial position, sound rates of exchange and generally confidence in its monetary system'.

The Convention thus contained the self-help commitment that Marshall had invited. Europe had agreed that dollars alone would not make for a successful European recovery programme. It planned to be self-supporting at the end of four years.

It should have come as no surprise that the elaboration of commodity

[13] OEEC (1948).

and sector programmes and the procurement of ECA-financed imports dominated Marshall Plan activities during its first year and more. The efforts were successful up to a point. Shortages of goods were substantially eased, and production levels began to reach and surpass prewar levels. Belgium, Germany, and Italy soon introduced currency stabilization programmes that brought their inflation rates under control; the other countries had more difficulty. Intra-European trade recovered much more slowly than production. Moreover, the disappearance of the dollar shortage—the so-called 'dollar gap'—seemed unlikely to be realized within the prescribed four-year period.

The OEEC was charged with the division of US aid from its earliest days. The process centred on reviewing and co-ordinating country programmes to arrive at equitable recommendations to ECA. The first decision, in September 1948, was the fruit of a co-operative and harmonious effort. A year later, the division of aid became an acrimonious and divisive exercise. US aid was planned to decline annually after the first year, but the countries did not perceive a commensurate reduction in their need for dollars in the second year.

Ultimately, the Chairman of the OEEC Council, Baron Snoy of Belgium, and Marjolin were charged with recommending a division of ECA aid that might be endorsed by all OEEC members with a minimum of further negotiations.[14] They could do so only by including funds that ECA intended to keep in reserve rather than allocate to individual countries. The Council's response to their recommendation was indeed unanimous: every country denounced it as unfair. United only by their common dismay, the members grudgingly accepted the report. The usefulness of dividing US aid as a method of promoting European co-operation appeared to be at an end. Thereafter, any question about aid division used the percentages in the Snoy–Marjolin formula. Reopening the allocations seemed likely to breed more argument than agreement. Harriman was so outraged about the division of the reserve fund that he gloomily predicted it would probably be the end of American aid to Europe.[15] Fortunately, that was not the outcome.

A new approach was needed. Both the OEEC Secretariat and the ECA organization, in Washington as well as in Paris, concluded that the chief focus of the OEEC should henceforth be the liberalization of trade and payments.[16] However, efforts within the OEEC to multilateralize payments and free trade from restrictions had produced more machinery than results by mid-1949, as a more detailed account that follows will demonstrate.

The collapse of the British convertibility experiment had forced Britain

---

[14] Roll (1985), 73. Recommendation approved by OEEC Council (31 Aug. 1949). OEEC C(49)141.
[15] Marjolin (1986), 223.
[16] 'Oral History Interview with Lincoln Gordon' (17 July 1975). Harry S. Truman Library.

to tighten its foreign exchange controls and enter into bilateral payments agreements with other European countries. By 1949, the 'universalists' in Washington believed that a devaluation of European currencies, reinforced by tighter anti-inflationary monetary policies, would allow Europe to move out of the 'transition' to the free system of non-discriminatory trade and payments prescribed by the Bretton Woods agreements. Rumours in Washington prompted excessive speculation, which compelled such devaluations in September 1949.

Neither European governments nor ECA believed these devaluations would permit an early lifting of exchange controls and discriminatory trade restrictions while balancing Europe's accounts with the dollar area. By that time, Europe's economic and political problems seemed too fundamental and intractable. To all those struggling to overcome them, an early move to convertibility appeared neither practicable nor realistic. Freeing intra-European trade and payments would be difficult enough. If it could be achieved at an early date, however, it could prove to be an essential step toward convertibility.

INTEGRATION OF WESTERN EUROPE

The idea of a united Europe is at least as old as Charlemagne and as new as the latest nation state that hoped to extend its hegemony over all the Continent. During the interwar period, some nurtured the dream of unifying Europe through a voluntary merger of the sovereignty of the existing nation states. This occurred largely in intellectual circles, with modest support from political leaders who were out of power. Altiero Spinelli of the Italian resistance issued a manifesto in 1941 that led to the General Declaration of July 1944—a proposal for a federal structure for Europe, endorsed by resistance leaders from most European countries.[17]

Jean Monnet, a prominent French statesman, and some of his associates in wartime London were attracted to the idea as they exercised responsibilities for planning economic reconstruction on the Continent. However, most leaders of the governments-in-exile were more concerned with re-establishing a political base upon their return. All were understandably concerned with how they would be received and how they could attract political support from populations whose loyalties had been strained by occupation, warfare, and economic deprivation.

The difficulties of the immediate postwar years brought statesmen in power to embrace the European idea—de Gasperi and Sforza, Schuman, Adenauer and Bevin, Spaak, Stikker, and Beyen. However, few political

---

[17] Pollard (1981), ch. vi.

leaders were ready to yield much of their newly regained sovereignty and mandates to a supra-national state. The early proposals were thus economic in character, designed to capture support for a measure of economic unification without raising the more sensitive issues of political sovereignty.

As leaders struggled with extremely difficult economic problems, some were attracted by the notion of a European economy cast in the mould of the continental United States. Both world wars had demonstrated the superior capacity and productivity of the US economy. Both in Europe and the United States, that performance came to be attributed to the size of the US market and the free flow of goods, money, and people within its vast borders. If such conditions could be established in Europe, it was thought, the use of resources could be greatly improved. Thereafter, competitiveness with the United States might become possible. Some even argued that only under such conditions could Europe hope to become competitive while meeting the demands of its people for rising living standards. This path differed from the one envisioned by the 'universalists', and conflicts between them and the 'regionalists' soon broke out.

Much attracted by the idea of a united Europe, the US Congress made it a major objective of the first European Recovery Act. Congressional support for the political and economic unification of Europe has never flagged. It was reiterated in numerous pieces of legislation and with particular urgency throughout the Marshall Plan years.

The Italian Foreign Minister, Count Sforza had proposed to the CEEC that a customs union be established in Europe, as the appropriate European response to the US challenge. Supported only by France, he obtained agreement to no more than the formation of a study group. Its report was inconclusive, but Italy and France entered into a more serious, albeit unsuccessful, effort to establish a customs union of the two countries, as the Benelux countries had done in January 1948. At a formal meeting of the CEEC, the US Under Secretary of State, Will Clayton, also failed to persuade European leaders of the advantages of a more inclusive customs union.

The United Kingdom was not at all attracted to these ideas. This was understandable, given its priorities and its poor estimate of the Continent's prospects. The British Treasury saw the customs union proposal as 'contributing nothing to the major problem of viability'.[18] The British had insisted from the beginning that the OEEC be under the control of the participating governments. They had successfully opposed French efforts to create an OEEC structure with considerable power and authority.[19]

[18] Cairncross (1985), 284.
[19] Lord Franks 'Lessons of the Marshall Plan Experience', in OECD (1978), 21.

Nevertheless, at the same time that it opposed delegating authority to OEEC international officials, the British Cabinet approved a very affirmative stance with respect to European co-operation.[20]

There was a general agreement that there was no alternative to a policy of full support for closer economic co-operation in Western Europe . . . even at the cost of considerable changes in the economic structure of the United Kingdom and some loss of the advantages which we now enjoy over other European countries. . . . His Majesty's Government should adopt it in a positive and optimistic way and should give a strong lead to the other participating countries.

The Cabinet had before it a joint memorandum by the Foreign Secretary (Bevin) and the Chancellor of the Exchequer (Sir Stafford Cripps). It was based on a strongly worded memorandum by Otto Clarke, then responsible for co-ordinating Marshall Plan work in London. Bevin was to state that policy to the CEEC, and the Commonwealth governments were to receive explanations.

Early in 1949, however, a more reserved policy was promulgated. Prime Minister Clement Attlee summarized the cabinet committee discussion by saying, 'We should not embark on a policy of cooperation on the assumption we were ready to extricate the other countries from their difficulties at the cost of sacrificing ourselves. But we should be prepared to initiate a policy of multilateralism, and to take some risks.'[21]

An October 1949 document was even more negative. It described the earlier decision in brief as 'one under which His Majesty's Government were not to involve themselves in the economic affairs of Europe beyond the point from which they could, if they wished, withdraw'.[22] The risks not to be run were made explicit—loss of responsibility for budgetary and credit policy and management of reserves, opening to European decision the size of strategic dollar-earning and dollar-saving United Kingdom industries. Relations with the US and the Commonwealth were to take priority over relations with Europe. For that reason alone, the United Kingdom could play only a limited part in European union.

Britain's repeatedly expressed reluctance to participate in moves that would limit sovereign independence had already led Monnet and other Continental leaders to look to a smaller grouping of Continental countries. Some countries might be ready to relinquish sovereignty if it would help in easing their most urgent problems. Six countries—France, Italy, Germany, and the Benelux countries—would soon begin negotiating French Foreign Minister Robert Schuman's proposal for a coal and steel

---

[20] Cabinet Meeting Minutes (8 Mar. 1948). CM (48) 20th Minute 2. PRO PREM 8/980.

[21] Economic Policy Com. Minutes (26 Jan. 1949). EPC (49) 5th. PRO CAB 134/220.

[22] 'Proposals for the Economic Unification of Europe'. Memo by Sec. of State for Foreign Affairs and Chancellor of Exchequer (25 Oct. 1949). CP (49) 203. PRO PREM 8/1434.

community.[23] They required about two years to reach an agreement, which took effect in 1953. Thereafter, this Community of Six evolved slowly. The next agreements—on Euratom and a Common Market—were signed in 1957.

In the late 1940s, it was even more difficult to get European countries to agree on drastic innovations. Unless new proposals would address the dollar problem immediately and directly, governments preferred to retain full sovereignty.

INTRA-EUROPEAN PAYMENTS AND COMPENSATIONS SCHEME [IEPS]

Freeing intra-European trade from its network of debilitating restrictions seemed relevant to both the dollar shortage and the integration of European economies. It promised markets that would be easier to penetrate than the North American market, a better division of labour, and more efficient use of resources. With a larger European market, European industry might achieve a scale that could compete successfully in North America. The theory had considerable appeal, but it was ignored in practice as each country focused on its need for dollars and everyone was reluctant to finance intra-European trade.

Repeating the pattern of the interwar period, each country wanted to earn a surplus in intra-European trade and to be paid for it in dollars. At the very least, each was unwilling to incur a dollar liability for imports from other European countries. Even Britain planned to reverse its historical trade deficit with the Continent and run a sizeable surplus; it succeeded in 1946 and 1947. Taken together, such efforts by all European countries had to be self-defeating; every country could not be in surplus with all other participating countries as a group. Neither arithmetic nor good sense would permit it.

Intra-European trade began after World War II on the basis of bilateral agreements. Most of them provided for limited credit margins, after which settlement had to be made in gold. By 1947, the credit lines were near exhaustion, with little chance of repayment. Debtors sought new credits and, when they were not forthcoming, cut back their imports. The expansion of intra-European trade came to a halt. Payments arrangements became completely jammed as each country sought bilateral balance.[24]

At the CEEC meetings in 1947, a more modest proposal for integrating European markets than Sforza's customs union gained some acceptance.

23 Mayne (1970), ch. vi, describes evolution of Schuman Plan.
24 ECA (1949), 98.

A Committee of Financial Experts proposed that European currencies be made transferable into one another. Each country with a bilateral credit should be permitted to use it to offset debits in its commercial relations with any European country. The CEEC referred this proposal to a Committee on Payments Agreements, which developed an even more modest proposal—a multilateral clearing agreement based on the bilateral agreements. For the clearing, monthly bilateral balances would be reported, offset, and the net debts divided proportionately between all the net creditors.

By November 1947, well before the Marshall Plan was enacted, an Agreement on Multilateral Monetary Compensation was signed by France, Italy, and the Benelux countries. They designated the Bank for International Settlements (BIS) as the agent to which countries would report their bilateral balances each month. That was a halting first step that would turn into a giant leap three years later. Eight other CEEC countries, unwilling to allow any automatic compensations, joined on a limited basis. They only reported balances and reserved the right to permit multilateral compensation. As a result, very little compensation occurred: countries seldom consented to non-automatic compensation. They preferred bilateral bargaining and control to the risk of losing dollars.

When ECA started to issue procurement authorizations for purchases in Europe, the logjam in intra-European payments began to break up. In its first six months, ECA issued over $200 million in such authorizations. But the system satisfied neither ECA nor the European participants. When ECA dollars were used for purchases within Europe, ECA reduced its aid to the seller country by the dollar amount of the sale. It did so on the theory that the seller could use its dollar proceeds to pay for imports from outside Europe. In practice, however, these deductions proved difficult to manage.

A more important objection to the system was that European sellers preferred to sell goods for ECA dollars. This hampered the expansion of intra-European trade on a non-dollar basis. 'The web of financial and commercial relations on which European trade could depend when the Marshall Plan was over' was not developing.[25]

The OEEC Secretariat suggested an alternative system, called the Intra-European Payments and Compensations Scheme (IEPS). It was adopted by all OEEC members in October 1948, but its mechanism was only a limited improvement. Nor was the modification, negotiated with considerable difficulty in mid-1949, much more satisfactory.

The 1948 IEPS was based on estimates by the participating countries

25 Diebold (1952), 31.

of their expected bilateral surpluses and deficits. The prospective creditors then agreed to grant 'drawing rights' to their prospective debtors. Each creditor agreed to permit its bilateral debtor to 'draw' from that creditor an amount up to the size of its estimated deficit. ECA then provided the creditor with an equal amount of 'conditional aid' that could be used to pay for dollar imports.

One difficulty with this scheme was that ECA had to establish the total aid available per country long before the amount of conditional aid could be determined. Thus the latter did not increase the aid creditor countries received. It did enable them to extend credit needed to maintain their markets in Europe, while their own need for dollars was covered by ECA.

Since all countries receiving aid participated in the scheme, the BIS as agent could automatically offset surpluses and deficits and effect some multilateral clearing. However, the IEPS agreements contained a debilitating proviso: automatic clearing was limited to cases where it would not increase any bilateral balance. The BIS was also authorized to use any available drawing rights automatically to settle balances remaining after the clearing. But clearings that would increase bilateral balances could only be effected with the consent of every country involved. Rarely could the BIS clear automatically without increasing any bilateral balance. As in the first compensation system, permission for non-automatic clearing was seldom granted.

The scheme did make 'possible an expansion of intra-European trade by creating drawing rights. It did little, however, to get trade out of the ruts created by bilateral arrangements.'[26] The drawing rights and offsetting together covered about 43 per cent of the gross deficits and surpluses of the participating countries, but the offsetting itself contributed hardly more than 5 per cent.

Given the extensive history of failure in balance-of-trade forecasting, one wonders how any system based on predictions about bilateral trade balances could work. In fact, the estimates were thrown further off than usual by the unanticipated devaluations of 1949. As a result, unused drawing rights were a major preoccupation during the last months of the system.

Valiant attempts to improve the multilateral character of the scheme were made early in 1949 in connection with its renewal in July.[27] ECA wanted the drawing rights to be freely transferable among OEEC countries. As a major grantor of drawing rights, the United Kingdom stoutly resisted. Already feeling unwelcome pressure from Washington and the markets to devalue the pound, the United Kingdom feared that such transferability would only increase its need for dollars.

[26] Diebold (1952), 64.
[27] Henry Wallich, 'Notes on the Intra-European Payments Plan' (5 Apr. 1949). Comments on proposals by ECA, Arthur Smithies, Robert Triffin, and Albert Hirschman. Then in Foreign

The negotiations produced some tense moments for the leading ministers who represented their governments at the OEEC. Britain's Chancellor Cripps reluctantly agreed that 25 per cent of the drawing rights might be transferable, after a heated and protracted dispute with his Belgian counterpart, Paul Spaak. According to Marjolin's memoirs, the decisive meeting was held at 1.00 a.m. on the night of 1 July 1949.[28] It was attended by Cripps, Harriman, Spaak, Sir Edmund Hall-Patch (UK Chairman of the OEEC Executive Committee), Maurice Petsche (French Minister of Finance), and himself. Based on a note dictated at the time, Marjolin's account bears eloquent testimony to the participants' capacity for compromise on behalf of the common interest. Compromise was an essential ingredient of the Marshall Plan's successes. Unfortunately, this one permitted no more than the continuation of a badly flawed system.

Intra-European trade did expand under the successive IEPS agreements, but largely as a result of rising production levels and the increasing availability of exportable surpluses, especially from Germany. US aid financed the granting of drawing rights by the creditor countries, thereby permitting somewhat freer purchasing within Europe than would have occurred under completely bilateral arrangements. More than some mitigation of bilateralism would be needed, however, if the prospects for intra-European trade were to be bright after the end of the Marshall Plan.

Perhaps the most lasting benefits of IEPS were the establishment of uniform accounting and the reporting of monthly bilateral balances to the BIS. The latter was an important psychological and practical step in preparing the ground for a more multilateral system. Data reported to the BIS revealed all the opportunities for multilateral offsetting; the refusals of permission underlined the inadequacies of the system. Over the 21-month life of the IEPS, only 2 per cent of the gross deficits reported to the BIS were covered by offsetting compensations.[29] Few countries were satisfied with the system, but few were prepared to incur the risks that a freer system would have created for creditors and debtors.

The United Kingdom was particularly adamant. Its foreign trade turnover was a third of the total for all participating countries. Its relatively large market enhanced its bargaining position in concluding bilateral agreements. It was succeeding in running surpluses in its trade with the Continent, reversing a traditional deficit. UK officials attributed these surpluses in part to their bilateral bargaining. With a weak overall balance-of-payments position, they were reluctant to give up the bilateral

Research Division of Federal Reserve Bank of New York, Wallich later served for 13 years as a Governor of the Federal Reserve System. Federal Reserve Files.

[28] Marjolin (1986), 218-20.
[29] BIS, *Twenty-First Annual Report, 1950-51*, 237.

arrangements. The United Kingdom would have liked all the participating countries to use sterling to settle their bilateral surpluses and deficits. Equally concerned about their own dollar shortages, the Continental countries were not enthusiastic about accepting payments in pounds sterling that were not freely convertible into dollars.

As the Marshall Plan approached its half-way mark, the walls of the bilateral trading fortress seemed capable of withstanding every assault. A proper system for promoting intra-European trade on a durable basis was still waiting to be born.

2   Proposals and Outbursts

The ECA Administrator, Paul Hoffman, was an early convert to a united Europe, and he preached his message to Americans and Europeans alike. His principal policy advisers in Washington encouraged such advocacy and were, in turn, stimulated to proffer ideas and advice on how to proceed. Economic integration as a prelude to political federation seemed to be the most feasible approach.

The first prerequisite for integration was the elimination of quantitative restrictions, then the most important trade barrier within Europe. Administered by means of bilateral agreements, they limited the amount of each commodity countries imported from each other. They were supplemented by payments restrictions, which controlled sales of foreign exchange in an attempt to maintain a balanced payments position with each trading partner. By mid-1949, ECA officials in Washington and Paris were agreed that the United States must lead a far more ambitious effort to break down these barriers.

The problem had to be raised to a political level where major agreements could be reached, at least in principle. Only the US government had the authority to force the issue, particularly because firm British opposition was probable. On this matter, Hoffman was prepared to be uncompromising about demanding a major forward move.

At the European senior civil servant level, efforts to find agreement on lowering trade and payments barriers had long been frustrated. For months, Marjolin and Frank Figgures (a senior UK Treasury official serving as Director for Trade and Payments in the OEEC Secretariat) had been producing carefully reasoned documents arguing for the elimination of all quantitative restrictions on intra-European trade. They had gained support from only a few Continental governments and no significant response from Great Britain.

Hoffman's 'Single Market' Address

Hoffman was persuaded that Europe would not be viable by the end of the four-year Marshall Plan unless much more integrated economic arrangements were in place. He decided to stake his own prestige on a dramatic initiative. He knew he might have to accept integration within smaller groupings, but he sought the integration of all western Europe.

First he lectured the OEEC heads of delegation, the permanent representatives of the member governments in Paris, on 16 August 1949.[1] In no uncertain terms, he asked for concrete steps to ensure that Europe would become a single market as soon as possible. The OEEC had already decided to establish a list of goods that all members would trade freely among themselves without quantitative restrictions. Hoffman commended the decision as a good starting point, but only the first of the specific measures that should be taken. The list of goods had to be important in intra-European trade. Transferability between European currencies was also essential, and tariff barriers should be reduced. His statement was a preliminary announcement. The OEEC ministers themselves were his real audience.

Two weeks later, Harriman's deputy, Ambassador Milton Katz, formally informed the Secretary General by letter that ECA intended to reserve $150 million from the aid appropriation for the US financial year 1950. The largest part of these funds would be used to encourage the reduction or elimination of trade barriers. It would be a sort of second line of foreign exchange reserves, available to deal with temporary difficulties caused by measures to free trade and payments.[2] The permanent members of the OEEC Council were startled and dismayed to learn that funds for countries would be reduced to create the reserve.

Thus forewarned, Bevin dispatched a personal message to Secretary of State Dean Acheson on 25 October 1949. It conveyed British concerns about any proposals that might be forthcoming for closer economic groupings in Europe.

In summary, the principal objective of our policy is to reconcile our position as a world power, as a member of the British Commonwealth, and as a member of the European community. We believe we can effect this reconciliation but that, if we are able to do so, we cannot accept obligations in relation to Western Europe which would prevent or restrict the implementation of our responsibilities elsewhere.[3]

Hoffman, nevertheless, followed through with his intended address to the cabinet-level meeting of the OEEC Council on 31 October. The draft of his speech had already been the subject of a major contretemps between ECA and State Department officials. Hoffman himself finally acceded to Acheson's request that he change the word 'unification' to 'integration',

---

[1] 'Declaration of Mr. Hoffman, (16 Aug. 1949). OEEC C(49)127.

[2] OEEC Sec. General, 'General Reserve Fund'. Memo transmitting Amb. Katz's letter (1 Sept. 1949). OEEC C(49)143.

[3] Cabinet Papers Annex B to CP (49) 203 (25 Oct. 1949).

a bit of semantics that had more significance within the US administration at the time than it did for the European audience.

Hoffman called for 'nothing less than the integration of the Western European economy . . . a single large market within which quantitative restrictions on the movement of goods, monetary barriers to the flow of payments and eventually all tariff barriers are permanently swept away'.[4] Some 36 years later, a similar but more far-reaching goal was established for the year 1992 by agreement among the Common Market governments. (By then, they included most countries that had belonged to the OEEC.) In 1949, the single market idea seemed hopelessly romantic and impractical.

Hoffman went on to say that 'a substantial measure of coordination of monetary and fiscal policies' would be necessary. In the absence of such integration, 'a vicious cycle of economic nationalism would again be set in motion' at the end of the Marshall Plan, because Europe's dollar balance would be precarious and its foreign exchange reserves would be inadequate.

After Hoffman's speech, the Council adjourned for a full day of study before responding. Sean Macbride, the Irish Minister for External Affairs and a subsequent recipient of the Nobel Peace Prize, provided a ringing endorsement before the adjournment. He asserted that 'they [the OEEC ministers] should have given themselves the same advice 12 months ago'.[5] When the ministers reassembled, most of the others responded positively, but much more cautiously. Cripps firmly reiterated reservations about integrating the British economy into that of Europe 'in any manner that would prejudice the full discharge of these other [Commonwealth and sterling area] responsibilities'.[6]

Nevertheless, the ministers did enact a decision that recognized 'the need to form a single large market'.[7] Though its language was guarded and vague, the decision provided a direction and framework for further work by the permanent representatives. Prodded by the Secretariat, they had to address the question of how to implement that decision.

Of greatest eventual significance was a modestly worded section agreeing to 'widen the area of transferability of currencies among Member countries by suitable measures in the next intra-European payments scheme'. The decision also contained a previously negotiated agreement to remove quantitative restrictions on at least 50 per cent of imports on private account in each of the categories of food, raw materials, and manufactured goods. That agreement represented a timid first step toward liberalizing intra-European trade. For others to follow, European governments would

---

[4] 'Statement by the ECA Administrator' (31 Oct. 1949). OEEC C(49)176.
[5] 'Minutes of the 75th Meeting' (31 Oct. and 1, 2 Nov. 1949). OEEC C/M(49)22.
[6] 'Statement by the Chancellor of the Exchequer' (1 Nov. 1949). OEEC C(49)182.
[7] 'Decision Regarding Further Measures of Cooperation' (2 Nov. 1949). OEEC C(49)181.

first have to know their currencies were fully transferable into one another. Until the kroner and lire they earned from exports could be turned into guilders and pounds to pay for imports, they were unlikely to risk removing much control over the trade itself.

Hoffman's requests for a 'record of accomplishment and a programme' to be ready early in 1950, for 'really effective action' and for a 'realistic plan to meet the fundamental requirements' would require further thought. His staff were, of course, already polishing proposals they had long deliberated. The essential features of what was to become the European Payments Union were about to be placed on the OEEC table.

THE PROPOSALS

Bissell's Plan

Six weeks after Hoffman's 'single market' address, on 10 December 1949, Richard M. Bissell came to Paris to attend a meeting of the OEEC heads of delegation. As ECA's Assistant Administrator for Program, he submitted a proposal for an Intra-European Clearing Union.[8] Its fundamental purpose was to promote the rapid elimination of quantitative restrictions on trade in goods and maximum possible freedom for the purchase and sale of services.

To achieve these goals, the union would establish full transferability between all western European currencies; thus countries would no longer feel impelled to balance their accounts bilaterally. Each country's surpluses with others in the union would be offset automatically against its deficits, making earnings in any European currency equally valuable. Each country would be expected to seek balance with all members of the union as a group, thus minimizing the need for dollars to settle imbalances. To accommodate temporary fluctuations in country positions and to permit some leeway for adjusting economic policies to regain balance, each country would have access to credit from the union.

ECA's proposal was presented as a preliminary and informal attempt to elaborate Hoffman's statement on integration. Bissell stressed that the general principles were important, not the details. Yet virtually all the details he provided were incorporated into the EPU Agreement approved seven months later, on 7 July 1950. Agreement came, however, only after prolonged and sometimes heated debate and manoeuvring on the part of OEEC governments and ECA.

[8] 'Trade and Payments Arrangements'. Draft working paper (9 Dec. 1949). Submitted by ECA to heads of del. (10 Dec. 1949). Circulated by Trade and Finance Directorate (16 Dec. 1949). OEEC TFD/DL/1950/1.

Bissell was one of Hoffman's first staff appointments. Possessing great skills in dealing with people, Hoffman focused his own efforts on persuading the American public, the Congress, and his cabinet counterparts at home and in Europe to support the purposes of the European Recovery Program. Bissell provided intellectual leadership for the staff and rigorous supervision over operating policies and the use of funds entrusted to ECA by the Congress.

Bissell was pragmatic as well as intellectual. He soon assembled a staff whose mix of skills matched the agency's needs for innovative policies, solid economic analysis, and strong administration. A member of the economics faculty at the Massachusetts Institute of Technology, Bissell sought creative ideas and critical insights from his staff. He appeared to enjoy staff debate, posing hard questions and sorting out conclusions that had merit. He insisted on factual evidence to support recommendations and readily absorbed detailed briefings. His legendary capacity for facts may have prompted the story that, as a child, he memorized railroad timetables. In wartime Washington and later as Executive Director of Harriman's Citizens Committee on Foreign Aid, he had learned the ways of Congress and the bureaucracy. His keen intellect, mastery of evidence, and calm demeanour made him an effective spokesman at Congressional hearings—and a formidable opponent of policy-makers in the Departments of State and the Treasury who did not share his views.

The memorandum with which Bissell confronted the OEEC was the fruit of eighteen months of formulation and reformulation, of discussion and dispute within ECA and with other US agencies. The ideas were drawn from many sources, European and American. Their conception is described in detail in Appendix A, 'Where Did the Ideas Come From?' As it turned out, Bissell and his staff's protracted threshing out of various proposals had produced one that best suited their own purposes while accommodating the divergent interests of the European governments.

OEEC Secretariat Proposal

Ever creative and diligent, the OEEC Secretariat had already used Hoffman's speech and the subsequent OEEC decision as a launching pad for its own proposal. Within a few weeks, on 1 December 1949, it was ready to circulate the third draft of a report prepared by its Trade and Finance Directorate, under Figgures's leadership.[9] An independent thinker, Figgures took his status as an international civil servant seriously. He had few hesitations about offering ideas that departed from official

[9] OEEC Trade and Finance Directorate, 'Third Draft of Trade and Payments Arrangements' (1 Dec. 1949). US Archives. ECA Bissell Files. Circulated as memo by Sec. General (19 Dec. 1949). OEEC TFD/DL/1950/2.

British policy, nor was he loathe to persuade his compatriots to alter their position.[10]

The Secretariat report proposed that all payments restrictions on transactions between European countries be eliminated by 1 July 1950. To speed up the freeing of trade, quantitative restrictions on at least 85 per cent of each member's imports from other participating countries were to be removed by the same date. Moreover, no less than 75 per cent of trade would be liberalized in each of three groups of imports—food and fuel, raw materials, and manufactured goods.

The Secretariat recognized, as had ECA, that its goal for liberalizing trade was ambitious. To achieve it would require full transferability of European currencies. The mechanism it proposed was a pool of member currencies. Each country would contribute amounts of its own currency equal to 10 per cent of its visible trade (i.e. trade in goods, not services). In addition, ECA would contribute a fund of $500 million. Membership in the pool would be limited to countries that accepted the trade liberalization objectives *and* implemented them by agreed dates. The money in the pool would be used to settle the surpluses and deficits of each member.

When the pool's supply of a net debtor's currency exceeded 135 per cent of its share in the pool, the debtor would be asked to repay the excess in dollars or another European currency within a set period, such as three years. The pool would replenish its own supply of each creditor's currency when it dropped below 65 per cent by selling dollars or by borrowing at a market rate of interest.

Under the Secretariat proposal, debtors would have a very large range of deficits that could be settled without any payment in convertible currency (gold or dollars). Those who ran deficits beyond that range would have to accept a fixed schedule of repayments over a set period. Net creditors similarly would have to finance their surpluses by extending credit over a wide range. Thereafter, they would receive dollars or would lend to the European pool with the backing of the pool's dollar resources. Creditors would thus be protected from having to lend to individual countries with weak currencies.

Once their quotas were exhausted, countries would have to jump from financing an intra-European deficit or surplus entirely through credit to settling entirely with gold or dollars. In that respect, the plan suffered from the same major drawback as the bilateral payments agreements. Credit came to an abrupt halt when the margins were used up and payments had to be made in gold.

[10] e.g. F. Figgures draft memo, 'Next Steps in European Cooperation' (28 Apr. 1949). Written 'primarily for the eye of Sir Stafford Cripps'. OEEC FF File.

Also Figgures letter to John Lithiby, a senior official of the Bank of England and also Alternate Member of BIS Board of Directors (11 Apr. 1950). Bank of England OV 46/39.

EPU Principles à la *Bissell*

The Secretariat paper had received little consideration from the OEEC delegations when Bissell submitted his memorandum. ECA suggested a more sophisticated mechanism, employing different incentives. A debtor would pay some gold at an early stage; but during the life of the Union, it would not assume a defined commitment to repay any credit to which it was entitled. A creditor, on the other hand, would have to extend increasing amounts of credit if its surpluses persisted. These provisions were designed to create pressure on every member to introduce monetary and fiscal policies conducive to a balanced intra-European position. By including the sterling area, the clearing union would embrace a sufficiently diverse trading area to make such a balance practicable.

The liberalization provisions would include all current account transactions—payments arising from purchases and sales of goods and services. Only capital transactions were excluded, as they had been from similar provisions in the IMF Articles of Agreement. The spectre of capital movements spreading the Great Depression from country to country still haunted the Continent. An international obligation to free capital movements from exchange restrictions was almost unthinkable, except for a very capital-rich country like the United States or Switzerland.

Like the Secretariat, ECA proposed a quota for each country based on the size of its current account transactions with the group as a whole. However, a local currency pool would not be necessary. A modest percentage of each country's quota would constitute a credit margin to be used automatically for settling surpluses or deficits, free of any accompanying payment in gold or dollars. Thereafter, settlements within the quota would be partially in gold and partially in credit. As a country used up successive percentages of its quota, an increasing proportion of gold would be paid by debtors and a decreasing proportion of gold would be paid to creditors.

The system would thus be a transitional arrangement between full convertibility into gold and dollars and the existing state of minimal convertibility in intra-European payments. Under the bilateral payments agreements, gold or dollars were used to settle intra-European accounts only after credits were exhausted. The Bissell paper suggested that over the balance of the Marshall Plan period, the percentage of gold settlements might be gradually increased.

The proposal called for certain administrative arrangements that were at least as important as the automatic settlements mechanism. Their purpose was to maintain continuous consultation and mutual reviews of each country's policies and its overall position in the union. A proposed board of directors would be able to provide facilities (perhaps in the form of loans) to extreme debtors, but only if they would adjust their policies to permit a return to equilibrium within the system.

Bissell proposed an even more far-reaching trade objective than the Secretariat. Quantitative restrictions on intra-European trade should be completely eliminated by the end of 1950. Bissell wanted a scheme that would maintain a free intra-European trade and payments system after the end of US aid under the Marshall Plan. The ambitiousness of his trade liberalization goal was a deliberate challenge to vested interests whose inefficient enterprises were being protected under the cover of a scarcity of foreign currency. With their markets sheltered from imports, they could avoid modernizing their plants or upgrading their products to meet foreign competition.

To attract European participation in the clearing union, the US offered to allocate ECA dollars for its support. ECA would finance structural deficits and surpluses for the balance of the Marshall Plan period. It would also finance the union's net dollar outflow, since, at any settlement date, debtors might pay for a smaller proportion of their deficits in gold or dollars than creditors would receive for their surpluses. More ECA funds would be available to finance temporary advances by the union to a country in difficulty.

Facing a mid-January deadline, the OEEC was then busily engaged in preparing its *Second Interim Report.* That report was to be a major element in ECA's request to Congress for the third year's Marshall Plan appropriation. In conversations with the Secretariat and delegation heads, Bissell pointed out that some description of new trade and payments arrangements would have to be included in the plan of action proposed by the OEEC for the ensuing year. With next year's Congressional appropriation at stake, the OEEC could hardly refuse.

Britain's Proposal

Cripps and his advisers had left the 31 October OEEC Council meeting well aware of the momentum that had been created. Lest it elude UK control, Cripps wanted to regain the initiative. Upon his return, the Bank of England was asked to prepare a description of how a European clearing union might work.[11] At the time, the Bank was preoccupied with Sir George Bolton's dream of expanding European participation in the sterling area. Bolton was then a Director of the Bank and the United Kingdom's non-resident Executive Director of the IMF. By late November, a committee in London had prepared a memorandum proposing that most

---

[11] Interview with John Fforde, Bank of England historian (11 May 1987). BIS EPU Archive.

European countries be given transferable account status in the sterling area.[12] They would be able to use sterling to offset payments imbalances with one another and with any other country that had such status. The idea was dismissed after other British officials concluded that transfers of sterling between the European and non-European participants would have to be controlled.

Four days after Bissell's presentation, the UK delegation submitted its own hastily drafted proposal, noting that it had reached similar conclusions independently.[13] The Chancellor had summarized its contents for the cabinet's Economic Policy Committee only on the very day the document was presented in Paris.[14]

The British paper agreed that a new payments scheme was needed to replace the 'obsolete' IEPS at an early date. It married the Secretariat's currency pool to a proposal, first developed in 1947 by the CEEC Financial Experts, to multilateralize credit margins in the bilateral arrangements. Its principal new idea was that the pool would be used only as a last resort, after exhausting bilateral credit and other existing resources, such as sterling balances. The pool would receive ECA dollars, which would be allocated in advance for the account of anticipated structural debtors and creditors. The pool should be large enough to finance all normal fluctuations without any settlements in convertible currency. Only after country quotas were exhausted would individual debtors have to settle partly in gold.

The memorandum also reiterated some long-standing United Kingdom positions—retention of its bilateral payments agreements, minimal use of gold in intra-European settlements, the availability of sterling as the vehicle for transferring European currencies, and opposition to any new European institution with power to interfere in the internal policies of member countries. The British document received minimal support and little serious consideration in the ensuing work on the OEEC's second report. The United Kingdom delegation found itself in the difficult position of registering reservations about proposals that were acceptable to both the US and most other European delegations.

Hall-Patch, who headed the UK delegation, was also Chairman of the OEEC Executive Committee and thus responsible for drafting the *Second Interim Report*. The actual work had been entrusted to a working party headed by Eric Roll, a minister in the UK delegation. Hall-Patch proposed that Hubert Ansiaux, the Chairman of the OEEC Intra-European

---

[12] European Economic Cooperation Com. memo, 'Future of the IEPS' (24 Nov. 1949). ER (L) (49) (320). PRO T 232.

[13] UK del. memo, 'The Future of Intra European Payments' (14 Dec. 1949). OEEC TFD/DL/1950/3.

[14] Economic Policy Com. (14 Dec. 1949). EPC (49) 159. PRO CAB 134/224.

Payments Committee, should join Roll's working party. At a meeting of the Executive Committee on 15 December 1949, the French representative said that the treatment of payments in the report should be referred instead to a subcommittee of financial experts, with Ansiaux in the chair. The OEEC Council concurred, and the first meeting of Ansiaux's committee was set for the following week. Thus the process of devising new intra-European payments arrangements did indeed elude UK control.

Financial Experts Report

A forceful presence at any meeting, Ansiaux combined great substantive and negotiating skills. Then a Director of the National Bank of Belgium, he had gained both experience and recognition for expertise in international financial affairs. He had been Chairman of the CEEC Committee of Financial Experts and was still an Executive Director of the IMF and an Alternate Member of the Board of the BIS. Conscious of the inherent opportunity in this new assignment, he directed his boundless energies to developing a report acceptable to his committee, while keeping in mind his own country's position as Europe's principal intra-European creditor on current account.

Ansiaux's subcommittee met briefly on 23 December, as scheduled, but adjourned for a short Christmas holiday until the 28th. Three weeks and seventeen meetings later, at midnight on 21 January 1950, it completed its work and submitted its third draft for Council consideration.[15] It would be difficult to identify a precedent for this achievement.

The Experts met without any of the usual formalities of international committees. They were all senior officials of central banks and ministries. While each tried to protect his government's position and interests, the pressure of time permitted little formal reporting or reference to authorities for instruction. Even ECA's normally voluminous reporting was occasional and sketchy. The sole record of the meetings consists of some hastily prepared, unnumbered notes circulated within the Secretariat. The members debated, and sometimes co-opted other experts from their capitals on particular technical points. The Secretariat drafted and redrafted points of agreement and disagreement until consensus could be reached on a full document. The discussions served primarily to clarify and modify an early January proposal that clearly bore Ansiaux's stamp.

On the whole, the subcommittee included the same men who had

---

[15] Final Experts' text is 'Payments Arrangements' (24 Jan. 1949). OEEC TFD/DL/1950/9 (3rd revision). Published in OEEC *Second Interim Report* (Jan. 1950). Final *Second Report* (Feb. 1950) contains section on 'How a European Payments Union Might Function', 232–6. These texts contain some amendments after Exec. Com. discussions (25, 28 Jan. 1950) and Min. meeting (31 Jan.–1 Feb. 1950).

devised and managed the earlier compensations agreements. Guillaume Guindey, both a philosopher and a financial expert, was Director of International Affairs for the French Ministry of Finance. F. A. G. Keesing came from the Dutch Ministry of Finance; Suardus Posthuma was both Executive Director of the Netherlands Bank and a long-established professor of economics in Rotterdam. Hugh Ellis-Rees was a British Treasury official with extensive European experience, assigned to his country's delegation to the OEEC with the rank of minister. The Italian government borrowed Giovanni Malagodi and Alberto Ferrari from the Banca Commerciale to represent Italy. Sigmund Hartogsohn of the Bank of Denmark and Roy Bridge of the Bank of England were other important participants. These men welcomed the opportunity to propose a new system embracing full transferability of European currencies, multilateral credit, automatic compensation, and the replacement of grants of drawing rights by repayable credits.

At an early meeting, they agreed on a name, the European Payments Union (EPU). They proposed a management with strong discretionary powers. This met Bissell's requirement for an effective means of inducing countries to adopt appropriate policies and of arranging special assistance needed by individual members. One of the subcommittee's first decisions was to invite the Bank for International Settlements to serve as Agent for the operations of the Union.

All the Experts were quite prepared to recommend that European governments should themselves finance intra-European credits to cover seasonal and other temporary fluctuations. For longer term credits, they proposed that ECA dollars be put into a special fund to provide backing. Moreover, ECA would be expected to finance the deficits of countries like Austria, Greece, Iceland, and Turkey, which were unlikely to achieve intra-European balance over the remaining years of the Marshall Plan.

The Experts also felt that seasonal credits should be repaid if they remained outstanding for very long and that longer term credits should be accompanied by an increasing scale of payments in convertible currency. Accordingly, once the line of short term credit was exhausted, debtors and creditors alike would have to turn to a medium or long term credit line with the Union, settling partially and increasingly in gold or dollars as they used it up. They thus rejected Bissell's suggestion that creditors receive a decreasing proportion of gold as their cumulative surplus increased. As conservative financial technicians, the Experts sympathized with Ansiaux's support of intra-European creditors like Belgium. He insisted that such countries could not be expected to finance intra-European surpluses to any considerable extent, so long as they needed dollars to pay for their own persistent deficits with the dollar area.

The Secretariat proposed quotas for the system totalling about $2 billion, roughly 8.5 per cent of its estimate of recent intra-European turnover on current account. Half would be short term, the rest medium or long term. The Experts did not demur, though the exact size of the quotas was left for later discussion.

Short term credit would have to be redeemed when it had been outstanding for twelve consecutive months. At the insistence of the UK and Scandinavian members, the possibility of extending this to two years was added. The relationship between the EPU and existing payments arrangements for the use of sterling was also left open, for lack of agreement with the same officials.

The Experts' system was 'harder' than either the Secretariat's or Bissell's and very much harder than the one proposed by the United Kingdom. (In the jargon of the time, 'harder' meant less credit.) The Experts proposed that payments in gold would enter the system as soon as the seasonal credit line was used up. Even short term credits would have to be repaid in convertible currencies if they remained outstanding for very long. Apart from the structural debtors, other members would undertake to finance persistent deficits with gold or dollars after a specified delay. The Bank of England thought the Experts were trying to restore the gold standard; indeed Bridge referred to the even milder ECA proposal as a 'modified and inchoate form of gold standard'.[16]

Henry Tasca had been assigned to represent the US. Then Director of Harriman's Trade and Payments Division, he had helped put the finishing touches to the Bissell proposal. In earlier years, he had served as an influential US financial adviser in Italy and as an Alternate US Executive Director of the IMF. A skilful negotiator, he limited his interventions with the OEEC Experts and did not try to promote each specific idea in the Bissell proposal. On his shoulders fell the arduous responsibility of registering and explaining US opposition to suggestions that threatened either the essential objectives of the scheme or full participation by all OEEC members. As his assistant, Tasca had promptly recruited Robert Triffin from his post as the IMF representative in Paris. Triffin was a consummate financial technician, eagerly advancing ingenious and usually successful methods for solving the mechanical problems posed by an automatic clearing system.

Apart from technical issues, the Americans confined themselves largely to three points: (1) assuring ECA control over the funds it would provide directly and indirectly to support the system; (2) emphasizing the link with trade liberalization; and (3) insisting on a powerful supervisory authority.[17] ECA/Washington suggested to the US negotiators that

[16] Bridge, 'Events in Paris 18th January to 2nd February' (3 Feb. 1950). Bank of England OV 46/39.

[17] These points reinforced in Amb. Katz's letter to Sec. General (7 Jan. 1950). OEEC C(50)7.

Ansiaux's proposals put too little onus for adjusting policies on the larger creditors, while asking debtors to assume gold obligations they might be unable to fulfil.[18] Intent on getting an agreed report, Tasca and Triffin were loathe to challenge Ansiaux's sway over the members of his committee on this issue.

With very few changes, the Experts report passed through the Executive Committee and permanent Council and then was issued as part of the *Second Interim Report*. A ministerial meeting on 1 February approved publication of a shorter version in the final OEEC *Second Report*. It included all the essential points, but omitted or toned down controversial questions, primarily those of concern to the British and Scandinavians.

THE OUTBURSTS

In Europe, the first outcry against the Experts' proposal was voiced by the Governor of the Bank of England, Cameron Cobbold, at a BIS board meeting in Basle early in January. Later in the month, Cripps protested in Paris, both verbally and in a hostile memorandum. These alarums were preceded by an equally vehement attack on the Bissell proposal by the Managing Director of the International Monetary Fund, the US Executive Director of the Fund, and the staff of the US Treasury.

Although it was winter, these outbursts were like a summer storm. They burst over the landscape with sudden force and disappeared without much lasting effect. On the first day of February, the OEEC ministers decided to continue their studies of future payments arrangements 'on the basis of the paper submitted by the group of Financial Experts'.[19] More storms would follow, but the negotiations proceeded until the final issues were ironed out.

Attracted more by the scent of controversy at high levels than by the arid technical content of the proposals, the press reported the conflicts widely and with a modicum of accuracy. Most of the reports failed to emphasize that they had ended with agreement to pursue the negotiations, the most important fact.

Storms in Washington

Shortly after returning to Washington, Bissell had submitted his proposal to the US National Advisory Council on International Monetary and Financial Problems (NAC) without much negative reaction. On 29

---

[18] US tel. from Hoffman to Harriman. TOREP 341 (12 Jan. 1950).
[19] 'Minutes of the 86th Meeting' (30 Jan.–1 Feb. 1950). OEEC C/M(50)4.

December 1949, Frank Southard, then in his first year as US Executive Director of the IMF, presented a copy to Camille Gutt, the Fund's first Managing Director and a former Belgian Minister of Finance. Gutt was perturbed by what he thought was a challenge to the authority and responsibilities of the International Monetary Fund.[20]

Gutt's reaction was not shared by all his staff. André van Campenhout, then the Fund's General Counsel and later its Belgian Executive Director, told his ECA counterpart on 10 January 1950 that the proposed organization would strengthen the IMF. He suggested continual liaison between the two organizations but questioned the wisdom of Gutt's insistence on the Fund's institutional right to provide advice. He felt that any such offer of technical advice would be resented by European financial experts.[21] Indeed it was!

Nevertheless, Gutt forcefully presented his views to the IMF Executive Board on 12 January, emphasizing his jurisdictional concerns rather than objections to the substance of the proposal.[22] He felt that the proposal intended to establish a permanent financial institution similar to the IMF, encompassing Europe and perhaps the entire sterling area. If such a regional agency were necessary, the IMF should provide the machinery. Before governments that belonged to the IMF took any action, they should consult the IMF. He noted that the proposal made no mention of any link to the IMF.

The IMF executive directors from European countries found themselves in a difficult position. Work was proceeding in Paris under the aegis of their ministers, and they were not necessarily well informed. Their colleagues in Paris were financial experts, many of whom held more senior positions than they in the hierarchy of their governments. Moreover, four OEEC countries—Germany, Portugal, Sweden, and Switzerland—were not members of the IMF. Most of the non-European members of the Board supported Gutt on a matter that the European members considered to be primarily their own governments' concern.

Southard was a vigorous and sometimes passionate proponent of the IMF, who would dedicate the rest of his professional career to establishing it as the primary international financial institution. In later years, he would persuade US Treasury officials to relax their initial domination over the IMF's policies, to permit it to be more responsive to other members, and to ease their rigid stance concerning the use of its resources. Above all, he wanted the IMF to work and to have a constructive impact.

[20] Deshormes (1986).

[21] I. Stokes, ECA General Counsel, memo to Gordon and Tasca (10 Jan. 1950). US Archives. ECA Bissell Files.

[22] 'Proposed European Clearing Union'. NAC Staff Document 948, Attachment A (12 Jan. 1950). US Archives. Treasury NAC Files.

At the time, however, he shared Gutt's concerns, as did his Treasury colleagues.

After some debate in the IMF Executive Board, the Managing Director was authorized to record his views in a letter to each executive director. Southard brought the letter formally before the US National Advisory Council, where he and the staff strongly supported Gutt's position.[23] Four days after receiving Gutt's letter, the staff had a hostile memorandum ready for the NAC meeting at cabinet level.

Southard had told the staff that the jurisdiction of the NAC itself had been challenged. It was the first time that decisions had been made, negotiations begun, and testimony given to the Congress (by the ECA Administrator and the Secretary of State) without consulting the NAC. Southard felt the Europeans did not take the IMF seriously, and the US should not help them set up a similar institution in which the IMF had no voice. Furthermore, the Bissell proposal did not advance multilateral trade and dollar convertibility, the fundamental objective of US policy in this field. At the subsequent NAC meeting on 19 January, with Treasury Secretary John Snyder in the chair, the US Executive Director foresaw 'a strengthened soft currency area which might permanently discriminate against dollar trade'.[24] He felt there was no way of reconciling the proposal with US obligations to the IMF.

State Department representatives had warned the NAC staff that European economic integration was a joint State/ECA objective and that US political interests went beyond economics. At the full NAC meeting, Assistant Secretary of State Willard L. Thorp observed that the proposal would not necessarily create a permanent institution. He further reminded the NAC that, in August 1949, it had accepted the temporary discrimination against the dollar that would flow from earlier elimination of trade barriers within Europe.[25]

At staff-level meetings, Arthur Marget, adviser to the Federal Reserve Board, had emphatically supported the position of the IMF. However, at the NAC meeting, the Federal Reserve representative, Governor Matthew Szymczak, endorsed the Bissell proposal in principle, while hoping the system would involve less credit rather than more. Commerce and Agriculture registered pro forma opposition to any system involving discrimination against US exporters.

Sure of their mandate and authority, ECA participants at the NAC staff meetings sat quietly and later reported the complaints and criticisms. However, none of those who had drafted the Bissell proposal attended the meetings. Arthur Smithies (ECA) did note that the realistic choice

[23] Department of State (1950), i. 815-19.
[24] US Archives. Treasury NAC Files.
[25] See Appendix A.

was not between EPU and convertibility, but between EPU and bilateralism. This was probably the most relevant factual observation in an otherwise extended theoretical debate.

Outside the meetings, ECA principals communicated with their State Department colleagues and with Szymczak.[26] Harriman later visited Snyder and reported that the Secretary's fears had been eased upon being assured that the proposal was not intended to liquidate the IMF.[27]

The result was a unanimous, noncommittal NAC action taken on 23 January 1950.[28] The language was crafted primarily by Governor Szymczak.[29] The NAC considered that the establishment of a European clearing union should meet certain conditions. Principally, it should not conflict with country obligations to the IMF; no participant should be prevented from moving to convertibility before the others were ready; US contributions should not be used by the union to make non-automatic loans to members; and the US should not participate in the management of the union. The US could have an observer, but only for the duration of the Marshall Plan.

Exchange rates—a more obvious point of jurisdictional conflict between the Bissell proposal and obligations to the IMF—went unmentioned. The IMF Articles of Agreement required countries to notify the IMF of the par values of their currency and to consult before altering them. Under Bissell's proposal, the EPU management could require countries to adjust their exchange rates or take other remedial action as a condition for receiving special credits. Neither the Secretariat proposal nor any of the versions of the Experts report proposed giving the EPU management authority over exchange rates. The IMF pointed out the possibility of the two institutions making conflicting recommendations on internal economic policies. However, it would have been difficult to sustain a legal basis for asserting the IMF's sole jurisdiction over such matters. They had been central to the work of the OEEC from its very outset.

Despite the NAC action, a representative of the US government sat at all meetings of the EPU Managing Board throughout its existence. He had the legal power to block further use of the US capital contribution, if the US was dissatisfied with any alterations in the terms of the final EPU Agreement. That he did not vote was a concession to the NAC decision, though hardly a very significant one. Moreover, the Union did provide non-automatic as well as automatic credits, both backed by the

[26] Bissell memo to Szymczak (21 Jan. 1950). US Archives. ECA Bissell Files.

[27] Gordon, letter to Tasca from Washington (25 Feb. 1950). US Archives. ECA/Paris Tasca Files.

[28] Action No. 383 at 147th meeting of National Advisory Council (23 Jan. 1950). US Archives. Treasury NAC Files.

[29] M. S. Szymczak, 'The European Payments Union'. Memo to Board of Governors (26 June 1950). Federal Reserve Files.

US capital contribution. By the end of 1953, the Europeans and the United States were agreed that convertibility had to be approached collectively, not country by country. However, these unmet conditions of the January 1950 NAC decision never again became a major issue within the US government.

What the NAC decision said was less important than what it did *not* say. It did not advise withdrawal of the Bissell proposal, nor did it advise ECA to cease its negotiations. ECA thus felt authorized to proceed. Harriman and his associates had a green light, though they knew they would have to proceed with some caution.

British Squalls

Ansiaux briefed the central bank governors on the preliminary views of the OEEC Experts on 9 January 1950, at the regular monthly meeting of the BIS. On behalf of his committee, he outlined the general principles that had been established thus far. The Governor of the Bank of England was taken aback by the impression among his fellow governors that the British supported these principles, apart from some minor reservations. He understood this to mean two British commitments: (1) 'to introduce a far more rigid control over the use of foreign-owned sterling' and (2) 'to offset liberalisation of imports and relaxation of exchange control by a domestic deflationary policy', similar to practices under the gold standard.[30] He told his colleagues that no British government could accept the policies and purposes behind the Experts' plan, as they had been explained to him.

The following week, Roy Bridge was sent to Paris to join Ellis-Rees at the Experts' meeting and attempt to salvage the situation. Thereafter, the Experts report was redrafted repeatedly, but the final version's principal concession to British (and Scandinavian) views was to note certain important points that remained to be worked out.

Chancellor Cripps arrived in Paris for OEEC ministerial meetings late in the month of January and registered strong objections to the Experts report, both orally and in a memorandum circulated to all delegations. He immediately told Hoffman of his doubts about the feasibility of reconciling a European clearing system with the existing sterling area.[31] He carried with him a brief, prepared in Treasury Chambers, that observed 'we should obviously deplore a system which led to the compulsory blocking of all sterling holdings in Europe. This would

[30] 'Note of a Conversation with Ansiaux', later joined by Frère, Auboin, Conolly, and Sir Otto Niemeyer (11 Jan. 1950). Bank of England OV 46/38.
[31] Bridge, 'Events in Paris 18th January to 2nd February' (3 Feb. 1950). Bank of England OV 46/39.

obviously be bad for the prestige of sterling. So, too, would be the complete substitution of clearing units as a means of settling international payments.'[32] The repetition of 'obviously' must have served to caution Cripps, an erudite barrister, about such reasoning. He did not mention the 'prestige of sterling' in his memorandum.

He did assert that the United Kingdom could not join the EPU if the Union were to be the sole lender and if all existing credit margins and balances would have to be given up or brought under the EPU's control.[33] The Experts' proposals were akin to a 'return to automatic gold settlements in Europe which, if it were attempted in present conditions of dollar shortage, would necessarily restrict trade'. Britain insisted on the right to reduce imports from any country to which it might be losing gold. The facilities of the EPU must be fully automatic, freely available with minimum intervention by the management of the Union. Finally, the management should have no power or functions that overlapped those of the IMF.

Cripps's position would have been even less acceptable to the NAC than either Bissell's or the Experts' proposals. He wanted fewer gold (or dollar) settlements in the system, thus minimizing any element of convertibility with the dollar world. Moreover, were the system to recognize the right to discriminate against Europeans who might be earning gold, it would justify *a fortiori* discrimination against the dollar area. Support for the IMF's jurisdiction was disingenuous: his brief reveals that its intent was to oppose powers for the EPU management to impose policy conditions on member countries. The UK certainly did not want the IMF to manage the EPU in view of the 'preponderant influence exercised in it [the IMF] by the Americans and nonparticipating countries'.

British officials in London had already sought support from those in the US administration who were said to be opposed to the Union. Bolton had visited the US Treasury representative in London and blasted the proposal as a return to the gold standard.[34] It would cause deflation in both the United Kingdom and the sterling area, as well as a 4 per cent decrease in intra-European trade. He felt that the UK Treasury people in Paris had been caught napping; the Belgians had put one over on them.

Cripps's hard line had been anticipated by the Continentals. Petsche (the French Finance Minister) had responded to Hoffman's October speech by proposing that the Finebel countries—France, Italy, the

[32] 'The New Payments System: Brief for the Chancellor' (23 Jan. 1950). Bank of England OV 46/38.
[33] 'Memo. by the Chancellor of the Exchequer of the United Kingdom' (27 Jan. 1950). OEEC C(50)30.
[34] L. Hebbard, memo of conversation (24 Jan. 1950). US Archives. ECA/Paris Tasca Files.

Netherlands, Belgium, and Luxembourg—should make their currencies convertible with one another. (The name Finebel had quickly replaced an earlier acronym, Fritalux, which carried a connotation of *pommes frites*.) Late in November, the Netherlands had sounded out Ambassador Katz about including all OEEC countries in the clearing union except the United Kingdom, Greece, Turkey, and western Austria.[35] Dirk Stikker, the Foreign Minister, and M. W. Holtrop, Governor of the Netherlands Bank, both felt that the sterling area would run an excessively large deficit. Its inclusion would require a much larger pool of dollars in the union. ECA offered some support to the advocates of Finebel, but it did not conceal its preference for a payments union that would include all OEEC members, including the UK and the sterling area. The Finebel idea soon collapsed over disagreement about whether Germany should be included. However, at the ministerial meeting held at the end of January, France and the Netherlands reiterated their willingness to form a regional payments union within the Continent if an OEEC-wide agreement proved impossible.

Hoffman continued to press for an agreed OEEC report for Congress. Supported only by the Scandinavians, Cripps's position became untenable. Dramatization of the controversy in the press did not help. With British elections looming in less than a month, Cripps decided to yield gracefully. At the final session of the ministerial meeting on 1 February, he agreed that the Experts report could be issued and negotiations resumed on the basis of that report. He promised that his delegation would do its utmost to bring the matter to a successful conclusion and saw no reason why such a result could not be worked out. Knowing he would be a key British representative in the negotiations, Bridge laconically reported that the Chancellor 'spoke too optimistically for my liking about the prospects for successful resolution of the outstanding differences'.

The negotiations would obviously be difficult. The OEEC Executive Committee assigned the task to the Payments Committee, chaired by Ansiaux. Its job was to reconcile the substantive proposals of the Experts with national interests, as perceived by the various participating governments.

The technical virtuosity of the Experts would not necessarily prevail in this assignment. Governments were influenced as much by political concerns and trading considerations as by the technical and financial feasibility of a payments union. Their perceptions of national interest, whether well founded or misguided, represented ideas that were as important to the negotiations as the conceptual ones. Unless they could be married to the principles and procedures propounded by the Experts,

[35] US del. tel. to Washington. REPTO 7549 (22 Nov. 1949).

it was unlikely that all members of the OEEC would join the European Payments Union.

3 Governments: Perceptions of National Interests

Hoffman's conception of European integration called for the free movement of goods, money, and labour within Europe. In the abstract, OEEC governments could accept this as a desirable goal, but they were less prepared for concrete measures to achieve it. The various proposals for a clearing union confronted them with specific steps and timetables that would change existing systems radically. These measures, more than the goal itself, brought national and jurisdictional interests into play. Squeezed by continuing economic and political difficulties, each OEEC member had to weigh the proposed changes against its own hopes and fears. Since governments had different perceptions of what would serve their own interests, conflicts were inevitable.

Within some governments, perceptions about the national interests at stake varied considerably. Different officials, politicians, and interest groups—with varying ideological values, responsibilities, and bureaucratic interests—vied with one another to influence the negotiating posture of their government. Each government had to adjudicate these differences, consider how its interests would be affected, and determine its priorities as it negotiated with other governments.

Persuading nearly a score of countries to sign an EPU Agreement required negotiators who understood the interests, real and perceived, of every government, not just their own. They also needed insight into which perceptions within each government were likely to prevail. Each government's priorities had to be accommodated sufficiently to achieve at least its acquiescence, without threatening interests that other governments considered equally important.

To succeed, the negotiators had to accept the reality of the perceptions of those in authority, to raise doubts where that might be effective, and to accommodate those that remained unshakeable. They had to be able to persuade colleagues within their own governments, or allies in other governments, of the wisdom of each concession. Accommodation, not confrontation, was the path to agreement.

The task of identifying, sorting, and reconciling the divergent interests fell heavily on the United States, and particularly on its Paris delegation to the OEEC. Harriman delegated most of the responsibility to Katz, his deputy. A distinguished legal scholar, Katz recognized the talents of his very competent staff and gave them considerable latitude. His quick grasp of their briefings on technical and policy issues enabled him to deal astutely with European cabinet ministers at critical junctures of the negotiations. Hoffman and Bissell provided home base support for their negotiating team, usually endorsing its judgements about necessary compromises.

As proponents of the plan for a clearing union and controllers of the aid for European recovery, the US negotiators were well situated to pursue the task. Since the US itself could expect no trading or financial advantage from the proposed EPU in the near future, its negotiators were well above the fray. Well-staffed ECA missions in each European capital could be asked to seek out local views whenever the negotiations bogged down. The Paris staff analysed the reports and tried to devise formulas that might be acceptable, while still preserving the kind of EPU they wanted.

THE UNITED KINGDOM AND SCANDINAVIA

The US proposal for a European clearing union was launched at a particularly difficult time for the United Kingdom. Britain had emerged from World War II justifiably proud of its accomplishments. It was determined to continue to play a major role in world affairs alongside the United States and the Soviet Union. Britain had contributed fully to Allied planning for the postwar world and felt that it had earned the equal role to which it aspired. It accounted for more than a quarter of all intra-European trade in goods and services, and its pound sterling was transferable over large parts of the world.[1]

However, the UK's war effort had grievously eroded its economic base. Britain's authorities were well aware that its immediate postwar economic capabilities would not support its aspirations to remain a great power. Nevertheless, they hoped to reconstruct Britain's economic base while playing a major power role *and* meeting domestic demands for large increases in publicly financed services and housing.

For this Herculean task, the British counted on the support and co-operation of what they had traditionally presumed to be assets: the British Commonwealth, the sterling area, and a 'special relationship' with the United States. They discounted Europe, regarding it more as a potential drain than contributor. These three assets thus became the publicly reiterated and unquestioned priorities of Britain's international economic policy. Through repeated disappointments and recurrent economic strain, those priorities persisted for more than a full decade after the end of the war.

[1] BIS, *Nineteenth Annual Report, 1948-49*, 126.

Cabinet discussions and policy papers prepared in Britain's Economic Policy Committee, the Treasury, and the Bank of England reveal a considerable intellectual effort to devise means of capitalizing on these presumed assets. That effort was handicapped by a reluctance to confront policy alternatives realistically. In crisis after crisis during the postwar years, 'making do' and 'muddling through' tended to substitute for difficult choices. Attempts to devise international and economic policy proposals also suffered from the inadequacy and even the absence of economic analysis of other countries' economic policies and prospects. The proposals that were generated were remarkably weak in anticipating the probable reactions of other countries. The latter were preoccupied with their own interests and were very conscious of Britain's weak economic base. Whitehall's approaches either neglected or were oblivious to that reality. As a result, British negotiators were constantly forced to deal with other people's proposals or with counterproposals that commanded more international support than their own.

Assessments in British archives of the economic interests of the United States, the Commonwealth, and the sterling area are more rhetorical than analytical. Economic contributions by these 'assets' regularly fell far short of what Britain's political aspirations required. Most other countries wanted Britain to take hard decisions about restraining its domestic economy. Yet even the Conservative government that succeeded Labour late in 1951 was reluctant. Neither party found it easy to tell the 'assets' that Britain could not satisfy the economic demands placed on it. The exodus of economists from government service after the end of the war undoubtedly contributed to such deficiencies in policy-making.[2]

After the 1947 experience, the US Congress was most unlikely to finance another attempt at sterling convertibility unless the prospects for success were very good indeed. UK policy advisers persistently hoped otherwise. US economic interest in sterling convertibility required an accompanying end to discrimination against US exports. British officials repeatedly thought the US might settle for less.

British authorities then regarded the sterling area as an indispensable bond linking Commonwealth countries to the United Kingdom. However, many sterling area members held sizeable sterling balances, largely representing debts incurred by the UK during the war. The 1945 US loan agreement suggested that these debts be consolidated or cancelled. The holders felt these balances were legal obligations and would probably have regarded unilateral repudiation as sufficient reason for leaving the sterling area. A suggestion that India limit its drawings on such balances provoked resentment because others, such as Australia, had not been

---

[2] Cairncross (1985), 54–6.

asked to accept a similar limitation. Discussions with the US in 1949–50 about taking over some of the balances also came to naught.[3] Restrictive agreements were concluded about the use of these balances, but they were not very effective during repeated sterling crises—in 1947, 1949, 1951-2, and 1955-6.

A further inducement for continued participation in the sterling area was freedom of access to the London capital market. That privilege produced a flow of capital from Britain that rivalled the volume of aid received under the Marshall Plan.

Apart from profits to traders and financial institutions in London, the economic benefits to Britain from sterling's role as a trading and reserve currency may not have been commensurate with the costs. That possibility apparently was not seriously considered in British official circles. A seeming reluctance to face the matter underlines the role of political aspirations in British economic policy-making. 'The prestige of sterling' was a recurrent theme in the London memoranda.

In fact, few European countries then wanted to hold sterling in their foreign exchange reserves. A desirable reserve currency must both inspire a high degree of confidence and be widely acceptable in financial transactions. Benelux central bank governors had lively memories of 1931, when the Bank of England assured them that sterling would not be devalued, only days before it was. It was no secret that British reserves of gold and dollars had fallen below $2 billion in 1949, while sterling liabilities were of the order of $9 billion. Nor did the inflation-prone British economy, with its heavy restrictions on internal markets and external trade, render its currency very attractive. Limitations on the use of sterling were hardly compatible with the restoration of confidence.

The United Kingdom also had a different vision of its economic relations with Europe than did Hoffman, his ECA associates, or the Continentals. Britain's payments agreements with Europe had been intended to 'reestablish sterling as an international currency and London as a financial centre and at the same time bring the European countries more closely together and identify the United Kingdom with the strengthening of Europe'.[4] The British Ambassador to the United States, Oliver Franks, explained to Secretary Acheson that the issue for the United Kingdom was whether the sterling area was to be subordinate to the EPU, superior to the EPU, or co-equal with it.[5]

To be sure, trade with Europe was then of limited importance to the United Kingdom, and it resisted a system apparently designed for

[3] Economic Policy Com. Minute 1 (25 May 1950). EPC (50) 15th. PRO CAB 134/224.
[4] Cairncross (1985), 285, summarizes a discussion between senior officials on 5 Jan. 1949.
[5] Sec. Acheson and Amb. Franks, memo of conversation (13 Apr. 1950). US Archives. State Department 840.10.

countries whose trade within Europe was much more significant. Moreover, it had some concern lest increasing competition, especially from a resurgent Germany, become a serious problem for Britain within a free and multilateral intra-European system. The prospective expansion of the European market held little allure. Yet the share of other OEEC members in British trade almost doubled in the ensuing years, expanding from 22 per cent in 1948 to 42 per cent in 1970. In 1949, however, British authorities hardly considered such a development possible.

In retrospect, it is difficult to understand why Britain regarded the economic prospects of the Continent to be so much poorer than its own. Its government files show no studied analyses that might have warranted such a view. Events proved just the contrary to be true. Nevertheless, that assumption appeared unchallenged in the government's policy papers at the time.

Perceptions of the UK's interests involved fears as well as hopes. The British were especially apprehensive about assigning gold an important role in settling international accounts. This concern went back to the views of Keynes and the British delegation at Bretton Woods, when UK authorities wanted nothing to do with a gold settlement system. Gold evoked memories of the pre-1914 gold standard, which tolerated wide fluctuations in the business cycle and sometimes forced the adoption of deflationary policies. After the war, the UK stock of gold was indeed badly depleted and inadequate to finance its trade and cover its liabilities. A substantial increase in sterling reserves during 1950, after the 1949 devaluation, failed to give British authorities enough confidence to risk any further drain. Having paid £30–40 million of gold annually to Belgium and Switzerland, they wanted to bring such payments to an end.[6]

Further fears were kindled by the spectre of an OEEC administrative body with the power to recommend fiscal and monetary policies. The British government did not want to entertain such recommendations from the more orthodox financial circles that held power in much of the Continent. Nor did it fancy contesting policy advice in a European forum in which each country participated as an equal.

Given such very different perceptions of its interests, it is not surprising that the United Kingdom reacted with some heat to the latest strain on the 'special relationship' created by Hoffman's speech and Bissell's proposal. Bevin asked Acheson to specify just what the United States meant by European economic integration.[7] The US Embassy in London reported to the State Department that the British resented a 'common

---

[6] Economic Policy Com. (7 Mar. 1950). EPC (50) 7th. PRO CAB 134/224.
[7] Sec. Acheson and Foreign Min. Bevin, memo of conversation in Paris (11 Nov. 1949). Department of State (1949), iv.

American attitude that they were just another European power'.[8] Sensitive to the US Treasury's demands for convertibility and non-discrimination at an early date, British officials felt that the US was still determined to break up the sterling area. They saw the different pressures from the various US agencies as conflicting, irreconcilable, and impossible to satisfy.

While these were the considered perceptions of the British government, some voices dissented. David Eccles, a Conservative member of Parliament, told the ECA mission chief in London that important British circles were not at all convinced of the correctness of the Treasury position.[9] R. F. Kahn, perhaps Britain's most creative academic economist after the death of Keynes, hailed the EPU agreement. 'The introduction at last of convertibility inside Europe will prove a most important achievement,' he wrote.[10] UK representatives to the OEEC (especially Hall-Patch and Roll) followed their instructions faithfully, though their colleagues were well aware of personal reservations. Bridge also came to see that the EPU might be advantageous to Britain, but his views made little impression on his superiors at the Bank of England. Denis Rickett, a Treasury official who was Prime Minister Attlee's Principal Private Secretary, regarded the negotiations only as an effort for a third—and improved— IEPS. Edward Playfair (Treasury) saw the potential benefit of an EPU at an early stage. When Hugh Gaitskell, newly appointed as Minister of State for Economic Affairs, took control of the negotiations, he relied heavily on Playfair.

The Scandinavian countries were very dependent on the British market. Their socialist governments were pursuing economic policies comparable to those prevalent in Britain. Essentially, they felt that their interests were tied inextricably to Britain's, and they supported the UK position throughout the negotiations. The Danes were particularly concerned about agreeing to reduce quantitative trade restrictions while other countries maintained much higher tariff barriers on imports than they did.[11] The Norwegians wanted to be able to impose discriminatory trade restrictions against any large creditor whose exports to their market might require large gold payments. They were also the sole supporters of Bissell's suggestion that creditors receive decreasing percentages of gold as they moved up the scale of their quotas.[12]

[8] US Embassy London tel. to Washington (7 Jan. 1950).

[9] W. J. Kenney memo to Harriman and Hoffman (6 Apr. 1950). US Archives. ECA/Paris Tasca Files.

[10] Kahn (1950).

[11] Danish memo to Financial Experts (15 Dec. 1949). OEEC TP(49)61.
Also 'Statement by Mr. Rasmussen', delegate for Denmark (2 Feb. 1950). OEEC C/M(50)4, Annex I.

[12] 'Statement by the Delegate from Norway' (10 Jan. 1950). OEEC C/M(50)1, Part I, Annex B.

THE FUTURE COMMUNITY OF SIX AND SWITZERLAND

Six countries were soon to begin negotiating a Coal and Steel Community and some years later would conclude a Common Market agreement. They were Belgium, France, Germany, Italy, Luxembourg, and the Netherlands. Each had specific interests in the proposed payments union but no basic reservations. They claimed to be willing to organize a multilateral payments system among themselves, if it proved impossible to agree on a system including all OEEC members.

Belgium was in a unique position and thus became one of the major protagonists in the negotiations. Its coal and steel were urgently needed throughout Europe, and it persistently ran substantial surpluses in intra-European trade. Some of its exports to Europe were derived from processing raw materials and assembling components bought from the dollar area. Hence it needed large amounts of dollars to pay for its imports and struggled to find a way to convert its European surpluses into dollars.

Tight fiscal and monetary policies restrained both internal demand and inflationary pressures. Investment lagged behind that of most other OEEC countries receiving Marshall Plan aid. Reluctantly, Belgium had to offer credit margins in its bilateral payments agreements or lose European markets for its exports. Marshall Plan aid had financed some of both its imports from the dollar area and its European surpluses. Nevertheless, credits to other European countries limited the availability of funds for domestic investment. Believing its government budget to be too restrictive, a returning ECA official characterized the Belgian economy at the time as one with an abundance of automobiles, but no highways on which to drive them.

ECA tried to persuade the Belgian government to ease its fiscal and monetary policies to finance larger investments. The National Bank of Belgium's orthodox Governor, Maurice Frère, resisted strenuously, demanding instead an end to Belgian credits to European countries. Affable and delightful on social occasions, Frère could be very rigid about financial issues. He represented an older generation of European central bankers who stressed the importance of monetary policy in sustaining non-inflationary growth. By monetary policy, they meant restrained creation of credit; control of the aggregate supply of money entered the conceptual apparatus of European monetarists only many years later.

It was inevitable that Frère should recoil from the EPU proposal, with its provision for automatic credits. He feared that Belgium might have to finance substantially more credit to Europe than was already outstanding. Ansiaux, his younger Director, wanted a more flexible approach. Foreign Affairs Minister Paul van Zeeland strongly supported the European idea and understood Belgium's commercial stake in European markets. Like van Zeeland, Ansiaux saw, at an early stage, Belgium's interest in clearing arrangements and freer intra-European trade and payments. However, he also negotiated for a hard system, with as little credit and as much payment to creditors in gold and dollars as possible.

The delegates of the Federal Republic of Germany took their place at OEEC Council tables on the same day as Hoffman's 'single market' speech, 31 October 1949. Until then, two delegations, headed by the occupying powers, had represented Germany. A Bizonal delegation was led by United Kingdom and United States officials, and a French Zone delegation by French civil servants.

The Bizone trade and payments position had resembled Belgium's, showing intra-European surpluses and large dollar deficits. With reviving production and substantial trade liberalization, that position began to change. By October 1949, Germany had begun to run deficits with its European trading partners. Hans Karl von Mangoldt, head of the permanent German delegation to the OEEC, so informed the Council early in January 1950, foreshadowing the future EPU's first major crisis. However, he supported the Experts' proposals and only asked that other members ease restrictions on imports from Germany.[13] At the end of the same month, Franz Blücher, the German Vice-Chancellor and Minister for Relations with the Marshall Plan, again called attention to the very rapid deterioration of Germany's balance of payments with nearly all member countries.[14]

Germany's role in the negotiations was restrained, as its delegation sought to gain acceptance in European circles and to avoid controversy. It focused its concerns on the possibility of using existing resources— mostly the sterling it had accumulated under its compensation agreement. Otmar Emminger, a thoughtful and articulate participant in international monetary discussions over the next three decades, represented Germany at the financial meetings. Under firm instruction, he had to confine his interventions largely to private discussions.

The Netherlands was a persistent debtor in intra-European trade after the war. Its government vigorously pursued a high investment policy, but its central bank and financial officials were equally vigorous in advocating a tight monetary policy. Though the latter officials had yet to gain an upper hand in domestic policy formulation, they did represent the Netherlands as experts and supported limited credit in intra-European settlements. Foreign Minister Stikker was a firm protagonist of the OEEC and an integrated Europe. On 4 April 1950, he became Chairman of the OEEC Council, with the additional title of Political Conciliator.[15] He

---

13 'Statement by the Delegate from Germany' (10 Jan. 1950). OEEC C/M(50)1, Part I, Annex C.
14 'Statement by Mr. Blücher' (30 Jan.–1 Feb. 1950). OEEC C/M(50)4, Annex VI.
15 'Minutes of the 91st Meeting' (4 Apr. 1950). OEEC C/M(50)9.

performed this role faithfully, especially during the later stages of the EPU negotiations. A small country with the highest ratio of trade to GNP in Europe, the Netherlands supported every initiative for reducing trade barriers within Europe. Heavily dependent on the British market and in a relatively weak bilateral bargaining position, the Dutch repeatedly sought to mediate conflicts between the United Kingdom and other participants in the EPU negotiations.

France did not think the EPU proposal would affect its interests significantly. A relatively self-sufficient member of the European community, it had focused its economic policy on carrying out a large investment programme. Military efforts to maintain control over colonial possessions were a heavy drain on the government budget, particularly in French Indo-China. The French government used subsidies and wage and price controls to restrain the inflationary effects of its large budget deficit.

Protected by a strong network of tariffs and other restrictions, France's intra-European trade was in surplus in 1950. The French thought it unlikely that they would be much affected by proposals to eliminate the discriminatory aspects of these restrictions. French financial authorities had traditionally sought to enhance the role of gold in international settlements, and they supported that view during the EPU negotiations. Ultimately, France became a major user of EPU credit, especially after its struggle in Algeria erupted. But such an outcome would have been hard to foresee when the negotiations were taking place.

At the time, France was still apprehensive about admitting Germany to full status in European circles. The Finance Minister had proposed the Finebel scheme in the autumn of 1949. The other Finebel countries increasingly felt it important to add the German economy to any trading arrangement. France, in turn, became more interested in a still broader scheme in which the United Kingdom would participate as a counterbalance to German influence. France would have admitted the United Kingdom to a payments arrangement pretty much on the latter's terms.

Both Italy and Switzerland were exporters of so-called luxury products and tourist services to other European countries. In bilateral negotiations, they had little alternative but to provide credits if they wanted to retain markets. An end to quantitative restrictions and discriminatory regulations in intra-European trade would have served both countries' commercial interests.

Otherwise, their situations were very different. Italy ran large deficits with the outside world, as well as with many of its European trading partners. However, its accounts with the United Kingdom were in surplus. Thus Italy was particularly concerned that it be able to use its accumulation of sterling balances to settle its EPU accounts. Its political leaders were in the forefront of the European integration movement and sympathetic to the idea of a new European financial institution.

Switzerland, on the other hand, put more emphasis on the broader effort to accelerate European recovery. It endorsed the principles of the Experts report, while calling for members of the OEEC to restore financial stability and sound exchange rates.[16] Ambassador Gérard Bauer, head of its permanent delegation to the OEEC and Rapporteur Général of the Executive Committee, was an indefatigable EPU supporter. Wary of compromising its traditional neutrality, Switzerland avoided any involvement in political matters. It had joined the OEEC, nevertheless, largely to protect its economic interests.

The Swiss were both ready and eager to offer credits to the rest of Europe in exchange for sharply reduced barriers to their exports. The Swiss franc was freely convertible for residents of the dollar area, but it was subject to exchange controls for European countries with which Switzerland had bilateral trade and payments agreements. The Swiss hoped to benefit from an end to discrimination against their franc, the only really hard European currency at the time.[17]

THE UNITED STATES

In the United States, responsibility for international economic policy in the executive branch was divided between a panoply of virtually independent fiefdoms. President Roosevelt's proclivity for exercising control by creating new and competing administrative entities had carried over into the Truman Administration. Each agency managed the programmes for which it was responsible under the authority of Congressional legislation. Formal co-ordination among them was minimal, except on matters of very high policy. Informal interagency relations among staff at all levels did produce a considerable exchange of ideas and judgements. However, when differences arose, the responsible agency tended to press forward with minimal interference, unless the matter was referred to the White House. Not surprisingly, perceptions of national interest varied widely in the different centres of dispersed power.

The Economic Cooperation Administration (ECA) had been established by an Act of Congress as an independent agency to administer the Marshall Plan. It was instructed to heed the advice of the Department of State only on broad matters of foreign policy. The legislation also directed it to seek the advice of the NAC (National Advisory Council on

---

[16] 'Statement by Mr. de Salis', delegate for Switzerland (31 Jan.–1 Feb. 1950). OEEC C/M(50)4, Annex X.

[17] Minutes of the Bank Com. (29 June 1950). Swiss National Bank Files.

International Monetary and Financial Problems) on whether aid should take the form of grants or loans, on the terms for repayment of loans, and on the release of counterpart funds.

The NAC had been created under the Bretton Woods enabling legislation, which authorized US membership of the IMF and the World Bank. Chaired by the Secretary of the Treasury, it consisted of the Secretaries of State and Commerce, the Chairman of the Board of Governors of the Federal Reserve System, and the President of the Export–Import Bank. As a rule, attendance by cabinet officers other than the Secretary of the Treasury was undependable, particularly in Acheson's case. The NAC was to co-ordinate all agencies to the 'extent they make foreign loans or engage in foreign financial, exchange or monetary transactions'. In practice, the NAC's principal responsibility was to instruct the US Executive Directors of the IMF and the World Bank. Its staff was dominated by the Treasury's international finance officials.

The spirit, if not the letter, of the Bretton Woods Act gave the NAC jurisdiction over such matters as a European clearing system. ECA carefully avoided any confrontation over jurisdiction by submitting its ideas for NAC advice, though not necessarily before taking action. Similarly, the NAC and the Secretary of the Treasury avoided any confrontation with ECA that could only have been resolved by the President.

The Department of State itself comprised numerous smaller fiefdoms, whose independence could be controlled only at the level of the Secretary. Its economic bureau, headed by Assistant Secretary Thorp, had primary responsibility for trade policy and representation to the various economic bodies of the recently organized United Nations. Throughout its unsuccessful battle on behalf of the International Trade Organization, the bureau reflected a deep commitment to freeing trade on a global scale without discriminatory restrictions. Thus it tended to be allied with the Treasury in the conflict between regionalists and universalists, and it represented the Department at the NAC. Supporters of European regionalism were scattered throughout the Department, but they had yet to achieve the influence they would acquire in the subsequent Eisenhower Administration. Even so, they were able to secure State Department support for the EPU at the NAC, buttressed by Hoffman and Harriman's direct access to the Secretary.

ECA had ample Congressional authority and support for its proposal concerning the EPU. The 1948 legislation that authorized the Marshall Plan declared that it was US policy to encourage European countries to achieve speedily the advantages the US enjoyed through a large domestic market with no internal trade barriers. Congress subsequently strengthened the language in the legislation to emphasize its intent: support of European 'integration' became support of European 'unification'. ECA promptly submitted the EPU proposal to the authorizing committees of the Congress and received a ringing endorsement. Both Hoffman and Acheson gave strong support in their testimony. Indeed, at Hoffman's request, on 21 February 1950 the Congress agreed that $600 million (later reduced to $500 million) out of the next appropriation should be set aside and made available only for the benefit of countries that joined the EPU.

An ECA Policy Series, prepared by Bissell's staff, circulated widely within the agency. Among other subjects, its papers promoted European unification. They proposed a European central bank, a European currency, and a European fund to finance the adjustment of uneconomic industrial enterprises. Eventually they advocated initial unification by a smaller group of countries that might be readier to relinquish sovereignty than Great Britain and some other OEEC members. However, the only proposal along these lines that ECA ever urged on European governments was for an OEEC-wide clearing union. In that sense, it was the only true policy paper about European integration in the series.

Harriman and his staff in Paris were sceptical about the more far-reaching proposals for European union, preferring more realistic arrangements that might be acceptable to all OEEC countries. They were especially dubious about persuading the United Kingdom to surrender its sovereignty to a European supra-national body, a scepticism shared by the State Department. Bissell himself had registered similar reservations in 1948. He then thought the US should not like 'to see the British abandon an overseas orientation in favor of a European orientation' and that any such effort would be hopeless, as well as to the disadvantage of the United States.[18]

However, the elimination of trade and payments barriers within all OEEC Europe was clearly the policy of the United States. It was endorsed repeatedly, without reservation, by ECA in Washington and Paris and by the Secretary of State, as well as the Congress. That this would involve discrimination against US exporters, at least for a time, was acknowledged.

Most US policy-makers saw the interests of the United States primarily as the building of a strong Europe, able to sustain vigorous economic growth after Marshall Plan assistance came to an end. A significant element in this policy was to create a framework within which Germany could rapidly assume a full share in the economic life of western Europe. The elimination of intra-European trade and payments barriers was regarded as indispensable to these ends.

In the face of the dour outlook for the US dollar in the 1980s, it is

---

[18] Bissell memo to Hoffman (22 Sept. 1948). US Archives. ECA Bissell Files.

difficult to recall the relative strength of the US economy around 1950. Its foreign exchange reserves—held in gold—were almost embarrassingly large. Despite brief recessions in the late 1940s, production was far above prewar levels. The major US problem in export markets had less to do with competitive prices than the buyers' inability to pay with dollars. Foreign trade accounted for a very small fraction of US gross national production.

The United States at the time was a model 'good creditor'—providing grants and loans to other countries, encouraging foreign investment, reducing its own trade barriers, and accepting discriminatory treatment of its exporters. Stimulating economic growth abroad was expected to serve US interests in the long term, particularly if it eventually led to a return to both convertibility and non-discrimination on a global scale.

However, disagreement about the means and timing of global convertibility and non-discrimination was intense. The Treasury felt that with better fiscal and monetary policies, most European countries could move quickly to global convertibility, particularly in the aftermath of the 1949 devaluations. While heartily endorsing the devaluations, ECA felt that the dollar problem would not subside so quickly. Some of its officials felt that a progressive dismantling of restrictions against the dollar should be possible after the Marshall Plan was successfully completed. Others believed that the dollar problem was structural, requiring years of investment in modernizing production facilities, retraining and re-employing workers, and developing marketing organizations in the dollar world.

ECA also believed that transferability of European currencies into one another was an essential step in weaning European countries away from long-established government controls and from the interests of the entrenched bureaucracies who administered them. If European countries could be persuaded to abandon such practices within Europe, the risks of the further step of liberalizing on a global basis would seem less awesome and the benefits would be more demonstrable.

The importance of including Great Britain and the sterling area in the payments union was another point of conflict. At both the Federal Reserve Board and in ECA/Washington, individuals despaired of persuading the United Kingdom to accept a full role in the proposed EPU. They were prepared to go forward on the basis of the Continental countries who were willing to participate. Efforts to persuade the United Kingdom to join, they felt, would only delay the progress for which the others were prepared, or else lead to less meaningful arrangements. Nevertheless, during the EPU negotiations, the US team held very firm in seeking full British participation. That became the critical point of the early negotiations.

CONFLICT AND COMPROMISE

Given the perceptions with which the participating governments entered the negotiations, the major players had to be the United States, the United Kingdom, and Belgium. Each had to resolve different perceptions among its own officials, as well as disagreements with other governments. Ultimately, each entrusted final negotiating authority to those within its government who had come to see the overriding importance of a successful outcome. Each had to accept major compromises to reach an agreement.

The outcome of their efforts proved admirably effective in serving the purposes of all three countries, as well as of the other participants. The compromises fairly reflected a balance of the countervailing perceptions of the three major interested participants. The willingness of the negotiators to accept such a balance produced an agreement that served well the interests of the community as a whole.

4 Negotiations: The Long, Hot Spring of 1950

When the OEEC ministers adjourned early in February 1950, everyone agreed that the negotiations for a European Payments Union would have to be postponed until after the British elections. That meant the Payments Committee (the designated negotiating team) could not proceed with its work until mid-March. Time to complete the task was limited. At the end of June, the existing payments arrangements (IEPS) would expire, and new ones were essential to avoid chaos in intra-European trade.

The outbursts against the proposals in January had created an undertone that promised to prolong and complicate the work of the negotiating team. The play in the press may have softened the weaker antagonists by exposing their position to public view. The Payments Committee had been instructed to reach an agreement. Yet its members knew they could not ignore officials at home who did not want an agreement resembling either the Experts report or the Bissell proposal. As they struggled to reconcile the wishes of their own authorities with those of others, they were not very sanguine about the outcome. National governments do not readily compromise their perceived interests.

The negotiations centred on a succession of detailed technical proposals about how a European Payments Union might operate. Each protagonist devised a scheme that would satisfy its priorities and still meet a few of the preoccupations of other countries. As these self-serving schemes were rejected, new and even more ingenious ones were proposed, but to no avail. Then compromise proposals were offered, incorporating more conciliatory details. Finally, all the specifics were agreed in a way that everyone could accept.

THE PROTAGONISTS

The Negotiating Team

The key negotiators were the same men who had formulated the Financial Experts report. They were senior public officials, though most were rather young. All had risen to their present responsibilities through their own talents and achievements. They negotiated as professionals, conscious that each was expressing the view of a government, not necessarily a personal conviction. Each tried to persuade his authorities to accept necessary compromises. Under pressure from home bases, tempers flared on occasion, but calm was soon restored.

This was neither the first nor the last occasion these men would have dealings with one another. As weeks turned into months, mutual respect grew; old friendships deepened and new ones developed. Some of the participants would go on to serve on the managing body of the institution they had fashioned so laboriously. Their conduct during the negotiations foreshadowed both the methods and the accomplishments of that body, the eventual Managing Board of the European Payments Union.

Starting Positions

The lines for the negotiations were pretty well drawn and evident to all parties at the outset. Having won re-election, Britain's Labour government was not about to abandon its previous priorities. As the Chancellor had pointed out to the OEEC ministers in January 1950, Britain wanted a system that would disturb none of the existing arrangements for sterling— neither the holding of sterling balances, nor the transferability of sterling, nor the credits in British bilateral payments agreements. It wanted a system in which deficits and surpluses would be settled primarily through credit; gold payments would play a role only in extreme situations. It also sought the right to impose trade restrictions in a discriminatory fashion against extreme creditors. Finally, it opposed the creation of a new international financial body with authority to interfere in British domestic policies.

Most of the Continentals, led by Ansiaux, felt that gold payments had to have a major role to induce countries to strive for balance in their foreign accounts. Apart from the Scandinavians and structural debtors, the Continentals did not particularly expect to obtain large amounts of credit from the system, and they certainly did not want to extend much credit. The Belgians, of course, hoped to be paid in gold for most of their intra-European surpluses.

The US negotiators sought a new system that would include Britain and the rest of the sterling area, permit free transferability of all European currencies, and bring an end to bilateral trade and payments arrangements and to discriminatory trade restrictions within Europe. Their attitude toward gold and credit settlements was less extreme than that of either the United Kingdom or Belgium. They recognized that intra-European trade restrictions could not disappear with a risk of large gold payments hanging over the heads of deficit countries. On the other hand, the system had to involve enough gold payments to induce internal policy changes and lay the ground for eventual non-discriminatory trade with the dollar area. The US also wanted the EPU managers to have ample authority to influence domestic policies.

PROPOSALS AND REJECTIONS

The Central Bank Governors in Basle

None of the parties let any grass grow while waiting for the negotiations to begin. In Washington on other OEEC business in February, Ansiaux discussed payments arrangements with officials in the US Treasury, the Federal Reserve Board, ECA, and the IMF. On his return to Europe, he prepared a precise and detailed proposal for an EPU, including a draft statute, which he wanted to submit on behalf of Belgium.[1] His proposal was understandably even harder on the matter of credit than the Experts report. When he carried his draft to Basle for consideration by Governor Frère (and hopefully the other governors) at the BIS meeting on 13 March, he encountered unyielding opposition.

Frère told him that the central bank governors were agreed on a scheme that would require only half as much additional Belgian credit as Ansiaux was suggesting. Ansiaux replied that the US would never agree to fund an EPU in which the European creditors refused to extend additional credit and that the US would be supported by every European country except Belgium and Switzerland. Frère was unmoved, and Ansiaux's proposal was never submitted to the Payments Committee.

Most central bank governors were heavily influenced by Per Jacobsson, economic adviser to the BIS. He preached constantly and eloquently about using higher interest rates to control inflation, after which global currency convertibility should be introduced. The Experts' proposal seemed irrelevant to such aspirations. Jacobsson had little interest in an interim system of transferability within Europe. Roger Auboin, the French General Manager of the BIS at the time, shared these views.[2]

Ansiaux had also suggested that a board consisting of eight central bank governors should manage the EPU. The governors bristled at the thought. They had a positive distaste for establishing a European monetary institution that they feared might become permanent and rival the BIS. To accept authority 'to censure the policies followed by the different countries' was equally repugnant to them. It would appear presumptuous

---

[1] Minutes of the Board and Annexes A and B (14 Mar. 1950). National Bank of Belgium PV 729/10.

[2] Auboin memo, 'Unofficial Meeting of the Governors on 13 March 1950' on the proposed EPU. Bank of England OV 46/39.

if, acting as EPU managers, they should undertake to recommend fiscal or other economic policies. Even to seek such powers might threaten working relations with their governments.

The governors preferred an Auboin proposal that would maintain all existing payments arrangements and multilateralize only the existing bilateral credits. The promised ECA contribution to the EPU would be used to pay for two-thirds of debtor country deficits. Debtors would pay the remaining third in gold or dollars, using their reserves, third currencies, drawings on the IMF, central bank credits, private market credits, or whatever. The only credits European countries would offer would be those under the bilateral agreements. The system would operate for a maximum of two years; the Experts' ideas about medium or long term credits would thus become moot.

The governors had agreed to sponsor a proposal that would be attractive to few, if any, of the negotiating governments. It certainly would have received short shrift from US negotiators, and the document never surfaced in Paris. Frère and Ansiaux soon brought their differences before Belgian Foreign Affairs Minister van Zeeland. He authorized Ansiaux to continue to campaign for the Experts report, but instructed him to stop appearing to be the US advocate against the United Kingdom.[3]

Britain's Counterproposal

When British officials returned to London after the January ministerial meeting, they, too, set to work preparing a counterproposal. Their major focus was on devising a method whereby Britain could join the EPU without disturbing either the sterling area mechanism or its bilateral payments arrangements. Indeed, officials were so preoccupied with that effort that Chancellor Cripps, reviewing the ideas they presented, voiced some concern. He had to be reassured that the other points in his memorandum to the OEEC ministers were not being neglected.[4]

The Continentals and the US were prepared to accept the basic concepts of the Experts report. Since the British were not, they thought it only logical for the sterling area to join the EPU under different arrangements than those applicable to and acceptable to the others. This might even enhance the position of sterling, rather than reducing it to the status of another European currency. Marcus Fleming, of the economic section of the cabinet secretariat, had devised a technical proposal that would have permitted full sterling area participation. However, other

---

[3] Tasca memo to Katz, relaying a Triffin conversation with Ansiaux (16 Mar. 1950). US Archives. ECA/Paris Tasca Files.

[4] 'European Payments Union'. Note of a meeting with the Chancellor (20 Jan. 1950). Bank of England OV 46/39.

officials presented it to the Chancellor without much enthusiasm, and he rejected that alternative.

Two weeks after the February elections, a tendentious, nineteen-page UK proposal was handed to Ambassador Harriman in London, as well as to a few other European statesmen (Ansiaux, Stikker, and Petsche). It began by defending the overriding priority Britain attached to full employment in framing its economic policies and went on to describe in considerable detail the international management of sterling.

On the day the proposal was handed to Harriman, Cripps had his Ambassador in Washington deliver a personal letter to Hoffman. 'I hope you will not hustle us unduly on this matter or encourage others to insist on provisions which it is not and never will be possible for us to accept.'[5] Hoffman characteristically avoided confrontations, preferring to accommodate critics and ease tensions. In this case, his reply a week later was both adamant and cold. The American proposals could not be modified. Britain seemed to be reneging on the decisions taken by the OEEC Council immediately after Hoffman's 'single market' speech, though the US public had been 'avidly waiting to see whether the program agreed to will be implemented'. If the United Kingdom could not participate fully in the EPU, 'the restoration of a cordial relationship between the United Kingdom and the United States will be difficult of achievement'.

Thus rebuffed and seriously ill, Cripps largely withdrew from personal involvement in the negotiations and appeared to be seeking a way to adjust to the US position. His British junior ministers, led by Gaitskell, urged standing fast.[6]

The counterproposal would have provided for full clearing (multilateral compensations plus settlements in gold and credit) of all Continental surpluses and deficits. However, the United Kingdom would retain its bilateral payments agreements. It would agree with each of the participating countries on the extent to which surpluses would be held in sterling, as well as the extent to which deficits could be met from existing resources— sterling resources acquired previously. 'Existing resources' would become a key issue in the negotiations.

The British believed they could arrange each clearing in such a way as to avoid any gold payments unless the UK ran deficits with all of western Europe for an appreciable period.[7] They insisted on the right to reimpose discriminatory restrictions, without prior review, on any creditor whose surplus exceeded three times its gold-free obligation.

[5] Cripps letter (7 Mar. 1950). Hoffman reply (25 Mar. 1950). As copied from UK Treasury files by Travers. OECD EPU Archive Box 11.

[6] 'Oral History Interview with Milton Katz' (25 July 1975). Harry S. Truman Library.

[7] Economic Policy Com. Minutes (7 Mar. 1950). EPC (50) 7th. PRO CAB 134/224.

Four days after receiving this proposal, Tasca informed Ellis-Rees that it was not acceptable to the US.[8] It involved neither full currency transferability nor full clearing of intra-European current transactions. The incentives for countries to keep their intra-European surpluses and deficits within manageable proportions were much weaker than those suggested by either Bissell or the Experts.

At the same time, Tasca raised the possibility of extra US help. The US was prepared to recognize the special position of sterling and the real possibility that the UK might build up a very large EPU deficit over a short period. If certain deficits could be regarded as structural, the US might provide dollars to finance them. The UK might also be given automatic freedom under certain conditions to reimpose quantitative restrictions for a temporary period, but only on a multilateral basis and subject to EPU review. He hoped the UK paper would not be formally presented. Stikker expressed the same hope to Cripps and Bevin in London.

The United Kingdom, nevertheless, gave an abbreviated and less doctrinaire version of its proposal to the OEEC heads of delegation, though not as an official document. Afterwards, Ellis-Rees and Bridge held a private meeting to provide explanations and allay suspicions. They emphasized that the United Kingdom was prepared to give, but not receive, a quota, so that it might be a lender to, but not a borrower from, the Union.

The individuals invited to their meeting would later become the so-called Inner Group that negotiated the tough policy issues. They were largely the key figures from the earlier Financial Experts subcommittee— Ansiaux, Ferrari, Guindey, Keesing, Posthuma, Tasca, and Triffin.

After the initial meeting, Bridge reported that the Europeans were bewildered, and the Americans were not particularly friendly.[9] Ferrari had felt that the British proposal could produce a situation where the UK was a creditor to the EPU, but Italy and other countries would still have to increase their sterling balances.[10]

Ansiaux had observed that by refusing to grant bilateral credit to a country, the UK might draw gold or dollars from the EPU, while being an overall debtor. It could borrow from its bilateral creditors and obtain gold for its own bilateral surpluses. Bridge felt Ansiaux suspected a UK intent to discriminate against Belgian exports rather than lose gold. Ansiaux reported acerbically to van Zeeland that the UK would be able

---

[8] Tasca, memo of conversation (11 Mar. 1950). US Archives. ECA/Paris Tasca Files.

[9] Bridge memo, 'EPU—Paris Negotiations' (25 Mar. 1950). Bank of England OV 46/39.

[10] F. Conolly, notes on the meeting (27 Mar. 1950). BIS EPU Archive Box 13. Inner Group Folder.

to settle a gold debt to Belgium or Switzerland by paying the Union with Greek drachmae or Austrian schillings.[11]

Within a few days, the group met again at the UK delegation offices for official or semi-official reactions.[12] A new member had been invited to join—Knut Getz Wold, the Norwegian co-ordinator for the Marshall Plan. Guindey, Ansiaux, Keesing, and Ferrari all registered reservations about the British proposal, indicating they saw no need for the UK to demand a special position for sterling. Tasca emphatically reiterated objections he had voiced during his meeting with Ellis-Rees earlier in the month. Getz Wold was the only Continental who showed any flexibility on the issue.

Nonetheless, Ellis-Rees reported to London that the Continentals could be persuaded if the Americans would relent.[13] Washington, on the other hand, was convinced that the main thrust of the British proposal was to secure 'complete freedom to pursue domestic policies they want on purely national grounds and . . . to exploit all the benefits of their present bilateral trading arrangements'.[14]

Both in Washington and in the OEEC delegations, voices had begun to despair of persuading the United Kingdom to join the EPU as a full partner. Guindey would have accorded sterling a special position, but without giving the UK a unilateral option to decide which currencies it would put into the clearing. Ansiaux thought Britain should have no voice in the management if it were not a full member.[15]

US Federal Reserve staff reluctantly suggested accepting the British counterproposal as the best solution that was obtainable.[16] Harold Van Buren Cleveland, a major contributor to the initial ECA proposal, offered Bissell similar counsel, but Bissell preferred to pursue full participation. After discussions with other agencies, ECA authorized an offer to the UK of a special drawing right. It further offered to set up a special contingency fund to cover any unexpected dollar drain.[17]

Tripartite ABC Economic Talks

The British counterproposal was undoubtedly influenced by other international financial discussions that had been going on for some months

[11] Ansiaux letter to van Zeeland (27 Mar. 1950). Annex to Minutes of the Board. National Bank of Belgium PV 735/13.

[12] Figgures memo, 'Discussion of 31 March'. OEEC TFD-122/FF.

[13] Gordon (US del.), memo of conversation with Eric Roll (UK del.) (5 Apr. 1950). US Archives. ECA/Paris Tasca Files.

[14] Washington tel. to US del. Reports ECA/Washington views after meeting with reps. of other interested agencies. TOREP 2647 (31 Mar. 1950).

[15] Figgures memo, 'Discussion of 31 March'. OEEC TFD-122/FF.

[16] e.g. 'The British Proposal on the European Payments Union'. Memo by Albert Hirschman, adviser to Gov. Szymczak (29 Mar. 1950). Federal Reserve Files. Marget recorded similar opinion in letter to member of Tasca's staff (21 Mar. 1950). US Archives. ECA/Paris Tasca Files.

[17] Washington tel. to US del. TOREP 2647 (31 Mar. 1950).

in Washington. UK Treasury civil servants were meeting with US State and Treasury counterparts, under the aegis of a Tripartite ABC (American, British, Canadian) Committee established during the September 1949 sterling devaluation crisis. ECA personnel did not participate. The subject of these meetings—sterling convertibility—corresponded more closely to the aspirations of British officials than did any European regional payments arrangement.

The US Treasury was pressing for early sterling convertibility. Its officials pointed to Article 9 of the 1945 Anglo-American Financial Agreement, under which Britain agreed to refrain from discrimination in its use of quantitative trade restrictions. Although the Agreement had been suspended after the 1947 convertibility débâcle, the UK was still obligated to seek convertibility as soon as it could. British participants in the ABC talks, led by Leslie Rowan, were as eager as the Americans for sterling convertibility. Moreover, if they could persuade the Americans to offer the necessary support, European integration and the EPU would fall into insignificance. Their American counterparts in these talks had no more interest in a successful outcome to the EPU negotiations than they did. UK dispatches from Washington repeatedly affirmed a belief that eventually the US Treasury would win its dispute with ECA about convertibility and the EPU.

Despite their mutual interest in sterling convertibility, participants in the ABC discussions never overcame the basic problem of how to achieve it in the face of a worldwide dollar shortage. The US side saw the principal obstacles as the large volume of sterling balances held by countries outside Great Britain and the excessively expansionist economic policies of the British government. Senior Treasury officers in London, undaunted by such obstacles, produced a steady stream of suggestions for surmounting them.

An Anglo-American currency union was explored. It would have required either a pooling of foreign exchange reserves or $5 billion in US support for sterling, in addition to Marshall Plan aid.[18] British Treasury officials recognized that strong anti-inflationary, if not de-flationary, measures would thereupon have to be introduced in the UK. However, the Labour ministers rejected any commitment that would endanger their political priorities—very full employment, social welfare, and housing.

British officials then shifted their attention to US measures that might facilitate sterling convertibility. To name a few: the US could open its market to more sterling exports; it could provide special credits in the

---

[18] 'Currency Union with the U.S.A.' UK memo for Anglo-American-Canadian Economic Talks (Nov. 1949). PRO T 236/2400.

event of a US recession; it could fund part of the sterling balances; it could increase aid to South Asia in return for a South Asian agreement to freeze its sterling balances. US counterparts greeted none of these ideas warmly. Nor did they welcome suggestions that the US should not reduce Marshall Plan aid or require a resumption of payments on the 1945 loan, even though UK foreign exchange reserves were rising.

Frustrated by the lack of progress in these talks, British officials began to consider a kind of convertibility that would retain restrictions on imports from the US. 'If the Americans want convertibility and non-discrimination, they will get neither. If they are prepared to take convertibility without non-discrimination there is a chance.'[19] Since the Americans wanted both, they encouraged the British to develop further thoughts.

Not long after his appointment as Economics Minister in February 1950, Gaitskell began to take a personal interest in these talks among officials. He opposed showing any flexibility to the Americans or anyone else about a possible drain on Britain's gold reserves. In European as well as in dollar trade, he felt it unwise to accept non-discrimination, lest the UK lose gold. He wanted that point to be relayed to all concerned foreign governments. His Treasury subordinates preferred to continue noncommittal talks in the ABC forum. Thereafter, Gaitskell was determined to keep tight control over any further negotiations with the US at the civil servant level concerning convertibility and non-discrimination.[20]

On 11 April 1950, Cripps received a letter from the US Secretary of the Treasury, requesting a full statement on the trade and payments policies the UK expected to pursue. Snyder pointed to UK obligations under the 1945 Agreement. UK reserves were increasing, without any sign of an accompanying move to convertibility or non-discrimination. The letter arrived at a critical moment in the EPU negotiations. The Americans and Continentals in Paris were trying to devise a way to bring the UK into the EPU as a full participant.

Cripps's reply only suggested continuing discussions about con-vertibility in Washington. He wisely defined the essential conditions for sterling/dollar convertibility as much larger UK reserves and a US foreign exchange position in balance or deficit with the rest of the world. Indeed, convertibility did not come until after these two conditions were met. Cripps and Gaitskell both recognized that sterling convertibility would not be within their grasp in the near future. The officials serving them still hoped to find a short cut.

As the ABC track with the US government seemed to be at a dead

[19] Official Com. on Economic Development ED (W) (15) (14 Mar. 1950). Quoted in Travers notes on UK Treasury files. OECD EPU Archive Box 17.
[20] Williams, P. M. (1979), 219.

end, Gaitskell became more attentive to the possibility of an acceptable outcome to the Paris negotiations. In Paris, at least, the US was showing some flexibility. He wrote in his diary after talking to Harriman and Katz that 'in the battle we shall have to fight [with the IMF and the US Treasury over convertibility and non-discrimination], ECA might become our allies.'[21]

A New Ansiaux Proposal

After rejecting the UK counterproposal in a desultory session, the small group meeting unofficially with Bridge and Ellis-Rees declared a hiatus. Further meetings were postponed for a few weeks to give everyone time to reflect and reconsider.

Two things had become clear. A cooling-off period was needed before trying to resolve major policy disagreements, and resolving them in the full Payments Committee was impractical. With seventeen European delegations represented, plus representatives of the US, the BIS, the IMF, and the World Bank, the Committee was too unwieldy and too public a forum for open discussion of important disagreements.

It was generally agreed that the same small group should continue to meet privately after the hiatus. It would tackle the thorny policy issues, while working parties dealt with the technical questions. Guindey invited the group to resume its meetings at the Louvre offices of the French Ministry of Finance. Thereafter, the 'Inner Group' met there or at the offices of the United Kingdom delegation, and Marjolin himself joined it.

The delegations that were not included in the Inner Group acquiesced in these informal arrangements. Subsequent meetings of the Payments Committee were confined to occasional reports by Ansiaux, who carefully veiled the contentious issues. Both Germany and Switzerland, later to play key roles in the operation of the EPU, graciously yielded to the necessity for a limited negotiating forum.

Early in April, Ansiaux developed a softer version of the central bank governors' proposal and obtained the concurrence of Frère, as well as the French, Italians, and Dutch.[22] The medium or long term credits would be dropped from the Experts' proposal. Surplus countries would settle entirely in credit, but the Union would repay them fully with gold after twelve months. Debtors would receive grants for half their deficits during the first year, financed out of the ECA contribution to the Union. The other half would be settled with their own resources or by drawing

---

[21] Williams, P. M. (1979), 221.
[22] 'OEEC—Payments Plan for 1950-51'. Annex to Minutes of the Board (7 Apr. 1950). National Bank of Belgium PV 738/16.

creditor currencies from the IMF. The IMF would put policy conditions on such drawings, not the EPU board.

The United Kingdom would thus be given its way on curtailing the managing board's power. In addition, creditor countries could either retain their sterling earnings or clear them through the Union as they pleased. Debtors could settle with any existing (sterling) resources at their discretion before using their EPU quotas. However, outstanding credit under the bilateral agreements would be paid off through the clearing over a three-year period.

Ansiaux reported to his Belgian colleagues that initial reactions to his scheme were encouraging, even from the Americans.[23] He and Triffin had established a close collaboration, and the latter undoubtedly saw in the scheme elements of his own proposal of the previous year.[24] Bridge's report to London was unenthusiastic; many points were still unclear.[25]

In fact, Ansiaux's proposal quickly united the US Treasury and ECA/Washington in firm disapproval. Ansiaux had suggested that EPU debtors should draw creditor currencies from the IMF and repay their drawings in the same currency. The IMF, however, had hitherto insisted that all drawings be repaid only in convertible currencies, and the US Treasury was not ready to change that policy. Gutt had sought its relaxation in 1948, and Triffin had so proposed in 1949. The idea was no more acceptable when Ansiaux proposed it in 1950. ECA had other objections; Bissell was not interested in financing a scheme that was unlikely to survive the Marshall Plan. The EPU capital would be used up in gifts to the debtors, and the Union would have no further capacity to extend credits or to induce debtors and creditors to adjust their economic policies. Such an EPU would represent little progress toward ECA's goal of European integration.

When the Inner Group reconvened late in April, it had before it Ansiaux's paper and a proposal Figgures had prepared in collaboration with Bridge. The Figgures paper was a virtuoso technical performance. It would have brought the United Kingdom into a technically workable system, but one which achieved neither full transferability nor an end to bilateralism.

At that meeting and at another two days later, heated debate in the Inner Group reached its zenith.[26] The UK rejected the Ansiaux proposal, the Continentals dismissed the scheme concocted by Figgures, and the

---

[23] 'OEEC—Payments Plan for 1950-51'. Minutes of the Board (21 Apr. 1950). National Bank of Belgium PV 741/10.
[24] See Appendix A.
[25] Bridge memo, dictated by telephone (19 Apr. 1950). Bank of England OV 46/39.
[26] Conolly, notes on meetings (26, 28 Apr. 1950). BIS EPU Archive.
Also Bridge report on the meeting (28 Apr. 1950). Bank of England OV 46/39.

US objected to both. All the negotiators assumed firm positions that left little room for compromise. Extreme statements poured forth. Only the British wanted so much as to discuss the Figgures paper.

Ellis-Rees made it plain that the UK would expect automatic credits even after the termination of the Marshall Plan in 1952. He went so far as to assert that a return to 100 per cent gold settlements would never be feasible.[27] Tasca insisted that surplus countries had to give credit in any system ECA would finance. Otherwise, he argued, debtor countries would restrict trade. Marjolin endorsed Tasca's point. Ansiaux could hardly have been surprised by Tasca's position, having predicted it to Frère less than two months earlier. Even so, he angrily responded that, in that event, Belgium would not join the EPU. The negotiations seemed to have reached an impasse.

SPECIAL RULES FOR BRITAIN?

The US negotiators meanwhile had turned their attention to devising an acceptable way for sterling to participate fully in the EPU. The question of European credits within the EPU seemed intractable, and calm would be restored by putting it aside for awhile. Borrowing points from both the Ansiaux and the Figgures proposals, ECA/Paris crafted an ingenious technical proposal for accommodating sterling.[28] Concessions were offered to British insistence on permitting OEEC countries to hold current earnings of sterling in their reserves and to use existing sterling balances to settle with the Union. However, limitations were also included that would minimize the risk that the EPU's capital would be exhausted by an avalanche of sterling injected into the clearing. After using existing resources, every country would report net bilateral positions fully to the Agent for offsetting, thus assuring full transferability.

The proposal was first submitted to Ansiaux, who modified it and gained the support of Italian, Dutch, French, and Swiss representatives. At the end of April, it was presented to the United Kingdom as another Ansiaux proposal, endorsed by the other Continental countries. The practical significance of this 'Continental proposal' proved to be minimal once the EPU began operations, as the ECA/Paris staff had anticipated. But it did offer the British a face-saving opening for a graceful withdrawal from their hitherto inflexible negotiating stance. Would they take the opening?

In London, British officials were divided about whether to accept the

---

[27] Memo on a meeting about the EPU (26 Apr. 1950). US Archives. ECA/Paris Tasca Files.

[28] ECA/Paris staff memo, 'Possible Reconciliation Between the EPU System and the Sterling System' (6 Apr. 1950). US Archives. ECA/Paris Havlik Files.

Continental approach as a basis for further proposals. Ministers still preferred bilateral offsetting; they 'would allow themselves to be driven back to the Ansiaux [Continental], or multilateral approach, only if retreat became necessary'.[29]

Early in April, the US State Department had begun to explore the possibilities of a high-level approach to resolve Anglo-American differences over the EPU.[30] Acheson discussed the issues with Ambassador Franks on 13 April. Subsequently, Harriman, Katz, and their staff prepared an *aide-mémoire* that Acheson handed to Bevin at the foreign ministers' meeting in London on 11 May 1950.[31] The Secretary stressed the importance of bringing the negotiations to a satisfactory conclusion on the basis of the Experts report, as modified by the Continental proposal for sterling area participation. He repeated the earlier offer of special dollar aid, as well as Tasca's initial suggestion to Ellis-Rees that multilateral quantitative restrictions might be reimposed in the event of significant reserve losses.

Three days later, Harriman informed ECA/Washington that Cripps had accepted the Continental proposal. The Bank of England 'continued to worry that the new EPU currency might threaten the special position of sterling'.[32] The British government, however, had given up unrealistic hopes that sterling might be held increasingly in European reserves and that it would play a much more important role in clearing intra-European accounts than any other OEEC currency. The UK had also given up any 'hope of getting sterling credit through the Union without the possibility of a loss of gold'.[33] On the other hand, it had gained recognition that the existence of sterling balances required special provisions in the EPU arrangements. In addition, the US accorded Britain special protection against possible gold losses. Thus was the first major hurdle of the negotiations cleared.

HOW MUCH CREDIT?

Gold and Credit Provisions

Having found an acceptable arrangement for the pound sterling, the negotiators had to address the role of gold and credit in settlements. If

---

[29] European Economic Cooperation Com. Minutes (17 May 1950). ER (L) 50 31st. PRO CAB 134/246. At this meeting, Playfair recapitulated UK consideration of EPU, from Continental proposal through early May discussions with Acheson and Harriman in London.

[30] ECA draft brief sent on request to State (10 Apr. 1950). US Archives. State Department 840.10. Revision sent by Bissell to Assistant Sec. Perkins (14 Apr. 1950). For Bissell's hard-hitting attack on British position and motives, Department of State (1950), iii. 646-52.

[31] For *aide-mémoire* text and comment, see Department of State (1950), iii. 655-7.

[32] Williams, P. M. (1979), 224.

[33] European Economic Cooperation Com. Minutes (17 May 1950), PRO CAB 136/246.

the UK wanted more credit, others wanted less. The British felt they were being pushed into another premature attempt at convertibility. At an IMF Executive Board meeting in mid-March, their representative had been outvoted after a sharp exchange of views. He had objected to an instruction to IMF observers in Paris to seek moderate credit and more gold or dollars in intra-European settlements. According to a Paris report, Gaitskell was 'pathological about gold settlements'.[34]

Having yielded to Acheson's urging, the UK now began to press for an EPU agreement that would be in accord with its purposes on the remaining issues. In a memorandum dated 19 May 1950, it formally recorded its acceptance of the Continental proposal respecting sterling arrangements.[35] The memorandum went on to make proposals concerning the role of gold and credit. The proposals were extreme, yielding very little to the views expressed earlier by other negotiators. However, Ansiaux soon discovered a change in the position of France, Italy, and the Netherlands. They, as well as the Scandinavians, were now supporting the British desire to minimize the role of gold payments.[36]

The amount of automatic credit in an EPU system would depend on the size of the quotas, the size of the gold-free fraction of the quotas, and the credit percentages available in the rest of the quotas. The British proposed large quotas, a large gold-free fraction, and substantial credit in the remainder. They suggested EPU quotas equal to 20 per cent of each country's intra-European turnover in 1949. (Turnover referred to total imports and exports of goods and services.) Borrowing would be free of gold payments for half of the quota. Thereafter, borrowers would pay increasing amounts of gold as they moved through the second half of their quotas. They would only settle with as much as 25 per cent in gold by the time their quotas were used up.

Creditors, on the other hand, would receive no gold as they ran surpluses up to a quarter of their quotas (5 per cent of the turnover). Thereafter, they would receive gold for a third of their surpluses until their quotas were exhausted. After half of a surplus country's lending quota had been used, other members of the Union would be entitled to impose discriminatory trade restrictions against it. Once its quota was exhausted, a creditor would be entitled to withdraw from the Union, if it preferred to cease settling by extending two-thirds credit. All credits would remain outstanding for two years, after which it would be decided

---

[34] Gordon, memo of conversation with Roll (15 Apr. 1950). US Archives. ECA/Paris Tasca Files.

[35] 'Proposals by the United Kingdom Delegation' (15 June 1950). Memo transmitting to Payments Com. proposals communicated informally to other dels. (19 May 1950). OEEC TP(50)62. The provisions for sterling—essentially the 'Continental proposal'—were discussed and generally accepted (23 May 1950). Intra-European Payments Com. Minutes, 108th. OEEC PC/M(50)9.

[36] Ansiaux letter to van Zeeland (26 May 1950). Attachment to Minutes of the Board (30 May 1950). National Bank of Belgium PV 752/1.

whether the Union should continue. If the life of the Union were extended, credits would remain outstanding until termination.

Ansiaux struggled to find a response that might be acceptable to his Belgian authorities and also find a sympathetic echo in Paris. The French and Italians, as well as the Americans, agreed that the British demand for credit was too large and that extreme deficit countries should not be allowed to impose import quotas that discriminated against creditors. However, they would go no further to satisfy Ansiaux than an offer to support a reduction in the size of the quotas suggested by the British, while accepting the UK settlement terms within the quotas. An outraged Frère talked to Wilfred Baumgartner, Governor of the Bank of France, who mistakenly informed him that Guindey had proposed to reduce the quotas from 20 to 4 per cent of turnover. Actually Guindey had suggested 12.5 per cent.

A meeting of the Inner Group on 26 May turned into an inconclusive haggling session.[37] With van Zeeland's authorization, Ansiaux offered counter-suggestions to each element in the British proposal. The quotas should be only 10 per cent of turnover, and the proportions of gold and credit in the settlements should be equal. His major concession was a gold-free credit segment equal to 10 per cent of the reduced quota. Cleverly, he now offered to accept Bissell's suggestion that creditors should receive decreasing percentages of gold as they ran through their quotas. However, gold payments to creditors would start at 75 per cent gold and decline to 25 per cent. Ellis-Rees was willing to be flexible about elements of the British proposal, but he found Ansiaux's 'not at all acceptable'.

Guindey made several unsuccessful efforts to mediate the dispute. His last suggestion was that quotas be equal to 15 per cent of turnover, of which the first third would be gold free and the rest would be settled half in gold. Ansiaux could not accept even that scheme; it would obligate Belgium to extend considerably more credit than his authorities would countenance.

The Katz-Gaitskell Compromises

The negotiations had once again reached an impasse, and time was running very short. In another month, the IEPS would come to an end, and the Americans showed no interest in helping to extend it. Without more US conditional aid, the IEPS arrangements would have no underpinning. Without an EPU agreement, a new wave of hurried bilateral

---

[37] Figgures memo to Marjolin records the meeting (30 May 1950). OEEC TFD-197/FF.

arrangements would probably be needed to prevent an extreme breakdown in intra-European trade flows.

Katz had visited Gaitskell in London in mid-April and again in May as he attempted to work out an agreement for the participation of sterling in a fully transferable EPU. As an OEEC ministerial meeting was scheduled for 2 June, Hall-Patch offered to arrange a private luncheon that day for Katz with Gaitskell.[38] At the formal session before the luncheon, Ansiaux reported the progress of the EPU negotiations, noting the major outstanding issues—the size of the quotas, the gold/credit settlement ratios, and consolidation of old debts.

After their lunch, Gaitskell asked to meet alone with Katz. He made it clear that he and the Cabinet—not the civil servants—would decide the terms of Britain's participation in the EPU. His mistrust and suspicions about US intentions were equally evident. He began by asserting that Britain would not submit to having the US impose the gold standard on it. A startled Katz denied any such purpose. After all, his negotiators fully recognized the significance of the dollar shortage, had vigorously insisted on the need for considerable credit in the system, and had proposed only a gradual introduction of gold into the settlements.

Gaitskell said that the British Cabinet still insisted on total EPU quotas of $5.2 billion (20 per cent of turnover), the first half of which would be gold free. The Cabinet wanted an overall credit/gold ratio of 2:1, as Guindey had suggested a week earlier, but could accept 3:2. However, if the overall proportion of credit were higher than 3:2, he could agree to a smaller gold-free quota.[39]

After this inauspicious beginning, the talks continued for two more days, with staff participation. By their conclusion, some semblance of 'the special relationship' had been restored. The two parties had come to a far-reaching agreement, subject to the approval of their governments. During the discussions, Katz was already on the telephone with Bissell to gain assent to the propositions on which he and Gaitskell were finding common ground.

Before leaving Paris, Gaitskell sent Katz a personal, handwritten note, expressing appreciation for 'your difficulties and efforts to settle on lines acceptable to us. I know you understand my personal position. I will let you know the outcome of my consultations with the Chancellor and the Prime Minister.'[40] On returning to London, he visited the US chargé the very next day to express his appreciation for the technical expertise

[38] 'Oral History Interview with Milton Katz' (25 July 1975). Harry S. Truman Library. Also Kaplan interview with Katz (23 Sept. 1986). BIS EPU Archive.

[39] Katz, memo of telephone conversation with Bissell and Foster on day of luncheon (2 June 1950). US Archives. ECA/Paris Harriman Files.

[40] US Archives. ECA/Paris Harriman Files.

and understanding of the United Kingdom's situation shown by the ECA officials in Paris. Gaitskell told the chargé that past troubles with ECA had resulted from the inflexibility of his associates, including Cripps.[41]

Gaitskell had apparently come to realize that ECA could acknowledge his own view of the dollar gap problem and accept the need for a two-world trading system (dollar and EPU), at least until European competitiveness had improved. Gaitskell's Bank of England and Treasury advisers had repeatedly rejected such a two-world system because it would be an anathema to the US. It was probably more of an anathema to them because it would diminish the prestige of sterling, especially if the non-dollar world were based on an EPU unit of account rather than on sterling. Gaitskell was less preoccupied with the international status of sterling; he had accepted the reality of its diminished role when the Cabinet acceded to Acheson's *aide-mémoire*.

Prime Minister Attlee and Cripps promptly agreed to accept the formula that Gaitskell had brought back to London.[42] The Katz–Gaitskell compromise was based on total quotas of about $4 billion or 15 per cent of turnover. They had thus adopted Guindey's mediation between the original British and Belgian views on the size of the quotas. They also agreed on an overall credit/gold ratio of 3:2.

However, the quotas would be divided into five equal segments, rather than the two preferred by the UK. The first fifth would be completely gold free for creditors and debtors alike. Thereafter, creditors would settle equally in gold and credit over the rest of their quotas. They would receive more gold than under Guindey's proposed compromise, though Belgium might well have to extend considerably more credit than Ansiaux had ever offered.

Debtors, on the other hand, would receive progressively less credit as they moved through their quotas, as Bissell had proposed. The second segment would be settled with 75 per cent credit; the third, with 60 per cent; the fourth, 40 per cent; and the fifth, 25 per cent.

Finally, ECA agreed to provide the United Kingdom with $150 million in conditional aid. Final agreement on terms for this aid was not reached until the last day of the EPU negotiations. On 7 July, letters were exchanged concerning what has come to be known as the Katz–Gaitskell Agreement.[43] As Acheson had proposed in May, the $150 million would indemnify the UK for loss of gold caused by debtors using previously existing sterling balances to settle their deficits.

[41] US Embassy London tel. to Washington and ECA/Paris (5 June 1950). US Archives. ECA/Paris Tasca Files.

[42] European Economic Cooperation Com. Minutes (7 June 1950). ER (L) (50) 35th. PRO CAB 134/246. Confirmed in Ellis-Rees letter to Katz (7 June 1950). US Archives. ECA/Paris Havlik Files.

[43] Exchange of letters reproduced in BIS, 'Second Aide-Mémoire for the Use of Central Banks', Annex 5 EP2 (20 Sept. 1950). BIS EPU Archive.

However, British concurrence on 6 June really resolved the last of the important financial issues that had prompted their refusal to participate fully in the European Payments Union. For the first time, a final agreement was now in sight.

Belgium's Problem

Resolution of Britain's difficulties had been achieved at the expense of Belgium's perceptions of its interests. Ansiaux had not been informed about the Katz–Gaitskell talks until he was confronted with a *fait accompli*.

He had chaired the EPU work of the OEEC from its beginning in the Financial Experts Committee with persistent dedication, patience, and brilliance. His efforts had been opposed throughout by his direct superior, Governor Frère. He devoutly wanted a successful outcome to the negotiations, but he now felt deceived. Triffin, with whom he had worked very closely, also was distressed.

Frère had travelled to Washington in January 1950, shortly after he had learned of the Bissell proposal. He visited Bissell, leaving a memorandum that firmly opposed any automatic credits.[44] He felt it unfair that countries should get credits though they had refused to straighten up their internal affairs. Throughout the negotiations, he had insisted that Belgium could not lend to Europe, unless it could recoup the equivalent in dollars.

Ansiaux had steadfastly opposed UK attempts to introduce easier credit into the Experts' proposal. He was sensitive to Belgium's isolated position as the only country expected to run persistent surpluses in intra-European trade. To maximize his negotiating leverage, he had taken the initiative with his own proposals. At first he was thwarted by Frère, later by his colleagues in the Inner Group. He had fastened considerable hope on the IMF loosening its purse strings. By early May, however, the Belgian authorities had been informed that the US and the IMF staff were both opposed to drawings on the IMF against European credits.[45] The US Embassy in Brussels reported that Frère insisted that Belgium could not raise the funds to give more foreign credits. The Belgian government might have a different view, but his position was firm.[46]

Katz was well aware of the Belgian problem as he negotiated with Gaitskell. The day before their first lunch, Ansiaux and two other senior Belgian delegates to the OEEC had asked ECA for an additional grant

[44] Frère, memo to Bissell (23 Jan. 1950) with Auboin note (12 Jan. 1950) attached. US Archives. ECA Bissell Files.

[45] Washington tel. to US Embassy Brussels. ECOTO 120 (1 May 1950). Department of State (1950), iii. 652–3.

[46] US Embassy Brussels tel. to State Department, Department of State (1950), iii. 652–3.

to Belgium of $100 million. Otherwise Frère might refuse to extend credit and force the issue into Parliament, where van Zeeland might be defeated.[47] ECA did not respond. Next came news of the US–UK compromise, followed by Secretariat turnover statistics. On the basis of the new figures, the proposed Belgian quota was raised from the $360 million they had been assuming to $433.8 million.

When an OEEC ministerial meeting convened on 12 June 1950, the British and Americans arrived in a state of elation over the very recent resolution of long-standing differences. Having finally overcome their own major policy disagreements, they were eager to settle the large number of other outstanding matters within the three weeks remaining for a timely EPU agreement. Some were relatively minor, but others would be of considerable concern to one government or another. Harriman had a special reason for wanting an early decision: he was about to return to Washington as Special Assistant to President Harry S. Truman. He planned to say his farewells to OEEC colleagues the following week as he turned his Paris responsibilities over to Katz.

Van Zeeland promptly asserted that Belgium was unable to accept the credit obligations of the gold/credit formula. The British and Americans responded with an unfortunate attempt to bulldoze him. Gaitskell insisted that persistent surplus countries must be following deflationary domestic policies and they should, therefore, be obliged to extend credits to their trading partners. Harriman agreed. At a private meeting, van Zeeland was told that for the next two years, Belgium would receive no more than the amount it might expect under the Snoy–Marjolin formula for dividing Marshall Plan aid. Moreover, all of it would be conditional on an equivalent Belgian credit to the EPU. That credit would have to be used before any Belgian surpluses would be settled within the quota, although the quota itself could be reduced to $360 million.

Harriman followed with a *note verbale* that van Zeeland regarded as an ultimatum: accept the proposals or stay out of the EPU. An experienced statesman with a well-deserved reputation for integrity and reasonableness, van Zeeland agreed only to transmit the *note verbale* to his Cabinet with his own unfavourable recommendation.[48] The Cabinet decided to reject the ultimatum and authorized representations in Washington.

Thereafter, Southard told the NAC staff about the formal protest registered by his Belgian colleague, Ernest de Selliers. A discussion of the Katz–Gaitskell compromises ensued. Marget (Federal Reserve) wanted the NAC staff to support the Belgian position. The US should not let

[47] Katz, memo of telephone conversation with Bissell and Foster (2 June 1950), US Archives. ECA/Paris Harriman Files.
[48] For Ansiaux's full account of these meetings, see Minutes of the Board (22 June 1950). National Bank of Belgium PV 760/9.

the United Kingdom call the tune, he said. The US negotiators in Paris had agreed to create a soft union, an unacceptable formula for moving Europe toward convertibility.[49]

Governor Szymczak promptly wrote to Hoffman about his distress at the soft arrangement that had been negotiated. He went on to propose that the gold-free credit margin be cut in half.[50] He felt that so much credit might induce countries to pursue unduly expansionary monetary and fiscal policies. Hoffman did not respond.

The Belgian problem was essentially resolved before the NAC could act. A compromise was arranged during the OEEC Executive Committee meetings on 16 and 17 June, though not without further acrimony.[51] As Political Conciliator, Stikker suggested that the Belgian quota might be reduced to $375 million. US aid to Belgium out of the last two Marshall Plan appropriations would remain at the Snoy–Marjolin formula level, estimated to be $160 million, but half would take the form of conditional aid and half the form of direct aid. (In prior years, only 12 per cent of Belgian aid had taken the latter form). Belgium's outstanding credits and sterling balances would be paid off through bilateral agreements to be reported to the OEEC. In the absence of a bilateral agreement, they would be amortized over a two-year period through the EPU.

Apart from holding out for a quota of $360 million, van Zeeland might have accepted this much, if the US were agreeable. However, Harriman would only agree to send Hoffman such a recommendation about further US aid to Belgium. To add to van Zeeland's dismay, Stikker had demanded, in return for these concessions, that Belgium agree to present an investment programme and switch its import purchases as far as possible from the dollar area to OEEC countries.

Both Harriman and Gaitskell strongly endorsed these demands. Van Zeeland was particularly taken aback by Harriman's position and asked for a written recommendation that Belgium restrict dollar imports. According to Ansiaux's report, Harriman replied that no US representative could write such a letter, but he fully approved of Gaitskell's point and believed that Belgium should practise a European policy rather than one based on the dollar. The tension abated, thanks to skilful drafting. The Executive Committee asked Belgium only 'to increase imports from participating [OEEC] countries relatively to those from non-participating countries'.[52]

None of the NAC agencies was pleased by this outcome. It reinforced

[49] Mc Cullough, memo to Bissell on NAC staff meeting (15 June 1950). US Archives. ECA Bissell Files.

[50] Szymczak letter (16 June 1950). Federal Reserve Files.

[51] Memo about Exec. Com. agreement (16–17 June 1950). US Archives. ECA/Paris Tasca Files.

[52] 'Minutes of 137th Meeting of Exec. Com.' (15, 17 June 1950). OEEC CE/M(50)21.

fears in Washington that the EPU would sustain a closed soft currency trading area, discriminating needlessly against US exporters and deterring members from moving toward convertibility. The Belgian government reserved its position about joining the EPU on these terms until the very last day. Meanwhile, other obstacles to an agreement among all OEEC members had to be surmounted.

FINAL HURDLES

EPU Management

Early British opposition to the kind of powerful management body recommended by Bissell and the Experts had soon found many sympathetic European ears. Only Ansiaux and the Secretariat ever provided much support for ECA's views on this subject. By mid-April, the matter had been pretty well settled. The powers of the managing group would be limited to those delegated by the OEEC Council; the managers would make recommendations to the Council, not directly to governments. Since Council decisions were bound by a rule of unanimity, countries could use their veto power to block unwelcome recommendations. This formula also allayed IMF concerns about the creation of a competitive body with power to make recommendations on financial policy to EPU members, most of whom were also signatories to the IMF Articles of Agreement. During the final days, the Payments Committee agreed to name the body the Managing Board of the European Payments Union.

As it turned out, fears about creating a powerful new institution were put to rest too easily. The Managing Board proved to be much more influential than most of its founding OEEC ministers had anticipated. In fact, they and their successors came increasingly to applaud the reasonableness of its decisions and to welcome the support offered by its recommendations concerning policies that were necessary, though politically unpopular.

Trade Liberalization

The ultimate purpose of the clearing, transferability, and credit arrangements was to induce countries to remove quantitative restrictions on intra-European trade. Everyone recognized that this would be far more difficult politically for governments to accept than the payments and financial arrangements. The latter were obscure to the public eye and somewhat removed from individual concerns. Trade liberalization, on the other hand, could affect individual livelihoods and draw the ire of threatened interest groups. Until a payments agreement itself loomed near, it was therefore difficult to focus much attention on the trade liberalization rules. The OEEC Trade Committee did not establish them until a special session held between 7 and 10 June 1950.

Countries had been justifying quantitative restrictions as essential to protect their balances of payments. Faced by the prospect that this justification would no longer obtain in intra-European trade, governments advanced other reasons for maintaining restrictions. Some frankly admitted an interest in protecting certain sectors of their economies from the competition of more efficient producers elsewhere in Europe. Low tariff countries feared to give up bargaining power in trade negotiations. Some felt they needed to retain quotas on some products for bargaining with others who would not give up theirs. Most governments feared paying a high political price at home if they removed restrictions too rapidly.

An agreement on 100 per cent liberalization from quantitative restrictions was thus not attainable at the outset of the new payments arrangement. The 50 per cent liberalization that had been agreed in October 1949 had been an easy first step. Countries liberalized products that they could produce competitively or that they did not produce at all. How much further would they go under the new payments system?

The initial answer was to move to 60 per cent by the end of 1950 and to consider moving to 75 per cent on 1 February 1951.[53] Detailed provisions were added:

1. After 30 June 1950, any removal or reduction in quantitative restrictions would be non-discriminatory as between OEEC members.
2. After 31 December 1950, the percentage of each country's trade that had already been liberalized would be made non-discriminatory.
3. Sixty per cent liberalization must apply to each of the three major categories of goods—food, raw materials, and manufactures.
4. The remaining restricted trade must be non-discriminatory.
5. Any reimposition of quantitative restrictions that might become necessary would be non-discriminatory.
6. Acceptable criteria for reimposing restrictions were closely defined.
7. A country could suspend its liberalization measures temporarily, but it must notify the OEEC, which would keep its situation under review.
8. If the measures were disapproved by the OEEC, the country must annul them.

---

[53] OEEC (1950a). Rules summarized in US del. circular tel. REPTO Circular 155 (13 July 1950).

'Exceptional' Creditors and Debtors

Early in the negotiations, it was clear that 'structural' creditors and debtors would require special provisions. Even before they began to use their quotas, they would have to settle surpluses and deficits with the Union without receiving or paying gold. US financing would be necessary, and it was agreed that the US should determine the amounts required after consulting the interested governments. No one wanted to repeat the acrimonious division of aid exercise that had led to the Snoy-Marjolin formula a year earlier. It was agreed that Lincoln Gordon, Director of Harriman's Program Coordination Division, would hold hearings and report his conclusions.

Gordon resisted the use of the term 'structural'. He felt that every member of a trading area as broad as the EPU's should be able to balance its payments with the rest of the area within a brief period, if it could introduce appropriate economic policies. He suggested that the countries be called 'exceptional' creditors and debtors. When the countries concerned protested, he suggested using 'initial positions' to describe the credits and debits he was to award. That bland, though accurate, appellation avoided any characterization of the countries.

The initial debit positions for the United Kingdom and Belgium had been established earlier in the negotiations. An initial debit position was also established for Sweden in the amount of its Snoy-Marjolin entitlement. ECA financed these debit positions by allocating the equivalent amount of dollars directly to each country.

Countries that felt they needed initial credit positions were invited to submit prompt written justifications. Gordon then began holding individual discussions. Awards for the first year of the EPU were made subsequently to Austria, Greece, Iceland, the Netherlands, Norway, and Turkey. Denmark, the Federal Republic of Germany, and Portugal also sought such initial credits, but Gordon rejected their justifications. On 4 July, Katz sent Marjolin a letter notifying him of the results of the hearings.[54]

Two days later, a ministerial committee chaired by Karl Gruber, the Austrian Foreign Minister, met to discuss the ECA letter. The only question that arose concerned ECA's willingness to consult with the OEEC and the Managing Board about initial positions for the second EPU year, 1951/2.[55] The following day, Blücher said that Germany agreed to join the EPU, though he expressed regret that ECA had not

[54] Sec. General, 'Initial Positions in the EPU'. Note to Joint Com. on Trade and Payments (5 July 1950). OEEC TP(50)78.

[55] Record of a meeting (6 July 1950). OEEC TFD/DI-245.

taken account of the Federal Republic's request for an initial position.[56] The rejection soon led to the EPU's first crisis—and its first success.

Most of the credit positions were balanced off against the debit positions established for the expected creditor countries. The US had agreed to provide the EPU with a grant of $350 million as its initial capital. However, the initial credits exceeded the total amount of initial debits by $79 million, a potential liability against the $350 million.

The Turkish position was awarded as a loan, repayable to the EPU, as was part of the Norwegian position. The rest of the credit positions were grants to the recipient countries.

In the light of subsequent events, eyebrows may be raised at the decision to award grants to the Netherlands, Norway, and Austria, but only a loan to Turkey. The first three were soon to establish their credit worthiness, while Turkey continued to experience more than its share of problems in servicing foreign debts. These decisions may seem like another example of the idiosyncrasies of balance-of-payments forecasting. However, as a neutral country, Turkey was spared war damage and emerged from World War II with substantial foreign exchange reserves. With the Soviets threatening its borders, it had become a candidate for assistance under the Marshall Plan. In contrast, the Dutch and Norwegian economies had been severely victimized by the war, and both countries were pursuing large and effective investment programmes with the help of ECA aid. Austria was still occupied by four powers and awaiting a peace treaty.

The Last Obstacles

After mid-June, the OEEC had to meet continuously, at every level, to conclude a timely EPU agreement without reservations by any of the prospective member countries. Ansiaux's Payments Committee had prepared an initial document for submission to the Executive Committee at ministerial level on 16 June.[57] Additions and textual changes were made repeatedly to accommodate the views of one delegate or another.

At this stage, technical decisions were reached on how the automatic mechanism would function. Early in the negotiations, the Payments Committee had established several working parties to address these matters. All the issues were resolved by the technical experts and agreed in the Payments Committee, without requiring the intervention of cabinet ministers.

The Committee recommended that bilateral positions be offset multilaterally at the end of each month. Every country would settle its net

---

[56] 'Minutes of 102nd Meeting' (6–7 July 1950). OEEC C/M(50)20, Part I.
[57] 'Proposals for a European Payments Union' (15 June 1950). OEEC CE(50)61 (First Revision).

balance with the Union on a settlement date fixed by the Agent. The cumulative principle would apply: if a country ran a succession of monthly deficits followed by monthly surpluses in the same amount, the later surpluses would offset the earlier deficits. All accounts and operations would be denominated in a unit of account, equal to the gold content of one US dollar. Between the settlement dates, central banks would provide whatever credit was necessary; they would be repaid on the settlement date without having incurred any exchange risk.

Today it may seem curious that a protracted controversy about liquidation rules should arise in the thick of debate about whether and how to create the EPU. At the time, the Dutch wanted to be sure that the Union would continue until full convertibility could be established. They particularly wanted assurance that the EPU capital would not be depleted, in part to assure creditors that their loans to the Union were backed by hard currency. As a potential large creditor, Belgium was also a very interested party in this matter. These concerns made liquidation procedures a hotly contested issue. On liquidation, the remaining capital funds would presumably be distributed, as well as the remaining debts and credits.

It was largely Professor Posthuma's suggestions that led to acceptable liquidation rules. The remaining capital and any other convertible assets would be distributed among the creditors. Residual debts would be divided among all members on the basis of the Snoy–Marjolin formula. Thus, at the time of liquidation, no creditor would have to collect the sums due to him exclusively from the net debtors in the Union, presumably those with the least ability to pay. The liquidation rules came to be referred to as the 'Posthuma formula'.

Other issues also surfaced in the final hours. The Swiss sought a larger quota than they would receive under the 15 per cent of turnover rule.[58] That was readily granted, but the Swiss also wanted assurance that they would receive at least 50 per cent gold payments for surpluses beyond their creditor quota. They also sought commitments that tourism to Switzerland would be liberalized and that their specialties, such as watches and chocolate, would be included in the products liberalized by other countries. Like the Belgians and Dutch, the Swiss did not withdraw their reservation until the very last day. Last minute drafting changes mollified Swiss and Dutch reservations about provisions for non-discrimination in trading commodities that remained under quota restrictions.

As of 5 July 1950, the OEEC had yet to find an accommodation for all the countries. A number of points were still in dispute, though none seemed really critical. The NAC had met on 29 June and continued to

[58] 'The Swiss Case'. Record of a special meeting (22 June 1950). OEEC TF/DI-222.

voice concerns about the amount of credit in the EPU system. However, with the Belgian problem resolved, it had no issue on which to base advice to ECA, despite continued misgivings. In these circumstances, Katz telephoned Hoffman and asked for authority to endorse the agreement in principle, but only if the remaining reservations were withdrawn and all OEEC governments were prepared to agree.[59] Otherwise, Katz wanted to refuse to support an extension of the IEPS, even though intra-European trade might become chaotic as a result. He particularly sought authority to act irrespective of the latest criticism at the NAC meeting. Hoffman agreed a day later, and on 7 July 1950, the last European reservations were withdrawn. The OEEC Council then decided to form the EPU for a two-year period, subject to a review at the end of the first year.[60]

The final agreement could not be signed until the promised US aid was available. Not until 18 September 1950 was Katz able to provide the OEEC with formal notification.[61] The ECA appropriation for 1950/1 first had to be enacted. Then the United States obligated $350 million directly for the EPU and formally announced its allotments of initial debit and credit positions. Katz also notified the OEEC that about $100 million more would be available for special assistance initiated by the US or recommended by the OEEC.

Three years had elapsed since a European regional payments system had first been placed on the international agenda at the CEEC meetings. It was almost a year since Hoffman had called for a single European market. But it was barely more than nine months since negotiations had begun in earnest, after Bissell pressed the OEEC heads of delegation to consider his proposal. The pregnancy had run its full term. The EPU could commence operations.

From the beginning, the threat of abortion had hovered over the negotiations. Time and again it was averted through imaginative leadership and a persistent search for compromise. Success in their careers had not made the members of the Inner Group, or their ministers, particularly complacent or arrogant. Products of an era of unparalleled destruction, they were impelled to create, construct, and concur. Theirs was an age that relished and nourished interdependence, and they were its ready and able servants.

Their spirit was reflected in an entry in Gaitskell's diary, written in August 1950. 'It is rather fun having participated in something which has really actually happened. I mean a new economic system which is definitely going to make some difference, whatever they may say.'[62]

But how well would it work?

[59] 'Oral History Interview with Milton Katz' (25 July 1975). Harry S. Truman Library.
[60] US del. tel. to Washington. REPTO 3793 (7 July 1950).
[61] Katz letter to Marjolin sent by hand (18 Sept. 1950). US Archives. ECA/Paris Havlik Files.
[62] Williams, P. M. (1979), 224.

Part Two

Crisis Management: The First Two Years
1950-1952

5 EPU System in a Nutshell

When the dust from the negotiations had settled, a radically new payments system, closely linked to new trading arrangements, was launched in western Europe. All OEEC members participated fully. Overseas countries and territories that were part of the currency area of a European country also participated indirectly in the payments system. In addition to western Europe, the EPU thus included most of Africa and much of Asia, as well as some territories in Central and South America. Signatories to the EPU Agreement were:[1]

Austria	Luxembourg
Belgium	The Netherlands
Denmark	Norway
France	Portugal
Germany	Sweden
Greece	Switzerland
Iceland	Trieste
Ireland	Turkey
Italy	The United Kingdom

The final EPU Agreement created: (1) a clearing union for payments made in any member currency; and (2) a Managing Board to supervise the operations and recommend improvements in the system. The Union was constituted for an indefinite period. After two years, the conditions governing the members' financial obligations were to be reviewed and perhaps renegotiated. The Union's financial year (FY) was to run from July to June,[2] beginning retroactively on 1 July 1950.

A second, simultaneous OEEC agreement established regulations for removing both quantitative restrictions on trade and limitations on the purchase of services from other OEEC members. The overriding purpose of the EPU clearing mechanism was to permit and induce countries to remove such restrictions on the free flow of goods and services within western Europe. Unlike its predecessors, the EPU achieved this aim by making member currencies fully transferable into one another. Transferability was the core of the system: member countries no longer had to be concerned about their bilateral balances; they need pay attention

---

[1] Ireland was included in the monetary area of the United Kingdom; Luxembourg and Trieste in those of Belgium and Italy respectively.

[2] In dates or time periods, 'to' is used inclusively here and throughout the book.

only to their balances of payments with the EPU system as a whole. As a result, they had no grounds for discriminating in trade with each other.

THE CLEARING UNION

The EPU clearing and settlements mechanism was the focal point of the entire trade and payments system. Its fundamental concept was embodied in a simple and ingenious method of establishing transferability.[3] The method involved four steps: (1) during any given month, central banks granted unlimited credit to each other; (2) the resulting bilateral balances were offset at the end of the month; (3) a net position was established for each member with the Union as a whole; (4) these debts and credits were settled partly in gold and partly in credit. A deficit country could settle either by transferring gold or by paying dollars.[4] Responsibility for these technical operations was delegated to a central agent, the Bank for International Settlements.

Under the original EPU system, all purchases of goods and services authorized by member countries continued to be cleared through their central banks. Each bank provided its own currency to pay for other EPU members' purchases in its country and recorded corresponding claims against the other members' central banks. At the end of every month, each central bank reported to the Agent its claims against other member central banks.

To clear the accounts each month, the Agent performed a series of calculations in accordance with a set of precise and pre-set rules. First, it converted into national currencies the claims reported by each pair of central banks. Then it offset them to establish a net bilateral balance. The bilateral balances were converted into EPU units of account, each unit equal to the gold content of one US dollar at the par value of each currency to the dollar. The next step was to offset the sum of the bilateral surpluses of each member currency against the sum of its bilateral deficits. That established each central bank's net monthly position *vis-à-vis* the EPU system as a whole. The final calculations involved the settlement of the net balances, determining how much of each net position was to be settled by giving or receiving credit and how much by paying or receiving gold or US dollars.

---

[3] For a detailed description of the EPU mechanism, see EPU Board, *Third Annual Report*, Annexes I and II (1953).
Also BIS, 'Second *Aide-Mémoire* for the Use of Central Banks' EPZ (20 Sept. 1950). BIS EPU Archive.

[4] At the time, the gold content of the dollar was firmly fixed at $35 per fine ounce. Hence the words 'gold' and 'dollars' were used interchangeably in describing the Union's accounts. These terms are also used interchangeably in this book.

All settlements were made with the Union, on a settlement date determined by the Agent, usually about two weeks after the end of the month. A surplus country received gold from the Union for part of its surplus. For the remainder, it was obliged to extend credit, receiving a claim against the Union in exchange. A deficit country paid gold to the Union for part of its debt and received automatic credit from the Union for the remainder.

As described in Chapter 4, the initial Agreement stipulated that net positions should first be reduced through the use of existing resources and initial positions. The residual accounting position of each member was then settled in credit or gold, within the quotas that had been established for each country. For most countries, the quotas were equal to 15 per cent of the sum of their payments and receipts in 1949 for trade in goods and services with all other EPU members.

Each month, the Agent calculated every country's 'cumulative position' from the beginning of the EPU. This determined the extent to which each had used its quota, be it as a creditor or a debtor country. Under the initial Agreement, the debtor quotas were divided into five equal segments, called 'tranches'. A cumulative debtor in the first *tranche* settled its position entirely with credit from the Union. Thereafter, it settled increasingly in gold as its cumulative position moved into successively higher *tranches* of the quota. Once a debtor quota was exhausted, the country had to settle entirely in gold, unless it sought and received a special credit on the recommendation of the Managing Board.

Creditor quotas were identical in size to the debtor quotas, but the gold/credit ratio progressed differently as the quota was used. Within the first 20 per cent *tranche*, cumulative surpluses were settled entirely by extending a credit to the Union; for the later *tranches*, settlements were all 50 per cent in gold and 50 per cent in credit. If a country ran cumulative surpluses in excess of its quota, the Managing Board had to propose to the OEEC Council how subsequent surpluses would be settled.

Countries with cumulative surpluses often had subsequent monthly deficits, and countries with cumulative deficits also frequently ran subsequent surpluses. In the case of such reversals of position, the 'last-in, first-out' principle was applied. The most recent credits to or from the Union were wiped out; gold payments most recently received from the Union or paid to it were returned. The system thus involved another form of compensation, the offsetting of positions over time.

Since the Union's payments to surplus countries could, and sometimes did, exceed its receipts from deficit countries, a working capital fund was required. The actual liquidity of the EPU—its convertible assets— fluctuated below and above the level of this working capital. On the basis of the capital fund, the EPU could recommend that *ad hoc* credits be given to countries in serious payments difficulties. The capital fund also served as security for the credits extended by surplus countries and as a source of confidence in the liquidity and continuity of the Union.

Originally, the gold/credit ratio was 40:60 if a country used its entire quota, although the percentages varied from *tranche* to *tranche*. Later on, the rules were changed to a flat 50:50 ratio of gold and credit for all settlements, with creditors and debtors alike. In the last years of the Union, that ratio was changed to 75 per cent gold and 25 per cent credit. The gold (or dollar) element in the settlements mechanism was both a disciplinary constraint on deficit countries and a method for partially converting European currencies into dollars. As the percentage of gold in the settlements mechanism increased, so did progress toward the full convertibility of European currencies.

TRADE LIBERALIZATION

The clearing system permitted payments to be made freely for all authorized transactions; the accompanying trade regulations were intended to broaden the range of authorized transactions to the greatest possible extent. The initial EPU Agreement was thus closely linked to the agreement on trade rules described in Chapter 4. Initially, countries were to liberalize 60 per cent of their imports on current account. By February 1951, that percentage had been raised to 75 per cent, and it was subsequently increased to 90 per cent.

Countries were encouraged to incur the risks of freer trade because the clearing mechanism yielded large economies in the foreign exchange needed to settle imbalances in their payments with one another. Automatic credit provided through the EPU further supplemented inadequate foreign exchange reserves.

In 1952, a Steering Board for Trade, comparable to the Managing Board, was established to supervise the implementation of the trade rules and to suggest improvements. In July 1951, a comprehensive set of rules for the liberalization of services was agreed and subsequently a Committee on Invisible Transactions (Services) was established to supervise these rules and to propose further liberalization measures. The clearing mechanism for payments thus had far-reaching consequences for freeing the underlying transactions that gave rise to them.

THE MANAGING BOARD

The initial EPU Agreement was more specific about the composition of the Managing Board than about its powers.[5] It had seven voting members,

---

[5] For a more complete account of the management of the system, see ch. 18.

each nominated by a government and elected by the OEEC Council. The terms were for one year, but members could be re-elected. They served as individuals performing a collective function, rather than as government representatives. The Chairman of the OEEC Payments Committee also attended Board meetings as a non-voting participant, responsible for keeping governments without nominees on the Board informed of its activities. Representatives of the Secretary General of the OEEC and of the Agent also participated. Only the US observer was appointed by his government as its official representative. Each member designated an Alternate, and the OEEC Secretariat provided a range of supporting services. The voting members of the board during its first two financial years (1950/1 and 1951/2) were:

Guido Carli (Italy)—Chairman
Pierre Calvet (France)—Vice-Chairman
Hugh Ellis-Rees (United Kingdom)—Vice-Chairman
Sigmund Hartogsohn (Denmark, 1951)
F. A. G. Keesing (Netherlands, 1951)
Hans Karl von Mangoldt (Federal Republic of Germany)
Suardus Posthuma (Netherlands, 1952)
Paul Rossy (Switzerland)
Knut Getz Wold (Norway, 1952)

Hubert Ansiaux and Hubert F. Havlik also attended the meetings as Chairman of the OEEC Intra-European Payments Committee and Representative of the United States Government, respectively. Frederick G. Conolly represented the Bank for International Settlements as Agent.

The Agreement said very little about the jurisdiction of the Managing Board, beyond making it 'responsible for supervising the execution of the present Agreement'. It was authorized to take decisions by majority vote, but only concerning the operations of the automatic clearing system and the management of the EPU capital fund. The Council was supposed to delegate specific powers to the Board. However, its 'Directives for the Application of the Agreement' and its 'Mandate' to the Managing Board were issued during the month of August 1950, when the weary negotiators were taking a well-deserved holiday.[6] Understandably, neither of these documents ventured much further in defining the authority of the Board to deal with policy issues. Probably that was just as well. Propelled into crisis management at its very first meeting, the Board used its vague authority to make such recommendations as it felt necessary to protect

---

[6] Council Decision, 'Directives for the Application of the Agreement for the Establishment of an European Payments Union' (18 Aug. 1950). OEEC C(50)254 and Addendum.
Council Resolution 'Concerning the Mandate of the Managing Board' (18 Aug. 1950). OEEC C(50)255 (Final).

and preserve the system. A more specific delegation of powers might well have limited its right to make proposals.

The means available to the Managing Board for crisis management fell into three categories. First, it could propose that a country reintroduce trade restrictions. If countries reimposed them on their own, the Board could recommend condoning the action or reversing it. However, extensive or prolonged use of restrictions would represent an admission of defeat for the system. Second, the Board had resources available for special credits, but these were limited, sufficient only to buy a bit of time for adjustment measures to take effect. To supplement the inadequacy of such measures, the Board assumed a more important responsibility—to propose changes in the policies of member governments that would restore balance to the intra-EPU payments of any country in crisis.

But what policy adjustments would be appropriate and effective? The Board was given no guidance, nor could it fall back on established precedents. Of necessity, it developed its own pragmatic *ad hoc* prescriptions about the appropriate mix of fiscal and monetary policies and of supporting measures, such as trade liberalization, debt repayment, and the freeing of capital movements. That established both its authority and its reputation.

6 German Payments Crisis of 1950/1

When the EPU Managing Board met for the first time, on 20 October 1950, it had to confront its first crisis. Expecting only to decide on regulations and working procedures, the Board instead faced a severe payments problem. The crisis involved the new Federal Republic of Germany, established as a republic and seated at the OEEC only a year earlier. Germany was, nevertheless, already resuming its role as a major trading country in western Europe.

Although the German situation presented an immediate and formidable challenge to the new payments system, the problem was resolved within six months. The system emerged stronger from the crisis, as did the Managing Board, its stature enhanced by the competence and effectiveness it had displayed. But success seemed unlikely when the Board first gathered at OEEC headquarters in Paris.

QUOTA EXHAUSTION LOOMS

The Agent's report for the first EPU clearing, covering the months of July to September, showed that Germany had already used 56 per cent of its debtor quota. The modest but persistent deficits noted by German representatives to the OEEC in January had swollen substantially. Like all EPU quotas, Germany's was intended to allow for surpluses or deficits over a two-year period. At the July–September rate, the German quota would soon be exhausted. Indeed, within another two months, it was used up.

What was the fledgling Managing Board to do? Some members simply wanted to wash the Board's hands of the problem, warning Germany to figure out for itself how it would pay 100 per cent gold when its quota was exhausted. Others suggested two possible actions: (1) advising Germany to suspend temporarily its measures of trade liberalization; and (2) making additional foreign exchange available to Germany for a limited period, through a special EPU loan.

After some debate, Guido Carli, Chairman of the Board, realized the members could not reach a consensus and thought further information might help. The Secretariat had prepared a factual report for the Board's use. The German member, von Mangoldt, had explained the position as viewed by his government and the steps taken to remedy it. His detailed statement was supplemented by three experts, brought to answer questions. Before making recommendations, the Board decided to seek a comprehensive, independent appraisal by some recognized authorities.

Accordingly, Alec Cairncross and Per Jacobsson were invited to visit Germany and report their findings to the Board at its next meeting, two weeks later. Previously an adviser to the British Labour government, Cairncross was then economic adviser to the OEEC. Jacobsson, subsequently Managing Director of the IMF, was economic adviser to the BIS. The two men thus had well-established international reputations, but brought to their task quite different preconceptions about economic policy. The Board hoped the German government would regard their report as authoritative and persuasive. It further hoped the experts would provide a solid, current, and factual analysis that could serve as the basis for a wise decision, acceptable to all members of the Board. Their aspirations were fully realized.

'Are the Germans Rocking the Boat?'

The deficits were a sensitive political issue, both inside and outside the Federal Republic. Strong prejudices toward a former enemy country still existed. Newspaper headlines that the Germans were 'rocking the boat (again)' expressed what many observers feared.

Embarrassed by the international attention their deficits received, German authorities were determined to solve the payments problems themselves. The new administration consisted of civil servants untainted by the Nazi past and younger staff filling up the ranks. Anxious to establish their competence and credibility at home and abroad, they were distressed by the implication that they lacked the efficiency or authority to deal with the crisis. Above all, there was a general and genuine desire to prove that the Federal Republic was a reliable partner in the new efforts for economic co-operation in western Europe.

Striving for full acceptance within the OEEC, the Germans were stung by accusations that they were 'rocking the boat' of European economic co-operation. At the time, they were in the midst of negotiations for a European Coal and Steel Community with France, Italy, and the Benelux countries (the Schuman Plan). They were also expected to contribute to the Western defence effort. For these reasons alone, the possibility of suspending or allowing Germany to withdraw from the EPU was never taken seriously. The Americans, as well as France and the United Kingdom, would have opposed it.

West Germany's position was further strengthened by its fast growing importance as a European trading nation. Half of the increase in intra-European trade between 1948 and 1950 had resulted from growth in German purchases. In some trade relationships, the increase was even greater. German imports from the Netherlands, for example, had risen more than eightfold between 1948 and 1950; its imports from Denmark, nearly tenfold. As Cairncross observed, 'For this reason the solution of the German problem was of far greater interest to the Members of OEEC than the solution of similar balance of payments difficulties in most other Member countries.'[1]

An abrupt suspension of German imports was in nobody's trading interest. It would have reduced the exports of EPU partners, many of whom were enjoying the benefit of trade surpluses (the counterpart of Germany's deficits). Countries with surpluses could build up credits in the EPU as a cushion against any future deficits and thus reduce the chance of having to settle in gold. In effect, Germany's deficits eased the initial EPU period for many trading partners.

Why a Deficit?

Today the Deutsche Mark is one of the strongest currencies in the world, having appreciated substantially in value over the years. Yet it first appeared on the international scene as the weakest currency in the EPU. Part of the explanation for its early problems is that the outbreak of hostilities in Korea hit the German economy at a particularly difficult moment.

In 1950, the Federal Republic was an infant state, still coping with the aftermath of war, the postwar occupation, and the division of Germany. An amalgam of the three western zones, it had been occupied by Allied powers with different ideas about Germany's future. That had impeded its economic recovery. Its political evolution was similarly slow, beginning with a Bizone and expanding to a Trizone, before becoming an independent, although not yet sovereign, republic.

In the first years of the occupation, economic life in the western zones was paralysed. Whereas other European countries received funds to rebuild their economies, aid provided by the occupation powers was merely 'to avoid disease and unrest'. Restrictions on what the Germans were allowed to produce also curtailed economic expansion. The first steps to promote recovery came with the Marshall Plan and the currency reform of 1948. In some ways, that reform sealed the division of Germany.[2]

In addition to reconstructing devastated cities and industries, the West German authorities had to cope with an influx of more than 9

---

[1] Cairncross (1951), 1.
[2] Möller (1981), 355.

million refugees from the east, a number that exceeded the population of Belgium and Luxembourg. Initially, most of the refugees could be accommodated only in the less damaged rural districts, despite the paucity of job opportunities. To employ them required a second phase of absorption—the creation of new jobs, the construction of new housing, resettlement, and other measures. That daunting task was tackled with remarkable results; 70 per cent of the refugees eligible for work were gainfully employed by mid-1950.

West Berlin was another serious problem. Severed from its agricultural hinterland and from many of its markets, it required multiple forms of assistance from both the West German authorities and the Allied powers. The latter became particularly 'visible' with the American/British airlift during the Soviet blockade of the western sectors of the city. From June 1948 to May 1949, approximately 1.5 million tons of foodstuffs, coal, and raw materials were flown into the beleaguered city. They were delivered on 196,000 flights, at intervals of only two to three minutes.

In spite of these problems, German production and exports had increased rapidly following the currency reform of 1948. Industrial production accelerated, doubling in two years, while exports doubled each year. In 1948, the volume of exports of finished goods was barely 12 per cent of the level in 1936; less than a year later, it had almost reached that level.[3]

These increases pointed to a strong recovery. Yet Germany's economy in 1950 lagged in comparison to most other western European countries because postwar reconstruction had started much later. The delay also affected the evolution of Germany's balance of payments. Its deficits peaked later than those of France and the United Kingdom, as Otmar Emminger pointed out in his essay about the EPU (see Table 1).[4]

The delay in Germany's recovery exacerbated its payments problems. Its EPU quota of $320 million proved to be too low, because Germany's share in 1949 intra-European trade was well below its long term trading position. Furthermore, as the German economy started to pick up in the summer of 1950, demand for raw materials burgeoned, though stocks were extremely low. Encouraged by the occupying powers, the Bank deutscher Länder (then the central bank for West Germany) eased credit policies to help absorb the refugees and reduce the high rate of unemployment. Easier credit enabled German manufacturers to finance more imports.

[3] Cairncross (1986b), 109-17.
[4] Emminger (1951), 641.

Germany's need for foreign exchange to pay for imports peaked as US aid was being reduced. Its foreign exchange reserves were still extremely low, amounting only to about $180 million, or less than 5 per cent of annual imports in June 1950. US aid deliveries had shrunk from about $1.35 billion in financial year 1948/9 to only $480 million in calendar year 1950. As a result, imports shifted substantially from the dollar to the EPU area, enlarging Germany's EPU deficit.

TABLE 1.   *Current Account Balances: West Germany, France, and the United Kingdom, 1947–1950 (in millions of US dollars)*

Period	West Germany	France	United Kingdom
1947	− 527	−1,833	−2,247
1948	− 875	−1,680	− 324
1949	−1,053	− 269	− 120
1950	− 673	+ 389	+ 627

Source: Emminger (1951), 641.

After the outbreak of the Korean War in June 1950, the fear of shortages added to the demand for raw materials, and German importers participated heavily in the international buying wave. They were in a position to do so because import restrictions, as well as credit policies, had been eased. In spite of the handicaps that still plagued the West German economy, Professor Ludwig Erhard, the German Economics Minister, liberalized German imports even more than the OEEC obligation of 60 per cent.

A convinced free-marketeer, Erhard had instituted a deregulation programme to spark Germany's rebuilding and recovery. Immediately after the American-led currency reform in 1948, he abrogated many domestic controls and restrictions, including most food rationing. He wished to extend this policy increasingly to the foreign sector, since he wanted West Germany to be a spearhead in the move to freer international trade and currency convertibility. As a result, two-thirds of German imports from the OEEC area were freed from quantitative restrictions shortly after the EPU agreement was reached.

To a certain extent, the buying wave in Germany and some other countries was triggered by rumours of an imminent revaluation of sterling. These rumours, by no means ill-founded, sparked rapid changes in Germany's payments, as buyers hastened to pay and sellers delayed billing for sterling area products. These changes were estimated to be responsible for $130 million of the $300 million net cumulative deficit with the EPU for July to October.

GERMANY'S FIRST CURBS

By the Managing Board's first meeting, the German authorities had already taken a series of measures to curb the booming import demand. As of 1 October 1950, the Bank deutscher Länder had increased minimum reserve requirements for commercial banks from 10 to 15 per cent for sight deposits and from 4 to 8 per cent for time deposits. The Bank also put a ceiling on the issuance of bankers' acceptances, on the rediscounting of bills of exchange, and on credits against collateral (Lombard credit).

Furthermore, importers were obliged to deposit 50 per cent of the DM cost of the goods when they obtained or renewed a licence. These deposits had to be transferred to blocked accounts at the regional central banks, thus decreasing the cash liquidity of the commercial banking system and making imports more onerous. In addition, the German government reduced the scale on which non-liberalized import licences were issued and cancelled all outstanding licences for liberalized imports not covered by a contract. About $600 million worth of licences were cancelled, cutting the total amount of outstanding licences with EPU countries almost in half.

The Managing Board noted these steps with approval in the minutes of its first meeting. But it also 'considered that such measures could have been taken earlier' and might need to be intensified.[5] In the Board's view, these measures appeared unlikely to reverse tendencies before the German quota and foreign exchange reserves were exhausted.

Increasing Pressure, Tough Choices

Responding to the Board's request for a prompt analysis, Cairncross and Jacobsson arranged to begin work in Frankfurt within a week. In the meantime, the Germans were being urged to take further action. They knew the Managing Board had arrived at a provisional conclusion favouring suspension of import liberalization. On 24 October, they heard from the Americans. Jean Cattier, chief of the ECA mission in Frankfurt and principal financial adviser to US High Commissioner John J. McCloy, telephoned Wilhelm Vocke, President of the Bank

---

[5] EPU Board Minutes, 1st Session (20–22 Oct. 1950). OEEC MBC/M(50)1, Part 2.

deutscher Länder. Cattier told Vocke that McCloy favoured suspending liberalization and the early reimposition of trade controls.

As part of the Korean War effort, the US had passed a Defense Production Act, introducing production priorities and regulatory measures for a number of commodity markets. The Americans expected their allies to take similar action. Concerned that Germany was buying excessive amounts of scarce raw materials, they pressed for restrictions.

On the day after Cattier's intercession, Jacobsson stopped in Frankfurt on his way to Sweden. He advocated a different approach, strongly advising his German counterparts against suspending liberalization of imports. Given the gravity of such a decision, he recommended that they wait for the report of the experts. That night he wrote to Auboin that 'Cessation of liberalisation would be such a serious measure that one should not do it without serious thought and analysis . . . the situation is less bad than it looks.'[6]

A firm believer in monetary policy and central bank co-operation, Jacobsson pressed Vocke instead to seek an increase in the German discount rate. He pointed out that it was better to act independently rather than under pressure from outside. Given the state of the financial markets, Jacobsson thought a change in the discount rate would be effective. He warned the German central bankers that it would make a 'lamentable impression' if they were to wait any longer.

Central Bank v. the Chancellor

On the following day, the German central bank council increased the discount rate from 4 to 6 per cent. It was a drastic measure, taken at a time when monetary action generally was not deemed a particularly effective instrument of macroeconomic policy. The increase was politically significant as well, because it prompted the first major confrontation between the new and independent central bank system and the Federal government.

The German central bank had been established as an independent body, somewhat like the US Federal Reserve System, on which it was modelled. Government representatives had no vote on its council, but they could delay (though not stop) implementation of its decisions. Although the constitution gave the council considerable autonomy and authority, its willingness to exercise them had not been tested when the payments crisis arose.

Ordinarily, the council met at the central bank's headquarters in Frankfurt. The meeting of 26 October—an extraordinary event—was

[6] Jacobsson (1979), 239.

held in Bonn, in the official residence of Chancellor Konrad Adenauer. Attended by several cabinet members, the session lasted eight hours. During the deliberations, Adenauer strongly opposed any increase in the discount rate, arguing that it would delay and undermine reconstruction efforts in Germany. Erhard was sympathetic to the council's position and supported the increase. Angry that the council members refused to accede to his wishes, but aware of the constraints on his authority, Adenauer bowed grudgingly to their decision. In the eyes of the German public, the event established the bank's independence and enhanced its stature. Thereafter, it was widely regarded as a reliable guardian of a sound Deutsche Mark.[7]

Rather than suspend liberalization, Germany opted to 'wait and see', producing a mixed reaction from trading partners. Smaller countries like Denmark, Ireland, Norway, and Switzerland objected to Germany's continuing commitment to the liberalized sector. They complained that the import cuts fell exclusively on the non-liberalized sector, which included a high proportion of agricultural products and other goods imported from them. France and the United Kingdom, whose exports to Germany were on the liberalized list, took the opposite view, and Germany was not pressed to take further action.

Two days after the central bank raised the discount rate, Cairncross arrived in Frankfurt, where Jacobsson joined him. Cairncross made it clear that he did not at all like the increase in the discount rate, and objected strongly that any such decision had been taken before his arrival.[8]

THE EXPERTS RECOMMEND

The Jacobsson/Cairncross Mission

The Jacobsson/Cairncross mission played a crucial role in the German payments crisis and in shaping subsequent German policy. Its recommendations were exceedingly effective, far more so than even the Managing Board had expected.

Two men of different backgrounds and persuasions were teamed up. Nevertheless, they worked well together and appreciated each other. In his diary, Jacobsson remarked, 'I have liked Alec Cairncross very much. He holds a problem in his head; is practical; willing to

---

[7] Emminger (1986), 20.
[8] Jacobsson (1979), 242.

adjust his views if he meets a spirit ready to make certain concessions in favour of his views.'[9]

Although starting from different positions, both men reached a similar diagnosis of the German situation and were prepared to make the same recommendations. Cairncross wrote that their agreement was 'to some extent a fluke, since, in other circumstances, I could imagine a real difference of views. It did not seem to us, however, that credit restriction, liberalisation, and increasing economic activity and employment would prove incompatible by the spring of 1951.'[10]

In fact, their report was more authoritative precisely because two men with different perspectives had reached the same conclusions and agreed on recommendations. This added weight to their findings, especially among OEEC members, who also had diverse conceptions of appropriate monetary, credit, and trade policies. Jacobsson's daughter and biographer, Erin Jacobsson, believes that her father never fully realized the extent of the differences within the OEEC. Nor was he fully aware of the help Cairncross gave in securing the Managing Board's acceptance of their recommendations. Unlike Jacobsson, Cairncross did not view the German problem as 'a test case for monetary and credit policy and liberalisation. It was a straightforward liquidity crisis in an otherwise healthy economy.'[11] Both experts had no difficulty in agreeing on the desirability of mutual self-help, on Europeans lending money to help a European country in a crisis, and on the lasting goodwill this would create in Germany.

The pair had less than a week to prepare a detailed diagnosis. As most of the hotels (and most of the city) were still in ruins, they worked, one on each side of a large dining-room table, in the central bank's guesthouse in Frankfurt. They interrupted their writing for a series of appointments in Frankfurt and Bonn, returning to their drafts late at night. They met with cabinet members, central bank directors, other senior officials, and representatives of the banking and business community to gather information and learn their views.

A meeting with the US High Commissioner centred largely on occupation costs. According to Cairncross, 'He kept telling us that Eastern Germany had managed to put together 27 divisions and he could see no reason why Western Germany should not support an equal programme. . . . If it were necessary to go back on liberalisation that might ease the problem of finance. This we just could not see.'[12]

Jacobsson warned the Americans against pushing Germany to discard

[9] Jacobsson (1979), 242.
[10] Cairncross (1986a), 207-11.
[11] Jacobsson (1979), 242-3.
[12] Cairncross (1986a), 5.

liberalization. If the Germans did so, 'people would say that another measure pressed on Europe by the Americans had shown itself unsuitable and impossible (as in 1947 the convertibility of sterling)'. With the Germans, Jacobsson turned the argument around, asserting that the suspension of liberalization would be a first-rate piece of propaganda for eastern Germany and a blow to the policies sponsored by the United States in western Europe.

Results of the Mission

On 3 November, the experts discussed their findings with the Managing Board; their sixty-page analytical report followed on 20 November.[13] It was updated later in the month with a complementary document on economic and financial developments in Germany.[14]

In its own reports to the OEEC Council, the Managing Board drew heavily on the diagnosis of the independent experts:[15]

The independent experts believed that the fundamental German position had developed favourably in most respects even in the autumn. The difficult balance of payments position had been created in part by errors of policy and judgment but, even more, by a number of accidental factors. . . .

The independent experts felt that over the next few months there would still be a trade deficit and, if it were at the rate of September (when imports were not really abnormal), the trade deficit from the beginning of November 1950 up to the end of January 1951 would be about $170 million. . . .

As regards the period after the end of January 1951 . . . there was a reasonable chance of equilibrium being reached and a surplus gradually achieved because of the continued improvement in the German production and the strong foreign demand likely to continue, and provided that the credit measures already taken were maintained and certain further measures were taken . . .

The experts also felt it essential that the German government adhere to its intention to maintain a balanced budget.

The experts' key conclusion was that Germany's trade would be balanced at a relatively high level by the spring of 1951. Both men were persuaded that the underlying situation had sufficient elements of strength for this to happen, provided the adjustment policies were pursued with some vigour. The corrective measures they suggested

[13] Jacobsson and Cairncross, 'Consideration of Germany's Position' (20 Nov. 1950). OEEC MBC(50)13.

[14] Jacobsson and Cairncross, 'Recent Economic and Financial Developments in Germany' (2 Dec. 1950). OEEC MBC(50)25.

[15] EPU Board Report, 'The Position of Germany in EPU' (6 Nov. 1950). OEEC C(50)315 (1st revision).

were based on confidence that this would be the outcome. 'My reading of the situation', Cairncross later wrote, 'disposed me to think that a country whose exports doubled annually, whose currency was clearly undervalued, and whose price level was still falling in the middle of world inflation, was most unlikely to suffer for long from balance of payments difficulties.'[16]

Although the experts were convinced that their diagnosis was sound, the Managing Board accepted it hesitantly. Cairncross attributed the scepticism to a strong feeling that Germany had pursued unnecessarily reckless policies. Under the circumstances, some countries undoubtedly felt other remedial measures were needed.[17]

Von Mangoldt was torn between conflicting roles. He had headed his country's first permanent mission to the OEEC, the first international institution to give Germany a seat after the war. He now sat on the board of a new international body, not as a representative of Germany, but as an independent member. Charged with acting in the EPU's best interests, he felt he could not be an advocate for his country. Yet he was close to the highest levels of its government and was its nominee. He resolved the dilemma by providing extensive factual material on Germany's situation at every Board meeting, by inviting German experts to explain the position of the German government, and by excusing himself from the Board's formal deliberations when it was time to agree on recommendations.

A Credit with 'Conditionality'

On 6 November 1950, the Managing Board agreed that the EPU should give Germany a special credit if it would accept certain conditions, in substance those recommended by the experts. Germany should continue its restrictive monetary policy. It should maintain the present exchange rate of the Deutsche Mark, with no further devaluation. (The Economic Advisory Council to the Federal Ministry for Economic Affairs, composed of leading German professors of economics, voiced the only support for devaluation. Neither the independent experts nor the German authorities saw any reason for it.)

In addition, Germany should abstain from any form of deficit financing, by the Federal as well as by the Länder governments, and should increase taxation at an early date by reducing depreciation allowances and increasing the turnover tax on selected items. Some

[16] Cairncross (1986b).
[17] Cairncross (1951), 4.

supplementary measures were added, e.g. to promote exports and develop the capital market.

The Managing Board recommended to the OEEC Council three lines of action to deal with the German payments problem. First, the EPU would grant Germany a special credit of $120 million. This would cover about 60 per cent of a deficit of some $200 million that Germany was expected to incur from the beginning of November 1950 to the end of March 1951. After March, its trade was expected to balance. In drawing on this credit, Germany would pay up to $60 million in gold, i.e. one-third of any deficit up to $180 million above its quota. The remainder of the deficit could be covered by drawing on the unused portion of Germany's quota in the EPU, about $20 million. The credit would bear interest at 2.75 per cent and be redeemable in six equal instalments between June and September 1951.

Second, in return for the credit, Germany would implement a programme consistent with the experts' recommendations and subject to the approval of the EPU Managing Board and the OEEC Council. Third, the other countries in the EPU should endeavour to liberalize goods of interest to Germany, to grant generous quotas to German goods not on their free list, and to refrain from seeking unreasonably large quotas for their own exports to Germany.

The German government responded with a comprehensive stabilization programme, presented to the Managing Board and approved at its meetings early in December. On 13 December 1950, the OEEC Council, in turn, approved the Board's recommendations and the extension of a credit of $120 million to Germany.

'The special credit was duly extended,' Cairncross recalls, 'although not without a good deal of expostulation and protest. . . . But in the end it was agreed to give Germany a helping hand. The Americans stood aside and for the first time in the postwar period the European nations were united in offering financial aid to one of their number. It was an investment in German goodwill that yielded large dividends in subsequent years.'[18]

The Americans did not contribute to the financing of the special credit other than by tolerating a temporary drain that the German drawings placed on the EPU's capital. Hubert Havlik, the US Representative to the Managing Board, later recalled his government's attitude. Ambassador Katz 'felt very strongly that the crisis had been brought on by willful action of the German authorities. It looked as though they decided to take advantage of their position and import as much as possible' by expanding domestic credit. Katz concluded

---

[18] Cairncross (1986b), 8-9.

that if the European Payments Union wanted to extend a credit to the Germans, let them do it. But the US should not put up any more money for the EPU as part of a loan operation for Germany. 'Washington took a rather more lenient view . . . but Katz put his neck on the line . . . and he won his point.' [19]

The German programme did not foresee a suspension of liberalization, emphasizing instead short and medium term adjustment measures. The Managing Board approved these measures but insisted on closely monitoring their execution. The monitoring procedures required key German officials to appear at the monthly Board meetings for questioning about their progress. The German government was also required to submit monthly memoranda for the Board's review. Germany tried to follow the Managing Board's recommendations faithfully. It did not resist the conditionality of the EPU credit, despite the stringent requirements.

The Managing Board emphasized that the special credit was not 'political' but 'commercial', backed by collateral. The collateral was an account with the Federal Reserve Bank of New York, into which the German central bank deposited dollars received from sources other than foreign trade or aid. Most of these receipts were from expenditures by American soldiers and tourists in Germany.

SUCCESS IN THE BALANCE

Putting on the Brakes

As Jacobsson saw it, the German policy gamble was on whether or not the credit and tax measures would bite hard enough to change the deficits into surpluses by the spring of 1951.[20] In the early months of that year, the Managing Board's review indicated that the braking distance would be somewhat longer than expected. During the preceding period of easy credit, the Bank deutscher Länder had refinanced obligations that had yet to be repaid. Anticipating shortages, German citizens drew on their savings and started to hoard goods, particularly after the Chinese intervention in Korea. Public opinion polls showed that more than half the population feared the Korean conflict would lead to a war among the world powers. Experience with two runaway postwar inflations had made the public apprehensive about a further increase in prices.

Under mounting pressure, the Bank felt obliged to resort to an

[19] 'Oral History Interview with Hubert F. Havlik' (Apr. 1980). Harry S. Truman Library.
[20] Jacobsson (1979), 243.

emergency braking device. In February 1951, in an unprecedented and never repeated move, it ordered a complete stop to all new lending by commercial banks. It further ruled that the volume of short term bank credit had to be reduced by DM 1 billion within a couple of months and on a selective basis.

This measure had to be implemented by the regional central banks and gave rise to immense administrative problems. The German central bank system already faced some criticism for being 'too federal' and therefore constitutionally incapable of maintaining effective monetary control. The Managing Board asserted, 'Whether or not the constitutional arrangements can be justly blamed, there has been less unified and purposeful direction of the Central Banking System than is desirable in a crisis . . . the central direction of the German Central Banking System must be strengthened.'[21]

The Americans, who had been godfathering the system to a large extent, were equally critical. Cattier asked the central bank leadership to report its conclusions about the obvious shortcomings of the system. The head of the central bank council, Karl Bernard, dispatched a firm reply. He maintained there were no grounds for assuming the central bank, as then constituted, could not stand up to further tests in the future. Bernard also told Cattier he saw no reason to change the system. But in their response to the OEEC, the German authorities mentioned the preparation of a new law that would replace the Bank deutscher Länder with a new Deutsche Bundesbank.

Other critics, within and outside the OEEC, voiced an opposing view. They attacked the central bank's restriction of credit when unemployment was high and appeared to be growing.[22]

Import Restrictions After All

The German situation in February 1951 seemed bleak indeed, and tension mounted as worried officials and monitors looked for signs of improvement. Jacobsson and Cairncross had predicted that March would be the turning point, but Figgures saw 'no clear trend yet'. Instead, February reports grimly implied that Germany was likely to exhaust its special credit by the middle of March. Before the end of February, Germany had used more than $90 million of the $120 million. The insufficiency of the remaining credit led to a new rush for import licences.

On 22 February, the German government suspended import

---

[21] EPU Board Report, 'German Programme of 12 March' (22 Mar. 1951). OEEC C(51)95.
[22] Cairncross (1986b).

liberalization at the advice of the central bank council. The Managing Board convened immediately. It supported the suspension, noting that 'because of the marked deterioration in the position, Germany could not do otherwise than take emergency measures.'[23] The Board advised Germany to stop issuing import licences altogether, until a new import programme had been prepared. Though virtually no new licences were issued after 21 February, those issued earlier remained valid.

To protect the EPU's capital and alert Germany to its situation, the Board announced that it could not recommend granting any additional credit, once the special credit was exhausted. The Board assured the OEEC 'that there is no need for apprehension that the German government may be unable to reimburse the special credit granted to it'. Apparently some members feared default and had to be given assurances that the collateral was sound.

As the month of February drew to a close, Germany's credit was almost used up. The government's remedial measures—denounced at home as too strict, and abroad as not strict enough—had apparently multiplied its problems without diminishing its deficits. With no sign of improvement, Vocke was near despair. In a letter dated 26 February 1951, he told Adenauer, 'Dear Mr. Chancellor, as it shows, it is well possible, perhaps even likely, that by the end of March we shall be confronted with the void . . .'.[24] Vocke's letter made it clear that he would prefer to have Germany withdraw from the EPU rather than accumulate more foreign debt.

Concerned about their German market, the British authorities would have been willing to provide more help. They would have been receptive to freeing the German collateral, prolonging the EPU special credit, or even increasing the German quota. They thought that further financial assistance would probably be required to keep Germany in the EPU.[25] Cairncross agrees, in retrospect, that Germany should have been granted a somewhat larger credit line. 'In relation to the uncertainties ahead, $120 million proved just a little too low . . . as the credit was near the lower rather than the upper limit [of the $100–200 million] that we suggested.'[26]

Germany's decision to suspend trade liberalization triggered hectic OEEC action. The Council set up a Special Restricted Committee, in accordance with Article 14 of the Code of Liberalisation, to consider

[23] EPU Board Report, 'Position of Germany in the European Payments Union' (24 Feb. 1951). OEEC MBC(51)18.

[24] Ludwig-Erhard-Stiftung (1986), 275.

[25] London Com., 'The German Deficit in the EPU' (19 Mar. 1951). EPC (51) 29. PRO CAB 134/229.

[26] Cairncross (1986b).

the German import programme, submitted on 12 March 1951.[27] A mediation group of three independent experts was appointed a few weeks later to propose to the German government how new import licences should be apportioned among OEEC member countries.[28] The situation was complicated, and there were no rules. The OEEC had no experience with a country reducing its trade liberalization from 65 per cent to zero.

In its handling of the crisis, the OEEC virtually took control of Germany's imports. The mediation group first vetted the issuance of German import licences for goods slated to arrive in April and May 1951. Then it fixed a ceiling of $31 million for additional imports in April. The total was divided into categories of imports, defined in great detail as to essential and non-essential goods and on a country-by-country basis. These restrictions led to considerable haggling among Germany's suppliers and, as a result, to widespread dissatisfaction.

The Managing Board's report on the German import programme sharply reiterated its continuing dissatisfaction with the implementation of German policies to restrict demand.[29] In earlier reports, it had stressed the importance of the speedy enactment of new fiscal measures. Disappointed that this had not happened, the Board advised the Council that 'during the critical period ahead, no assistance from fiscal policy can be expected, and a correspondingly heavier burden must, therefore, be thrown on credit policy . . .'.

Nor was the Board content with monetary measures. The same report notes, 'It is disturbing that there should not have been, since the 31st October, any significant decrease in the credits granted by the Central Banking System.'

Ironically, Germany's decision to suspend all liberalization of imports and the OEEC's drastic responses may have been unnecessary. Although no one was then aware of it, Germany's position had already begun to improve.

Vanishing Act: Germany's Deficits Disappear

The OEEC accepted the temporary suspension of German import liberalization as a necessary precaution, but Jacobsson did not. He felt personally involved in an adjustment achieved mainly through credit and fiscal measures, not import restrictions. According to his biographer, he was 'heartbroken' and felt 'never as lonely as he did

---

[27] The Special Restricted Com. met and submitted two reports to the OEEC Council: (22 Mar. 1951) OEEC C(51)96 and (27 Sept. 1951) OEEC C(51)315.

[28] Decision of the Council (7 Apr. 1951). OEEC C(51)112 (Final).

[29] EPU Board Report, 'German Programme of 12 March' (22 Mar. 1951). OEEC C(51)95.

in those days'. At their February 1951 meeting at the BIS, some central bank governors had ignored him; others begged him to reconsider his orthodox approach and 'save his career and reputation'.

'Could I have advised differently?' he asked in his diary. The answer came soon enough. For the first time, Germany showed a surplus in its EPU accounts at the end of March, exactly as Jacobsson and Cairncross had predicted. The surplus ($11.3 million) appeared before the suspension of import liberalization could have had any appreciable effect.

Germany continued to run surpluses in April and May and, by the end of May, repaid the EPU special credit in full, five months before maturity. The Managing Board informed the OEEC Council 'that in its view it was no longer desirable to recommend to the German Government month by month what should be the amount of its imports from the EPU area'.[30] It thought Germany would be able to pay for imports from the EPU area at a monthly rate of $170 million, as compared with about $220 million before suspension.

Nevertheless, OEEC committees continued to monitor the German import programmes very closely, even though the German payments position improved month after month. The Managing Board, too, maintained 'that Germany should proceed with caution'. The shock of such large deficits had been so deep-seated that the OEEC insisted on practising crisis management long after the crisis had disappeared.

By the end of the year, Germany had completely reversed the cumulative deficit that had peaked at $457 million in February 1951. Its EPU account even showed a small surplus. At the beginning of 1952, Germany resumed import liberalization under the normal OEEC rules, freeing 57 per cent of imports on private account. After three months, it moved to 76 per cent.

By the spring of 1953, Germany was the largest creditor of the EPU, though it had further liberalized its EPU imports to 91 per cent. From then on, it was Germany's extreme and growing creditor position that created headaches for the Managing Board and the OEEC.

CONSEQUENCES AND LESSONS

The Federal Republic of Germany became the object of a major international rescue operation very soon after the war. That experience

---

[30] EPU Board, *First Annual Report* (1951), 23.

had an impact on German attitudes and policy far beyond the crisis itself.

Its government was favourably disposed toward the OEEC and the EPU, the first organizations to treat Germany as an equal. Upon joining the Union, Germany intended to keep a low profile. Instead, it found itself the focus of embarrassing international attention, obliged to ask for help and accused of rocking the boat. The payments crisis and the stringent conditions attached to the EPU credit forced Germany to co-operate in unprecedented ways. Indeed, the monitoring procedures and restrictive measures were so severe that other countries took pains to avoid a similar predicament.

Isolated from new developments in economic analysis in the 1930s, German economists had had little exposure to modern economics and the Keynesian jargon in common use outside Germany. Civil servants received a crash course in both, as a by-product of the sometimes gruelling hearings at the EPU. The German experts soon improved their ability to present their case and defend their opinions. The senior civil servants had grown up in a Schachtian environment, with its emphasis on tough bargaining for bilateral advantages in trade. They were deeply impressed that Germany had been granted a special credit—and astounded that it was permitted to reintroduce import restrictions without any retaliation from OEEC partner countries.

Under Germany's new constitutional arrangements, authority was divided between the Federal and Länder governments and their respective bureaucracies, thus delaying the hammering out of programmes and the implementation of policies. Other obstacles arose in dealing with a parliament that was not exactly outward-looking. Another vexing legacy from the past was an aversion to strong government. These drawbacks sometimes tested the nerves of Germany's partner countries and the OEEC Secretariat, as indicated in minutes of meetings and office memos. 'The nature of the German constitution with its divide of responsibilities between the Federal and Land Governments has been a further brake on progress and has strengthened the influence of those who wish to drag their feet . . .' was the short-tempered remark in a UK government memo.[31]

On the other hand, as Cairncross notes, 'there were no less than four international organisations that could take decisions reacting directly on Germany's balance of payments,' including the OEEC.[32] The International Ruhr Authority had power over the allocation of German coal and steel. The Allied High Commissioners had various

---

[31] London Com., 'The German Deficit in the EPU' (19 Mar. 1951). EPC (51) 29. PRO CAB 134/229.

[32] Cairncross (1986b), 1.

veto powers and a large bill for occupation costs. The ECA mission provided most of the funds that covered the German external deficit. Not surprisingly, these relationships complicated the handling of the German case and made it difficult to reach decisions that could be implemented rapidly.

Inside the German government, the payments crisis was instrumental in streamlining the decision-making process and administrative procedures. This occurred much earlier than it might have in less critical circumstances. The burden of international responsibility had indeed been learned the hard way, but the experience was not without its benefits.

The payments crisis also tested the prevailing economic doctrine in Germany and its main spokesmen. When the crisis was at its height, Erhard's personal reputation was as battered as that of his free market principles. His views had never been very popular with the British High Commission, and they came under increasing fire from the Americans. The latter saw the payments problems as another sign that more regulation was warranted as part of the defence effort. In a letter to Adenauer, McCloy called for a major modification of the free market economy in response to changed circumstances.

Emminger, who by that time had joined the leadership of the Bank deutscher Länder, believed that certain factions in the US High Commission had been waiting for this opportunity to press for changes in the regulatory direction. The German government made certain concessions to these pressures, but, according to Emminger, Erhard did not take them very seriously. He considered them only temporary and of limited economic importance. More important, his views were under attack domestically, even within his own party. He found an ally in the central bank and sided on all major issues with its leadership.

The restoration of equilibrium to German payments within a relatively short period of time repaired Erhard's reputation completely. He then pursued his previous policy unflinchingly and led the German economy on to the 'miracle' that is closely linked to his name. He immediately set the convertibility of the Deutsche Mark as the next goal of German external economic policy.

Internationally, the success of German adjustment policies was no less important. Sound management of the payments crisis bestowed a formidable reputation upon the EPU and its Managing Board early in their existence. Thus, Triffin recalled, 'This dynamic and successful handling of a major crisis endowed the young Managing Board with a prestige and authority far beyond the most optimistic expectations of the promoters of the EPU agreement.'[33] G. L. Rees reached a similar conclusion.[34] 'The entire episode of Germany's intra-European payments difficulty was one which reflected considerable credit both upon Germany's monetary authorities for their willingness to cooperate with the representatives of the newly formed EPU and upon the Managing Board for its unobtrusive competence in handling the situation in spite of the lack of previous experience.'

The Board itself expressed relief and satisfaction. 'Great patience and restraint have been shown by all members, not least by Germany. The Board wishes to record its gratitude to the Federal German Authorities for the assistance which they have given during these difficult months. At all times they have been willing to produce all information asked for and to send officials to discuss the problems with the Board.'[35]

Particular credit was given in OEEC circles to von Mangoldt's role. His absolute frankness and avoidance of technical manoeuvring disarmed critical colleagues on the Managing Board, who came increasingly to trust his integrity. In 1952, he succeeded Carli as Chairman of the Board. His election had its roots in the esteem he had earned during the difficult months of the payments crisis.

The German payments crisis set an international precedent for the formation of macroeconomic policies and for policy mixes in times of crisis. It contributed decisively to a renaissance of monetary policy. As the *Federal Reserve Bulletin* stated in December 1951, 'The success of Belgium and Germany in overcoming post-Korean inflationary pressures is largely the result of their credit policies.' And Erin Jacobsson observed, 'Within the next years all industrial countries which had not yet started to use monetary policy took some measure in this direction. . . . The use of monetary and financial policy to control the economy also made it possible to dismantle the remains of the wartime controls.'[36]

For the EPU, the German payments problem was only the first of several crises. In the years ahead, it served as a model for international crisis management. The Managing Board, the German government, and the other members of the OEEC all accepted responsibility for resolving the problems. Their success demonstrated the advantages of close co-operation and mutual assistance. It also showed that impressive results can be achieved by energetic adjustment measures, particularly if directed and followed up by an effective international institution.

[33] Triffin (1957), 182.
[34] Rees (1963), 131.
[35] EPU Board, *First Annual Report* (1951), 24.
[36] Jacobsson (1979), 245.

As one caught in the centre of the crisis, Vocke could later reflect on its significance, not only for Germany but for others. Addressing the German group of the International Chamber of Commerce on 23 May 1951, he hailed Germany's 'first credit'.

Some people say that this credit was not needed at all. They allege that it merely exposed us, quite unnecessarily, to foreign interference. To this I could reply that the credit, and the use made of it, have been an enormous benefit to our economy. The credit was the first part of the help given to us, while the second part was the fact that foreign countries maintained their liberalisation in respect to Germany, while we were relieved of the corresponding obligation on our side. . . .

This ought to be borne in mind by those who complain that other members of the EPU are interfering in our affairs. After all, we could never have got through if they had not so interfered. The EPU is above all a valuable means of overcoming nationalism in currency matters, and of educating people to think in international terms.[37]

Vocke was often reminded during his next seven years in office of another passage in his address:

It would be highly desirable that the EPU should attack the problem of those creditors which have extreme creditor positions with the same thoroughness and force that it has applied to the problem of deficits. . . . The future fate of the EPU, and its success in the expansion of trade and liberalisation, are to a large extent in the hands of the creditor countries.

At that time, Vocke would have found it unbelievable that his remarks would soon apply to his own country. Indeed, the future fate of the EPU was largely in Germany's hands, as it became the Union's most extreme creditor within two years.

---

[37] Vocke, 'The First Year of the European Payments Union'. Address delivered at the Conference of the German Group of the International Chamber of Commerce (23 May 1951). BIS EPU Archive.

7 Coping with Rearmament

The ultimate test of an international monetary system is its ability to absorb and survive blows from unexpected major events. The European Payments Union was born at the onset of severe payments imbalances, coped successfully with the consequences, and survived. The EPU Agreement had yet to be concluded when North Korean troops, apparently with Soviet support, marched into South Korea on 25 June 1950. At the time, the Marshall Plan itself was only at the half-way mark.

The economic repercussions of the Korean invasion exacerbated the German payments crisis, the first test of the system. During the next two years, every other EPU country reached a position critical enough to require the Managing Board's serious attention. To a greater or lesser degree, crisis management became standard operating procedure for the infant system. It faced a very different environment from the one in which it had been created.

AN UNEXPECTED ENVIRONMENT

The invasion of South Korea had consequences that extended far beyond President Truman's decision to intervene militarily. It marked the beginning of US determination to build and maintain a military establishment capable of deterring the Soviet Union, while expecting its allies to do the same. Pursued now for nearly four decades, that policy has had profound effects on the US economy. It has also transformed US political and economic relations with the rest of the world, and especially with its European friends.

To be sure, the Soviet threat had become increasingly evident. More than a year earlier, in April 1949, the North Atlantic Treaty Organisation (NATO) had been created. Its membership included all western European countries except for the traditional neutrals and a still not independent Federal Republic of Germany. The US Mutual Defense Assistance Act of October 1949 had authorized the provision of military equipment to European forces. In September 1949, the first Soviet nuclear explosion had further heightened concern. Before Korea, however, rearmament had consisted of more talk than substance. The US was still reducing its military establishment from World War II levels.

Many of its European allies had pared their military forces drastically, but reluctantly, after World War II. They wanted to retain important roles on the international scene and therefore felt that a substantial defence establishment was essential. Britain continued to maintain a large military programme, with occupation troops in Germany and other forces stationed throughout the Middle and Far East. So did France and the Netherlands, as they sought to maintain positions in South East Asia, North Africa, and in their colonial territories elsewhere. All three countries kept troops stationed in the Third World, where they were repeatedly embroiled in hostilities. As a result, Britain and the Netherlands were spending a higher proportion of their GNP on national defence in 1950 than was the United States, and the French proportion was nearly as large.[1]

In Korea, the United States soon found itself involved in a bitter war, barely five years after the end of World War II. Its priorities inevitably shifted to military matters, and it urged its NATO partners to do likewise. With their economic reconstruction still incomplete, the European NATO countries were apprehensive, but their initial response was nonetheless substantial. Still under the shadow of World War II, political leaders assumed that defence needs should have a priority claim on resources. The members of NATO all agreed on the necessity of responding to the menacing Soviets by demonstrating their determination to rebuild their armed forces. In the process, European governments tended to underestimate their economic limitations and overestimate the assistance the US would provide for their rearmament.

In September 1950, a month before the Managing Board first met, ECA mission chiefs were called to Paris and asked to urge participating countries to initiate large increases in arms expenditures as quickly as possible. They were told ECA would accept some deterioration in 'civilian investment, social welfare and sound financial policies' for a few years to close the gap in military strength with the Soviet bloc.[2] However reluctantly, ECA now acknowledged to its missions that Europeans might have to reimpose trade controls in some cases, though tougher fiscal and monetary policies would be preferable.

Convertibility, freer trade and payments arrangements, and internal financial stability thus became secondary, though still important, goals. During the autumn of 1950, the OEEC Council met at ministerial level on several occasions to consider its Secretary General's memorandum on 'Urgent Economic Problems'. (The title was an OEEC euphemism for the economic implications of rearmament that satisfied the sensitivities of its non-NATO members.) At the same meetings, proposals for liberalizing 75 per cent of intra-European trade were considered and approved.

---

[1] Mayne (1970), 193.
[2] Washington tel. to US del. TOREP 7999 (16 Sept. 1950).

Several ministers expressed the view that trade liberalization would ease the burden of rearmament by reducing costs and that non-inflationary financing would facilitate removing trade restrictions.

Governments, however, found it difficult to control price increases. The impact of higher raw materials prices on world markets could not be contained. Larger military budgets required tax increases that were difficult to enact, given already high rates of taxation. Between June 1950 and June 1951, retail prices in western Europe rose on the average by 12 per cent.[3] In country after country, governments became embroiled in serious political difficulties, more or less related to the resurgent inflation.

The Marshall Plan had asked Europe to state its needs and define the contribution it could make through self help. The rearmament programme used a different approach. NATO established defence requirements in the form of a Medium Term Defence Plan, largely defined by the US military, and then began to prod members to implement it. Most European countries responded with substantial increases in their defence budgets, though scarcely enough to satisfy the requirements.

Finally, at their meeting in Ottawa in September 1951, the NATO ministers organized a high-level burden-sharing analysis under 'Three Wise Men'—Harriman, Monnet, and Sir Edwin Plowden (UK). They were given the impossible assignment of arranging an equitable sharing, among sovereign states, of the costs of rearmament programmes established by the military.[4] They could not and did not succeed, though some *ad hoc* bargaining occurred before and during the NATO ministers' meeting in Lisbon in February 1952. The more important outcome was a realization that the requirements could not be met as quickly as the NATO military would have liked.

US aid to Europe, nevertheless, continued to emphasize rearmament rather than economic objectives. A somewhat reluctant supporter of the new priority, Hoffman had left his post as the head of ECA toward the end of 1950. He was succeeded for a while by his deputy, William C. Foster. The new foreign aid legislation submitted to Congress early in 1951 was called the Mutual Security Act. The Marshall Plan itself was formally terminated at the end of 1951, six months ahead of schedule. The ECA organization was renamed MSA, the Mutual Security Administration, and the US Congress provided it with funds to support the expansion of European military capabilities. The US also provided dollars by buying military equipment in Europe and by financing NATO infrastructure (construction of military bases and transportation and communications networks). However, the transition from one type of aid

---

[3] OEEC (1951), 9.
[4] Schelling (1955), 6–10.

to another was not smooth, and a number of countries experienced severe shortages of dollars for a period.

The Korean War also resolved hesitations about devising a framework for a German contribution to the defence of western Europe.[5] By October 1950, Monnet had persuaded the French Defence Minister, René Pleven, to propose a European Defence Community (EDC) comprising the six countries already negotiating a Coal and Steel Community. After nearly four years of reformulations and negotiations, the EDC proposal was rejected by the French Chamber of Deputies. Only thereafter, in 1954, was Germany admitted first to a military alliance called Western European Union and then to NATO, arrangements then acceptable to all western governments. Peace treaty limitations also slowed the pace of Italian rearmament. As a result, both Germany and Italy were able to meet foreign demands for the products of their heavy manufacturing industries, while production capacity in other NATO countries was diverted to rearmament.

This wholly unexpected environment led to economic stresses that severely tested the EPU throughout its first two years. Both the automatic clearing mechanism and the Managing Board were called upon to show their mettle. They bent, but they did not break. By the time the first renewal was approved in mid-1952, the new system had established its worth and its ability to deal successfully with major unforeseen circumstances.

INITIAL EXPECTATIONS FOR THE EPU

Negotiations for the EPU Agreement had been heated and intense in the final months. The negotiators were completely preoccupied with identifying specific provisions that would be acceptable to the numerous interested parties. By that time, the disagreements were about how the EPU would affect national interests, not about whether the new system would function successfully in any major crisis. Korea was hardly mentioned during the fortnight of negotiations preceding the decisions of 7 July 1950.

Before Korea, the economic portents had suggested that the system should experience little difficulty at the outset. By mid-1950, the favourable effects of the 1949 devaluations and of reduced rates of inflation were very apparent. Intra-European trade was expanding, trade restrictions were being eased, and the result was much better balance. As early as the previous February, the OEEC had drawn attention to a tendency

[5] Mayne (1970), 170-218.

toward balance in intra-European trade that had followed the devaluations.[6] Some subsequent observers felt that the reduction of surpluses and deficits within Europe during the first half of 1950 helped lay the groundwork for an EPU Agreement.[7] One suggested that acceptance by the United Kingdom was 'due in part to the rapid increase in her reserves of foreign exchange in the first half of 1950'.[8]

Even the initial positions allotted to the presumed persistent debtors and creditors were considerably smaller than their net use of IEPS drawing rights in the preceding year (see Table 2). The initial credits that debtors received were only 70 per cent of the drawing rights they had needed a year earlier.

TABLE 2.   *Initial EPU Credit Positions and Use of IEPS Drawing Rights, FY 1949/50 and FY 1950/51 (in millions of US dollars)*

	Net Utilization of Drawing Rights, FY 1949/50	Initial Credit Balances Allotted, FY 1950/51
Austria	90	80
Greece	130	115
Netherlands	80	30
Norway	80	60
Turkey	60	25
TOTAL	440	310

Sources: BIS, *Twenty-First Annual Report* (1951), 218; EPU, *First Annual Report of the Managing Board* (1951), 13.

Initial debits were reduced even more sharply. During the last year of the IEPS, ECA had provided $703 million in conditional aid to a dozen OEEC members in return for their granting drawing rights to European trading partners. Under the EPU, conditional aid was needed to finance surpluses with the Union as a whole, not bilateral partners. Thus, for the first year, it was allotted to just three countries—Belgium, Sweden, and the United Kingdom. A total of only $201 million was enough to fund their initial debit balances, including $150 million for the United Kingdom.

ECA had obviously expected the incentives in the EPU system to strengthen the tendency toward equilibrium in intra-European trade and

6 OEEC, *European Recovery Program: Second Report* (1950).
7 e.g. Diebold (1952), 86.
8 Cairncross (1985), 272.

payments, despite a higher level of exchanges resulting from trade liberalization. To minimize the obligatory extension of credit, countries with surpluses would reduce them by expanding internal demand for imports and by lifting restrictions on imports. The need to pay increasing amounts of gold as cumulative deficits mounted would force debtors to check inflationary pressures and promote exports to their European partners.

The IMF staff concurred, but took small comfort from its conclusion. It reported to its Executive Board in June 1950 that the EPU scheme would provide for debtors practically gold-free means of payment during the first year of operation and some probability of gold payments in the second year. The staff had apparently concluded that the EPU arrangements would lead the debtors—apart from those with initial credit balances—to keep their intra-European deficits within the segment of their quota that could be settled entirely with credit, a mere 3 per cent of their 1949 turnover. The staff feared that such an intra-European system would retard progress toward convertibility.

Federal Reserve Governor Szymczak's last-minute protest about the 'softness' of the EPU was apparently based on staff advice that relied heavily on this IMF forecast. An analyst at the Federal Reserve Bank of New York took a different view. In a memorandum to the bank's president, he concluded that deficit countries would soon be faced with heavy gold payments. 'Debtors probably will not reach the stage of quota exhaustion, but will probably find the gold payments onerous enough to require the imposition of trade restrictions or withdrawal from the Union at some previous time.'[9] In retrospect, the Federal Reserve analyst proved to be at least as prescient as those more closely involved in making decisions. In truth, however, he paid no more attention to the effects of the Korean War than did the negotiators.

ECONOMIC EFFECTS OF THE KOREAN WAR

The effects of the Korean War showed up in the European economy in two stages. The first lasted about nine months and was marked by scare buying, much higher raw materials prices, and sharp increases in the military budgets adopted by NATO members. By the spring of 1951, however, the raw materials boom was over. Governments began to realize that military expenditures could not be usefully increased as rapidly as planned. Beginning in March 1951, a number of countries curtailed their military expenditure plans, tightened their fiscal and monetary policies,

[9] P. D. Sternlight memo, 'The European Payments Union' (2 Aug. 1950). Federal Reserve Files.

and sharply reduced rates of price inflation. Some were slower to act and did not succeed in stabilizing price levels until mid-1952.

Differences in the magnitude of military programmes and in the timing of anti-inflation policies inevitably led individual members of the EPU along different paths. Both their internal economies and their balances of foreign payments fared very differently. However, by January 1954 the OEEC could report with assurance that 'the general inflationary trend which set in after the outbreak of the war in Korea has disappeared, and Western Europe's balance of payments, particularly its dollar balance, has improved . . .'.[10] The actual turning-point had been a full year and a half earlier. Nevertheless, the different roads to stability pursued by various members created numerous hazards for the newly formed European Payments Union.

Stage 1: June 1950–March 1951

Immediately after President Truman announced that the US would help defend South Korea, public and private stockpiling increased sharply, precipitating heavy demands from North America for both raw materials and finished manufactures. Most European countries followed suit. By the early months of 1951, the prices of wool and rubber had risen by 200 per cent, of tin and Egyptian cotton by 170 per cent, and of hides and wood pulp by 100 per cent over their June 1950 levels.[11] Since the principal sources of supply of such materials were within the monetary areas of the United Kingdom and France, and more or less under their control, those two countries were slower to join the rush to buy. Instead, they reaped benefits from the sharply higher foreign exchange earnings of their overseas territories.

A number of NATO countries—Belgium, Denmark, the Netherlands, and Norway—announced increases of 50 per cent or more in their military budgets. However, the United Kingdom and France assumed the major burdens. France was then facing the costs of heightened hostilities in Indo-China, as well as building up its European defence capabilities. By mid-January 1951, Britain had increased its military programmes from £2.6 billion to £5.1 billion for the three financial years beginning in March.[12] French military expenditures in 1952 were 66 per cent larger than in 1951.[13]

Soaring raw materials prices and expectations about rising defence budgets combined to stimulate a roaring double-digit inflation. National

[10] OEEC, *Progress and Problems of the European Economy: Fifth Annual Report* (1954), 7.
[11] OEEC (1951), 13.
[12] Cairncross (1985), 215.
[13] OEEC, *Progress and Problems of the European Economy: Fifth Annual Report* (1954), 85.

wholesale price indices in North America and in the OEEC were all 10–20 per cent higher in the first quarter of 1951 than their 1950 averages. Despite direct controls in most countries over wages, prices, and rents, both the cost of living and labour costs rose substantially.

During this period, the United States raised its discount rate, legislated two tax increases, and kept its budget in approximate balance. (This was strikingly different from the way it financed the subsequent war in Vietnam.) Nevertheless, its wholesale prices jumped 11.5 per cent during the second half of 1950. Avidly buying raw materials, the US helped inflate their prices. As a result, its imports from overseas members of European currency areas were twice as large in the first half of 1951 as in the corresponding period of 1950. The non-European members of the sterling area were thus able to convert a 1949 deficit of $400 million with the US into a surplus of the same magnitude in US financial year 1950/1. Since sterling area reserves were held in London, the United Kingdom's official holdings of gold and dollars were given a substantial boost.

For the first time since the outbreak of the war, European foreign exchange reserves increased. UK reserves reached nearly $3.9 billion by the end of June 1951, $2.5 billion more than the low point in 1949.[14] French reserves had increased to more than $900 million by the end of March 1951, a fifth more than at the end of 1949.[15] Dutch reserves rose by more than a third in 1950 alone. Exuberance about this happy turn of events masked an important fact. The increases were based largely on earnings by overseas members of European currency areas, who acquired matching claims against the foreign exchange reserves.

The increase in UK reserves was so dramatic that its Marshall Plan aid was terminated by mutual consent before the end of 1950. The IMF and the BIS had repeatedly called attention to the critical need for much larger foreign exchange reserves, if European countries were to move successfully to convertibility. However, the US executive branch had repeatedly told the Congress that aid was needed to finance shortages of essential goods and services, not accumulations of foreign exchange. The Congress was not expected to take kindly to appropriating grants of economic aid for countries that were saving foreign exchange, particularly in a wartime atmosphere.

Stage 2: April 1951–June 1952

By the end of the first quarter of 1951, scare buying of raw materials had come to an end, prices began to drop, and private sector inventories

---

[14] EPU Board, 'Report by Mr. Ellis-Rees', 23rd Session (23–30 May 1952). OEEC MBC/M(52)5, Part II, Annex I.
[15] EPU Board, 'Report by M. Calvet' (20 Feb. 1952). OEEC MBC(52)12.

started to decline. In the United States, a dramatic change occurred in Federal Reserve policy, as its board ended rigid support of the market for government securities. Reserve requirements were increased, the expansion of bank credit slackened, and a mild recession began, despite sharply rising defence expenditures. Prices and wages stabilized, and the demand for imported goods fell off.

European overseas territories increased spending, based on their earlier accumulations, just as their current foreign exchange earnings were beginning to fall. British and French defence expenditures began to mushroom at the same time, as previous sharp programme increases started to take effect. Neither government thought it had much room for tax increases, and both were slow to use monetary policy to choke credit expansion. Wholesale prices rose 8.5 per cent in the UK and 17.5 per cent in France between the first quarters of 1951 and 1952, a period in which wholesale prices in North America declined slightly. As a result of these internal and external developments, the foreign exchange accounts of France and England sharply deteriorated and their reserves plummeted. From the March 1951 peak to the end of the year, France lost $300 million in reserves; UK reserves fell by $1.5 billion during the second half of the year.

Belgium and Germany had tightened monetary policies earlier, and the increase in their price levels now came to an end. They began to show surpluses in their foreign accounts and to increase foreign exchange reserves. The Netherlands tightened its monetary policy in March 1951, after a new government took office. During the second half of that calendar year, it earned a surplus on its current account for the first time since the end of the war.

Early in 1952, Britain and France joined the others in using monetary policy to restrain inflation. By the second quarter, wholesale prices were falling in both countries. Their foreign exchange positions thereupon improved considerably, fortified by an increased flow of dollars from the US defence and mutual security programmes. By the end of the EPU's second year, in June 1952, the OEEC countries as a whole were earning a surplus on current account with the rest of the world, and foreign exchange reserves were increasing in almost every country.

Individual European countries, however, fared very differently over the course of the two years after the outbreak of the war in Korea. Britain and France rode a roller coaster; the Dutch experience was similar, if less extreme. German and Italian resources were less strained by increased rearmament expenditures. They ran deficits to build inventories in 1950, found expanding markets for their exports in 1951, and saw their foreign exchange reserves grow. Belgium also made raw materials purchases in 1950 at the expense of its foreign exchange reserves and was able to recoup handsomely from export markets in 1951. The Scandinavian members of the EPU benefited from sharply increased shipping incomes in 1951, as well as from a buoyant market for their exports. However, they were as slow as Britain and France to tighten monetary policies and restrain inflation.

THE IMPACT ON INTRA-EUROPEAN PAYMENTS

The Korean War produced a series of economic surges that ebbed and flowed at different times among European countries, their associated territories, and the United States. The fluctuations in overall foreign exchange positions, described in the preceding paragraphs, were matched by comparable volatility in net positions within the EPU area. How could it be otherwise, given the overwhelming proportion of member country foreign exchange transactions that occurred within the EPU monetary area?

TABLE 3.   *Intra-European Payments Surpluses and Deficits, FY 1948/49–FY 1951/52 (in millions of US dollars)*

	Under the IEPS		Under the EPU	
	1948/59[a]	1949/50	1950/51	1951/52
'Structural' Debtors				
Austria	− 71	− 87	−104	− 38
Greece	− 90	−143	−140	− 84
Iceland	n.a.	n.a.	− 7	− 6
Netherlands	−147	−107	−271	+ 476
Norway	−103	−115	− 80	+ 20
Turkey	+ 6	− 84	− 64	− 97
Other Members				
Belgium	+268	+302	+236	+ 566
Denmark	− 19	− 8	− 69	+ 45
France	−201	+203	+196	− 630
Germany	+ 91	−141	−285	+ 584
Italy	+215	+ 90	− 30	+ 194
Portugal	− 93	0	+ 59	+ 29
Sweden	+ 82	+ 75	− 60	+ 286
Switzerland	n.a.	n.a.	+ 11	+ 160
United Kingdom	+ 62	+ 16	+608	−1,509

[a] For the nine months during which the first IEPS Agreement operated.

Sources: BIS, *Twenty-First Annual Report* (1951); EPU Managing Board, *First* and *Second Annual Reports* (1951 and 1952).

Intra-European positions had been fairly stable under the IEPS and even tended to diminish in size (see Table 3). With the exception of France and Germany, all countries that were in surplus in one year were in surplus both years. The same was true for countries in deficit. In addition, the surpluses and deficits were of relatively modest proportions. This was to be expected under the IEPS system, in which every country strove for balance with each partner. The imbalances were even smaller during the second IEPS year than in the first, though the IEPS Agreement in the first year covered only the last nine months of the financial year.

Under the EPU system, countries were supposed to have more flexibility and larger net positions. The Korean War exaggerated these changes, making country net positions in the EPU even larger and more volatile. Twelve of the fifteen participating currency areas ran intra-European deficits in at least one of the first two years.

As expected, some so-called structural debtors ran EPU deficits in both years and needed considerably more US aid to finance them than their initial positions allowed (shown in Table 2). It was surprising, however, that two of them—Norway and the Netherlands—ran a surplus the second year. Only Belgium, Portugal, and Switzerland had surpluses in both years. All other members were in deficit one year, in surplus the other.

In the aftermath of Korea, the magnitudes of the imbalances began to explode. In both financial years 1948/9 and 1949/50, the sum of country surpluses and deficits had been about $700 million a year each. In the first year of the EPU, this aggregate jumped by over 50 per cent, exceeding $1.1 billion. In the second year, it more than doubled again, reaching nearly $2.4 billion.

To understand these statistics, one must remember that the EPU was a closed system, clearing only payments to and from members of its currency areas. Every payment was also a receipt elsewhere in the system; the sum of member deficits was always equal to the total of member surpluses. Large changes in the position of any one member of the system—and especially of a large member—had to be reflected in compensatory changes elsewhere. Hence the sizeable deficits run by Great Britain and France in 1951/2 and by Germany and the Netherlands in 1950/1 meant equally sizeable surpluses for their major trading partners— Belgium, Germany, and the Netherlands in 1951/2 and Belgium, France, and Great Britain in 1950/1. The EPU's bookkeeping system and settlement arrangements made debtors and creditors very aware of imbalances—and the implications for each other. But assigning responsibility for correcting them was nonetheless a contentious issue—and remains so today.

HOW DID THE MECHANISM FARE?

The automatic mechanism of the EPU was designed precisely to accommodate large reversals in the position of its participants. The volatility of the first two years prompted full use of the compensations mechanism. Nearly a third (31 per cent) of the monthly bilateral deficits and surpluses incurred during that period were compensated over time.[16] Deficits incurred by member countries in some months were cleared against surpluses they earned in other months and vice versa.

The multilateral compensations principle proved to be even more important than the compensations over time. About 43 per cent of the bilateral deficits were cleared through surpluses that the same countries earned in the same month in their payments relations with other countries.

Compensations thus settled nearly three-quarters of all the monthly bilateral deficits and surpluses incurred by members over the first two years of the Union. Only 23 per cent of bilateral deficits were settled through such compensations under the previous two IEPS agreements, and the volume was much smaller. EPU members were thus able to risk, incur, and settle bilateral imbalances without using gold or dollar reserves, at least up to a point.

The system was designed to cope with speculative activity, and it did so effectively during the economic turmoil of the Korean War. During this period, speculation derived primarily from rumours about exchange rate adjustments. Markets anticipated an adjustment if they saw a continuing series of monthly deficits (or surpluses). Such rumours were recurrent, but nothing happened. The speculators scurried for cover, once they realized an exchange rate was unlikely to be adjusted. Rumours about a revaluation of the pound sterling and later about a devaluation of the pound and the French franc were particularly important. They affected not only the reported monthly balances of Britain and France but also those of their trading partners.

With omnipresent exchange controls and no international money market, much of the speculation was accomplished through so-called leads and lags. When rumours spread about a devaluation, importers accelerated paying their bills and exporters delayed cashing in theirs. Monthly deficits based on central bank foreign exchange balances thus became larger than the underlying flow of trade. They quickly turned around, however, once the traders were satisfied that devaluation was unlikely. Rumours about a possible revaluation worked in the opposite direction, causing larger surpluses than were warranted by actual trade flows. In both cases,

---

[16] Data concerning EPU operations over its first two years from EPU Board, *First* and *Second Annual Reports* (1951 and 1952).

monthly positions that central banks reported to the Agent exaggerated the underlying economic situation. The EPU's mechanism for compensations over time evened out these exaggerations, but the very magnitudes of the reported deficits or surpluses were worrisome until the actual reversal began.

Credit and Gold in EPU Settlements

Many in Washington had feared that the EPU would prove to be a very soft system, in which payments in gold or convertible currencies would play little or no role. These fears were belied by the results of the first two years of operations. The size of the imbalances and their volatility were much too great to be settled only by compensations and automatic credit.

Although some considered the quotas and the initial 20 per cent gold-free *tranche* to be over-generous, convertible currencies were used at the very first settlement. The first operation had covered the accounts retroactively from June to September 1950. In that first settlement, three countries passed beyond the gold-free portion of their quotas. Germany paid $31 million to the Union, while France received $40.8 million and Portugal $1.8 million.[17] The Union had to dip into its capital for $11 million to settle these accounts.

During the first two years, the deficits and surpluses remaining after offsetting still totalled $1.9 billion each. Debtors had paid gold to settle 36 per cent of their debts and received slightly more than 50 per cent in credit from the Union. The US government financed the balance in dollars, since it had undertaken to pay for the deficits of structural debtors. Over $1 billion in credit was outstanding, sums owed to the Union by debtors and by the Union to creditors. However, almost all the debts had been outstanding for only nine months or less. One cannot resist observing how much 'harder' were these early EPU credits than the commercial bank loans or the government-insured export credits granted in the 1970s. Not only were a third repaid automatically as borrowing countries earned surpluses, but their use had to be accompanied by increasingly substantial gold payments.

The gold-free quotas had not lasted very long, and the role of gold in the settlements grew steadily. In the second year, gross payments of gold to creditors and by debtors to the Union were more than twice as large as in the first year. The total turnover of gold and dollar payments between the Union and its members was almost $2.9 billion over the first two years. Debtors had paid the Union nearly $1.3 billion in gold or

---

17 US del. tel. to Washington. REPTO 5635 (14 Oct. 1950).

dollars out of their own funds to settle monthly deficits over the two-year period. Creditors had received $1.4 billion from the Union. During the 21 months of the two IEPS agreements, gold and dollar settlements had amounted to only $255 million.[18] Thus convertibility under the EPU, though partial, was still much more substantial than under its predecessor.

The EPU Liquidity Squeeze

In the latter months of 1951, the volatility in country positions threatened the liquidity of the EPU itself. Britain and France moved from extreme creditor positions to cumulative deficits with the Union. Under the rules, they paid no gold at all while they used up the first fifth of their debtor quotas. For a second fifth, they paid in gold for only a quarter of their deficits. Because their quotas were the largest in the system, the flow of gold payments to the Union dropped sharply. Meanwhile, a number of cumulative creditors were entitled to gold for half of their surpluses. The difference between the Union's receipts and payments had to be covered out of its capital, and the EPU's convertible assets fell, dropping to $176 million in October 1951.

A few creditors had neared the end of (or indeed exhausted) their quotas, and they wanted full payment in gold for succeeding surpluses. The Board refused, fearing further depletion of the Union's capital. With the convertible assets falling and creditor demands for gold rising, the Board first turned to the US for help. At its October 1951 meeting, it asked Havlik whether the US might add to the Union's capital.[19] While not excluding the possibility, he promptly countered that the problem should be considered first a European responsibility. The Board thereupon briefly contemplated turning to the deficit countries as possible contributors. Neither Ellis-Rees nor Calvet nor Getz Wold felt that such countries could reasonably be asked to pay more gold to the Union. Their deficits with the dollar area were then rising and their foreign exchange reserves were too low. Posthuma and Ansiaux both supported this position of the deficit countries.

The Board asked the Secretariat, the Agent, and the Alternates to analyse the adequacy of the Union's convertible assets. The reports concluded that it was quite possible that the assets would run out. The Board judged that a minimum of $200 million should be kept on hand at all times to assure confidence in the solvency and continuity of the Union.

Though the assets began to increase again at the November settlement,

---

[18] OEEC, 'Statistical Examination of the Functioning of the IEPS Agreements' (12 Nov. 1950). OEEC C(50)322.

[19] UK del., 'Record of Discussions at 16th Session of the Managing Board' (25 Oct.–7 Nov. 1951). PRO T 230/211.

the Board continued to press Havlik about the possibility of a further US contribution. Belgium had become especially insistent about being paid in gold for its post-quota surpluses (as described in the next chapter). It had even threatened to withdraw from the Union. An addition to the EPU capital would have made it possible for the Board to accommodate Belgium. After the January meeting, Havlik met privately with the Chairman and the Vice-Chairmen to explain the US position before announcing it at the next Board meeting. He declared that the US had decided not to ask Congress for more funds for the EPU. US interest in the Union had not lessened at all, but the problem could and should be solved primarily by the Europeans.[20]

In March 1952, the Board submitted its report concerning the renewal of the Union for a third year.[21] The report stated that the minimum additional amount required for the Union's capital assets was $178 million. The problem was put before the OEEC ministerial meeting on 28-9 March. William E. Draper, Jr., then US Ambassador to both NATO and the OEEC, advised that the 'problem of supplying the additional contributions required was wholly one for the European countries to decide'.[22]

Dirk Stikker, the Dutch Foreign Minister, had become Chairman of the OEEC Council. He was scheduled to accompany Queen Juliana to Washington the following week and used the occasion to discuss a US capital contribution with both Acheson and Harriman. Harriman reiterated what had already been said by the US officials in Paris, emphasizing that a new contribution could be made only out of funds voted by the Congress to support increased European defence efforts.[23]

In fact, the Union's convertible assets rose continuously during the first half of 1952. Both France and Britain moved to the upper ranges of their debtor quotas and beyond, settling their continuing deficits increasingly in gold. France needed a special credit in the spring. But by July 1952, both countries were able to meet the payments, because US aid and defence expenditures were producing a larger flow of dollars.

Nevertheless, a cautious Managing Board persuaded OEEC members to agree to make temporary contributions in the form of gold loans of up to $100 million, if the Union's gold and dollar assets should fall below $100 million.[24] All agreed to pay in proportion to the size of their quotas, and the creditors agreed that their contributions should be called up first.

---

[20] US del. tel. to Washington. REPTO 599 (1 Feb. 1952).

[21] EPU Board Report, 'The Operation of the Union after 30 June 1952' (16 Mar. 1952). OEEC C(52)64.

[22] 'Minutes of the 172nd Meeting' (28-9 Mar. 1952). OEEC C/M(52)9, Part II.

[23] Netherlands Amb. in Washington, tel. to OEEC in Paris (10 Apr. 1952). OECD EPU Archive Box 32.

[24] EPU Board, *Second Annual Report* (1952).

Ultimately, the 'maximum drain' forecasts turned out to be much too pessimistic and the need to call up contributions never arose.

Although a system crisis did not occur, the possibility forced some soul-searching in Europe about the value of the EPU. Despite their individual difficulties, all countries responded affirmatively to the Managing Board's request for financial support. Funds from Europe would be forthcoming, if necessary, to assure that the EPU would continue to function smoothly and effectively.

SURVIVAL WITH FLYING COLOURS

The clearing and settlement system itself survived the effects of the Korean War with flying colours. In the process, the EPU helped its members cope with their own payments difficulties. Many had quickly mounted large rearmament efforts on top of their economic recovery programmes. Despite subsequent reductions in over-ambitious plans, they still made substantial progress with both rearmament and reconstruction. As the individual imbalances were brought under control, countries recognized that the system had indeed been helpful and that its continued operation was essential.

The automatic credit and compensations provisions had enabled governments to pursue ambitious goals with less constraint than their own foreign exchange reserves alone would have permitted. However, the limited size of the quotas and the provisions for gold payments did force countries to try to bring their payments position within the Union into balance before long. Most succeeded in doing so.

Trade liberalization moved forward on the whole, despite balance-of-payments difficulties. Progress in that area was neither uninterrupted nor all that had been hoped for. Nevertheless, ECA's initial fears that rearmament would necessitate tighter trade restrictions were not generally realized.

During the negotiations to establish the EPU, a number of countries had agreed to compromises concerning their perceived interests. After the Union had operated for two years, their gains from the system were easier to identify than their losses. Debtor countries, in particular, were given an important measure of flexibility in managing their economies. It is also fair to assume that the system exercised a well-measured restraint on their behaviour, since most did adjust their policies effectively and successfully toward balance within the system. Surplus countries had to provide credit. But the system enabled their export and transit trade industries to thrive, free of discrimination by countries trying to rein in their deficits.

All EPU members felt the economic repercussions of the Korean War, which contributed to crises in one country after another. When the prospect of exhausted quotas loomed, governments were forced to submit their programmes and policies for the Managing Board's review. They could seek relief in the form of additional credits and aid or by retreating temporarily from their trade liberalization commitments without facing retaliation. But they would have to adjust their policies toward balance within the system. They could expect the Managing Board to recommend such policy adjustments, as it had in Germany's case, if they did not take appropriate steps on their own.

8 Countries in Dire Straits

The negotiators of the EPU Agreement understood that membership would imply acceptance of 'interference' in economic policy-making. Countries had to adjust policies to keep their intra-European payments in approximate balance, or at least to keep imbalances within their EPU quotas. Otherwise, their continued participation in the Union might be threatened, and the Managing Board would have to intervene. However, it was not expected to do so very often, since critical situations should only occur sporadically and develop slowly. At least for the first two years, these expectations proved much too optimistic.

At one time or another during this period, every EPU member was in danger of exhausting its quota, and many did. A remedy was found in every case, largely through internal policy changes that reversed or ameliorated the country's position. In only a few cases did the Board endorse increased trade restrictions and then only for a temporary period. Some situations were eased through special assistance out of EPU funds or through 'special resources'—funds provided by the US government to settle the deficits of persistent debtors who had exhausted their initial credit positions. Greece, Austria, Iceland, and Turkey received such assistance after the Board had questioned delegations from capitals, analysed their situations, and made its recommendations.

The individual payments imbalances varied in their nature, intensity, and duration. In the case of countries with large EPU quotas, the crises did threaten the system. Indeed, Britain, France, and Belgium contemplated measures that would have effectively terminated their participation in the EPU and might have ended the system itself. Though the difficulties of the smaller countries may not have menaced the survival of the EPU, they were, nevertheless, very serious for their governments. Most European countries were still very short of foreign exchange reserves. Such international money and capital markets as existed were essentially closed to them, and payments imbalances were thus of momentous importance.

A brief account follows of how the Board handled the payments problems of several members. In these instances, as in others, its proposals were tailored to the specific problems and sensitivities of each country at issue. Every situation involved a different combination of political and economic circumstances. Having inherited no precedents, the Board did not try to invent a standard pattern into which every country must fit. It never concealed its strong preference for fewer specific controls over private economic activity. Above all, however, it sought corrective measures that were workable and acceptable to the country at issue. In sensitive political situations, it was willing to offer recommendations or cogent analyses instead of imposing conditions for assistance. It would even delay preparing a written report. Yet countries were expected to take the necessary steps, whatever the form in which the Board's views were expressed.

SOME CRITICAL CASES

The Netherlands

The Netherlands had been awarded an initial credit in recognition of persistent previous deficits with Europe, arising out of ambitious programmes for rebuilding and developing its roads, ports, industry, and housing. After the invasion of South Korea, the government announced a large rearmament effort, on top of its continuing recovery programmes. Ensuing inflationary pressures intensified the demand for more imports, which were already growing as a result of trade liberalization and private stockpiling. Early in 1951, a cabinet crisis erupted.

In 1950/1, direct dollar receipts from ECA were substantially larger than the Dutch deficit with the dollar area. While this increased its foreign exchange reserves, deficits with the EPU area were still very large. With quota exhaustion impending, the Managing Board requested a formal review of the Dutch situation for its February 1951 session.

Keesing, the Dutch nominee on the Board, resisted at first. He said that policy adjustments were being prepared, but decisions awaited resolution of the political situation. The Dutch certainly did not want the German precedent—nor its internal policy recommendations—to be applied to their country. Keesing noted that Dutch gold reserves were adequate to permit 100 per cent gold payments to the EPU if his country exhausted its quota and that the Netherlands was prepared to pay.[1]

In fact, the new government applied to its own ailments medicine that was very similar to what the Managing Board had prescribed for Germany. Taxes were increased, subsidies were reduced, and the rate of growth in military expenditures was restrained. The central bank raised its discount rate from 3 to 4 per cent and placed ceilings on bank credit. As a result, the banks were soon forced to rediscount their loans with the central bank.

If anything, these measures may have been too stringent, since they transformed the large Netherlands EPU deficit of 1950/1 into an even

[1] US del. tel. to Washington, Managing Board meetings of 4-8 Jan. 1951. REPTO 148 (10 Jan. 1951).

larger surplus in the succeeding year. After Germany, it became the first major EPU deficit country to swing into the surplus column. Belgium helped by lifting restrictions on Dutch agricultural exports. So did developments in the French and British monetary areas.[2] When price inflation accelerated in those countries early in 1952, the Netherlands increased its exports to them much more than its imports from them. Pending a correction of their situations, France and the UK ran large bilateral deficits with the Netherlands, exaggerating the improvement in the latter's EPU position.

Still concerned about the near exhaustion of its deficit quota, the Netherlands sought an increase for the second EPU year. With considerable reluctance, the Board agreed to a modest one. By May 1952, the Netherlands' surplus was so great that the Board felt some moderation was in order. The Dutch thereafter relaxed their restrictive monetary policies, and their EPU surpluses declined.

The United Kingdom

Though reluctant at first to join the system, the United Kingdom was a major early beneficiary of the EPU arrangements. This was freely acknowledged within the British government near the end of the EPU's first year. At that time, the United Kingdom was in substantial surplus in the EPU and had lent over $300 million to the Union. Gaitskell, by then Chancellor of the Exchequer, asked for an analysis of what had happened and what would have happened had there been no EPU.

The Treasury's response concluded that the UK had been getting 'one pound in cash dollars for every one pound of credit extended'. . . and 'some good and worthwhile assets for which the U.K. could be grateful later on'.[3] The Bank of England's reply was more grudging. It felt that without the EPU, a greater reduction in sterling balances would have occurred, and sterling would have been used more by other Europeans as a means of settlement. However, the Bank did concede that there would have been 'smaller gold and dollar receipts in some trades, discrimination against the sterling area in order to finance raw materials purchases, . . . less trade generally in Europe and increased U.K. holdings of [individual] European currencies [rather than credits in the EPU]'. Speculation in October 1950 concerning a revaluation of the pound had led traders to lead their payments and lag their billings in sterling. This produced a movement into sterling of funds equivalent to £40 million. These reports should have provided Gaitskell with some comfort about

[2] EPU Board Minutes, 'Statement by Mr. Posthuma', 23rd Session (23–30 May 1952). OEEC MBC/M(52)5, Part III, Annex I.

[3] Travers, notes on UK Treasury Files. OECD EPU Archive Box 22.

the concessions which he had persuaded the Cabinet to make a year earlier. The rest of 1951 would provide very little further comfort.

In February 1951, Ellis-Rees had explained the British surplus to the Board, calling attention to the speculative inflow. He noted that the UK had already removed quantitative restrictions from 87 per cent of its trade with other members and had doubled travel allowances, to the then extravagant sum of £100 per year per person. Though he expected the UK surplus to diminish, he agreed to remind the Dominions and the Colonies that they no longer had any financial reason for discriminating against imports from any country in the EPU area. He guessed that surpluses would shrink to a rate of £100 million per year, about a third of the rate during the first months of the EPU.

New rumours of sterling revaluation produced a further speculative inflow of funds in April. Ellis-Rees offered another statement to the Managing Board at its May meeting, assuring members that any further UK surplus in the EPU 'would be moderate in size and attributable largely to the rest of the sterling area, rather than to the U.K. itself'.[4]

By July, the pendulum had swung much further than he had predicted. Sterling area deficits in the EPU were distressingly large, and the loss of dollar reserves began to accelerate from month to month. The Labour government fell in October, weakened by the loss of cabinet members through death, ill health, and the resignation of those who opposed the large increase in armaments programmes. The new Conservative government promptly took some modest restrictive measures, including a reduction in its OEEC trade liberalization to 61 per cent.

A sceptical Managing Board invited a delegation from the United Kingdom to its meeting at the end of November 1951. The delegation reported on the measures taken, including a small increase in the Bank Rate from 2 to 2.5 per cent and a reduction in travel allowances to £50 per year. Concerned about the prospective exhaustion of Britain's EPU quota, as well as its trade deliberalization, the Managing Board asked some two dozen searching questions.[5] Posthuma had succeeded Keesing on the Board in September 1951 and soon became an energetic participant in the discussions. On this occasion, he sharply protested against the resort to import restrictions, noting the severity with which cuts in food imports had fallen on the Netherlands. As expert civil servants, the UK delegation could give only optimistic and defensive replies. Recognizing the gravity of the problems inherited by the new British government, the Board issued a very patient and limited report.[6] It only noted the

---

[4] EPU Board Minutes, 9th Session (17-22 May 1951). OEEC MBC/M(51)6, Part III.

[5] EPU Board Minutes, 17th Session (26 Nov.-5 Dec. 1951). OEEC MBC/M(51)14, Part III.

[6] EPU Board Report, 'The Position of the United Kingdom in EPU' (7 Dec. 1951). OEEC C(51)378.

seriousness with which all other members would be affected by UK deliberalization and emphasized that trade restrictions would not strike at the causes of the UK's difficulties.

As the UK deficits mounted, the Swiss imposed export controls, ostensibly to enable Switzerland to stay within its quota through mid-1952. Paul Rossy, the Swiss member of the Board, had at first opposed his country's decision to join the EPU, but he came increasingly to value the benefits it received from participating in the system. He was seldom reluctant to express pointed opinions in rather direct language. In this instance, he first claimed that the tighter controls were necessary because Swiss production could not be increased sufficiently to meet all the demands for its exports.[7] Switzerland had placed financial ceilings on exports to the sterling area and to France, which was also running large deficits with Switzerland and the EPU as a whole. The United Kingdom felt particularly aggrieved and claimed discrimination. The Board considered the Swiss measures to be 'contrary to the spirit of the Agreement for EPU'.[8] Rossy's reaction was characteristically forthright. His country was not willing to run surpluses and provide credits necessitated by the unsound fiscal and monetary policies of its major partners in the EPU system.

By February 1952, Britain was about to exhaust its EPU quota, and its foreign exchange reserves were dangerously low. London considered asking the Managing Board for a special credit. After the Treasury and the Bank of England carefully compared the present circumstances of the UK with those of Germany when it sought such a credit, the British quickly decided against making a request. 'We should also bear in mind that if OEEC granted a Special Credit, it would certainly expect its policy recommendations to be accepted by the UK and would try to exercise close control; it would, no doubt, also want to be supplied with information on every aspect of UK affairs that was remotely relevant.'[9]

Pressed by the severity of their situation, the British were also contemplating convertibility with a floating rate. But the government decided instead to announce stern fiscal and monetary restraints in its March Budget. In most respects, the measures were strikingly similar to steps the Board itself might have recommended.

The Bank Rate was raised to 4 per cent, and substantial cuts were announced in the domestic budget. Some price subsidies were abolished,

---

[7] EPU Board Minutes, 'Statement by Mr. Rossy', 19th Session (21–9 Jan. 1952). OEEC MBC/M(52)1, Part I, Annex.

[8] EPU Board Minutes, 20th Session (11–16 Feb. 1952). OEEC MBC/M(52)2.

[9] Guy Watson (Bank of England), letter to E. R. Copleston (UK Treasury) (14 Feb. 1952). Copleston replied 'that we had come to the same conclusion as yours and for the same reasons . . .', PRO T 237/93.

and publicly financed investments were severely curtailed. Travel allowances had been lowered again in January to £25 per year. The outer sterling area had reversed its trade liberalization, and the UK itself now further restricted its own OEEC liberalization to 46 per cent.

At the time, British gold and dollar reserves had been drawn down to $1.7 billion, and by May its EPU quota was fully exhausted. Fortunately, at the May meeting of the Managing Board, Ellis-Rees could already point to a sharp decrease since March in the UK deficit.[10] By September, the United Kingdom was again regularly running surpluses with the Union. The fiscal and monetary measures had worked, and the Board wondered when trade liberalization might be resumed. However, by the end of 1952, the UK had other irons in the fire.

France

The volatility of the French position over the first two years of the Union was just as dramatic as the British. France was an early surplus country, accumulating $271 million by the end of March 1951, largely as a counterpart to the German deficit. Pierre Calvet, French Vice-Chairman of the Board, had not been involved in the EPU negotiations. He assumed his new role with great seriousness, both as a responsible international expert and as the proud representative of his country. During his first major presentation to the Board on behalf of France, he had predicted that the French surplus would be considerably reduced in the near future.

The Board, none the less, had recommended in February 1951 that France liberalize more than 75 per cent of its imports from other OEEC members and consider suspending its relatively high tariffs and customs duties. Calvet thereupon submitted a list of eleven French measures, all of which relaxed foreign exchange controls and had been taken since the EPU came into force. The measures were far-reaching for an economy with a long record of restrictive practices in its foreign economic relations. They covered travel allowances and capital movements as well as trade.

In April 1951, France ran its first monthly deficit, as both Germany and the Netherlands reversed their previous deficits. Thereafter, France was continually in deficit to the Union. By March 1952, its cumulative deficits totalled $445 million. Frank and direct as usual, Calvet had taken a pessimistic view of French prospects in the course of Managing Board discussions as early as November 1951.[11] He noted heavy speculation against the franc because of uncertainty regarding French capacity to

---

[10] EPU Board Minutes, 'Statement by Mr. Ellis-Rees', 23rd Session (23–30 May 1952). OEEC MBC/M(52)5, Part II, Annex I.

[11] UK del., 'Record of Discussion at the 16th Session of the Managing Board' (20 Nov. 1951). PRO T 230/211.

continue financing the war in Indo-China and at the same time undertake a vast rearmament programme. Uncertainty about the amount and timing of US military assistance was, at the time, a considerable preoccupation for the French authorities.

Early in February 1952, France suspended trade liberalization completely, and severely tightened all foreign exchange controls. Calvet submitted a long memorandum about the gravity of the French position.[12] France had twice raised its discount rate during the previous autumn, applied more stringent quantitative restrictions on credit, and required its banks to turn in to the Exchange Equalisation Fund their increased holdings of EPU currencies. Nevertheless, French foreign exchange reserves had shrunk to a critical level, and a cabinet crisis was in full swing. Calvet admitted to a series of mistaken judgements, by both French and foreign authorities, concerning the strength and capabilities of the French economy during its period of convalescence in 1950. He had also prepared a despairing private memorandum about his government's inability to take necessary decisions that would radically alter France's economic and financial policies.[13]

By the end of February, France's cumulative EPU deficit was expected to exceed 80 per cent of its quota. The Board invited France to send experts to its March meeting and listened for two days to an exposition by a team of eleven, headed by M. de Clermont Tonnerre, Secretary General of the French Interministerial Committee for Economic Cooperation. The Board's interrogations covered the entire gamut of French economic policy, with particular emphasis on credit and monetary policy.[14]

By that time, Belgium was as concerned about its large credits to the Union as was France about its deficits. Calvet met with Frère and Ansiaux in Brussels to ask for a $100 million loan. The Belgian Prime Minister and Finance Minister were willing to agree, if the loan could be marketed and thus reduce the government's burden of financing its credit to the EPU.[15] Frère proceeded to Paris to work out appropriate loan terms with Baumgartner, Calvet, and Guindey. The arrangement they worked out would have reduced both the cumulative Belgian surplus and the French deficit, each by $100 million. Belgium would accept French bonds payable in dollars or Swiss francs. They might be marketable in the US or in

---

[12] EPU Board, 'Statement by Mr. Calvet on the Position of France' (14 Feb. 1952). OEEC MBC(52)12.
[13] Calvet gave a copy of the memo (14 Feb. 1952) to Frère and Ansiaux during his visit to Brussels. Minutes of the Board (29 Feb. 1952). National Bank of Belgium PV 946/1, Annex 1.
[14] EPU Board Minutes, 21st Session (7–20 Mar. 1952). OEEC MBC/M(52)3, Part III.
[15] Minutes of the Board (29 Feb. and 4 Mar. 1952). National Bank of Belgium PV 946/1 and 947/1.

Switzerland, possibly with the assistance of the BIS. The US Representative vigorously opposed the arrangement because it would weaken pressure on both France and Belgium to adjust their policies.[16]

Unhappy about this proposed lapse into a bilateral credit system, Carli proposed that the EPU itself should extend a $100 million special short term credit to France. With the prior concurrence of both Calvet and Ansiaux, the Managing Board agreed. The credit was granted without any of the conditions that had been attached to the German credit.[17] Calvet had asserted that France would not accept 'assistance if it were accompanied by conditions or entailed the supervision of French commercial and financial policy'.[18]

However, the Board also submitted a detailed report to the OEEC Council. The report concluded that the 'solution for the problem of the French disequilibrium does not lie simply in restrictive measures; the real remedy . . . must consist in an attack by the Government on inflation and price rises . . . a strong budgeting policy, designed to eliminate the present total deficit, is essential . . . the French Government should be prepared to reinforce these [credit] restrictions . . . the Government should endeavour to prevent wage increases substantially exceeding increases in productivity'.[19]

'To eliminate the present *total* [budget] deficit' was indeed stern advice. Such blunt language, specifically directed to the government of a major country, is rarely to be found in any report prepared by an international body in the 1980s. Obviously, the spirit of the times has changed, and the acceptability of international advice has been severely diminished. The Board's recommendations to France were no less severe than those it had offered Germany, though its pressure was exerted very differently. The newly reconstituted French government did move in the direction indicated. It also repaid the EPU credit within three months, with the help of an increased flow of receipts from the US defence programme.

The French measures had reduced imports and stopped the increase in prices. The speculators responded by reversing their operations against the franc. During the second quarter of 1952, France even ran a small surplus in the EPU. The effectiveness of the measures taken in February and March produced such remarkably quick results that Ellis-Rees was moved to remark, with some exasperation, that 'I shall consult them another time if it ever happens again to see how it is done.'[20]

[16] As reported by Ansiaux. Minutes of the Board (11 Mar. 1952). National Bank of Belgium PV 949/1a and B.

[17] See ch. 6.

[18] EPU Board Minutes, 21st Session (7-20 Mar. 1952). OEEC MBC/M(52)3, Part I.

[19] EPU Board Report, 'The Situation of France' (25 Mar. 1952). OEEC C(52)81.

[20] EPU Board Minutes, 'Statement by Mr. Ellis-Rees', 23rd Session (23-30 May 1952). OEEC MBC/M(52)5, Part II, Annex I.

Nevertheless, both French authorities and the Managing Board remained apprehensive. In May 1952, Governor Cobbold and Rowan (UK Treasury) visited Paris. The Finance Minister, Antoine Pinay, and Governor Baumgartner told them that if Britain moved to convertibility with a floating rate, France might follow suit. The statement was disingenuous. Guindey had been urging Pinay to devalue the French franc, only to meet with stubborn refusal. Upon hearing that British authorities were contemplating a floating rate for the pound, Guindey inquired in London and learned that Churchill had already vetoed the idea. Assured by Guindey's report that the British government would not act, Pinay agreed to let his currency float downwards, but only if the British moved first.[21] The Managing Board's next annual report offered veiled support for Guindey's advice. 'The restoration of France's position is not yet complete and much remains to be done before the situation can be considered as not merely stabilised but really sound.'[22]

Belgium

By far the most traumatic situation concerned the Union's major creditor, Belgium. Months before the EPU Agreement was up for renewal, Belgium was threatening to withdraw. A variety of Byzantine provisions had to be arranged to satisfy its needs, while protecting the Union. The search for acceptable solutions was prolonged and strenuous, but a way was found, with some co-operation from both the International Monetary Fund and the US government.

The Belgian government had threatened to stay out of the system during the last days of the negotiations, essentially because it saw no way of implementing the system's initial premiss. It consistently rejected the notion that all members should seek balance over time in their foreign exchange accounts with other members of the system as a group. For a long time, Belgium had been a surplus country—and a substantial creditor—in its relations with the rest of Europe. It expected that situation to continue and was unwilling to accept an obligation to seek balance within the EPU.

Belgium had achieved internal price stability by the end of 1948, much earlier than virtually all its European trading partners. It was among the first OEEC countries to liberalize imports from Europe to the extent of 75 per cent. Furthermore, Belgium had lifted limitations on imports from the dollar area much sooner than the others. Its overall foreign exchange

[21] As recounted by Guillaume Guindey, memo of conversation with one of the authors (2 Dec. 1987). BIS EPU Archive.
[22] EPU Board, *Second Annual Report* (1952), 29.

payments and receipts tended to be in balance, with a dollar deficit matched by a European currency surplus.

Price stability and a balanced overall foreign exchange position had been achieved, however, at substantial cost—less investment in modernizing facilities, slower economic growth, and relatively high unemployment. In every year from 1949 to 1953, a smaller percentage of Belgium's civilian labour force was employed than in 1948. No other OEEC member reported such poor results. Nor was Belgium's record in restraining inflation under the pressure of the Korean War boom any better than those of most other European countries.

Under the circumstances, both the OEEC and the Managing Board, as well as ECA, felt that Belgium could well afford a more expansionist policy and a redirection of exports from Europe to the dollar area. With the inauguration of the EPU, European discrimination on currency grounds against Belgian exports had ceased. Countries that had previously felt obliged to discriminate because they lacked means of payment had increased their imports from Belgium disproportionately. These measures had undoubtedly increased the latter's EPU surpluses.[23] However, the Belgian authorities—and its powerful central bank, in particular—insisted that its intra-European surpluses principally resulted from the inflationary policies practised by other member countries. They argued, though not very convincingly, that Belgian credits to Europe hampered its own ability to finance urgently needed domestic investment.

Immediately after the outbreak of war in Korea, Belgian production and exports to the US rose sharply, but Belgium ran a most unexpected deficit in its EPU accounts over the next five months. By the beginning of 1951, a strict monetary policy was checking the inflationary pressures induced by the Korean War, but at the cost of further production or employment increases. The Belgian structural surplus with the rest of the European currency area then reappeared—with a vengeance. By the end of July 1951, Belgium had wiped out its earlier EPU deficits and used up 84 per cent of its creditor quota.

With exhaustion imminent, the Managing Board proposed a 'rallonge', a temporary extension of the Belgian quota. Further surpluses would continue to be settled on the basis of 50 per cent gold and 50 per cent credit, a proposal accepted by Portugal the previous February, when its creditor quota was at a similar critical juncture.

The Belgian government argued for 100 per cent gold payments, noting that its hard currency foreign exchange reserves had declined. As a concession, Ansiaux was authorized by his Minister of Finance to accept a $140 million rallonge, to be settled on the basis of 75 per cent gold, 25

---

[23] EPU Board, *First Annual Report* (1951), 33.

per cent credit.[24] The Managing Board refused to recommend a gold ratio of more than 50 per cent.

In July, September, October, and December 1951 and again in March 1952, Ansiaux reluctantly acquiesced to the addition of one limited *rallonge* after another to the Belgian quota. For the first two of these increases, he persuaded his government to agree to 50 per cent settlement in gold. For each of the others, the Managing Board set a limit on the amount of gold that the Union would pay to settle Belgian surpluses. If the surpluses were larger than the specified sums, Belgium would have to extend credit for the balance.

Neither the Belgian government nor the Managing Board found these temporary arrangements very satisfactory, but no better solutions seemed available. The Board realized it could not expect Belgium to accept an open-ended commitment to extend credit to the EPU with very little prospect of early repayment. On the other hand, it could not afford larger gold payments to Belgium, lest the convertible assets of the Union be reduced to a dangerously low level.

Belgium could be relieved of extending credit to the EPU only if the debtors would pay in more gold or if the US would increase its capital contribution. Neither of these alternatives was realistic. The Europeans and the US had also become critical of the Belgian defence effort. Ansiaux went to Washington in September 1951, prior to the NATO meeting in Ottawa on burden-sharing. During his visit, he learned that UK officials were adamantly opposed to departing from the 50:50 settlement ratio unless Belgium accepted a substantial increase in its NATO contribution.[25]

At that point, Belgium seriously considered withdrawing from the EPU. Its Cabinet decided to settle post-quota EPU surpluses directly with each country from which they were earned, rather than agree to continuing large EPU credits. Article 16(6) of the Agreement permitted such action, but everyone realized that such a solution meant a serious retreat to bilateralism. Again Ansiaux persuaded his government to agree to another *rallonge*.

The Belgian government was faced with continuing to extend large credits or restraining its surpluses. Ansiaux recommended the latter course in no uncertain language. Despite the reluctance of the Minister for Commerce, the government decided to introduce strong measures to limit exports of goods and services to the EPU area, as well as imports of speculative capital.[26] Imports from the dollar area would also be restricted to encourage Belgian importers to seek supplies from EPU sources. The elimination of transit trade originating in the dollar area was a prime

[24] Minutes of the Board (10 July 1951). National Bank of Belgium PV 874/17 f.
[25] Minutes of the Board (18 Sept. 1951). National Bank of Belgium PV 893/9.
[26] 'Statement by the Delegate for Belgium', at the 157th Meeting (17 Oct. 1951). OEEC C(51)333.

target of these measures. Revaluation of the Belgian franc was rejected, as was a surcharge on Belgian exporters that would be paid to Belgian importers.[27]

In January 1952, the Board had started discussing how to operate the EPU after its initial two-year period had ended. Ansiaux 'strongly asserted that it was entirely unreasonable to ask Belgium to sign a new Agreement extending EPU which did not provide definite arrangements for settlements with Belgium for the period to be covered by the extension'.[28] In bilateral meetings, he asked the US to endorse this view at the Managing Board and at the OEEC Council.[29] The US should offer proposals for consolidating existing debt and 'hardening the system'. Credit should be drastically curtailed for debtors who failed to take corrective internal monetary action.

The Managing Board had consistently asserted that Belgium could not expect to earn large amounts of dollars through the EPU, while European countries as a whole were seriously short of dollars to pay for their current imports. During the spring of 1952, a line-up emerged of debtor countries (France, the Netherlands, Norway, and the UK) against the two creditors (Belgium and Switzerland). The creditors wanted 100 per cent gold settlements; the debtors felt that creditors should reorient their basic economic policies in the light of the continuing dollar shortage. Havlik reported that the debate over these conflicting views became 'extremely warm' at some points.[30]

By the end of June 1952, Belgium had a cumulative accounting surplus in the Union of $789 million, $424 million of which had been settled by extending credit to the Union. The credit exceeded Belgium's obligation within its quota by $223 million. Fortunately, the convertible assets of the Union had increased each month after October 1951, as deficit countries reached and exceeded the upper ranges of their quotas. By the end of June, the convertible assets had risen to $460 million.

With more assets in hand, the Managing Board was finally in a position to work out a longer term compromise with Belgium. It agreed to pay off $123 million of the Belgian post-quota credit in gold in July 1952. A further $50 million in credit would be settled by equal annual gold payments over a five-year period, with the first payment to be made after June 1953.

A proposal by Havlik and Draper led to the settlement of an additional $50 million of the Union's debt to Belgium.[31] That debt was formally

---

[27] Minutes of the Board (2 Oct. 1951). National Bank of Belgium PV 902/11.
[28] US del. tel. to Washington. REPTO 599 (5 Feb. 1952).
[29] Havlik, memo of conversation (7 Feb. 1952). US Archives. ECA/Paris Havlik Files.
[30] US del. tel. to Washington. REPTO 901 (20 Feb. 1952).
[31] US del. tel. to Washington. REPTO 2247 (23 May 1952).

transferred to France and the United Kingdom, who agreed to pay it off by delivering defence products to Belgium. The US would actually pay for the products, as part of its offshore procurement programme in support of NATO. For all practical purposes, the US thus contributed another $50 million to support the continuation of the EPU.

Given these arrangements, Belgium agreed to settle further post-quota surpluses on the basis of the 50:50 ratio, up to an amount of $250 million. It actually ran a small deficit over the course of the EPU's third year, with declining surpluses in the first half more than matched by deficits in the second half. By the beginning of the calendar year 1953, Belgium was able to lift the additional restrictions on dollar imports it had imposed at the height of its EPU crises. After mid-1952, it also progressively withdrew its measures for restraining exports to the EPU area.

Nevertheless, one more concession was needed to satisfy Belgium in the mid-1952 EPU negotiations. It obtained from the IMF the line of credit it had sought repeatedly since discussions had first begun about an IEPS system. OEEC member governments agreed to endorse a Belgian request to the IMF for a credit of $50 million, based on the sum to be repaid in instalments by the EPU.[32] The credit would be reimbursable to the IMF only on the dates at which Belgium itself would be paid.

Draper and Havlik flew to Washington to seek US approval at a cabinet-level meeting of the NAC.[33] Southard, still the US Executive Director of the IMF, proposed that Belgium be given a drawing right to $50 million, and he helped negotiate an agreement with Governor Frère, who had come to Washington for that purpose.

Though the IMF approved a Belgian drawing, it refused to make explicit the link to Belgium's EPU credits. The IMF also disclaimed any intention of establishing a precedent. Nonetheless, the Belgian credit was, in fact, the first IMF 'standby' decision, which later became its principal method of permitting countries to draw funds. The Belgian credit thus turned out to be a more important incident in the life of the IMF than it was for Belgium or the EPU. Belgium never drew the funds permitted by its IMF standby credit.

THE MANAGING BOARD'S FIRST TWO YEARS

The unexpected size and volatility of country imbalances forced the newly appointed Managing Board to mature very quickly. Critical situations,

---

[32] Brussels cable to Selliers, Belgian IMF Exec. Director (9 June 1952). Contains text of OEEC appeal to IMF. US Archives. ECA/Paris Havlik Files.

[33] Minutes of 195th Meeting of NAC (18 June 1952). Reprinted in Department of State (1952-4), vi. 83-5.

well beyond the capacity of the automatic mechanism alone, descended on the Board with unrelenting regularity. It responded to each issue with a sensible mixture of firmness and flexibility, so that its conclusions were both acceptable and effective.

By the end of its second year, the Board had acquired an unusual degree of prestige and influence. The Union had been preserved and renewed. Trade and payments liberalization within Europe had proved to be both possible and valuable, even in a wholly unexpected and stressful economic environment. Despite some temporary retreats, the process of freeing and multilateralizing economic relations was moving forward. How the Board worked—the ingredients for its achievements—is recounted in Chapter 18. However, the story of the EPU during the Korean War would be incomplete without some interpretation of the Board's role in containing the economic dislocations of rearmament.

In the broadest sense, the Board helped gain acceptability for macroeconomic policy, though the term itself was hardly known at the time. Fiscal and monetary measures then became the principal policy tool for controlling inflation. Direct controls over prices, rents, and wages were eased or eliminated; rationing virtually disappeared; and subsidies were sharply reduced. As one country after another threatened to exhaust its debtor quota, the Board consistently urged readjustment through restrictive fiscal and monetary policies. Some countries adopted such measures before the Board acted, knowing the kind of recommendations that would be forthcoming.

Countries that threatened to exhaust their creditor quotas received correspondingly appropriate advice—remove trade restrictions and use fiscal and monetary measures to promote increased demand for imports. Over the first two years, such recommendations were addressed at various times to the United Kingdom, France, Portugal, Belgium, Italy, and Sweden. Switzerland was urged to consider larger exports of Swiss capital through the Union. In every case, these creditors complied with some or all of the Board's injunctions.

By the spring of 1953, Marjolin could quip, during a visit to Washington, that the OEEC had achieved a consensus about appropriate economic policies—Robbins to counter inflation and Keynes to reduce unemployment. Lionel (Lord) Robbins, a highly regarded professor of economics at the University of London, advocated tight government budgets and restrictive monetary policies as the best antidote for inflation. Maynard (Lord) Keynes is probably best known for recommending that government budgets be unbalanced at times of high unemployment. Inflation was the more prevalent problem in the EPU's early years, but most members of the Managing Board felt closer philosophically to Robbins in any event.

At every opportunity, the Board urged freer trade on countries whose EPU position was sufficiently favourable to risk larger payments in the system. Its recommendations to extreme debtors were always accompanied by recommendations to all other members to remove their restrictions on the kind of goods the debtor country had available for export. To redress their imbalances, prospective extreme creditors were urged to liberalize imports beyond the levels established by the OEEC Council for all members. They were also urged to consider unilateral reduction or suspension of tariffs and customs duties.

Over these two years, the Board persevered in pressing such policies on member countries, and they were effective. By mid-1953, all of western Europe had achieved a degree of price stability unknown since the outbreak of the Second World War. Payments imbalances within the EPU area were narrowing noticeably and becoming much less volatile. During its third year, the aggregate of monthly surpluses or deficits fell back from almost $2.4 billion in the second year to less than $900 million, though trade and other transactions cleared through the Union continued to grow, and restrictions were fewer. The proof of the pudding was indeed in the eating—and the flavour was good.

It would be presumptuous to claim that the Board alone was responsible for these policies and results. Obviously, the governments of EPU member countries adopted them and made them work. But the Board was a major instrument in changing attitudes about appropriate economic policies.

The Marshall Plan had been preoccupied at first with microeconomic matters—shortages of specific commodities and the investment needs of individual industries. After the outbreak of the Korean War, many governments attempted to pile a large defence effort on top of existing programmes for promoting investment and social welfare. The resulting inflationary pressures could not be controlled by microeconomic devices. Government after government was toppled in 1951 in the aftermath of the resulting inflation.

Their successors were more open to fiscal and monetary remedies, and the Board's recommendations helped senior civil servants persuade cabinets to take the necessary decisions. Those decisions might have been taken anyway, though not necessarily as promptly. The fact that they were taken and succeeded lent the Managing Board a stature that belied its youthful existence.

The EPU Agreement had provided the framework for the Managing Board's 'interference' in this way in the economic policy-making of its members. Government experts co-operated by appearing before the Board to review the economic situation of their country in unprecedented detail. They did so not only because of the Agreement but also because most found the Board's review useful for decision-making at home. Even the possibility of a review was useful. For example, reluctant to face a Managing Board examination, the Danish government took steps to check internal demand, first in November 1950 and again in March–April 1951. Taxes were increased, the discount rate was raised to 5 per cent, subsidies were reduced, and a system of compulsory savings was introduced.

The Board, in turn, was willing to tailor its advice to the particular situation and sensitivities indicated by the expert delegations and by the member of the Board from the country under review. Its recommendations eschewed preaching and emphasized specific policies without excessive detail. Though the deliberations could become heated, the conclusions were pragmatic. A contemporary monetarist, Keynesian, or supply-side ideologue would find them deficient in theoretical and/or practical content, and the economic events that followed undoubtedly left something to be desired in every case. Nevertheless, country positions did move toward balance in almost every instance. Moreover, the rapidity of that movement was often startling. The system itself was able to continue with increased effectiveness and without compromising the purposes and principles that motivated its creation.

The View from Washington

One final episode testifies to the widespread appreciation of the Board's role during the post-Korean rearmament period. It involved the US Secretary of the Treasury and the NAC staff, who were still unreconciled to the establishment of the EPU. Staff members had read the reports of the US Representative to the Managing Board. They knew the Board was contributing effectively to resolving international financial problems and to improving the internal economic policies of its members. The Board's stature had been much enhanced by a solid record of achievement. Meanwhile, the Marshall Plan and then rearmament had kept the IMF on the sidelines. With the reappearance of a severe dollar shortage, convertibility seemed even further off than when the EPU was first authorized. Early in 1952, there was no question that the EPU would somehow be extended.

Hoffman and Bissell, its original and powerful protagonists, had left government service. The NAC staff felt that the renewal provided an opportunity to revise US policy toward and relations with the EPU. Their ideas were framed as advice to former Ambassador Harriman, who was then the White House co-ordinator of both the military assistance programme and the economic aid programme administered by MSA.

Two alternative drafts, both rather hostile in tone, were prepared for a mid-March meeting of the NAC at cabinet level.[34] Neither version

---

[34] Both drafts are reproduced in Department of State (1952-4), vi. 11–16.

contained a single positive statement about the EPU. The more negative of the two wanted to limit its extension to 'not more than one year'.

At the meeting, Harriman initially sought to soft pedal controversy by opposing only the one-year limitation. 'To announce that the EPU was to be extended for only one year more would have very definite adverse political effects both in Europe and the United States', reversing previous US support for the EPU as a factor in European integration.[35] He listed some major EPU contributions, noted the current financial difficulties in Europe, and cautioned against giving the impression that the US was changing its attitudes and policies.

Snyder responded by repeating the Treasury's long-standing fundamental objections to the EPU—its conflict with the IMF and the General Agreement on Tariffs and Trade (GATT). It did not serve the US interest in convertibility and non-discrimination. He could not agree that the EPU had been an outstanding success. As the controversy sharpened, Harriman found little support. The State Department was represented by senior civil servants of a universalist persuasion, who recorded without much enthusiasm Secretary Acheson's personal support of the EPU. The meeting ended by referring the drafts to the staff for revision.

At the following staff meeting, Treasury officials agreed to drop the one-year extension clause, but wanted to maintain the completely negative tone of their original draft.[36] The EPU was to be regarded only as a transitional organization, pending full currency convertibility. The US should oppose any action by the Union favouring measures to impose discriminatory restrictions on transactions with the dollar area. The future of the EPU in form and function should be primarily a European problem. US representatives should participate only as observers and should endeavour to further the objectives of US policy. The only such objectives specified in the draft were 'the financial and commercial policies as set forth in IMF and GATT'. Their new draft was presented at a subsequent NAC meeting that month.

Harriman again attended and listened patiently to the discussion, with dismay bordering on outrage. He observed only that he had not had time to follow the matter as closely as he would have liked, because of the pressure of presenting the new Mutual Security programme to the Congress. A week later, he sent Secretary Snyder a four-page, single-spaced letter, with copies to the other members of the NAC. It bristled with

[35] Minutes of the 190th Meeting of the NAC (13 Mar. 1952). Reprinted in Department of State (1952-4), vi. 16-26.

[36] Draft action prepared at NAC staff meeting (13 Mar. 1952), with Harriman's amendments. NAC Document 1273 (2nd revision). US Archives. ECA/Paris Havlik Files.

indignation.[37] He also enclosed a modified version of the NAC draft action. His letter observed that Acheson shared his concern.

Harriman's modified action asserted that the US should continue to support effective measures for a satisfactory functioning of the EPU during the defence build-up. It explicitly recognized the contribution of the EPU toward transferability of European currencies and trade liberalization among participating countries, including trade required for the current large-scale European defence programme. The EPU should be regarded as leading to closer European integration, as well as being transitional to convertibility and non-discrimination. The US representative at the Managing Board should pursue a broader set of objectives than the NAC staff had specified, including the NATO defence effort and the promotion of economic unification and political federation in Europe.

Harriman's letter carefully traced the history of US involvement in the creation of the EPU, including solid and continuing Congressional support for promoting European unification. It noted that NATO had adopted a resolution at its recent Lisbon meeting, endorsed by the US as well as all other NATO members, recommending 'the adoption of effective measures to provide during the defence buildup a satisfactory functioning of the EPU'.

The following statements in his letter went to the core of his (and Acheson's) disagreement with Secretary Snyder and the NAC staff:

A withdrawal at this time of U.S. interest in the EPU or U.S. support for the EPU could lead to a loss of confidence in U.S. leadership and U.S. policies in Europe.

In my view it is consequently out of the question that the U.S. should adopt an attitude of disinterest or neutrality toward the EPU, or abandon its moral support of the system and its participation in discussions of EPU questions.

NAC Action No. 546, dated 5 May 1952, was approved unanimously through a telephone poll.[38] It did not deviate from Harriman's modified draft.

---

[37] Harriman letter to Snyder (8 Apr. 1952). US Archives. ECA/Paris Havlik Files.
[38] NAC Action 546, 'European Payments Union' (5 May 1952). NAC Document 88. US Archives. Treasury NAC Files.

Part Three

Negotiating for Convertibility
1952-1955

9 From ROBOT to Istanbul: An Overview

FIRST SIGNS OF ECONOMIC RECOVERY

The second two years of the EPU, July 1952 to June 1954, were the most serenely satisfying for the economies of Europe in many a year. By the beginning of 1954, the OEEC could flatly report that 'Inflationary pressure has on the whole been eliminated in Western Europe.'[1] The tiger had finally been caged and would remain under control for another year or so.

Meanwhile, economic activity in the OEEC areas as a whole expanded steadily. Gross national product (GNP) increased in real terms by 5 per cent in both 1953 and 1954; Germany's economy grew at the rate of nearly 8 per cent and the rest of western Europe's at about 4 per cent.[2] Industrial capacity and productivity also grew, as investment in durable equipment increased by 15 per cent over the same two years. Meanwhile, life was improving noticeably for the general public. The volume of house-building rose by more than 30 per cent, and purchases by private consumers increased by 10 per cent in real terms.

Capping these signs of significant recovery, independence from further foreign assistance appeared on the horizon. Over these two years, Europe achieved an approximate balance in its current transactions with the rest of the world. The Marshall Plan had ended, but some US economic aid continued to support European rearmament. Furthermore, some of the decline in aid was offset by a flow of receipts from North American military expenditures in Europe. The combination of continued US economic support and a balanced account on current transactions produced a large increase in aggregate foreign exchange reserves of OEEC countries. Reserves rose by 50 per cent during the second two years of the EPU, from $8.1 billion to $12.0 billion.

A more discouraging indicator was Europe's failure to increase its exports to North America very much. Fortunately, however, imports from the US and Canada were only slightly more than $4 billion per year in 1953 and 1954, well below the $5.5 billion rate of 1951 and 1952.

Various explanations were given for the absence of growth in European

---

[1] OEEC, *Progress and Problems of the European Economy: Fifth Annual Report* (1954), 24.

[2] OEEC, *Economic Expansion and its Problems: Seventh Report* (1956), 84. The data in this section are primarily from this report.

exports to North America. Europe's productive capacity was limited, and its industrial productivity still lagged, inhibiting European manufacturers from looking to North America for markets. After the outbreak of war in Korea, Europe had a higher rate of price inflation than North America. This reduced the competitive edge it had gained from the 1949 devaluations. However, the OEEC consensus attributed much of Europe's export problem to a high US tariff and to fears that US protectionist pressures would choke off any significant foreign penetration of its market.

TABLE 4. *EPU Surpluses or Deficits and Cumulative Positions, FY 1952/53 and FY 1953/54 (in millions of US dollars)*

	Net Surpluses or Deficits		Net Cumulative Positions
	FY 1952/53	FY 1953/54	June 1950 to June 1954
Austria	+ 42	+106	+ 5
Belgium	− 33	− 55	+ 658
Denmark	− 17	− 92	− 132
France	−417	−149	− 973
Germany	+260	+518	+1,081
Greece	− 28	− 40	− 291
Iceland	− 4	− 5	− 22
Italy	−223	−210	− 268
Netherlands	+139	− 42	+ 304
Norway	− 59	− 61	− 179
Portugal	− 23	− 19	− 45
Sweden	− 44	− 37	+ 144
Switzerland	+ 85	+ 73	+ 326
Turkey	− 50	− 94	− 303
United Kingdom	+371	+107	− 394
TOTAL	+/−897	+/−804	+/−2,563

Source: EPU Board, *Fourth Annual Report* (1954), 16.

At the same time, intra-European trade was booming. By 1955, it was estimated to be more than 50 per cent greater than in 1950. The increase between 1952 and 1954 alone was 27 per cent.

With demand in all European markets expanding, the barriers to increasing exports to other European countries were falling away. By mid-1954, 81 per cent of private intra-European trade had been freed of quantitative restrictions, and seven of the sixteen countries had reached or surpassed 90 per cent.[3] In mid-1952, the overall liberalization percentage had been only 66 per cent.

The monthly deficits and surpluses reported to the EPU also fell sharply during the Union's third and fourth years.[4] The aggregate of $2.4 billion in the second year fell to below $900 million in the third and to slightly more than $800 million in the fourth. Moreover, the system was moving toward greater balance as five cumulative creditors and debtors in the first two years reversed their positions in the next two. Table 4 shows net surpluses or deficits of member countries in the EPU's third and fourth years, as well as their cumulative positions at the end of June 1954. The totals for both surpluses and deficits are necessarily equal because the EPU was a closed system (as explained in Chapter 7).

As shown in Table 4, Belgium's small deficits in both the third and fourth year of the Union somewhat reduced its huge cumulative surplus of 1952. Italy and Sweden had also been cumulative creditors in the first two years, but both ran deficits in the second two. Britain, on the other hand, earned surpluses in much of the third and fourth year and thus offset some of its huge deficit of the second year. Some structural debtors showed signs of leaving that category. Austria earned surpluses in the EPU, and Greece reduced its deficits substantially. Both had devalued their currencies in the spring of 1953.

The other countries did add to their imbalances with the system during the second two-year period, but only four cases seemed at all worrisome. The Netherlands added to its previous surplus in the third year, but ran a deficit in the fourth. The German and Swiss surpluses continued to mount in both years. So did the French deficits, though they were significantly lower in the fourth year. At the conclusion of the EPU's fourth year, Germany was by far the largest cumulative creditor in the Union, and France was much the largest cumulative debtor.

The continuing German and Dutch surpluses shifted the consensus on the Managing Board away from its initial goal of having countries achieve balance within the system. Previously, only Belgium and Switzerland had challenged this aim, preferring instead a target of global balance. As Germany and the Netherlands came to recognize that they, too, were likely to be persistent creditors, they also wanted a harder system in which EPU surplus countries could earn more convertible currency and give less credit. To that end, Posthuma and von Mangoldt joined the Belgian and Swiss representatives in forming an informal creditors' club. Though their own countries (Italy and France) were running large deficits

[3] OEEC, *From Recovery towards Economic Strength: Sixth Report* (1955), i. 128.
[4] EPU Board, *Fourth Annual Report* (1954).

at the time, Carli and Calvet sympathized with the creditors' point of view and sought to have the system accommodate them as much as possible.

THOUGHTS TURN TO CONVERTIBILITY

With reserves increasing, inflation under control, and a high rate of economic growth, the perspectives of economic policy-makers changed. As their immediate problems became less pressing, they could begin to think about long-standing objectives that had hitherto seemed out of reach, including free convertibility of their currencies into dollars. Freeing trade and payments on a global scale was a goal to which European governments were committed. The Bretton Woods Agreements, the Anglo-American Loan Agreement, the OEEC Convention, and the EPU Agreement itself all attested to that commitment. Early in 1952, well before economic stability was firmly rooted in Britain or on the Continent, the UK government was again considering convertibility. By mid-1954, its subsequent initiatives had established convertibility as a serious and pressing issue.

Washington 'universalists' were, nevertheless, suspicious about the seriousness of that commitment. They feared that Europeans were becoming increasingly comfortable with the protection that the sterling area and EPU arrangements afforded their producers. Those arrangements involved discriminatory barriers to North American competition.

Europeans' interest in convertibility was genuine; it was not based merely on a sense of obligation to their American allies or to the international commitments they had assumed. Convertibility on a global scale would benefit the citizens of their own countries and other areas that used their currencies. It would free their consumers and businesses to spend and invest wherever they pleased, freedoms they had been denied for over two decades. For European governments, achieving convertibility would also be an international symbol of renewed political strength. Reservations and differences among them did not involve *whether* they wanted convertibility, but only how and when to achieve it.

At the same time, both the British and the Continentals saw Europe's foreign exchange resources as still insufficient and the dollar gap as a persistent phenomenon. The dollar shortage, in the prevalent view, was temporarily concealed by evanescent US aid and military expenditures, as well as by import restrictions. Full convertibility was inconceivable until these conditions were corrected. All European governments were agreed that the first steps toward full convertibility would have to be strictly limited. Their divergent interests, however, led the British and most Continentals to very different conceptions about which limitations should be removed first.

The British wanted first to establish sterling as a reserve and trading currency on a par with the dollar. With US help, they hoped to go-it-alone, allowing each of the Continentals to follow at its own pace. They sought to terminate the EPU, to end the market for cheap sterling, and to eliminate the restrictions that prevented reopening a free market for foreign exchange in London. These priorities led them to propose, as a first step, a convertibility limited to the free exchange of currencies currently earned by non-residents of the sterling area. The shortage of dollars would be controlled by floating exchange rates, by supplementary reserves to be provided by the IMF and the United States, and by continuing trade restrictions. These limitations would be removed progressively as conditions permitted.

The Continental approach was institutional, founded on the success achieved by the EPU and its closely associated trade liberalization programme. Most Continental officials saw currency convertibility as a means, not an end. The end was to liberalize the underlying transactions—trade, services, and capital movements—that currencies financed. They sought convertibility first for their own residents, attaching little importance to encouraging others to use their currencies. Continental creditors also wanted to earn more convertible currencies to increase their foreign exchange reserves prior to convertibility.

Consequently, the Continentals preferred a gradual approach to convertibility involving all the major OEEC trading countries. They wanted to increase the role of gold and dollars in settling EPU accounts, through repayment of old debts and credits and through a progressively greater use of convertible currencies in settling new intra-European surpluses and deficits. If the EPU were thus refurbished, stable exchange rates could be maintained, as well as pressures for sound economic policies and intra-European trade liberalization. It would also provide more incentive for liberalizing imports from the dollar area. Once 100 per cent gold settlements were possible, currency convertibility would become a reality *de facto*, and discrimination would make little economic sense.

These differences in interests and approaches produced an intellectual ferment that seethed for some three years. Within the British government, the first convertibility proposal, named ROBOT, appeared as early as January 1952.[5] In the ensuing disagreements, both internal and with the Commonwealth, ideas proliferated, only to be discarded or repeatedly revised.

---

[5] See ch. 10.

As the Continentals got wind of these ideas, the Managing Board's discussion of convertibility centred on criticizing what the British had in mind, in so far as that could be ascertained. Early in 1953, some Board members began to formulate their own approach to convertibility, only to meet with firm British resistance. The British approach foundered, however, not only on Continental resistance, but also because the US refused to provide the necessary support. The US shared Continental doubts about whether the UK economy was then strong enough to sustain a convertible pound. Like the Continentals, it was critical of much of the British proposal and concurred in many of the positions taken by the Managing Board.

Thereafter, the British began to take measures consistent with the Continental approach—without accepting it in principle. Step by step, they lifted trade restrictions on imports from the EPU and the dollar area. They also reopened a London foreign exchange market for the major European currencies, and later a gold market. None the less, the British refused to accommodate Continental insistence on refurbishing the EPU until the spring of 1954. By the middle of 1955, agreement was reached on a truly collective approach. It included arrangements that should take effect when circumstances would permit currency convertibility, trade liberalization, and non-discriminatory trade arrangements with the dollar area. By the time that agreement was concluded, however, Britain was again experiencing balance-of-payments difficulties. At the 1955 IMF annual meeting, a short time later in Istanbul, the UK had to indicate an indefinite delay in its move to convertibility.

Unlike its promotion of the EPU, the US offered no specific programme or proposals for a European move to convertibility. To many US officials, the British seemed more eager for convertibility than the Continentals, and they warmly welcomed the British initiative. However, the US could not support the specific proposal with which it was confronted early in 1953. It was also attracted by the Managing Board's institutional approach. Under these circumstances, it offered cautious nurturing and guidance to both the British and the Continentals, but no comprehensive initiatives of its own.

The following chapter is an account of the evolution of the British approach, its presentation to the newly installed Eisenhower Administration in March 1953, and the diplomatic US rebuff. The succeeding chapter describes the development of the EPU Managing Board's more deliberate institutional approach to convertibility. The final chapter of Part Three is an account of the consensus about convertibility arrangements that was finally reached within the Managing Board and the OEEC. The three chapters overlap in time. The first two run from early 1952 until mid-1954. The third begins early in 1954 and continues to September 1955.

10 A Dash to Convertibility?

In October 1951, Britain's Conservative Party returned to office, committed to major changes in the direction of economic policy. The balance-of-payments crisis discussed in Chapter 8 was in full swing, and the new government acted promptly, but cautiously. It increased the Bank Rate modestly, reduced expenditures on housing and the military somewhat, and introduced new import restrictions. Results were slow in coming, however.

By January 1952, foreign exchange reserves were still declining, and official forecasts saw no end to the trend. The new Chancellor of the Exchequer, R. A. Butler, had been the major force in reshaping his party's platform and leading it to victory. Now he had to seek acceptable emergency measures to announce in the March Budget.

He responded to advice from several key civil servants, including some who had resisted full UK participation in the EPU in 1950. Sir Leslie Rowan, spearhead of the 1949–50 convertibility discussions in Washington, had returned to London as Second Secretary in charge of overseas finance. Otto Clarke of the Treasury, as well as Governor Cobbold and Sir George Bolton from the Bank of England, also found a much more attentive ear in Butler than in his predecessors.

They soon beguiled the Chancellor with a proposal for a frontal attack on the foreign exchange problem, a precipitous dash to sterling convertibility, based on a floating exchange rate. The proposal was given the code-name ROBOT in a highly restricted government file of the time. Its adoption would have resulted in 'killing the European Payments Union', to quote its authors, well before its second birthday.[1] For the British economy itself, ROBOT was hazardous.

Butler was an articulate, intelligent, and conciliatory politician, but he had little background in economics or international finance. He was outranked in the new Cabinet only by two elder statesmen, Churchill and Anthony Eden, both rather infirm. Seeking an early major achievement in his own area of responsibility, he found ROBOT very attractive.

A desperate Cabinet, eager to resolve the country's economic crisis, teetered dangerously on the edge of the precipice for six weeks, but then retreated. According to Cairncross, the controversy over ROBOT was

---

[1] Chancellor of Exchequer memo, 'External Action', second draft (26 Feb. 1952). PRO PREM 11/140.

'perhaps the most bitter of the postwar years in Whitehall'.[2] His book presents a fascinating account of the proposal and its rejection, first at a cabinet meeting on 29 February and finally on 30 June 1952.

The code-name ROBOT suggested an automatic regulator, but it also derived from the names of its originators: *Ro*wan, *Bo*lton and *Ot*to Clarke. Proponents hoped that convertibility—and the depreciation of sterling that would probably result from letting its exchange rate float in the markets—would stop the drain in reserves, end the markets in cheap sterling, and rehabilitate sterling as an international currency. All externally held sterling would become convertible.

When he presented ROBOT to the Cabinet, Butler proposed five measures: (1) permit sterling to float within limits, say $2.40-$3.20; (2) block 90 per cent of all foreigners' sterling balances; (3) require all sterling area countries to retain full exchange control; (4) fund not less than 80 per cent of sterling balances held by independent sterling area countries; (5) reopen the London Gold Market at the highest possible price for newly mined gold from the sterling area. He said that a 'substantial increase in short-term money rates' was an integral part of the plan.

He urged haste to avoid 'a major catastrophe to our economy in the next few months'. Even if catastrophe could be avoided without ROBOT, 'It is highly likely that at some stage we shall have to take drastic action in our external economy, of a character which is most unpalatable.'[3]

Two of the Prime Minister's most trusted lieutenants led the opposition to ROBOT. Sir Arthur Salter was an economist Churchill had selected to assist Butler as Minister of State for Economic Affairs. Lord Cherwell, then Paymaster General, had long been Churchill's closest adviser and confidant. Donald MacDougall, who had been the economic adviser in the OEEC Secretariat, assisted Cherwell. Salter relied on two veteran cabinet economic advisers, Edwin Plowden and Robert Hall.

From the text of the Chancellor's memorandum, Cherwell compiled a long list of consequences, which Butler himself admitted would be adverse both at home and abroad. Cherwell characterized them as 'formidable objections'.[4] On the domestic side, he emphasized the certainty of rising prices and wages, and heavy unemployment. On the foreign side, he stressed the probable departure of some members from the sterling area and ill will on the part of the US and other NATO partners. Nor was he sanguine that depreciating the pound by means of a floating rate would stem the loss of foreign exchange reserves.

[2] Cairncross (1985), 234-71.

[3] Chancellor of Exchequer memo, 'External Action', second draft (26 Feb. 1952). PRO PREM 11/140.

[4] Paymaster General memo, 'The Balance of Payments' (26 Feb. 1952). Cherwell sent this memo to Churchill together with a sharply worded covering letter (26 Feb. 1952). PRO PREM 11/140.

Along with his memorandum, Cherwell sent Churchill a personal letter that described the plan as 'a reckless leap in the dark involving appalling political as well as economic risks at home and abroad in the blind hope that the speculators will see us through'. Churchill concurred, and the full Cabinet turned down ROBOT at the end of February.

Two weeks later, Churchill voiced a longing for the day when 'we could free the pound'. Cherwell responded with an even more acerbic personal letter underscoring the consequences in melodramatic prose.[5]

If a 6% Bank Rate, 1 million unemployed and a 2/- loaf are not enough, there will have to be an 8% Bank Rate, 2 million unemployed and a 3/- loaf. If the workers, finding their food dearer, are inclined to demand higher wages, this will have to be stopped by increasing unemployment until their bargaining power is destroyed. This is what comfortable phrases like 'letting the exchange rate take the strain' mean.

Churchill sent this letter to Butler with a note: 'This is a formidable statement . . . No decision is called for at the present time but all should be borne in mind.'[6] In 1952, no British political leader believed that the electorate would tolerate a large increase in unemployment.

As Cherwell had urged in February, the Bank Rate was raised again, and the March Budget included further restrictive measures, which stopped the haemorrhaging of UK foreign exchange reserves. By the end of March, Butler had agreed at the OEEC to extend the EPU for another year, to mid-1953. Churchill had asked the Chancellor about the disadvantages if the EPU had to be abandoned. Butler's reply concluded that 'a reversion to the straight-jacket of bilateralism' would be damaging to the European economy and to the European defence effort and that the UK had more to lose than any other country. Cherwell also responded with an endorsement of the EPU, and Churchill wrote to the Chancellor that the Paymaster General's note 'has comforted me a lot'.[7]

Despite the improved economic situation, the Bank of England tried to revive ROBOT, and the debate continued for some months. Cobbold and Rowan's visit to Paris in May 1952, noted in Chapter 8, was an attempt to demonstrate that it would find some favour on the Continent. At an informal meeting of some cabinet members on 30 June 1952, Butler put ROBOT forward for the last time, again without success. In his memoirs, he admitted that opposition to ROBOT was widespread among the elder statesmen in the Cabinet. He felt, nevertheless, that the Cabinet's decision to reject a freely floating pound was 'a fundamental mistake'.[8]

---

[5] Cherwell, 'Setting the Pound Free'. Letter to Churchill (18 Mar. 1952). PRO PREM 11/137.

[6] Churchill note to Chancellor of Exchequer (20 Mar. 1952). PRO PREM 11/137.

[7] Chancellor's reply to Prime Min., Cherwell's reply (24 Apr. 1952), and Churchill's comment. Quoted in Travers notes on UK Treasury Files. OECD EPU Archive Box 33.

[8] Butler (1971).

AN ATLANTIC PAYMENTS UNION

ROBOT's critics were both impressed and disturbed by the strong attachment its proponents had to an early move to convertibility based on a floating rate. In July 1952, Cherwell and MacDougall submitted to the Chancellor their own approach to convertibility, an alternative to floating the pound sterling while a severe dollar shortage persisted.[9] They suggested an Atlantic Payments Union, an APU to succeed the EPU.[10]

The United States, Canada, and the individual members of the sterling area would be added to the membership of the EPU. The dollar would be declared a scarce currency at the outset, permitting other members to discriminate against exports from the dollar area. Onerous terms of settlement with persistent creditors would provide an incentive for other members to discriminate against them.

The authors argued that this would be the most effective way to move toward convertibility and eventual non-discrimination. Like the EPU, the APU would institutionalize continuous consultation with members, now including the United States, about their internal economic and foreign trade policies. The US would thus be under persistent pressure to adjust its policies so as to attain a better balance in its international trade and payments.

UK officials thoroughly analysed the scheme, and its difficulties soon became apparent. The US Congress would have to vote both for foreign exchange controls and for granting automatic credits to the proposed union. As first proposed, an APU would have led to the break-up of the sterling area, since each country in that area would have its own quota within the union and would have to manage to live within it. Payments relations with non-members, such as Latin America, would be a further problem.

In the summer of 1952, the UK government was preparing for an Economic Conference of Commonwealth Prime Ministers, to be held in December. A preparatory meeting of Commonwealth officials was scheduled for September. At that session, an amended version of the Atlantic Payments Union was proposed, but very tentatively.[11] Only Ceylon responded very positively, and the proposal was never put forward officially to the prospective North American members.

[9] A few years later, MacDougall elaborated the basis for his pessimistic view of the dollar problem in a widely discussed book, *The World Dollar Problem* (1957).

[10] The plan was referred to the Preparatory Economic Com. for the Commonwealth Economic Conference. PEC(52)7. See Travers notes on UK Treasury File concerning the Atlantic Payments Union. OECD EPU Archive Box 17.

[11] Commonwealth Economic Conference. Preparatory Meeting of Officials, 'Report on Finance and Trade', Annex II, 'An Extended Payments Union' (15 Oct. 1952). CEC(O)(HD)(52)1 (Final). PEC(52)41. PRO T 236/3072.

However, the success of the EPU during its first two years stimulated others to envisage adding the US and Canada to its membership. Minister Frank Aiken of Ireland so proposed at the OEEC Council meeting in June 1952. Marjolin entertained the same notion during the early autumn of 1952 as he prepared ideas for the first OEEC annual report to be issued after the termination of the Marshall Plan. Consideration in Washington was neither serious nor prolonged.

THE 'COLLECTIVE APPROACH'

The scheme that UK officials did promote at the preparatory meeting of Commonwealth officials was a so-called 'Collective Approach to Convertibility'.[12] It was more like a trot than a headlong dash. Its purposes were similar to those of ROBOT, though Britain's circumstances by that time were no longer desperate. Like ROBOT, the scheme would involve a floating rate for sterling, but without specifying any limits. Again, the privilege of converting sterling into any other currency would be confined to non-residents of the sterling area, but it would be available only for their current account transactions. Permission would still be required to export capital, and the clear intent was to refrain from readily licensing such transactions.

Unlike ROBOT's go-it-alone scenario, the Collective Approach would involve the sterling area, the United States, and some European countries—France, Benelux, and later Germany. They would be consulted in advance and asked to support or join the move. However, the timing would not be 'collective'. Sterling would become convertible on a date of the United Kingdom's own choosing. A target date of June 1953—or within the succeeding year—was floated during informal discussions. The starting-gun for the trot was thus cocked, for all to see.

Another difference from ROBOT was the stipulation of prearranged measures for protecting Great Britain in the event that convertibility proved difficult to sustain. The ROBOT controversy had led Butler and his advisers to recognize the risks inherent in then making sterling convertible. Eager for the political and economic benefits, they devised more safeguards for Britain's foreign exchange reserves than just ROBOT's floating rate.

As initially conceived, the preconditions for Britain's Collective Approach were: (1) an exchange fund, to be supplied by the United States and managed by the United Kingdom, the United States, Canada,

---

[12] 'Convertibility of Sterling', memo to Mins. by working party of officials (30 Aug. 1952) as attachment to 'The Objectives of External Economic Policy', draft memo for submission by UK del. to Preparatory Meeting of Officials (1 Sept. 1952). PEC(52)16 and PEC(52)18. PRO CAB 130/78.

France, and the Benelux countries; (2) a concerted plan for Commonwealth and European countries to remove quantitative restrictions progressively, though discrimination could continue against a persistent creditor; (3) a strict emergency escape clause to be incorporated in the new trading rules; (4) retention of imperial preference on tariffs and a relaxation of the existing GATT rules against any new preferences; (5) modification of the IMF and GATT to conform to these new policies; (6) adoption of good creditor policies by the United States. The scheme was predicated on a commitment by all participating countries to follow internal policies that would enable them to attain and maintain a sound balance-of-payments position.

The EPU would have survived no more under such a Collective Approach than under ROBOT. However, British proponents did not consider that to be a defect. They had never been fully reconciled to the Labour Cabinet's decision to join the Union.

Approaching the Commonwealth

At the preparatory meeting in September 1952, Commonwealth countries raised objections to every single feature of the Collective Approach.[13] Some felt they would have to move slowly in easing import restrictions, and others preferred to begin by relaxing restraints on dollar spending. However, South Africa was eager for Britain to introduce a floating rate, anticipating an increase in the sterling price of its gold exports. Canada, a dollar rather than a sterling area country, avidly sought sterling convertibility and a relaxation of sterling area restrictions against its exports. When it had decided to float its currency against the US dollar in 1950, the IMF and US had acquiesced reluctantly, noting but not approving the decision. Thus Canada would have welcomed a floating pound and a change in the IMF rules to permit approval of a floating exchange rate.[14] These countries, and others, argued for changes in the British plan to remove elements likely to be most objectionable to the US and the global institutions.

All delegations, except the one from the UK, felt that the proposals relating to imperial preference would be 'untimely and inadvisable'.[15] They all doubted the wisdom of asking for the right to discriminate against a persistent creditor. Most questioned the proposed new exchange

[13] Cherwell memo to Cabinet Preparatory Com. summarizes Commonwealth country criticisms (24 Oct. 1952). PEC(52)44. PRO CAB 130/78.
See also Commonwealth Economic Conference. Preparatory Meeting of Officials, 'Report on Finance and Trade' (15 Oct. 1952). CEC(O)(HD)(52)1 (Final). PEC(52)41. PRO T 236/3072.
[14] Horsefield (1969), 272-5.
[15] Commonwealth Economic Conference. Preparatory Meeting of Officials, 'Report on Finance and Trade' (15 Oct. 1952). CEC(O)(HD)(52)1 (Final). PEC(52)41. PRO T 236/3072.

fund, to be managed by a small group of countries. Preferring to work through the IMF and the GATT, they suggested that the IMF should be asked to provide standby credits to countries undertaking convertibility operations. If its resources were inadequate, further bilateral credits might be sought. A joint committee of the IMF and the GATT might be set up as a 'forum for discussing the whole complex of finance, trade and associated problems'. Such a committee would be responsible for supervising the liberalization programme and the use of the proposed emergency escape clause.

The Chancellor modified the Collective Approach to meet these suggestions, though he insisted on retaining a provision for reinforcing imperial preference.[16] On 3 November 1952, the full Cabinet agreed that the United Kingdom should put forward the amended proposals to the Commonwealth prime ministers, but only as a basis for discussion.[17]

Cherwell's opposition was as unrelenting as it had been to ROBOT. He contended that convertibility and a floating pound would have a disrupting, not stabilizing, effect on the economies of the West. Early convertibility with a flexible rate would be very dangerous and extremely damaging if it later had to be reversed. He preferred a more gradual approach, and several cabinet ministers shared his apprehensions about a premature move. They were 'fortified by the assurance' that the UK would reserve the right to make the final judgement about whether conditions were suitable.

The modified plan was presented to the Commonwealth prime ministers early in December. The Commonwealth countries insisted that the United Kingdom should discuss the plan with the US government before making any specific proposals to European governments. They were willing for the United Kingdom to present the plan to the United States as having Commonwealth support, but would not tolerate a joint initiative.[18] Several countries had difficulty in accepting a flexible rate for sterling; India had reserved its position on this issue.[19]

While the British were moving the Collective Approach through the Commonwealth forum, the EPU Board formulated a different view about the approach to convertibility. UK and US participation in its discussions was awkward, the former because of instructions neither to reveal nor to

---

[16] Chancellor of Exchequer, 'The Collective Approach to Convertibility'. Note proposing amendments to original plan, in light of meeting of Commonwealth officials (24 Oct. 1952). Bank of England OV 44/59.

[17] British Cabinet meeting (3 Nov. 1952). CC(52) 92nd Conclusions. The Cabinet had before it Butler's note, memo from Eden C(52)376, and a summary of Cherwell's objections C(52)377. Eden recommended that modified proposals be put forward at Commonwealth Conference.

[18] Jasper Rootham, memo to Bolton concerning an Ellis-Rees memo (8 Jan. 1953). Bank of England OV 46/58.

[19] Rowan, memo to Sir Edward Bridges (29 Apr. 1953). Bank of England OV 44/60.

prejudge the Collective Approach, the latter because of the interregnum between US administrations. However, both reported the discussions to their capitals in considerable detail. In addition, Ellis-Rees carefully summarized Continental views and concerns in a separate memorandum.[20] Only the US government proved very attentive to the reports.

Would the Americans Agree?

The Collective Approach was meant to restore some of the tattered international prestige of sterling and to reinforce the sterling area. The London foreign exchange market would have reopened, and the market for 'cheap sterling' would have been more controllable, if not wholly eliminated. The City was eager for foreign exchange business, and Cobbold repeatedly advocated sterling convertibility to open up the market.

However, the commercial advantages that the US expected to flow from convertibility would be very limited. To be sure, non-residents of the sterling area would be able to spend sterling freely in the US and would have little incentive to discriminate against US suppliers. Members of the sterling area might press the UK for similar treatment, but higher tariff barriers (imperial preference) could restrain spending on dollar goods. Of greater importance to the US was UK insistence on elaborating the rules for removing quantitative restrictions only after a year or so of experimentation with a floating convertible pound.

Moreover, fluctuating exchange rates challenged the par value system enshrined in the IMF Articles of Agreement. Exchange rate stability might well be the sacrificial price of the Collective Approach. In return for a vague and undefined promise of non-discrimination in the future, the US would be asked to supply funds, to reduce its own trade barriers, and to accept modification of the IMF. Would the new US administration be sufficiently attracted by the approach to do all of that? At the British Cabinet meeting on 3 November 1952, Cherwell had predicted it would be 'most unlikely that the Americans would agree to contribute'.[21]

Approaching Washington

Days after his prophetic statement, the US held elections and voted the Republican Party into office for the first time in twenty years. The British Conservative government, itself in office for only a year, expected the new administration to respond sympathetically to its proposals for

---

[20] Ellis-Rees memo, 'The Commonwealth Conference and the OEEC' (25 Nov. 1952). PRO T 230/213.
[21] British Cabinet meeting (3 Nov. 1952). CC(52) 92nd Conclusions.

convertibility and freer trade. President Dwight D. Eisenhower's initial State of the Union message, delivered on 2 February 1953, suggested the US might respond if other countries took steps to create dependable currencies and to enlarge their trade with each other. British hopes surged on reading this guarded offer.

The new US Secretary of the Treasury, George Humphrey, had little experience in international finance. He was an instinctive supporter of free markets and a critic of government restrictions on business. His first priority was to eliminate the deficit in the budget prepared by the previous administration. Like the Republican administration that took office under Ronald Reagan more than a quarter of a century later, Humphrey was firmly opposed to a tax increase. Unlike that successor, his target for budget cuts was international security, including foreign aid as well as defence. His President would even have welcomed a slowing down in NATO rearmament goals.[22]

Humphrey's Under Secretary, W. Randolph Burgess, was a prominent banker who had long urged anti-inflationary fiscal and monetary policies and currency convertibility. As president of the American Bankers Association, he had campaigned against ratification of the Bretton Woods Agreements, but in office he became a firm supporter of the IMF. Burgess kept intact the international finance staff inherited from the previous administration, including Southard and Assistant Secretary Andrew Overby.

Butler and his advisers had high hopes that this team would be predisposed to their plan, and they were eager to present it at the earliest possible moment. However, they soon became aware that the new administration had other priorities as well. While heading NATO's armed forces prior to his presidential campaign, President Eisenhower had become an articulate advocate of an integrated Europe. With his Secretary of State, John Foster Dulles, he placed a high priority on the then current negotiations for a European Defence Community. The EDC would have permitted German rearmament under the blanket of a common military force and a common military budget of the six countries that had formed the Schuman Plan. The new Mutual Security Administrator, Harold Stassen, was a leader of the liberal wing of the Republican Party. He was well attuned both to US international responsibilities and to the sensitivities of domestic constituents about barriers to US exports. With cabinet rank, he administered the continuing US aid programmes for Europe and the developing areas. As ardent a supporter of European

---

[22] Memo of discussion at 138th Meeting, National Security Council (25 Mar. 1953). Department of State (1952–4), ii, Part I, 258 ff.
Also Special Meeting (31 Mar. 1953), ibid. 264 ff., and 139th Meeting (8 Apr. 1953), ibid. 287 ff.

integration as Hoffman had been, he had inherited the primary US responsibility for OEEC and EPU affairs.

All of these men were concerned about the effects of a premature liquidation of the EPU on European integration. They well knew that the finances of both the Schuman Plan and the European Defence Community were based on an EPU through which accounts could be settled at fixed exchange rates. Stassen, among others, placed a high priority on trade liberalization, including an early reduction in European restrictions on imports from the US. He was well briefed about the Managing Board's discussions of convertibility and about Continental uneasiness regarding the British descent on Washington.

The British tried to address these sensitivities by rewriting the Collective Approach paper. The major elements of the plan were retained, but the rhetoric was muted. The title was changed to 'A Collective Approach to Freer Trade and Currencies'.[23] An exhortation for 'trade, not aid', first enunciated by Butler in March 1952, was featured. The UK emphasized 'its awareness that its proposals carry important consequences for other Western European countries'. It aimed to strengthen the western European economy and 'provide a more solid foundation for Western European political and military strength than the present arrangements can possibly do'. The internal policy language became more specific—tighten credit, check the growth of government expenditures, reduce food subsidies and physical controls on the economy, and reduce taxation.

As for the convertibility arrangements proper, only enough flexibility was sought in the exchange rate to make the convertibility operation possible. The official parity would not be changed, and the objective would be to maintain exchange rate stability.

Financial support was sought only in the form of a standby IMF credit, but the US government would have to provide additional funds to the IMF for the credit to be sufficiently large. The credit would not be used to fill continuing balance-of-payments deficits. It was needed only to deal with short term fluctuations, to provide confidence in sterling, and to deal with potential pressures for converting sterling balances.

Once non-resident convertibility was a success, limitations on residents of the sterling area would gradually be removed. The UK would eliminate trade restrictions and discrimination as fast as compatible with avoiding additional strain on the sterling area's balance of payments. The proposed new escape clause was introduced in the text *sotto voce*, its use to be justified in an international forum. Freedom to increase imperial preference

---

[23] UK memo, 'A Collective Approach to Freer Trade and Currencies'. Submitted to US Administration (10 Feb. 1953). Bank of England OV 44/59.

by raising tariffs against other countries would be sought in the GATT, to be used 'as and when this may from time to time be necessary'.

A Diplomatic Rebuff

A large British delegation, headed by Eden and Butler, embarked on the liner Queen Elizabeth at the end of February 1953 to approach the Eisenhower Administration. Butler discovered that his 'economic brief was pretty unintelligible', and he spent long hours in his cabin trying to put it into 'plain language'.[24]

Dulles had sent Eden a warning about the risks of his (and possibly the Chancellor's) appearing in Washington prematurely. It would be better to wait until the Commonwealth economic plan had been discussed in detail with US experts and the Americans saw some prospect of success.[25] However, Butler and Eden were determined to proceed and had not been further discouraged about coming. The Chancellor wanted to be back in London by 10-12 March for Budget preparations. They left with Churchill's blessing and a long list of questions hurriedly prepared by US advisers after receiving the Collective Approach document.

When they landed in New York, UK Embassy officers met them with the news that the US would not provide the requested financing.[26] The British had hoped for at least $2 billion, in addition to their $1.3 billion of normal drawing rights in the IMF.

Secretary Humphrey was not given to careful reading of long memoranda. He simply thought that $3 billion was a lot of money. Burgess was a reflective man whose strong ideological convictions were not matched by an appetite for confrontation. Although favourably disposed to the British proposal, he was unlikely to dispute Humphrey's decision. Later, during the 1956 Suez crisis, Humphrey suggested that the British seek a $1.3 billion drawing and standby from the Fund, rather than the $750 million they had tentatively and timidly requested.[27] Humphrey then preferred to go 'all out'. But not in 1953.

Dulles had asked Lewis Douglas, Truman's Ambassador to Great Britain, to act as his deputy for these discussions. Douglas enlisted John Williams and Walter Stewart, another academic economist, to advise him. Stassen recruited Bissell, who had left government service a year earlier,

---

[24] Butler (1971).

[25] Letter from New York, signed J. R. G., to Evelyn Shuckburgh, UK Foreign Office (7 Jan. 1953). Sent to Prime Min. office. Reports conversation with Sec. of State Designate Dulles that evening. PRO PREM 11/431.

[26] Interview with Lincoln Gordon (autumn 1986). By 1953, Gordon was in London as US Min. for Economic Affairs. He accompanied British del. on its journey to the US.

[27] Southard (1979), 20.

to assist him. Otherwise, the US side consisted of newly appointed officials of the Eisenhower Administration and holdover civil servants.

Douglas was predisposed to support the British, but Williams's perceptive analytical mind made him cautious. After the meetings, Douglas was asked to prepare recommendations to the President about the UK Approach. Not until July did he submit his views, in a six-page, single-spaced letter. While recognizing the importance of sterling and the desirability of convertibility, he concluded that 'more remains to be done if sterling is to acquire sufficient strength and resilience to stand the vigorous test of convertibility.'[28] His report was referred to a newly appointed President's Commission on Foreign Economic Policy, chaired by Clarence Randall, then president of a major US steel company.

The Washington Meetings

The British delegation, led by Eden and Butler, continued its journey from New York to Washington for thirteen abortive meetings over a period of six days.[29] The opening session at the State Department, on 4 March 1953, was attended by Dulles, Humphrey, Stassen, Douglas, Burgess, Bissell, and Gabriel Hauge (the President's Administrative Assistant for Economic Affairs). Dulles began by stating that the principles in the British memorandum were in accord with US thinking, but it would not be possible to answer Mr Eden's questions offhand.[30] Eden thereafter absented himself from most of the meetings, apart from those concerned with the communiqué. He and Dulles met to discuss international political issues. Butler was left to deal with US concerns about his Approach.

The following day, Dulles noted substantial issues such as the size of the support fund, the effect on western Europe, the nature and timing of discussions with western Europe, and whether the UK economy was sufficiently strong and flexible to sustain the proposed operation.[31] A well-briefed Butler replied in impressive detail about UK economic policies and prospects and about the sterling balances. He was vaguer

[28] Lewis Douglas, letter to the President (6 July 1953). Cobbold met with the President, Amb. Douglas, and Hauge (30 June 1953). Thereafter, he received copy of Douglas letter. Bank of England OV 44/60.

[29] Thirteen formal meetings. Rapporteurs in each del. prepared summary minutes. UK minutes, numbered US/UK(53)1-13, Bank of England OV 44/60. US minutes, numbered 384-9, report only 6 meetings, Department of State (1952-4), vi. Some statements understandably recorded in only one of the sets of minutes.

[30] UK Minutes. Meeting at State Department (4 Mar. 1953). US/UK(53)1, Bank of England OV 44/60.

[31] UK Minutes. Meeting at State Department (5 Mar. 1953). US/UK(53)4, Bank of England OV 44/60.

about how European trade liberalization could be maintained after the proposed move to convertibility.

As concerns the EPU, he said that it would not be possible to run an EPU system in which some currencies were convertible and others were not. The IMF should provide credit to Europe after the EPU was ended. That credit could be supplemented by a new fund in Europe consisting of the US stake in the EPU plus any other residual EPU assets. Perhaps the Managing Board could be retained and have some responsibility for the IMF credits.[32] Later he referred to the EPU as a 'nice little working mechanism' but not a worldwide approach. Responding to a question about a UK advance in intra-European trade liberalization, Rowan said the UK did not wish to go back into deficit with the EPU.[33] In reply to a question from Douglas, Butler thought the UK would require $2.5 billion, including $1.3 billion from the IMF quota, plus an additional $700 million for the sterling area. Europe would also have claims, but 'it was a mistake to compare the European currencies to sterling.'[34] Europe-blindness, characteristic of British policy since 1949, still persisted and was thus displayed to the new US administration.[35]

The US side felt that a premature move to convertibility would be fatal and a further $2 billion would be difficult to find if the risks were too great. The risks might be greatly reduced if in the meantime both countries intensified efforts to create an underlying pattern of production and trade that would help to sustain convertibility.[36] In a final interview with Butler, Humphrey said 'he would be satisfied to see convertibility introduced when there was a reasonable prospect of assuring the necessary trade pattern'. He felt that a $2 billion credit 'should not be necessary if things were to be properly managed'.[37] In effect, he reiterated views previously expressed by the Continental members of the Managing Board.

The US was also uncertain about how well it could perform in the matter of the requested 'good creditor' policies. Dulles and Humphrey both said it would be dangerous to give the impression that the US could change its trade policy on the scale implied in the UK proposals. The UK had asked the US to reduce its tariff unilaterally, simplify its customs regulations, and remove its discriminatory restrictions on shipping, its

---

[32] US Minutes. Meeting at State Department (5 Mar. 1953). No. 385, Department of State (1952–4), vi.

[33] US Minutes. Meeting at US Treasury (6 Mar. 1953). No. 387, Department of State (1952–4), vi.

[34] US Minutes. Meeting at State Department (5 Mar. 1953). No. 386, Department of State (1952–4), vi.

[35] The term 'Europe-blindness' was suggested by John Fforde, historian of the Bank of England.

[36] UK Minutes. Meeting at State Department (5 Mar. 1953). US/UK(53)4, Bank of England OV 44/60.

[37] UK tel. 135 from New York (10 Mar. 1953). Marked for Prime Min. from Chancellor of Exchequer. PRO PREM 11/431.

tying of Export–Import Bank loans to US exports, and the Buy American legislation. Bissell observed that the US payments surplus would be substantially covered by continuing military outlays and offshore procurement. His prediction was not so much as recorded in the UK minutes, though it later proved correct.

On the third day, the meetings moved to the US Treasury, where Humphrey chaired the US side. Noting that the US regarded the UK proposals as premature, Butler doubted the usefulness of continuing the talks on existing lines.[38] Burgess hoped that the UK proposals would be treated as 'in suspense', rather than abandoned. It was agreed that the communiqué should not give a discouraging impression and that subgroups should proceed with discussions of the various issues.

At the subsequent meetings, the only ray of encouragement the UK might have gleaned was a Southard statement that there was no *legal* obstacle to prevent a country that had a fluctuating rate from drawing on the IMF. Responsible under the IMF Articles of Agreement for a par value system, the IMF staff was extremely critical of the possibility that a fluctuating rate for sterling might be introduced. Echoing the concerns of Cherwell and MacDougall, Williams suggested that a flexible rate would give rise to internal difficulties for Britain and might generate a wage/cost spiral. A Bissell query about permitting flexibility in the exchange rate without convertibility drew a critical reply from Rowan.

The US Treasury registered surprise at the size of the figures the UK had mentioned. It felt the IMF could not offer more than $1 billion in support and thought it would be 'politically impossible to increase the US contribution to the Fund at this stage'.[39]

Stassen expressed concern that confidence in trade liberalization might be destroyed if the communiqué suggested an end to the EPU. He referred to the difficulties that UK deliberalization had caused to Italy and France and their consequent demand for more US aid.

The Collective Approach may have seemed more methodical than ROBOT to the British Cabinet, but it looked like a 'dash to convertibility' to the US. At least with respect to international trade and payments, it seemed to threaten the special relationship that Gaitskell had re-established during the EPU negotiations. Though the message took some time to sink in, the British had been told to develop an approach to convertibility with their European colleagues and at the more measured pace the Continentals preferred. They left Washington, warned that the prospects were dim for two major preconditions of the Collective Approach—a large support fund and sharply reduced US trade barriers. Nor were

---

[38] UK Minutes (6 Mar. 1953). US/UK(53)5, Bank of England OV 44/60.
[39] UK Minutes of Sub-group at US Treasury (7 Mar. 1953). US/UK(53)10, Bank of England OV44/60.

they encouraged to contemplate a freely floating exchange rate for sterling.

Butler's report to the British Cabinet did not gloss over his rebuff, and Eden endorsed his statement.[40] The Americans 'doubted whether its [the British] economy was yet sufficiently strong or flexible to sustain the risks involved in making sterling convertible and they had indicated that the time was not yet opportune for putting these proposals into effect'. Nor were they 'disposed at this early stage of their Administration to ask Congress to approve the drastic measures which would be required . . .'. Butler reported, 'in American thinking the reduction of restrictions in world trade should precede any movement towards greater convertibility of currencies.' He did not mention that US views differed very little from those expressed by the Continental members of the Managing Board.

An OEEC ministerial meeting had been scheduled for 23 March 1953, at which the UK was to explain its plans and report on the talks in Washington. Butler told the Cabinet that it would be inexpedient to disclose formally to the OEEC ministers details of the proposals evolved at the Commonwealth Conference. Obviously the EPU would have to be renewed for another year, until July 1954. A Bank of England suggestion for only a six-month renewal found no support in Whitehall.[41]

Approaching Europe

Under the circumstances, Eden and Butler gave a bravura performance at the OEEC ministerial meeting.[42] They gave no indication that their sterling convertibility plan had been put in abeyance. Eden called for collective action to free trade and currencies over as much of the world as possible. In Washington, 'We neither sought nor received commitments.' Butler outlined his collective approach with eloquent rhetoric, but little detail. He took particular care not to mention flexible rates.

Butler went on to announce a decision to increase liberalization of UK intra-European trade from 44 to 58 per cent, including an increase in liberalization of manufactured goods from 21 to 65 per cent. Quotas for two commodities would be liberalized with special attention to the needs of France and Italy, and the annual tourist allowance would be raised from £25 to £40 per year.

The Continental responses stressed satisfaction with the liberalization measures and the agreement to renew the EPU for at least another year. Virtually everyone emphasized the importance of freeing intra-European trade, and most expressed caution about any move to convertibility that

---

[40] British Cabinet meeting (17 Mar. 1953). CC(53)20th Conclusions, Minute 3. PRO PREM 11/431.

[41] Memo on meeting at the Treasury (10 Mar. 1953). Bank of England OV 44/60.

[42] 'Minutes of the 209th Meeting' (23-4 Mar. 1953). OEEC C/M(53)8.

might imperil it. The ministers instructed the OEEC to study how and what conditions would permit an orderly transition from the present EPU to a wider system of trade, payments, and credit.

Immediately after the ministerial meeting, Rowan led a team of British experts to answer questions about the Collective Approach. The success of the Managing Board had led the OEEC to create a parallel Steering Board for Trade in March 1952. An unusual joint meeting of the Managing Board and the Steering Board was arranged to hear Rowan and his team. Southard and Bissell joined the regular US representatives at the meeting. The Chairman of the Steering Board, Baron Snoy, presided.[43]

The Europeans asked more specific questions about British plans than had the Americans. The British experts were not very reassuring on intra-European trade liberalization. They hoped to progress up to the date of convertibility and to maintain the degree of liberalization already attained during the first stage of convertibility. After about a year, it should be possible to begin writing new global trading rules.

Rowan said exchange rates should be allowed to fluctuate within wider margins, but he refused to be more specific. Britain hoped that some other European countries would make their currencies convertible at the same time as it did. Pegging European currencies to sterling (rather than the dollar) was not an essential part of the plan, but Britain hoped for exchange stability within Europe and would try to reach an understanding with individual countries. Initially, the United Kingdom did not expect to provide any credit to countries outside the sterling area, nor would it remove exchange controls on capital transactions. Convertibility on the Swiss model, permitting continued membership in the EPU, would not be possible for a currency as important as sterling.

Undaunted by the March meetings in Washington and Paris, Rowan returned to the US in April. He later reported, 'The most depressing talks we had were with Treasury officials—especially Mr. Burgess. In the first place the latter talked of the "demise"—which he later corrected to the deferment of Plan A—i.e. our plan—and the need for filling the resultant vacuum with an undefined Plan B.'[44] Burgess offered Rowan a personal suggestion—the United Kingdom might, as a first step, widen the spread of its exchange rate beyond the 1 per cent mandated by IMF regulations. Speaking personally, Burgess said he would 'smile' on a British approach to the IMF for funds to support such an operation.

Rowan returned again to Europe for bilateral meetings with the international financial officials of a few countries—France, Belgium,

---

[43] Joint Session of Managing Board and Steering Board, 'Summary Record' (25-6 Mar. 1953). MBC/M(53)3, Part I and SBC/M(53)5, Part II.

[44] L. Rowan, 'Visit to Washington' (19-21 Apr. 1953). Bank of England OV 44/60.

Germany, and the Netherlands. He tried to revive the original plan by gaining Continental adherents, but did not succeed. The UK was not ready to consider alternative approaches.

At the end of June, Rowan and his team returned to Paris for another joint session with the Managing and Steering Boards. He gave a forthright exposition about the need, in the new world trade rules, for countries to have the right to discriminate against an extreme creditor such as the United States. Otherwise, he added little to his previous presentation. Posthuma openly stated his dislike for linking convertibility to the abandonment of fixed rates. That would introduce a new element of risk and uncertainty in international trade. No one responded to Rowan's suggestion that it would be useful to know which other countries would join a British move.

WHY DID THE COLLECTIVE APPROACH FOUNDER?

The dash to convertibility proposed by the ROBOT team in February 1952 had been stopped completely by June. By the end of the year, the British government had proposed a trot to the same finish. After the Washington rebuff in March 1953, little scope was left for anything more than a stately walk, at a carefully measured pace. Indeed, that was how the goal was finally reached more than five years later, to the satisfaction of virtually all of Britain's trading partners.

The Collective Approach foundered because it failed to attract the prospective members of the collectivity. Even the Commonwealth prime ministers had offered only a reserved blessing for conversations with the United States. Other governments did not reject convertibility, but they saw few benefits and many risks in an early move, undertaken with inadequate foreign exchange reserves and a continuing dollar problem. They were much more interested in the trading benefits that might accrue from convertibility and could see few advantages in a hasty move, restricted to monetary arrangements.

The British descent on Washington was both premature and misguided. The Eisenhower Administration had barely taken office and was pre-occupied with sorting out its priorities and mastering its responsibilities. To be sure, it wanted convertibility, but at what price? The magnitude of the British request for financing would have required a Congressional appropriation. Even in the improbable event that room could have been found in the new budget, convincing the Congress would have been arduous, if not impossible.

Only a few years had elapsed since the Congress had been persuaded of the benefits of joining the IMF. A stable exchange rate system had been a major attraction, but the British now proposed a departure. Other countries might tie their exchange rates to a fluctuating pound sterling and hold part of their foreign exchange reserves in sterling rather than in dollars. That might be valuable to the United Kingdom, but it was hardly an inducement for a US Congressional appropriation. Furthermore, Congressional sponsors of European integration would regard the demise of the EPU as an important loss.

The trade safeguards in the UK Approach would also have been difficult for the Congress to accept. The British proposed to continue trade restrictions on dollar imports for about a year, and only then would new trade rules be negotiated. Thus, even if the US administration were inclined to bless the UK proposal, it would have had to negotiate far more specific commitments about sterling area foreign trade policies. The only immediate enticement for the US was a limited form of currency convertibility, an abstraction of more interest to a few large US banks than to the rest of the country.

The proposal had even less attraction for the Continentals. The EPU would doubtless have to be terminated. Europe would be divided between countries with convertible currencies and those without. The few Continentals who might have been ready to make their own currencies convertible—Benelux and Germany—had grave reservations about doing so while major trading partners were unable to join them. The inconvertible countries would then have every reason to discriminate against all convertible country exports to protect their foreign exchange reserves. Moreover, tying their exchange rate to a floating pound sterling could threaten their own internal financial stability. Above all, the Continentals foresaw the destruction of the intra-European trade liberalization programme on which their continuing economic expansion was founded.

Liquidating the EPU would mean giving up an important secondary line of foreign exchange reserves. The only concrete substitute would be less than $300 million in credit, based on the EPU's residual assets, to be reserved for the countries that remained inconvertible. The possibility that the Congress would provide the IMF with additional funds for Europe, as well as the United Kingdom, to draw seemed rather far-fetched.

As Vice-Chairman of the EPU, Calvet testified before the Randall Commission that 'the United Kingdom's reserves presently represent hardly three months of imports, Germany's and Italy's reserves three and a half months, France's reserves less than three months, and the same for Norway, Sweden and Denmark.'[45] The Continentals were not ready to dispense with the EPU under such circumstances.

---

[45] EPU Board, 'Statement by Calvet before the Randall Commission' (6 Jan. 1954). OEEC MBC(54)1.

THE RESULTS

A year of intensive preparation of a variety of proposals, followed by extensive international discussion, thus ended in frustration for the British. The only apparent result was the renewal of the EPU for a fourth year without significant change. Near the end of 1953, Chancellor Butler answered a Parliamentary interrogation with the statement that 'At the October [OEEC] Council meeting . . . I made it clear that we support the continuation of EPU in very much its present form until the time comes for a transition to a wider system.'[46] Gaitskell, now leader of the Opposition, could not refrain from an impish rejoinder: 'Does the Chancellor realise that that statement will give much satisfaction to many people in this country and in Europe?'

Something had been gained, however, though it was scarcely apparent at the time. Convertibility had been put on the table of a large number of governments as a practical proposition, whose time would come before long. It could no longer be treated as a theoretical goal to be achieved at some distant and nebulous date.

A new generation of officials, whose experience over the preceding two decades came from coping with discriminatory trade and payments restrictions, had to think through the implications of convertibility. What form might it take? What changes in internal economic policy would be required? How would trading relationships, capital movements, and payments for services be affected and managed? What would be the impact on key political relationships—with such overseas ties as the Commonwealth, the US, and the rest of Europe?

National interests had to be reviewed and priorities reassessed. Transferability of European currencies had prepared the way, but free competition with the dollar seemed like a further quantum jump, different in kind as well as magnitude. No matter how narrowly the first big step might be hedged—and the British proposed to make it as narrow as possible—convertibility would transform the basis for international transactions. Governments were forced to think it through during this period, and that very necessary intellectual process thereafter guided steady progress toward convertibility.

Another result was that the Managing Board established itself as the principal international forum for that intellectual process. Only after convertibility was finally achieved, in December 1958, did the IMF's 'activities become central to the international monetary system', to quote its official history.[47] The Managing Board's convertibility discussions had

---

[46] Hansard, House of Commons, 'Official Report of Tuesday, 1 Dec. 1953', 521 No. 21, 950.

[47] Horsefield (1969), 474.

informed the Continentals and cautioned the British. Through Williams, Bissell, and Stassen, the Board had a substantial influence on the substance of the US response to the Collective Approach. That response forced the United Kingdom to set aside its preference for an initial bilateral arrangement with the US. Increasingly, it had to seek the support of European colleagues, who in turn preferred to use the EPU Board and other OEEC forums. These positive outcomes were neither intended by the sponsors of the Collective Approach nor widely recognized at the time.

The foundering of the Collective Approach focused attention on the need for a 'Plan B', as Burgess had observed to Rowan's dismay. The British, as well as the Continentals, increasingly turned their attention to devising one. Unlike its role in 1949-50, the US was prepared neither to offer nor to sponsor an alternative proposal. Unwilling or unable to offer financing, it could not lead and did not try.

Reluctant to embarrass the British further or to discourage them from continuing to seek convertibility, the US refused to tell the Continentals what had transpired during the March visit to Washington. The French Ambassador, Henri Bonnet, had asked to be briefed, and Harold Linder, a holdover Acting Assistant Secretary of State, was assigned to brief him. Linder could only say that he was not at liberty to comment on certain specific ideas that had been touched upon.[48] The communiqué emphasized freer trade as well as currencies and noted a US promise to examine 'possible alternative suggestions', as well as the Commonwealth proposals. Such language was too subtle to reassure the apprehensive Continentals.

The British, in turn, never told them that Plan A had been rebuffed. In July, the Douglas report to the President provided more than an inkling. But the Continentals could not be sure until January 1954, when the Randall Commission report was published.

The latter report explicitly favoured 'gradual progress' rather than a 'dash' to convertibility. While expressing sympathy for a floating rate, it did not favour letting a foreign currency find its own level. Moreover, it endorsed the success of the EPU and advised against wrecking the Union before something better was available to take its place. Williams had prepared a careful and scholarly essay for the Commission that provided an incisive analytical foundation for these recommendations.[49]

Not long after the report was issued, the British began to repair their fences with Europe. Slowly but surely, they became more accommodating to the Continent about both trade and payments arrangements. The usually well-informed British magazine, the *Banker*, observed as early as

[48] Department of State (1952-4), vi.
[49] Williams, memo on Currency Convertibility (15 Dec. 1953). Department of State (1952-4), i, Part I, 340-8.

May 1953 that 'Europe is now in the saddle for the slow ride to convertibility.' In British argot of the time, Europe meant the Continent.

11 With Measured Steps: The Institutional Approach

In the spring of 1952, some British officials were still flirting with the daring dash to convertibility described in Chapter 10. By summer, rumours about ROBOT had crossed the Channel, and a reluctant EPU Managing Board was forced into what would be a long and gruelling controversy. The Board had just been through two years of incessant crises and was still grappling with a Turkish request for a special credit. Although the EPU had survived its initial buffeting in good shape, the very thought of a much wider system seemed decidedly premature to its Continental members.

Only two weeks after ROBOT's final rejection in June 1952, the Managing Board received a mandate to study convertibility. During the next year, the British pushed ahead with their Collective Approach and had their disillusioning encounters with the Americans. Meanwhile, the Continentals formulated a very different, institutional approach of their own.

PRELIMINARY DISCUSSIONS

Origins of the Mandate

Early in 1952, the OEEC Council asked seven distinguished academics to examine the problems of internal financial stability in member countries. Their analysis focused on the neglect of monetary policy in the postwar years. They also recommended that local currencies be made convertible, in keeping with the statutes of the IMF.[1] 'If it is treated not as something to be postponed to the Greek Kalends but rather as the constant preoccupation of practical policy . . .', convertibility would exercise a disciplinary influence on the domestic financial policies of member governments.

In July 1952, a temporary committee of ministers endorsed their conclusions. With an ear to the rumours emanating from London, the OEEC Council seized upon the endorsement to give the Managing Board an urgent assignment. It was instructed to 'carry out a preliminary study

---

[1] The group was chaired by Lionel Robbins (UK). Other members were C. Bresciani-Turoni (Italy), E. Lindahl (Sweden), A. Marget (US), M. Masoin (Belgium), J. Rueff (France), and E. Schneider (Germany). Final report submitted on 18 June 1952. OEEC C(52)173.

of the questions and problems that would be raised by the convertibility of currencies for payments on current account'.[2]

Marjolin himself made a rare appearance at the Board to press for a serious examination of the problem of convertibility. He even suggested that the Board delay publication of its second annual report long enough to include the results of its preliminary analysis.[3]

The Board responded by adding only a very few cautionary paragraphs to the report that was issued a month later.[4] It reaffirmed its own dedication to the goal of convertibility but doubted its imminence as a practical proposition. First, 'there must be further progress towards the establishment and maintenance of real equilibrium in the balances of payments of all members, the reduction of their dollar deficits, and the extension of the area in which a multilateral system of payments can operate.' Further consideration was delayed until the Board's October meeting.

What Is Convertibility?

By October 1952, Carli had yielded the EPU chair to von Mangoldt. Still in the dark about UK thinking, the Board remained unenthusiastic about the mandate it had been given. Under von Mangoldt's deft leadership, it nevertheless began a thoughtful analysis of the issues.[5] First it formulated the basic questions that had to be addressed.

What is meant by convertibility? Can convertibility be reconciled with the maintenance of quantitative import restrictions? Is it possible and does it make sense to limit currency convertibility to current transactions only? Is currency convertibility conceptually linked to fixed rates of exchange? Even so, can convertibility be achieved without at least a temporary recourse to fluctuating exchange rates?

In the Board's tentative answers, the first sketchy outlines of a Continental European viewpoint could be discerned. Carli was a skilled economist, with finely honed analytical powers. He called a convertibility that tolerated the maintenance of widespread quantitative import restrictions a 'caricature'. Ansiaux agreed fully with Carli that convertibility with continued import restrictions would be meaningless.

Rossy doubted that it would be possible to restrict convertibility to current transactions. 'The market would soon make it total.' Switzerland had once tried partial convertibility and had never suffered so great a

---

[2] OEEC Council, 'Recommendations Concerning Internal Financial Stability' (4 Aug. 1952). OEEC MBC(52)55.

[3] EPU Board Minutes, 25th Session (21–6 July 1952). OEEC MBC/M(52)7, Part I (Final).

[4] EPU Board, *Second Annual Report* (1952), 52–4.

[5] US del. airgram to Washington. REPTO A-607 (8 Nov. 1952).

capital loss as during the period when capital transfers were restricted. Ansiaux considered capital movements to be the 'regulator' of a convertible system; otherwise this role would fall exclusively on the exchange rate. Nor could he foresee an early move to convertibility without a steady and permanent capital flow from the US to Europe. That was unlikely to occur in the near future.

Rossy carried the discussion one step further by favouring another approach to convertibility 'within the framework of existing institutions, by gradually hardening the gold-credit ratio within the EPU, even if convertibility would in this way not be achieved this year or next year'. This was a first announcement of what became the institutional approach.

The tenor of this initial discussion ran counter to British thinking, but the British were poorly situated to resist. In August, Ellis-Rees had been promoted to head their OEEC delegation, and Bridge had been assigned to other responsibilities in the Bank of England. The new British nominee to the Managing Board was Alexander Grant, from the domestic side of the UK Treasury. For the convertibility discussions, he was instructed to seek a report that would keep all options open—and to offer no inkling of what the British government had in mind. 'Any British comments at the moment have to be cautious because we do not want to unmask our intentions—and we are not even sure what they are.'[6]

Making the best of a difficult job, Grant argued that there were many half-way houses to convertibility and that it would be a mistake to exclude any of them from further examination. That hardly sufficed to suppress opposition to a 'merely monetary' approach to convertibility without a concomitant abolition of trade and exchange restrictions.

On exchange rates, the discussion was less contentious. Most Board members believed that convertibility would be difficult to achieve on the basis of fixed exchange rates, within the narrow margins prescribed by the IMF's Articles of Agreement. A wider spread would probably be necessary. On this point, the Continentals hoped to be conciliatory to what the UK had in mind. Only later did they learn that Britain wanted no fixed limits on the floating of sterling, although it hoped for a stable rate.

A Unilateral Move?

When the Board reassembled in November 1952, more leaks had occurred about UK preparations for a Commonwealth Prime Ministers Conference, to be held shortly before a scheduled meeting of OEEC ministers in

[6] 'EPU and APU', internal note to Governor, Bank of England (12 Sept. 1952). Bank of England OV 46/58.

December. The Board's discussion therefore focused on the consequences for the EPU of a move to convertibility by one or a few countries.

Once again, von Mangoldt asked the Board to begin by identifying the major issues. Would it be possible for such a country to remain a member of the EPU? What would happen to relations between countries whose currencies became convertible and those that remained in-convertible? How would the EPU clearing operate if some countries introduced fluctuating rates of exchange?

The Board valiantly tried to formulate preliminary answers to such practical questions in the short time remaining before mid-December.[7] It concluded that fluctuating rates need not be an insurmountable obstacle to continued EPU membership. However, the Board agreed with the British that it would be difficult for a convertible member to remain in the EPU. Its currency would tend to become scarce, and other countries would try to earn such a currency and convert it into dollars, instead of allowing it to be spent within the EPU area. Only a dual system of convertibility, like Switzerland's, could be reconciled with continued participation in the EPU mechanism. The Swiss franc was convertible into other convertible currencies, but exchange restrictions applied to all non-convertible countries. The Board recognized that such an arrangement was not what the UK appeared to have in mind.

Its conclusions were incorporated in a preliminary report, circulated informally to the delegations assembled for the December ministerial meeting.[8] The Board was not pleased with its own efforts, undertaken without knowledge of British intentions. Nor were the British. They were still negotiating with the Commonwealth and had yet to approach the US. Any Board conclusions inconsistent with their plans could only complicate their other negotiations. A few weeks earlier, a telegram to Ellis-Rees had conveyed the Chancellor's view that 'We could not accept any [Managing Board] report with recommendations.'[9] The Board itself would have preferred to reason with the British before recording its views.

Since the British would not discuss their own concepts, the Board could report only on definitions and technicalities. However, through discussion of the issues, members reached consensus on a number of fundamental points. Grant and Getz Wold disassociated themselves from that consensus, though Getz Wold argued tenaciously that convertibility

---

[7] F. J. Portsmore, UK Alternate, 'Managing Board Discussion of Convertibility' (17–19 Nov. 1952). Bank of England OV 46/58, Nos. 107, 113, and 120. Also US del. circular tel. REPTO 84 (2 Dec. 1952).

[8] EPU Board Report, 'Preliminary Report on Some Aspects of the Problem of Convertibility' (11 Dec. 1952). OEEC TP(52)36.

[9] UK Foreign Office tel. to UK del. Paris for Ellis-Rees (13 Nov. 1952). PRO T 237/213.

would be premature at that time. The consensus can be summarized as follows:

The general economic preconditions for convertibility were not yet fulfilled. Foreign reserves were insufficient and payments equilibrium was lacking, both within Europe and with the dollar area.

Convertibility combined with continued foreign exchange restrictions offered very few attractions.

Breaking up the EPU would also end the OEEC trade rules and risk a return to bilateralism, at least in parts of Europe. Negotiating new rules would be lengthy and precarious.

The EPU itself would be a better vehicle for a concerted move to convertibility. Settlement rules within the system could be brought progressively nearer those governing payment relations with the dollar area.

Parallel to a 'hardening' of the EPU, dollar trade could be liberalized progressively. Thus, the EPU area and the dollar area would finally merge *de facto*—with respect to trade as well as payments. (As they finally did.)

The Tactics of Disdain

With the arrival of the new year, 1953, the Board's irritation came to a head. First, Ellis-Rees read a prepared statement to the OEEC Council, and Grant repeated it at the following meeting of the Managing Board.[10] The statement announced a UK intention to hold exploratory talks with the United States government on the transition to currency convertibility for sterling. Thereafter, if it was possible to formulate definite proposals, full discussions would be undertaken with European governments.

The Board's reactions ranged from disappointment to anger. It saw the statement as limited to describing a procedure, without any hint of the substance of British intentions beyond the vague announcements issued after the Commonwealth Conference. Grant could provide no further details.

Nor was the procedure at all satisfactory. Ansiaux and Calvet were bluntly critical. The Commonwealth Conference might have given a mandate to the UK, but the European nations had not. They had not even been consulted, though their vital interests were involved. Having reduced its own trade liberalization in Europe, the UK was hardly leading the way towards a 'wider' trade and payments system.

Other European countries also sought convertibility, and some were

---

[10] Ellis-Rees statement to Council (19 Jan. 1953). OEEC MBC(53)17. Board's reactions summarized in US del. tel. to Washington. REPTO 2322 (27 Jan. 1953).

better able to undertake it. They had no assurance that either their interests or those of Europe as a whole would be addressed in the US–UK conversations. Only bilateral discussions with European countries were intended, undercutting a multilateral approach and compromising the OEEC. Carli, Posthuma, Rossy, and von Mangoldt voiced similar resentment, although in milder language. Only Getz Wold expressed understanding for the British attitude and procedure.

As Ellis-Rees had anticipated, he encountered similar outbursts from his Council colleagues. Earlier, he had sent a memorandum and then gone to London with Marjolin to propose that the Continentals be 'put in the picture first'.[11] Otherwise, he reasoned, the UK could lose the leadership of Europe and the opportunity to shape its progress to greater unity along the lines 'we regard as most appropriate and convenient'. He had urged that the Commonwealth communiqué should refer to consultation with the OEEC and not merely with two or three selected European countries. He had returned to Paris empty-handed.

Whitehall proponents of the Collective Approach realized, of course, that the Continentals were unlikely to be persuaded that a purely monetary convertibility of sterling would serve their own interests. Prior negotiations with the Board, or with Continental governments, were bound to lead to an unacceptable watering down of the UK proposal, if not outright rejection.

If US support for the UK plan could first be assured, the Continentals might have to negotiate on British terms. London preferred, therefore, to risk initial European irritation rather than consult them first. The US would be even more difficult to persuade if it were privy to detailed European criticisms of the Collective Approach.

FORMULATING THE INSTITUTIONAL APPROACH

Perhaps London officials hoped their tactics would inhibit the Managing Board from recording further views about convertibility before their US visit. If so, they must have been disappointed by what ensued. In December 1952, the OEEC ministers had issued a routine directive for the Board to report on the renewal of the EPU after mid-1953. The Continental members saw in that assignment an opportunity to recommend improvements in the Union appropriate for progress toward convertibility. Six months of convertibility discussions had prepared the ground and sharpened their ideas. They were ready to prescribe how the EPU region should be opened up, with respect to both trade and payments.

---

[11] Ellis-Rees, 'The Commonwealth Conference and OEEC' (25 Nov. 1952). PRO T 230/213.

To open up trade, they proposed extending liberalization progressively to imports from the dollar area. Professor Posthuma's economic doctrines wholly accorded with those of the academic experts. 'It must be shown', he now declared, 'that EPU is not evolving toward a closed system . . . It must be demonstrated that EPU is not a "fortress" based on permanent discrimination against the United States . . .'.[12] Both Grant and Getz Wold protested. Grant saw 'no point in reducing trade discrimination against the dollar area, except as an insincere gesture for the purpose of getting more aid from the United States'. He did admit the dollar problem might be temporary. In that case, discrimination might be removed *pari passu* with the closing of the dollar gap.

As for payments, the creditors proposed an increase in the role of gold and dollars in the EPU. Outstanding debts could be repaid in instalments. In addition, or perhaps as an alternative, a higher ratio of gold to credit could be introduced for the monthly settlements. The creditors reasoned that the 40 per cent overall gold ratio that had prevailed hitherto reflected a 40 per cent convertibility of EPU currencies. Gradually increasing the ratio would lower the brick wall between the EPU and dollar area, layer by layer. At 100 per cent gold settlements, the wall would have disappeared.

Until that point was reached, the EPU would continue as a transitional arrangement. Proponents saw important advantages in prolonging a more convertible EPU. It would obviate the need for new trade and payments arrangements between European countries with convertible currencies and those that remained inconvertible. It would also avoid political and technical difficulties for the new European Coal and Steel Community and for the European Defence Community negotiators.

Hardening the EPU

A 'harder' EPU was scarcely a new idea. The Belgians had nearly refused to join the Union in 1950 because of its alleged 'softness'; they had threatened to withdraw early in 1952 unless their old debts were repaid in gold. In an attempt to meet these demands, the Managing Board had briefly considered—and quickly rejected—an increase in the gold ratio for debtors alone.

Only Rossy had offered solid support for Ansiaux's earlier efforts to harden the Union. Other members all felt that substantial credit was essential for continued trade liberalization, given low foreign exchange reserves and large balance-of-payments uncertainties. Creditors must take

---

[12] US del. airgram to Washington. REPTO A-821 (29 Dec. 1952).

measures to return to balance within the system and must not expect to earn dollars continually from the EPU.

By 1953, conditions had changed. Two more countries—Germany and the Netherlands—recognized that they, too, might well be persistent creditors in the Union. As early beneficiaries of the Union's 'softness', they had been reluctant to press deficit countries for more gold, even though their own surpluses were now accumulating. Nor were they willing to risk the deliberalization that might follow a reduction in credit available to deficit countries. With the Union's largest debtor—Great Britain— threatening an early move to convertibility, their reluctance no longer seemed warranted. Accordingly, von Mangoldt and Posthuma joined Ansiaux and Rossy in asking for a symmetrical increase in gold payments— by debtors and to creditors. As a first step, they suggested moving the gold ratio from 40 to 50 per cent. Carli supported his four colleagues despite Italy's balance-of-payments difficulties. Soon afterwards, Posthuma published a carefully reasoned article that explained the theoretical premisses of an approach to convertibility through 'improving the EPU'.[13]

The Bank of England would have endorsed hardening the EPU, much as it rejected a gradual, institutional approach to convertibility. Avid for early currency convertibility, it argued that excess EPU credit encouraged an 'unnaturally high level of intra-European trade with distorted price levels'.[14] The UK Alternate on the Managing Board proposed, in an internal Bank memorandum, to raise the gold percentage from 40 to 60 per cent, higher than the 50 per cent that the Continentals had gingerly suggested.[15] He would also have considered a scheme for repaying debts and credits outstanding for two or more years. Bank officials were thus ready to accept the logic of their own enthusiasm for sterling convertibility. The Treasury, on the other hand, insisted on keeping the Union's rules unaltered until the prospect for early convertibility was better defined. Grant was so instructed.

Getz Wold endorsed the UK's opposition to reducing the Union's credit element. Norway had run persistent deficits from the early days of the Union and expected to continue to do so. It had been borrowing as heavily as the private market would permit to finance its large and successful investment programme.

Getz Wold's views also had a strong philosophical underpinning, and he would elaborate them repeatedly throughout his tenure on the Managing Board. He felt that creditor countries should assume the major responsibility for correcting payments imbalances. They should take

---

[13] S. Posthuma, 'Notes on Convertibility'. Originally published in *Economia Internazionale* (1953), vi. 3. Reproduced in Posthuma (1982), 275–87.

[14] Jasper Rootham, memo to Bolton (8 Jan. 1953). Bank of England OV 46/58.

[15] Portsmore, 'Future of the EPU'. Internal memo (5 Jan. 1953). Bank of England OV 46/58.

measures to expand their economies, to remove all their barriers to imports, and to export capital. Responsibility for correcting imbalances in a payments system, whether regional or global, continues to be a controversial issue in the 1980s, despite three decades of debate and negotiation. How much of the initiative and the burden should be assumed by deficit countries or by those in surplus has never been resolved.

As the debate over hardening moved out into the OEEC corridors, adversaries ridiculed the proposals as a 'creditors' war-cry for hardening the onion'. On a more serious note, they warned that it would impede further liberalization within Europe. Nevertheless, after 1952, Getz Wold found little support for his views among Managing Board colleagues. British members were less well equipped than he to engage in doctrinal disputation with men like Carli and Posthuma. Nor was the British government then as single-minded about doctrine as about its specific proposal.

Calvet would have supported hardening as a matter of principle, but France's economic problems precluded his doing so. Language that made the proposal for a harder system less clear-cut would 'not drive him into the British camp'. He advised against firmly proposing a specific change in the settlement rules for the moment.

Grant was insisting that the EPU Agreement be revised to permit the UK (or any other member) to withdraw at any time, rather than only at the end of the financial year. In these circumstances, the Board majority decided it would be imprudent to press their proposals, and so they accepted Calvet's advice. Majority arguments for making the Union a more convertible system were included in the report the Board formulated late in February, while Butler was heading for Washington.[16] The only issue it asked the OEEC ministers to decide immediately was the right of a member to withdraw. Everyone understood that UK withdrawal would mean the end of the EPU.

Havlik summarized the Managing Board discussions and report in telegrams that circulated widely in Washington among Americans preparing for the British talks. Ambassador Draper sent a copy of the report, with a brief 'Dear George' letter, to Secretary Humphrey.[17] The letter called attention to one sentence that it quoted from the report: '. . . until a better payments system has been organized, the Union should be continued and improved in order to contribute to the achievement of the objectives of the Organisation and to allow a return to general convertibility.' Those

---

[16] EPU Board Report, 'Regarding the Future of the Union' (6 Mar. 1953). Report adopted during 34th session (16–21 Feb. and 4 Mar. 1953). OEEC C(53)71.

[17] William E. Draper, Jr., letter to The Honourable George M. Humphrey (2 Mar. 1953). US Archives. ECA/Paris Harriman Files.

in Washington who were sceptical about the British approach picked up the phrase about 'a better system' and repeated it regularly.

A Practical British Initiative

After their abortive mission to Washington, the British tried to maintain some momentum with their prospective, though reluctant, European partners. At the subsequent OEEC ministerial meeting, Eden and Butler announced trade liberalization measures. They also agreed to renew the EPU for another year without changing the withdrawal provisions.

Immediately afterwards, Grant told his Managing Board colleagues that the Bank of England would try to arrange a limited reopening of European private markets in foreign exchange. The proposed arrangement was for multilateral arbitrage of European currencies, a practical step indispensable to careful preparation for convertibility.

Freedom to engage in multilateral arbitrage permitted commercial banks in participating countries to trade foreign exchange with one another in order to eliminate discrepancies in the rates of exchange among the various currencies. The previous distortions in exchange rate quotations were not large, but arbitrage transactions permitted commercial banks to eliminate them while playing an active trading role. Arbitrage made 'the trans-ferability of currencies, inherent in the EPU system, a day-to-day reality in the foreign exchange markets', to quote a Managing Board annual report.[18]

Arbitrage did not affect the net positions of EPU members in the Union or the monthly settlements. Nor did it make European currencies more convertible, because there was no direct link with dollar markets. However, the bilateral balances that central banks reported to the EPU Agent dropped sharply. As a result of their new freedom, the commercial banks cleared on the market a significant portion of these balances.

Perhaps the most important effect of multilateral arbitrage was to force commercial banks to train a new generation of dealers in foreign exchange. In many countries, nearly a quarter of a century had passed since commercial banks were free to engage in such transactions. They had to seek out experienced personnel, reactivate retired foreign exchange dealers to train younger staff, and recycle administrators of foreign exchange restrictions into foreign exchange market operators. This British initiative thus prepared private banks for their role, once a move to convertibility could be undertaken. When currencies became convertible, the private banks would take over from the central banks and the Agent full responsibility for clearing and settling foreign exchange balances. Central

---

[18] EPU Board, *Fifth Annual Report* (1956), 67.

banks would only intervene on the markets to keep exchange rates within the declared margins.

INCONCLUSIVE ENCOUNTERS

Welcome as these UK steps were to the Continentals, disagreement about the best course to convertibility remained. Two very different approaches had been formulated by the time Butler returned from Washington, but neither the British nor the Continentals were ready for a definitive confrontation. Each side wanted to persuade the other and the Americans, but neither was prepared to negotiate or compromise. Both tried to advance their own views—but backed away from a fight.

The British hoped to maintain both the OEEC trade rules and OEEC discrimination against the dollar for a period after their move. If some major Continentals would join them, they thought agreement on such matters might be negotiable. If these partners would let their own rates fluctuate in tandem with sterling, so much the better. The prospective Continental participants did not relish these notions. They were pessimistic about persuading countries with inconvertible currencies to retain the OEEC trade rules under the conditions the UK proposed. Ansiaux caustically described British trade proposals as 'a leap into chaos and then try to organise it'.[19] The Continentals preferred their own cautious path to convertibility.

For von Mangoldt and other OEEC leaders, the path led first to Washington. Stassen had picked up a staff suggestion that the OEEC itself be invited to meet with the new administration. Such an invitation would underline a continuing US commitment to European integration and a willingness to deal with representatives of western Europe as a whole on major economic issues. In April 1953, an OEEC mission travelled to the United States. It was led by the Chairman of the permanent Council, Ellis-Rees, and received by the cabinet officers who had met with the British a few weeks earlier.

On the matter of convertibility, the Americans were even less prepared to negotiate with the OEEC than they had been with the UK. Von Mangoldt felt that the US administration was split and would take no stand on the convertibility issue in the foreseeable future. His impression was accurate. Stassen wanted to preserve the EPU and the OEEC trade liberalization programme, while encouraging the Board and the OEEC to press forward with dollar liberalization. Burgess wanted to encourage the

---

[19] US del. tel. to Washington. ECOTO 126 (15 Apr. 1953).

British to pursue convertibility at an early date. Under the circumstances, neither would speak his mind to the OEEC visitors.

At a State Department meeting on 10 April 1953, von Mangoldt referred to the Board's work 'on how to improve the functioning of the EPU and to strengthen its role'.[20] This could be achieved by raising gold payments or by debt repayment, thus increasing the extent to which European currencies were convertible into dollars. His audience was interested but not responsive, and he concluded that Europeans would have to decide among themselves the appropriate route to convertibility.

After von Mangoldt's return to Europe, Ansiaux submitted a document to the Board, elaborating in considerable detail the creditors' ideas about reforming the EPU into a more convertible system.[21] He offered five specific suggestions: (1) a 50 per cent gold/credit ratio; (2) a 20 per cent increase in quotas, thus maintaining the existing amount of automatic credit in the system; (3) larger gold payments to creditors for post-quota surpluses; (4) repayment of old debts in instalments; (5) raising interest rates on EPU credits to correspond to market rates.

Grant protested that this was a direct attack on the Collective Approach, as indeed it was. Upon reflection, the proponents of the institutional approach decided not to force a confrontation with the British, lest it result in a precipitous UK move to convertibility. Instead, they recommended continuing the Union for another year without any major changes.

Even in bilateral talks, the British received little encouragement from the governments they had identified as potential participants in the Collective Approach. From an economic standpoint, no country was then better able than Germany to undertake the risks of convertibility. Yet when Butler and Peter Thorneycroft (President of the British Board of Trade) met with Ministers Erhard and Blücher in London on 11–13 May 1953, they found no meeting of the minds. Erhard was not interested in non-resident convertibility. He saw convertibility as the removal of all restrictions on all transactions with foreign countries, and he said so repeatedly in speeches, at home and abroad. His preaching on 'real convertibility' earned his interpreter an internationally recognized nickname—'Miss Convertibility'.

Erhard's intense convictions also led him to criticize the EPU and the OEEC programme of gradual liberalization. He had only disdain for their 'liberalisation seesaw', which permitted countries to vary trade restrictions with EPU accounting positions. The British thus considered Erhard to be more of an irritant than an ally. On more than one occasion, von Mangoldt reminded him that German credibility in multilateral co-operation suffered from his freewheeling speeches.

---

[20] Von Mangoldt report to Bonn (25 Apr. 1953). G/17/53.
[21] Ansiaux, 'Proposals for the Prolongation of the EPU' (24 Apr. 1953). OEEC MBC(53)70.

An Unstable Truce

Agreement in June 1953 to renew the EPU for another year only reflected a truce. Neither the Continentals nor the British were prepared to retreat from their positions. The moment for compromise had not arrived. For one of the few times in the life of the EPU, the Board went public with its disagreements, in its *Third Annual Report*.[22]

A section on 'Possible Improvements in the Working of the Union' presented the institutional approach, listing Ansiaux's specific proposals. Another section on 'Problems Connected with Convertibility' mentioned the British proposals, though without specific details. The existence of two alternative and competing approaches was clear.

Meanwhile, the Board had been instructed to prepare a report on the British convertibility plan for a ministerial meeting at the end of October. The British Treasury finally provided the OEEC Secretariat with a summary of its proposals and agreed to a four-point condensation: (1) non-resident convertibility of currently acquired sterling; (2) a fluctuating dollar/sterling exchange rate without fixed limits; (3) maintenance of quantitative restrictions on imports and of exchange control restrictions during a transition period after sterling convertibility was initiated; (4) formulation thereafter of rules for using quantitative restrictions to protect the balance of payments. The principal world trading countries would establish these rules, and a new international body would administer them. The UK also listed preconditions for its move: an increase in IMF resources, increased UK foreign exchange reserves, improved US trade policies, and adjustments in the internal economic policies of members of the sterling area.

Once again, the Board had little zest for its mandate. Nor did its response lead to any agreement at the ministerial meeting. Although Ellis-Rees had concurred with von Mangoldt's suggestion that the report be short and interim, disagreement about its content was prolonged.[23] After only one year, Grant had been replaced by another Treasury official, John Owen, who was not well known to the veteran members of the Board. The Board did not think it useful to examine the UK proposals in detail, since the preconditions had not been met. Nor could Owen persuade his colleagues about the value of a 'What if . . .' report. Ansiaux even questioned the British preconditions. He thought an increase in IMF resources and a substantial change in US trade policy might be desirable, but not really necessary. Both Carli and Calvet stated that the internal economic situation of some important EPU countries (particularly their own) rendered premature any move to currency convertibility. Once

[22] EPU Board, *Third Annual Report* (1953), 87–94.
[23] US del. circular airgram. ECOTO A-112 (15 Oct. 1953).

again the Board's report asserted that conditions were not yet ripe.[24] It urged moving forward with trade liberalization for the present, both within Europe and with the dollar area. The Board preferred to deal with a problem it considered more immediate and realistic—improving the EPU.

As a result, the October 1953 ministerial meeting consisted of nothing more than long but inconclusive discussions about convertibility.[25] The ministers' views were no different than those of their representatives on the Managing Board. The British announced further liberalization of their OEEC trade to 75 per cent, but said they were unable to accept changes in the EPU system that would add to their financial burdens. Nonetheless, they wanted to maintain the momentum of their proposals. Erhard suggested a ministerial study group on convertibility, but gained no support. He even evoked a mild reprimand from Stassen, who preferred to use the existing OEEC organs.[26] The Managing Board was asked to submit proposals for renewing the EPU for a fifth year, beginning after June 1954.

REVIVING THE INSTITUTIONAL APPROACH

When the Board met in November 1953, the creditors introduced proposals for automatic and continuous repayment of credits outstanding for more than eighteen months. Posthuma, Ansiaux, and Hans Möller (the German Alternate) subsequently wrote a memorandum for further study.[27] In its *Third Annual Report*, the Board had featured debt repayment, with a sweetener for debtors. New credit facilities would be opened immediately for those agreeing to repay long-outstanding debts over a period of years. During the summer of 1953, the creditor countries had concluded that debt repayment might meet less resistance than an increase in the gold ratio.

To make their proposal even more palatable, the creditors now added a further offer. Debtors who subsequently ran monthly surpluses could recover any gold they had paid. This would require a new technical complication, which came to be called a 'gold sandwich *tranche*'. A 100 per cent gold *tranche*, corresponding to gold payments against debts, would be inserted into the quotas. The concept gave journalists a golden

---

[24] EPU Board Report, 'Payments Arrangements in Western Europe' (13 Oct. 1953). OEEC C(53)253.

[25] 'Minutes of 231st meeting (29–30 Oct. 1953). OEEC C/M(53)30.

[26] US del. circular airgram. ECOTO A-145 (7 Nov. 1953).

[27] EPU Board memo, 'Proposals for a Reimbursement Scheme and the Treatment of Extreme Creditors' (10 Dec. 1953). OEEC MBC(53)137.

opportunity to display their sense of humour. It also helped ingrain the notion that the EPU was a technical machine beyond the comprehension of laymen. Although complicated, the proposal was workable and constructive. It was attractive to countries needing more credit but reluctant to part for long with foreign exchange reserves.

By late 1953, all four major creditors had exhausted their quotas and were settling post-quota surpluses by extending 50 per cent credit. They now proposed to continue to do so only until their surpluses exceeded their quotas by 40 per cent. For the next 40 per cent, they sought 70 per cent gold settlements, and for surpluses twice the size of their quotas, 100 per cent gold.

Owen and Getz Wold again opposed these proposals, and debate continued throughout the winter of 1953–4. For the first time, the creditors' club voiced a reluctance to continue the EPU unless its demands were met. The financial strength of its members was growing, and they were taking steps toward convertibility. Germany was preparing to make its currency transferable throughout the non-dollar world and was liberalizing restrictions on dollar imports. The Dutch and Belgians were discussing the abolition of all exchange restrictions between their two countries. Emminger, now a Director of the German central bank, told the Secretariat that Erhard might force German withdrawal from the EPU during the course of 1954 if reasonable demands were not met.[28]

France and Italy were most vulnerable to this threat, and Calvet and Carli sought a compromise. If the Union were liquidated, France would have to repay some $300 million within three years, Italy about $100 million. Moreover, France would lose the chance to recover some of the $600 million in gold it had already paid the Union. Under EPU rules, it could recover that gold by running a series of EPU monthly surpluses.

Consequently, both France and Italy feared an early liquidation of the EPU, either as a result of a British move to convertibility or the withdrawal of some creditor countries from the system. Both countries began to explore the possibility of debt repayment on easier terms than the EPU liquidation rules provided. Italy had an additional reason for repaying its EPU debts. Reopening its EPU credit facilities by agreeing to a firm schedule for paying off debts would offer an effective counter to internal pressures for reducing liberalization.[29] As far back as mid-1952, Italy had liberalized 100 per cent of its European imports, and its officials were now resisting any retreat. The situation of the United Kingdom concerning debts was comparable to that of France and Italy. It would have to repay about $550 million if the EPU were liquidated.

[28] J. F. Cahan, OEEC Secretariat internal staff memo (11 Feb. 1954). OEEC JFC 90.
[29] US Embassy Rome tel. to US del. Paris. ECOTO 288 (8 Feb. 1954).

Britain Reclaims the Initiative

At the Managing Board meeting in March 1954, Owen made two major announcements concerning British measures to free the use of sterling.[30] The first was to widen its transferability, permitting sterling held by any country outside the dollar area to move freely from centres with a surplus of sterling to centres that were short. The second was to reopen the London gold market to all non-residents of the sterling area. Although neither measure permitted the convertibility of sterling to be extended to the dollar area, both were further preparatory steps, consistent with the gradual institutional approach.

At about the same time, Butler and Reginald Maudling (Salter's successor as UK Economic Secretary) decided to begin negotiations with the EPU creditors. However, they first met with the Anglo-Scandinavian Economic Committee to explain their decision to those who hitherto had been their principal supporters within the EPU. The Scandinavians agreed reluctantly to join the British in negotiating about debt repayment. But they insisted that the UK join them in demanding further trade concessions from Germany, then the major EPU creditor.

The British made their offer to the OEEC Council, not to the Managing Board.[31] On 2 April 1954, Ellis-Rees began by rejecting creditor proposals for a formal and continuous repayment scheme. However, he admitted that the EPU was '. . . in fact, in danger of grinding to a standstill'. Only some $200 million of credit was left for debtors. The UK therefore proposed an *ad hoc* contribution to reducing its past indebtedness. It would pay $84 million to the four major creditor countries, against a debt of $350 million it would have to assume toward them if the EPU were then liquidated. It would also agree to repay the remaining $266 million over a period of years. In return, it would expect these creditors to adopt 'good creditor' policies. Germany, in particular, should adopt a comprehensive programme of internal and external measures to keep its EPU payments position in balance. It should no longer continue to run surpluses, as it had for several years.

Still disdainful of the Managing Board, the UK wanted to open bilateral discussions immediately with the four major creditors. Roger Ockrent, head of the Belgian delegation to the OEEC, made a 'slashing attack' on the UK plan, primarily because of its bilateral character.[32] The US delegation further reported that the 'Dutch delegate matched Ockrent in bluntness and exceeded him in sarcasm'. The creditors initially

[30] EPU Board Minutes, 46th Session (15–20 Mar. 1954). OEEC MBC/M(54)3, Part I, Annex I.
[31] 'Basis of a Statement made by the United Kingdom Del. to the Council' (2 Apr. 1954). OEEC CES/296.
[32] US del. tel. to Washington. ECOTO 1362 (8 Apr. 1954).

assumed the proposal was part of a British plan to leave the EPU and move soon to convertibility with a floating rate. Its debt repayment proposal looked like an attempt to get easier terms than the EPU liquidation rules provided. Some debtors—Italy, the Scandinavian countries, and Ireland—generally supported the British proposal. It was referred to the Managing Board for study.

Moving Toward Compromise

At the April meeting of the Board, Calvet made an 'analogous' French offer, but 'with certain adjustments'.[33] France would repay or fund its entire debt to the EPU, making payments to all creditors. His proposal was more multilateral than the UK offer. It sought to continue and solidify the EPU as a system, while the UK wanted *ad hoc* bilateral agreements to render the EPU viable for only another year.

After reviewing the specific proposals, the creditors found few advantages in either of them.[34] Posthuma insisted on systematic repayment of all future debts. All the creditors noted that the entire amount of the debts to be amortized would be removed immediately from the books of the Union, and debtor quotas would be reopened simultaneously in the same amounts. Creditors would thus undertake new lending obligations before a penny had been paid under the bilateral amortization agreements. In addition, the creditors observed that the UK had accepted the suggestion about a gold sandwich *tranche*, but sought more than the creditors had offered. The entire amount of any debt to be repaid under an amortization agreement would be put into the sandwich, not just the amounts actually repaid.

The creditors had another two specific objections. The British were offering to pay off the debts over a seven-year period. The EPU liquidation rules provided for repayment over only three years, unless the bilateral partners agreed otherwise or the OEEC decided on a different period. Moreover, France and the UK were offering to repay in cash only 15 per cent of their outstanding debt to the EPU as a whole. This was less than half the amount the creditors might expect in the event of liquidation.

Such creditor reactions led to negotiations as intense as those concerning the original EPU Agreement in 1950. Discussions ensued at all levels. Governments held interdepartmental reviews, followed by bilateral meetings and cabinet-level debate. Primarily, however, the negotiations fell back on the Managing Board.

The result was a continuous advance toward a broader package of

[33] US del. tel. to Washington. ECOTO 1382 (13 Apr. 1954).

[34] US del. circular tel., 'Managing Board Discussion UK Debt Repayment Proposals. ECOTO 10 (29 Apr. 1954).

EPU reforms. The Union was refurbished, as well as renewed. The eventual package went beyond the earlier patchwork of self-serving proposals, achieving a better balance of interests between creditors and debtors. In the process, emphasis was refocused on the viability of the Union itself, rather than the interests of individual members. The end product was also a technically simpler arrangement. Happily, the gold sandwich *tranche*—and other complications—fell by the wayside.

THE REFURBISHED EPU

How was the final balance struck? How were the old debts amortized and new credit lines opened?[35]

As finally agreed, the repayment scheme was neither automatic nor continuous, as the creditors wanted, nor was it selective, as the UK proposed. Though participation was voluntary, all creditors took part and eventually all debtors, except for Greece, Iceland, and Turkey.

New credit was reopened only as old debts were repaid. Creditors could treat the remaining debt as a liquid asset on the books of the Union. If they ran deficits, their cumulative position in the Union would be reduced on the usual 'last-in, first-out' basis. They would settle by repaying the 50 per cent they had received earlier in gold and by drawing on their credit balances with the Union to cover the remaining 50 per cent.

Three-quarters of all the credit outstanding at the end of June 1954 was to be amortized, $858 million out of $1,142 million. Individual debtors agreed to repay in instalments from 60 to 90 per cent of their outstanding debts. Down payments on the amortized debt amounted to $224 million, as agreed bilaterally between debtors and creditors.

The EPU paid an additional $130 million to the creditors out of its assets. That left the Union with $414 million, well above the initial US capital contribution of $350 million.

The down payments, as well as the amounts repaid by the Union itself, were used to reopen immediate new credit lines. The debtors thus began the fifth year of the EPU with $590 million of actual borrowing facilities. Amortization payments would reopen their credit lines further, *pro tanto*. At the end of June 1954, before the adjustments of the reform package, only $204 million of new credit was still available to EPU debtors. Creditors accepted a new lending ceiling of nearly $1 billion.

The UK made a special arrangement with Germany. After a down

---

[35] Results incorporated in a further EPU Board Report, 'Renewal of EPU After 30 June 1954' (21 June 1954). OEEC C(54)161.

payment of $35 million, the remainder of its bilateral debt would be offset against German obligations to the UK under the London debt agreement of 1953.

At Last, a Higher Gold Ratio

Near the end of the negotiations, an equally important feature was added concerning a long-unresolved dispute about the Union's gold/credit ratio. The creditors had earlier given up their battle, but the Secretariat now offered a proposal in the interest of the Union itself.[36] All future surpluses and deficits that fell within the quotas should be settled on a flat 50:50 basis, for debtors and creditors alike.

This meant a major simplification of the EPU mechanism, and the debtors accepted it readily. Most were already settling deficits with more than 50 per cent gold, because they were in the upper *tranches* of their debtor quotas. The proposal also assured the future liquidity of the Union since all subsequent surpluses and deficits would be settled in identical proportions of gold and credit. The liquidity crisis of late 1951 could not reappear under this arrangement.

Significance of the Reform

The outcome of a year and a half of persistent wrangling was an agreement with advantages for both debtors and creditors. Firmly entrenched initial negotiating positions had yielded to realities and the need for compromise, but the compromises did not damage the major interests of any participant. Bilateral negotiations determined both the amounts and terms of the repayments, permitting each side to arrive at an acceptable bargain.

In EPU jargon of the time, debt repayment was generally referred to as 'debt consolidation' and was central to reforming the Union. In turn, the reform itself consolidated much more than debts and credits. By putting the EPU on solid footing until 'a better system' was available, it consolidated the institutional approach to convertibility. For the first time, the British appeared willing to permit the EPU to be the vehicle for joint progress toward convertibility.

The refurbishing also reflected a major change in the basic premiss upon which the Union was first organized. The emphasis henceforth would be on persuading countries to balance their foreign exchange accounts on a global basis, not on a regional basis. Countries in global balance could earn surpluses within the Union to offset deficits elsewhere

---

[36] 'Mechanism of EPU' (26 May 1954). OEEC TFD/DI 220 (1st revision). Initial secretariat proposal by Waters, clarified in memo by Cahan (26 May 1954). OEEC JFC-273.

and vice versa, without being vulnerable to charges of dereliction in their responsibilities to the system. If the system was still only partially convertible for the moment, full convertibility was now embedded in its philosophy.

The Union was hardened both by the 'consolidation' of old debts and by formally increasing the ratio of gold to credit in settling current imbalances. In practical terms, the higher gold ratio was insignificant because creditors were already receiving 50 per cent in gold and debtors were paying 50 per cent or more. But that symbolic step eliminated any future possibility of softer settlements through major reversals of country positions from cumulative surplus to deficit, or vice versa.

More important, the 1954 package set the stage for agreement on further hardening. Simplifying the settlement rules to apply equally to all members, whatever their debtor or creditor position, meant that further hardening would seem more equitable. A country's position within the *tranches* of its quota would lose all significance. Agreement on debt repayment also opened the way for additional amortization agreements in the course of subsequent EPU renewals.

The EPU became a more viable system, with more credit available to support further intra-European trade liberalization. In the absence of the reform, the system would have become as choked as the IEPS system was in 1949, and trade liberalization might have suffered.

With most members' foreign exchange reserves continuing to increase despite debt repayment, progress was encouraged toward dollar liberalization and other steps toward convertibility. During the year after refurbishment, aggregate reserves of EPU members grew by $1.4 billion. Only Denmark and Great Britain experienced a significant reduction, as a result primarily of internal economic developments rather than paying off debts to the EPU.[37] The redistribution of foreign exchange reserves within Europe through debt repayment was thus a relatively minor matter.

The US remained supportive but passive throughout the debate about the details of the reform package. It could welcome the final compromises without playing a partisan role. Thereafter, it concentrated on seeking further liberalization of dollar imports. This confirmed the Europeans' belief that they would have to decide among themselves how convertibility should be achieved. That would be the Managing Board's next major order of business.

---

[37] OEEC, *Seventh Report: Economic Expansion and its Problems* (1956), 127–38 and 257–72.

12 Charting the Course: The European Monetary Agreement

Although the British agreed to refurbishing the EPU in May 1954, they had yet to abandon their own plans for convertibility. Earlier that year, they had failed in another attempt to gain American support. Thereafter, they actively sought Continental endorsement of the essential features of their Collective Approach. The Continentals were given the impression that a British move to non-resident convertibility, probably with a freely floating rate, was imminent. Hence they agreed to further discussions.

This did not mean capitulation. They still had serious reservations about UK concepts and timing, preferring instead their own gradual, institutional approach. The stronger countries were already implementing convertibility for their own residents. Switzerland had never abandoned resident convertibility, and Germany and the Benelux countries were far down the road toward removing foreign exchange restrictions and ending discrimination. By November 1954, the Benelux countries had freed 86 per cent of their dollar imports, and Germany had freed 79 per cent of imports of manufactured goods from the dollar area.[1]

Although the stronger countries were moving toward convertibility, they were not ready to break up the EPU. They were wary of steps that might threaten European political co-operation and intra-European trade liberalization. The weaker countries were apprehensive about their balance-of-payments prospects. Both Italy and France maintained quantitative restrictions on almost all their imports from the dollar area, and France had just begun to resume intra-European liberalization. They were eager to delay a final move to convertibility and a resulting end to the EPU. The stronger Continentals concurred, preferring to await further recovery in the weaker countries before breaking up the Union. They also feared a premature British move, lest it rely too much on a floating rate and a depreciating pound sterling.

Charting a common course from such divergent approaches to convertibility seemed a formidable, if not impossible, task. Neither the Continental ministers nor the Managing Board relished the assignment. The negotiations for terminating the EPU at the moment of convertibility proved almost as difficult as those for bringing it to life. Economic and political changes in the United Kingdom itself eventually opened the

---

[1] OEEC (1957), 29 and 91.

door to agreement. But the British had a very different route in mind when they first turned to the Continent.

IMPASSE IN WASHINGTON

Seeking American support for a move to convertibility, the UK initiated discussions about an IMF standby credit early in 1954. The US was willing for the UK to have a credit of $1.3 billion, its full IMF quota, but no more. It thought that another $1 billion of IMF funds should be reserved for Belgium, France, Germany, and the Netherlands—other countries that might participate in a general move to convertibility.[2] The Americans also sought a better definition of post-convertibility trade arrangements than the Collective Approach memorandum had offered. Above all, they wanted the standby to obligate the UK to abandon all forms of discrimination in trade as soon as funds were drawn.

The British Cabinet was not ready for such a commitment. Only 4 per cent of UK imports of manufactured goods from North America had been liberalized, and British industry was demanding continued protection.[3] Controlling imports from the dollar area remained firm Conservative policy. In both the GATT and IMF forums, the UK had found it necessary to promise to end discrimination within one year of adopting convertibility. The Cabinet was loath to authorize steps that might trigger those promises.

By mid-1954, discussions with the US were near an impasse. To maintain some momentum for the Collective Approach, the UK began to look for reconciliation with the Continentals. Perhaps that would also weaken the rigidity of the US position. Intensive preparations were initiated to ensure successful negotiations with the Continentals, as well as with the Americans. A Collective Approach Committee of senior British officials, chaired by Sir Bernard Gilbert, was organized to address the issues.

THE MINISTERIAL EXAMINATION GROUP ON CONVERTIBILITY

For their May 1954 meeting, OEEC ministers had again asked the Managing Board to prepare a report on convertibility. Coming not long after the US had published the Randall Commission report (see Chapter 10), the assignment did not seem very urgent. Refurbishing the EPU was

---

[2] Louis Rasminsky, Canadian IMF Exec. Director, extract from note to Bank of England. Bank of England OV 44/62.
[3] OEEC (1957), 119.

a more pressing and immediate task. The Board's report on 'Problems of a Move to Convertibility' was admittedly a summary of previous studies that did not necessarily reflect the views of all members.[4] In the spring of 1954, specific constructive suggestions about arrangements for convertibility still seemed premature.

Butler had previously registered discontent with the attitude the Managing Board had displayed toward British proposals in its October 1953 report.[5] Annoyed by continued cavalier treatment, the British were determined to distance the Board from further work on the Collective Approach. Responding to Butler's initiative, the OEEC ministers adopted Erhard's suggestion of the previous October. A Ministerial Examination Group on Convertibility, with a limited membership, was established to consider trade, as well as financial, issues. As Chairman of both the OEEC Council and the Ministerial Group, Butler called a meeting for July 1954 at Lancaster House in London.

Cobbold, Bolton, and Rowan were once again pressing the Chancellor to move to convertibility.[6] Warm and affable in his personal relations, Governor Cobbold could be as tenacious as a bulldog about his official responsibilities. He was dedicated to restoring the prestige of sterling and opening up the London foreign exchange market to all kinds of sterling transactions. He bridled at the continued existence of two markets for converting sterling into dollars. The official market in London operated on the par value notified to the IMF, but sterling that was transferable among non-residents of the dollar area could not be sold there for dollars. An alternative market had grown up, primarily in New York and Zurich, where transferable sterling could be exchanged for dollars at a lower rate than the official one. 'Cheap sterling' was an anathema to a man deeply conscious of his responsibility for the currency. Moreover, the City of London resented the loss of foreign exchange business to other markets.

Aware of Cabinet reservations, Cobbold suggested not announcing convertibility as such, lest the US insist on a concomitant commitment to end dollar discrimination. Instead, the UK should seek an IMF standby agreement to support a preliminary step—unifying the exchange rates for transferable and American account sterling. He also warned that 'agreement on an IMF standby credit would take us further along the road and make reversal of policies more difficult . . . if we did not take the further step within six months or a year it might well lead to lack of confidence.'[7] Rowan endorsed this advice.

[4] EPU Board Report, 'Problems of a Move to Convertibility' (14 Apr. 1954). OEEC C(54)103.

[5] Cahan memo on recent visit to London (27 Oct. 1953). OEEC JFC-552.

[6] Otto Clarke, the other member of the ROBOT team, was no longer involved in external issues. He had been promoted to position on domestic side of Treasury in 1953.

[7] Rowan, 'Record of a Discussion at the Treasury' (3 June 1954). Chancellor, Governor of Bank of England, and senior advisers were present. PRO T 230/268.

Sir Robert Hall, chief of the cabinet's economic secretariat, urged greater caution, as he had since ROBOT burst on the scene. He felt that prudence called for first removing dollar discrimination gradually in both Great Britain and the rest of the sterling area. Much of the recent increase in dollar reserves, he also noted, had been matched by an increase in sterling liabilities.[8]

Butler refused to endorse Cobbold's proposal. He could not accept an implicit commitment about timing, nor was he willing to be bound politically by the public announcement of an IMF standby agreement. The Gilbert Committee turned to preparations for the OEEC Ministerial Examination Group. A substantial British paper was circulated in advance of the meeting and was first discussed at the preliminary meeting of ministerial deputies.[9]

The paper was basically a restatement of the Collective Approach. It contained six major proposals, each of which proved to be more or less controversial: (1) continue the OEEC trade rules for a transitional period after convertibility; (2) establish a European Fund that could lend to countries that might otherwise feel constrained to reduce trade liberalization or discriminate against the newly convertible European currencies; (3) negotiate new global trade rules in the GATT to ban quantitative restrictions for balance-of-payments reasons, as far as possible, but with an escape clause for discriminating against any persistent creditor; (4) use limited inter-central bank credits to replace unlimited EPU interim finance; (5) leave foreign exchange rate policy for each country to decide on its own; (6) establish an IMF-GATT Joint Advisory Group. Only the first two of these proposals survived intact.

For the first time in the convertibility debates, the British were aggressively seeking a European endorsement of their Collective Approach. They encountered a unanimous feeling that the kind of co-operation established in the OEEC was far more effective in handling trade and payments problems than would be possible in global organizations. The Continentals preferred to maintain an OEEC role in these areas after convertibility.[10]

Apart from agreeing that some sort of European Fund should be established, the formal London Ministerial Group meeting resolved very little. Stassen headed a large delegation that put forward US views. Although the language was mild, the variance with some British thinking was unmistakable. The Americans wanted full intra-European and dollar liberalization as rapidly as European balance-of-payments positions would

---

[8] Hall memo, 'Convertibility—Where We Stand' (21 June 1954). Bank of England OV 44/63.

[9] OEEC, 'Report on Convertibility'. Note by the UK del. (4 June 1954). OEEC GMC(54)1.

[10] Ellis-Rees report on June meeting of Deputies. UK del. tel. 465 (21 June 1954). PRO T 232/44.

permit. They were willing for the EPU residual assets contributed by the US to be transferred to the proposed European Fund. However, they would also welcome a European contribution. The IMF-GATT Advisory Group was unnecessary, though arrangements might be made for greater co-operation between the two organizations.[11] Under these circumstances, the Continental ministers could restrain their own criticisms for the time being.

After listening to the prepared statements, the ministers referred the preparation of arrangements for an orderly transition to convertibility to the group of deputies. The Deputies Group met in October and again in December before reporting to another meeting of the Ministerial Group in January 1955.

None of these meetings produced conclusive results. A better understanding was achieved about national attitudes toward the issues raised by convertibility. Disagreements did engage cabinet-level attention. However, the *ad hoc* meetings of the ministers and their deputies were better suited to exchanging views and achieving consensus about generalities than to meaningful compromise and the conclusion of final agreements. The financial issues surrounding a transition to convertibility, together with their broader trade implications, had repeatedly to be returned to the Managing Board. The Board had by then become a strong collegial entity, an institution with a capacity for finding a way to reach intra-European agreements and convert them into binding instruments.

Butler Slows the Pace

The January 1955 ministerial meetings marked a critical step forward in Britain's willingness to accommodate the Continentals. Preceding economic and political developments in the UK contributed to this change in attitude.

In his March 1954 Budget, Chancellor Butler had reduced business taxes, although the British economy was booming and unemployment was hardly more than 1 per cent. Inflationary pressures began to build thereafter, and the UK's foreign exchange reserves fell by $255 million in the second half of 1954. By 1955, early signs of a new sterling crisis were looming.[12] These developments forced a slowdown in the British convertibility timetable, and the UK became increasingly more amenable to Continental concerns.

Political factors also dictated a slower pace. The French had rejected the European Defence Community on 30 August 1954, evoking British

---

[11] OEEC Trade and Finance Directorate, 'Summary of Statements by Ministers', London meeting (15–16 July 1954). OECD EPU Archive Box 43, unnumbered internal document.
[12] Cairncross (1987).

concern about political disintegration in western Europe. Moreover, an ageing Churchill was expected to turn over the reins to Eden, after which an election would be held to confirm the new Cabinet, probably in the autumn of 1955.

At the Washington meetings of IMF Governors in September 1954, Butler and Maudling (UK Economic Secretary) had let it be known that convertibility was unlikely to occur until after a British election.[13] To Bolton's dismay, Secretary Humphrey was very relaxed when Butler told him that convertibility would be postponed because of UK domestic political difficulties. '. . . they do not really care what we do, whether we remain inconvertible or become convertible.'[14]

Under these circumstances, the January 1955 ministerial meetings identified three major issues and commissioned efforts to resolve them: (1) the European Fund; (2) post-convertibility trade arrangements; and (3) exchange rate policies. The first was assigned to the Managing Board; the second, to the Deputies Group. The UK preferred to refer exchange rates to the central bank governors and their technical experts at the BIS. The British also agreed that the EPU should be renewed for another year. That became the Managing Board's first and easiest task.

None of these matters could be resolved completely until an agreement was reached on the others. Between January and July 1955, separate but simultaneous negotiations were pursued on each issue. None was settled finally until all had been compromised and incorporated into a single agreement.

EXTENDING THE EPU

Tackling its first assignment with alacrity, the Managing Board began to consider the terms for EPU renewal after June 1955. Unlike earlier extensions, the disagreements that arose were low key, and compromises were readily achieved. Indeed, it proved to be the most harmonious renewal the Managing Board had thus far experienced.

At the very outset, the Board agreed that another general debt consolidation was unnecessary, though individual debtors might wish to make a voluntary arrangement. The French Finance Minister had already told his OEEC colleagues that France would repay its entire $80 million of unconsolidated EPU debt.[15] That took care of the only major remaining debt that had been outstanding for very long.

---

[13] Bolton, letters to Cobbold from Washington (24 Sept. and 2 Oct. 1954). Bank of England OV 44/64 and OV 46/65.

[14] Bolton letter to Cobbold (24 Sept. 1954). Bank of England OV 44/64.

[15] Edgar Faure, 'Statement to OEEC Min. Council' (13 Jan. 1955). OEEC MBC(55)4.

To no one's surprise, Posthuma promptly suggested raising the EPU gold settlement ratio to 75 per cent. Only Hartogsohn, who had again rotated with Getz Wold, rejected the idea flatly, for essentially the same reason that his Scandinavian colleague had so often propounded. Hardening would reduce the pressure on creditors to bring their EPU payments into balance. Calvet and Owen were reserved, but not outrightly opposed to Posthuma's suggestion.

A month later, in February 1955, the British Chancellor authorized intervention in the foreign exchange markets to support the transferable sterling exchange rate. It was a major step, taken at a moment when the rate for transferable sterling had dropped to $2.70 and 'cheap sterling' was distorting the markets. It brought sterling close to becoming a convertible currency, narrowing the discount on transferable sterling to about 1 per cent. Butler gained immediate cabinet approval for that decision with no warning of its importance and not much discussion.[16]

By the February Managing Board meeting, Calvet and Owen were ready to agree to 75 per cent gold settlements in the EPU. Increased French foreign exchange reserves enabled Calvet to accept an idea that he had long approved in principle. Owen's conversion to hardening was a logical necessity, given British support of the market rate for transferable sterling. Unless the EPU were hardened, other members would be tempted to use its interim finance to draw sterling and sell it for dollars in Zurich or New York. The 1 per cent discount would hardly deter members who settled only half of their EPU accounts in dollars. To be sure, such use of sterling drawings would be an abuse of Article 8 of the EPU Agreement, but the UK could hardly protest without risking a further loss of confidence in its already troubled currency. With only 25 per cent credit in EPU settlements, the incentive for such abuse would be much weaker.

Ansiaux, Carli, and Rossy tried to take advantage of the new situation by launching a trial balloon—settle current imbalances entirely in gold and offer *ad hoc* credits to members who had temporary difficulty in making payments. The European Fund could be started up to finance the *ad hoc* credits, as part of the EPU Agreement. All the creditors, of course, would have been in favour. Carli's support stemmed from a practical consideration, as well as from principle—Italy needed credit and, in fact, would receive a $50 million special credit from the EPU in April.[17]

Owen objected vigorously to the 100 per cent idea, and Calvet, as well as Hartogsohn, supported him.[18] All three agreed that a 100 per cent gold EPU would mean convertibility, while the ministers had instructed

---

[16] Cairncross (1987).
[17] EPU Board Minutes, 57th Session (13–16 Apr. 1955). OEEC MBC/M(55)4.
[18] US del. airgram to Washington. ECOTO A-640 (25 Feb. 1955).

the Board only to renew the Union. Calvet, however, indicated that he would be prepared to endorse such an EPU, as an interim step to formal convertibility, at some future date. The creditors thereupon withdrew their trial balloon. Calvet's response was precisely what they had in mind.

Owen's position precipitated a controversy in London. A senior Bank of England official advised that the UK decision to intervene in the transferable sterling market meant that 'we must join the 100% gold settlement party'.[19] That would provide the safest protection against abuse of the right to draw unlimited amounts of sterling under the EPU Agreement. The Chancellor and his Treasury advisers felt that such a move would require the UK to end discrimination against imports from the dollar area. The UK Board of Trade opposed hardening even to 75 per cent, lest it prejudice an OEEC move to 90 per cent intra-European trade liberalization, as agreed the previous January.[20] Cobbold pursued the matter of 100 per cent gold settlements with the Chancellor in March, but Butler decided to maintain the 75 per cent line.[21] He did agree that continued automatic EPU credit should be reconsidered if excessive amounts of sterling were drawn.

The Managing Board recommended an increase from 50 to 75 per cent gold settlements, with Hartogsohn alone dissenting. Otherwise, the Board reached an amicable agreement at its April 1955 meeting to renew the EPU for a sixth year, beginning in July.

A EUROPEAN FUND

Negotiations for a European Fund were only slightly more contentious. The Americans proved to be the principal source of controversy. The United Kingdom had suggested the creation of such a fund, based on the residual capital of the EPU, as early as its March 1953 presentation in Washington.

Under the original EPU Agreement, the residual capital would have been paid out to the creditors immediately upon liquidation, 'if the Government of the United States of America has not objected to the liquidation'.[22] Otherwise, the US could, in consultation with the OEEC, earmark the capital for the benefit of OEEC members, either individually or as a group. After the 1954 refurbishing, the residual capital amounted

---

[19] L. P. McC. (Lucius P. Thompson-McCausland), internal memo (1 Mar. 1955). Bank of England OV 44/65.

[20] R. P. F. (Roy Fenton), 'EPU/European Fund'. Report of meeting re Board of Trade's suggestion (14 Mar. 1955). Bank of England OV 46/18.

[21] Governor's note (18 Mar. 1955). Bank of England OV 46/66.

[22] OEEC (1950b), Annex B.

to $271.6 million and was unlikely to be drawn down further. Of this sum, $148 million was in liquid form, and $123.6 million remained in an EPU account at the US Treasury. These assets were thus available for a European Fund, given US consent.

Initially, the United Kingdom proposed that the OEEC ask the US to object formally to liquidation and earmark the residual capital for the European Fund. At the first meeting of the Ministerial Group in London, that idea met with general approval. The creditors were willing to yield their claims for the residual capital at the time of liquidation, and the US was agreeable to the transfer. However, the US favoured additional European contributions, and a number of Europeans agreed. The Scandinavians noted that their drawing rights in the IMF were much less than their EPU credit lines. The French and Italians, pessimistic about their short term balance-of-payments prospects, felt they might have difficulty in obtaining IMF drawings and would be dependent on the European Fund if they needed credit. In the autumn of 1954, Italy submitted a memorandum proposing a $1 billion Fund. The Ministerial Deputies agreed thereafter to recommend a $500-600 million Fund, to consist of the residual assets plus additional contributions by all OEEC members in proportion to their EPU quotas.

By the January 1955 ministerial meeting, the British were suggesting a different arrangement. The residual assets should be distributed to the creditors, in accordance with the normal liquidation rules. The European Fund would be set up thereafter, wholly on the basis of contributions by European creditors. The creditors would thus subscribe to the European Fund the dollars they received from the liquidation of the EPU.

The UK had changed its position largely because of an unexpected statement by Treasury Under Secretary Burgess that the US 'looked forward to continuing, on roughly the same basis, the association it had enjoyed with the EPU'.[23] Still at odds with the Americans about the conditions for an IMF standby credit, the UK thought it 'undesirable that they [the Americans] should have any right of control or veto over the operations of the European Fund'.[24] Calvet objected, preferring the Americans to have an effective responsibility in the new European Fund.[25]

In fact, the US hoped that the European Fund might become a major European financial institution once the EPU was liquidated. With Italy

[23] OEEC Trade and Finance Directorate, 'Summary of Statements by Ministers' London meeting (15-16 July 1954). OECD EPU Archive Box 43, unnumbered internal document. Burgess repeated that statement at the next meeting (12 Jan. 1955).

[24] Treasury Brief for Chancellor on 'Report from Deputies to the Ministerial Group on Convertibility' (1 Jan. 1955). PRO T 232/415.

[25] R. E. Heasman, UK Alternate, memo, 'European Fund' (20 Nov. 1954). Bank of England OV 46/65.

and France, among other OEEC countries, still heavily dependent on US aid, both the US aid programme and European integration would benefit if the stronger European countries accepted responsibility for helping the weaker ones.

The Europeans were much less sanguine. Minister Jens Krag of Denmark, speaking for debtor countries, pointedly observed that the Scandinavian countries 'did not consider that the proposed Fund was likely to be a very important institution, given its character as envisaged in the Deputies Report'.[26] The Continental creditors were willing to create a European Fund, though with no great enthusiasm. It might be useful for a few years, they thought, but hopefully its lending could be limited to the EPU residual assets.

Havlik had returned to the US the previous summer, and his post was still vacant. On the flight home from the ministerial meetings, Stassen decided to replace him with Kaplan (one of the authors of this book). A civil servant who had been the US official in charge of OEEC affairs, Kaplan joined the Managing Board at its February meeting with firm instructions to negotiate for as strong a European Fund as possible.

The British had hoped to rally a European consensus for eliminating an effective US voice and for basing the Fund's operations primarily on funds derived from the residual EPU assets. Ansiaux destroyed that aspiration at the outset of the meeting by suggesting that the EPU capital be drawn upon only to the extent that it was matched by fresh European contributions.[27]

Kaplan affirmed US resolve that its grant to the EPU should continue to be used multilaterally for the benefit of Europe. To that end, the US wanted to maintain its blocking right on the $271 million in the event that the Europeans decided to liquidate the European Fund. The US was prepared to relinquish the right to veto loans proposed by the management of the Fund. However, it wanted a commitment that the loans would not require borrowers to increase trade discrimination against non-member countries. Reporting these views, Owen wryly commented that 'the $271 million may prove to be some of the hardest earned dollars we were ever given.'[28]

The Board was not disposed to quarrel long with the US. It was much more concerned with the other major issues it had to resolve that spring. Firm but not inflexible about his government's views, Kaplan could compromise. At its March meeting, the Board reached agreement on

---

[26] Min. Examination Group on Convertibility Minutes (12 Jan. 1955). OEEC GMC/M(55)1.

[27] Heasman memo, 'American Attitudes Towards the European Fund' (23 Feb. 1955). Bank of England OV 46/66.

[28] Owen letter to Copleston, 'Transfer of EPU Capital to the European Fund and Call-up of Contributions' (25 Feb. 1955). Bank of England OV 46/66.

virtually every aspect of the constitution and operation of the European Fund. The British abandoned their position about how the Fund should be financed.

The Board proposed a European Fund of $600 million, based on the residual capital and on European contributions proportional to EPU quotas. European governments would make initial payments of $148 million, matching the liquid assets transferred from the EPU. Thereafter, funds would be called as needed *pari passu* from European governments and from the US Treasury account. Ansiaux and Alexandre Hay, the Swiss Alternate, favoured authorizing the European Fund to borrow on the private capital market, but the rest of the Board rejected that suggestion.

Contributions were defined and made payable in gold, to avoid burdening the Fund management with decisions about which member currencies should be used in lending operations or in short term investments. Owen would have welcomed the selection of sterling as the Fund's transaction and reserve currency, but he did not insist. Loans would be made for a two-year period and would not be renewable. Credits would be extended on a basis comparable to that of IMF drawings or EPU special credits, with policy conditions attached. Like the IMF, the European Fund could offer standby credits that might be arranged before the initial move to convertibility. After a three-year period, the Fund would be liquidated if countries representing half of its contributions decided to withdraw.

The only point that the Board left for Council decision was whether to defer the contributions of weaker members until other contributions had been paid in full. The Scandinavians were particularly adamant about having the contributions of the creditor countries called first. The Council agreed, and the contributions of Austria, Denmark, Greece, Iceland, Italy, Norway, and Turkey, totalling $57 million, were so deferred. Only Sweden remained recalcitrant, insisting that European contributions be proportional to foreign exchange reserves rather than EPU quotas. Finally, at the July 1955 meeting of the Managing Board, von Mangoldt proposed that Germany, France, and the United Kingdom share a $6 million increase in their contributions to permit a corresponding reduction in Sweden's.[29] Sweden accepted reluctantly at the subsequent ministerial meeting.

By April, except for this matter, the Managing Board had resolved the issues concerning a European Fund and had provided the OEEC ministers with a detailed report from which legal texts could be prepared.[30]

---

[29] UK del., 'Record of Discussion', 61st Session of the Managing Board (19 July 1955). Bank of England OV 46/47/42.

[30] EPU Board Report, 'The Renewal of the European Payments Union and the Establishment of a European Fund' (22 Apr. 1955). OEEC C(55)91.

Post-convertibility trade arrangements proved to be as politically charged an issue in 1955 as intra-European trade liberalization had been in 1950. The thorny problems were twofold: (1) how to maintain intra-European trade liberalization after some members made their currencies convertible; (2) how to cope with the non-discrimination commitment OEEC members had undertaken when most of them joined the IMF and the GATT.

OEEC Trade Liberalization

At the July 1954 meeting, other members of the Ministerial Examination Group resisted British insistence that the GATT should supplant the OEEC trade rules, once currency convertibility was firmly established. They were sceptical about the GATT's effectiveness and preferred to retain their own OEEC trade code. Perhaps the other Commonwealth countries could join their organization as associate members, as the US and Canada had done, and work out trade problems within the tested and effective OEEC forum.

When the ministers met in January 1955, they faced a major proposal from the Steering Board for Trade. The mandatory intra-European trade liberalization percentages should be raised to 90 per cent overall and to 75 per cent for each broad category—agriculture, raw materials, and manufactures. This was by far the most significant trade measure with which the OEEC ministers had been confronted.

Some countries were near to, or had exceeded, the proposed new goals and were prepared to accept them. Others pointed out that high tariffs, state trading, and a variety of artificial aids to exports were equally or more restrictive limitations on a truly competitive European market. The Steering Board had recognized these complaints and proposed some safety clauses, but more were required for an agreement.[31] The clauses softened the application of the new requirements to particular countries and to certain economic sectors, especially agriculture.

At this same meeting, Minister Victor Larock of Belgium, speaking for Benelux, observed that restrictive practices other than quantitative limitations put member countries on an unequal plane. The Benelux countries wanted action within the OEEC to reduce tariffs and all other types of trade limitations; the Swiss and Scandinavian governments supported that view. However, Thorneycroft, speaking for the UK, insisted that tariff reductions 'should be kept distinct from the elimination

---

[31] Council Decision, 'Concerning the Extension and Stabilisation/Liberalisation of Trade' (14 Jan. 1955). OEEC C(54)291 (Final).

of quotas' and should remain within the province of the GATT, where they were applied globally on a most favoured nation basis.[32] After the conclusion of the latest GATT negotiations early in 1955, the Continentals felt that the trade rules had been weakened, not strengthened, and their own attachment to the OEEC Code was reinforced.

These discussions planted some seeds for a European Common Market. Indeed, the six Coal and Steel Community countries held their Messina Conference within six months and there began to consider forming such a market. Marjolin and Harry Lintott (Deputy Secretary General of the OEEC and a former senior official of the UK Board of Trade) had made a number of trips to London in an abortive effort to persuade Butler and Thorneycroft to lead the OEEC towards a customs union.[33] Still adhering to its Commonwealth priority and its aspirations for a global role for sterling, the UK refused to take the OEEC route.

As a result, the only agreement that could be reached concerning post-convertibility trade rules was to keep the OEEC Code of Trade Liberalisation in effect for an indefinite period.[34] That decision notwithstanding, everyone realized that, after convertibility, the GATT would govern trade relations, including those between OEEC members.

Non-discrimination

As members of the GATT and the IMF, almost all OEEC countries had assumed stringent obligations about their trade policies. They had undertaken to eliminate quantitative restrictions and not to discriminate between any of the members of these worldwide organizations in administering permitted trade barriers. Their continuing postwar balance-of-payments problems had justified temporary exemption from these obligations. Following a declaration of convertibility, however, it would be difficult to sustain such a justification for very long. Reliance on the IMF for any necessary financial support would compound the difficulty. Discrimination as between two or more convertible currencies could be defended only if one of them were 'scarce', in the sense that the IMF itself was running out of that currency. That interpretation of the IMF Articles made it useless for debtor countries. After convertibility, the only solid basis for long continued discriminatory practices against any GATT or IMF member would be the formation of a customs union or a free trade area.

OEEC governments sought some way to avoid the rigidity of these obligations. The UK had first hoped to negotiate new trade rules, with

---

[32] 'Minutes of 270th Meeting' (13–14 Jan. 1955). OEEC C/M(55)1.
[33] Marjolin (1986), 245 ff.
[34] OEEC press release, 'Decisions of the OEEC Council' (29 July 1955). OEEC Press/A(55)40.

new escape clauses. However, neither the US nor other non-European members of the global organizations felt that flexibility about an early end to discrimination was warranted. In their eyes, the international payments situation was much improved over the early postwar years. The US had run balance-of-payments deficits continuously since 1952, of the order of $1-2 billion per year. Until mid-1954, almost all OEEC members had shared in the growth of European foreign exchange reserves. The most recent decline in UK reserves seemed attributable to its economic policies, not to a generalized dollar gap. The Europeans, on the other hand, saw the US as providing aid, not promoting trade, and were reluctant to count on the continuation of aid.

The IMF-GATT commitments were binding, however, and European governments appreciated the advantages of membership in these global organizations. They only wanted more flexibility and more possibility of escape from the obligations. After the GATT meetings in the autumn and winter of 1954-5 and the OEEC Ministerial Group discussions, Europe was faced with the fact that convertibility would mean severe pressure to reduce trade barriers of every variety and to bring discriminatory practices to an early end. Only the Six (the Common Market countries) were willing to take advantage of the sole escape available— and to accept its obligations.

EXCHANGE RATES

The most contentious problems about transitional and post-convertibility arrangements concerned exchange rates. They were so fundamental that final resolution of the other issues was made contingent on agreement about them. Not until the end of July 1955 was the controversy resolved. The EPU had to be renewed for a single month to permit time for the Managing Board to hammer out the final important details.

In 1953, the UK had unsuccessfully sought the right to leave the EPU whenever it chose to make its currency convertible. Its proposal in early 1955 was more modest—the transition from the EPU to the European Fund should occur whenever a group of countries holding 50-60 per cent of all EPU quotas decided to move to convertibility. The Continentals were then quite willing to agree, but made their concurrence subject to Great Britain's meeting two of their own major concerns. Agreement must first be reached on post-convertibility trade rules. Second, an acceptable solution to the question of exchange rate policies must be found. The latter condition became the key to an accord concerning transitional arrangements for convertibility.

Basic Issues

The Continentals had two major reservations about the British exchange rate proposals that had been presented to them. They preferred stable, if not fixed, exchange rates. Their central banks also sought an exchange rate guarantee comparable to that under the EPU. Negotiators sometimes also referred to the Tripartite Monetary Agreement of 1936, which provided a 24-hour guarantee.[35]

Most responsible officials felt some sympathy for the British desire to float their currency within a somewhat wider band than the 1 per cent above or below par value then permitted under IMF rules. However, IMF primary jurisdiction over members' exchange rate policies had been recognized from the very outset of the 1950 negotiations for an EPU Agreement. The Managing Board had always been careful not to tread on the toes of the IMF about exchange rates and hesitated now to become directly involved in UK exchange rate policy.

However, Great Britain's notion of floating without announced limits raised Continental hackles. Memories of competitive currency depreciation during the interwar years were still vivid. Floating rates would mean that any European country joining a British move would find itself on the horns of a distasteful dilemma. It could continue to peg its exchange rate to the then stable dollar. In that event, its foreign traders might be placed at a disadvantage against sterling area traders using a depreciating currency. Alternatively, it could peg to the pound sterling, a currency based on an economy considered to be weak, unstable, and overburdened with foreign exchange debts. If it chose the second alternative, its own financial stability might be threatened by dependence on an inflation- and depreciation-prone British economy. By mid-1954, the British knew that Germany and the Benelux countries had decided to continue to adhere to a fixed rate, tied to the dollar, after convertibility.[36] More closely linked to the British economy than most other European countries, the Dutch were still vexed by this dilemma. They were particularly adamant about the UK preserving a fixed exchange rate system.

The Continental central banks had a special concern of their own. Under the EPU, the interim finance they extended each month to other members was settled at a pre-fixed rate of exchange. Even if a partner devalued during the month, its accounts would be settled at the previous par value of its currency. Any central bank extending interim finance was thus guaranteed against loss when compensated at the monthly EPU settlement. For all practical purposes, cumulative credits also carried an effective guarantee. For example, a member that had not changed the par

---

[35] Kindleberger (1984), 397–8, describes the Tripartite Agreement.
[36] Rowan, 'Report to the Chancellor' (21 June 1954). PRO T 232/414.

value of its currency could prevent a change in the gold value of the unit of account and thus protect the gold value of the credits. (In later years, this latter guarantee was considered an ingenious contingency plan in the event of a change in the gold value of the dollar. Indeed, the Common Market initially copied the EPU's method of defining its own unit of account.) Central banks were reluctant to give up these guarantees after convertibility, unless they were replaced by others.

Retaining a Compensations Mechanism

The exchange rate issue was first attacked during the IMF Annual Meetings in September 1953. Ivar Rooth, Gutt's successor as Managing Director of the IMF and a former Governor of the Swedish Riksbank, chaired an informal discussion about British convertibility proposals among European Governors of the IMF and their representatives. US and Canadian Executive Directors of the IMF attended, as did J. Flint Cahan, who had replaced Figgures in the OEEC Secretariat.[37]

Reinforcing the position taken by Posthuma at an earlier meeting of the Managing Board, Governor Holtrop (Netherlands) opposed floating rates in no uncertain terms. Fluctuating rates might be adopted, but only in an emergency, as a temporary measure. Other Continental representatives supported him. Governor Frère suggested a compromise experiment—the IMF might permit temporary fluctuations of 3 to 4 per cent on either side of parity. Cahan reported that Maudling seemed to welcome the compromise, but Rowan and Bolton were more cautious.

A year later, after the British had begun to seek accommodation with the Continentals, the Bank of England devised a conciliatory suggestion. Central bank swaps might provide a way to maintain interim finance with an exchange rate guarantee. A central bank wanting to borrow another currency for no more than three months could draw a limited amount in exchange for its own currency at the then prevailing rate. Settlement would be effected by reversing the swap. The same amounts of each currency would be re-exchanged, so that the lender would suffer no loss in its own currency if the other currency had depreciated in the interim. The Bank of England was ready to institute such a system immediately, even while the EPU continued in operation.[38]

The Chancellor authorized the Governor to discuss that proposal with other European central banks, and a meeting was arranged during the

---

[37] Minutes of meeting in IMF Board Room (13 Sept. 1953). Cahan letter to Eric Wyndham White, Exec. Sec. of GATT, also reports and comments on the meeting. OECD EPU Archive Box 43.

[38] 'Intra-Central Bank Financial Arrangements', memo (13 Sept. 1954) and Bolton letter to Cobbold (25 Sept. 1954). Bank of England OV 46/65.

November 1954 session of the BIS. Bolton used the occasion to assure the other central bankers that the UK was committed to a policy of exchange rate stability, though it needed to be free to change its rate in the event of major crises—war, a US depression, or massive US inflation. The other central bankers seemed reassured and relieved by what they assumed was a major change in UK thinking about exchange rate policy. They were, however, reserved about the swap proposal.[39] The Continentals feared that bilateral swap arrangements might be accompanied by pressures for bilateral trade arrangements.

Since they were not members of the IMF, the Swiss neither participated in its discussions nor were they bound by its Articles of Agreement. They were thus best situated to press Continental preference for a fixed exchange rate system within the OEEC forum. With Rossy ill, Hay took the initiative. In November 1954, he circulated a paper stating that the EPU should not be dissolved before member countries had undertaken three obligations.[40] The first was to ensure continuing multilateral compensation of claims. The second was to settle residual balances in gold. The third was a central bank obligation to maintain exchange rates within agreed margins above and below parity.

At the December meeting of the Deputies Group and again at the January 1955 ministerial meeting, most Continentals supported the Swiss.[41] However, the United Kingdom considered the compensations idea to be impractical and unnecessary. The Swiss readily admitted that their interest in the scheme derived entirely from the exchange rate issue.

By late December 1954, the Bank of England had completed a fundamental reconsideration of its position on exchange rate policy.[42] It had come to recognize that widely fluctuating rates would not be consistent with maintaining confidence in sterling. All the prospective partners in the Collective Approach wanted a high degree of day-to-day stability. A margin of 3 to 4 per cent would 'give us reasonable freedom of action'. A review of sterling/dollar exchange rates during the 1931-9 period had raised questions about the validity of a previous assumption that the UK had then offset stresses by 'taking them on the rate'.[43]

An EPU Metamorphosis?

In January 1955, the Continental members of the Board devised another way of dealing with the exchange rate issue. During the first discussion

[39] 'Notes of a Meeting at the BIS' (12-13 Nov. 1954). Bank of England OV 46/65.

[40] E. R. Copleston, 'Europe and Exchange Rate Policy'. Internal memo (30 Nov. 1954). Bank of England OV 44/64.

[41] Min. Examination Group on Convertibility Minutes (12 Jan. 1955). OEEC GMC/M(55)1.

[42] Bolton letter to Rowan (23 Dec. 1954). Bank of England OV 44/64.

[43] Bolton later summarized results of study in memo, 'Sterling Exchange Between the Wars' (13 Jan. 1955). Bank of England OV 44/64.

about EPU renewal, they explored a gradual, rather than an abrupt, transformation of the EPU into the European Fund. They continued to refine that notion over the next few months.[44]

A kind of metamorphosis would take place in stages. The statutes of the European Fund would be incorporated into the EPU Agreement on the next renewal date. In the first stage, the EPU would shift to 100 per cent gold settlements, and the European Fund would start operating. The EPU compensations system would continue, but it would not prevent some members from permitting their currencies to fluctuate within wider margins than the others. The margins would, of course, have to be declared and guaranteed for every settlement. This first stage would begin when countries holding 50 per cent of EPU quotas so decided. Thereafter, each member would be able to announce, at a date of its own choosing, its withdrawal from the compensations system. After all countries had withdrawn, only the European Fund would remain.

Both Owen and Hartogsohn would have none of such a 'metamorphosis'. They wanted a clean break with the past on 'C-Day'—liquidation of the EPU and activation of the European Fund on the date of convertibility. They ventilated smoke screen arguments about the need for '. . . a start afresh, in order to signalise the end of the period of post-war transition and the achievement of one of the main purposes for which the EPU was formulated'.[45]

The replies were equally disingenuous. The EPU should not be swept away, since it was a symbol of European integration and trade liberalization. Metamorphosis would have the advantage of simplicity and might not require parliamentary ratification. It would permit *de facto* convertibility without invoking the non-discrimination obligations of the IMF or the GATT.[46] Moreover, it would reduce the risk of bilateralism in relations with OEEC countries that remained inconvertible.

These arguments about a post-convertibility compensations system mainly reflected concern lest the rate for sterling be allowed to float after Britain moved to convertibility. Metamorphosis would limit British exchange rate flexibility so long as the compensations system remained. The British could withdraw, but only at their peril. The others would remain in a convertible payments system that would not use the pound sterling. Understandably, Owen staunchly opposed any such optional system after convertibility. Roy Heasman, the UK Alternate, later reported

---

[44] Ansiaux report *re* Jan. Managing Board meeting. Minutes of the Board (22 Feb. 1955). National Bank of Belgium PV 1271/3.

[45] EPU Board Report, 'The Renewal of the European Payments Union and the Establishment of a European Fund' (22 Apr. 1955) OEEC C(55)91.

[46] US del. tel. to Washington. 'Main unresolved problems raised in February Meeting EPU Managing Board'. ECOTO 712 (24 Feb. 1955).

disparagingly about 'Ansiaux's efforts to organize a European currency bloc' after convertibility.[47]

Stability Without Commitment

A meeting was called in the Chancellor's room early in February 1955 to consider how to deal with the multilateral settlements idea.[48] Determined to keep exchange rate policy out of the purview of the Managing Board, Cobbold gained the Chancellor's permission to work something out directly with the other central banks. Earlier promises of 'stability without commitment' would be amplified. He would announce that if sterling were to move to convertibility at the present time, the UK would maintain its exchange rate within a spread of 3 per cent on each side of parity. Such an assurance was indeed given to the Continental governors at the February BIS meeting. A meeting of central bank experts was arranged a month later to discuss the technical implications of the new policy. The British hoped that their statement would reconcile the others to the disappearance of the compensations system after convertibility.

During the March meetings at the BIS, the Continental governors and their technical experts said that the 3 per cent spread was too large. Furthermore, they wanted advance notice of any subsequent British decision to change the spread. Cobbold and Bolton would promise no more than what they had already announced—stability without commitment and probably a spread of only 3 per cent.

Impasse and Reconciliation

At the following meeting of the Managing Board, the Continentals denied that their authorities had agreed to anything in Basle. They still preferred to retain the possibility of interim finance within a compensations system. They noted that the UK had offered assurances in Basle, but no commitments. The exchange rate issue remained at an impasse.

In April, the Board prepared a report to the OEEC ministers containing one of its few divided recommendations. The majority recorded its preference for metamorphosis, while the minority favoured a clean break. Each side elaborated its arguments.[49] The debate was resumed at a meeting of the Deputies Group in May, but to no avail. The Swiss

[47] Heasman letter to Fenton (4 Mar. 1955). Bank of England OV 46/66.

[48] 'Multilateral Compensations in Europe after Convertibility and Our Exchange Rate Policy'. Report of meeting of Chancellor, Governor, and senior staff (7 Feb. 1955). Bank of England OV 46/66.

[49] EPU Board Report, 'The Renewal of the European Payments Union and the Establishment of a European Fund' (22 Apr. 1955) OEEC C(55)91.

provided the Deputies with a detailed compensations scheme, but it failed to meet UK objections. This basic disagreement was referred to a ministerial meeting called for 10 June 1955.

The impasse could not have been resolved without a major decision in London, generated in part by Britain's deteriorating economic situation. In his 1955 Budget, Butler had again cut taxes, counting on a restrictive monetary policy to check inflationary pressures. That policy had failed, and major strikes had erupted.[50] By summer, transferable sterling was under pressure, UK reserves were dwindling, and the government remained unwilling to accept the implications of unifying the exchange rates for sterling. Under these circumstances, the Chancellor did not want to adopt an attitude at the June ministerial meeting 'which might be resisted and/or resented by the majority of Europeans'.[51]

Prior to the meeting, Posthuma and a colleague from the Netherlands Bank visited the Bank of England. They presented a note describing a compromise that the Dutch Minister would offer.[52] The scheme would maintain a compensations system after convertibility but discourage its use under normal circumstances. The system would be available for use primarily when members wanted to invoke the exchange rate guarantee that was implicit in its mechanism.

The mechanics of the Dutch compromise were imaginative but complicated. Countries would be able to draw a limited amount of interim finance from any other member's central bank. Each member would declare an exchange rate spread that would be guaranteed for the next settlement and until further notice. However, it would settle interim finance at the upper limit of the lending country's margin for its currency, the most unfavourable rate for the borrower. This would keep most clearing transactions in the market-place and deter misuse of interim finance. Central banks could also include in the clearing balances any funds acquired other than through interim finance—most likely from their commercial banks. Such funds would also be settled at the upper limit of the currency put into the settlement.

The Chancellor was unwilling to risk further speculation about some change in exchange rate policy that he might have in mind. Therefore,

---

[50] Cairncross (1987).

[51] Bolton, 'Multilateral Compensation'. Internal memo (18 May 1955). Bank of England OV 46/66.

[52] Heasman, 'Dutch Scheme for Continuation of a Clearing Mechanism after the Liquidation of the EPU' (7 June 1955). Memo of conversation. Bank of England OV 46/67.

Also 'Multilateral Compensations after the Liquidation of the EPU' (9 June 1955). Bank of England OV 46/67, Annex.

Posthuma, 'Outline of a Clearing Mechanism After Liquidation of the European Payments Union'. Submitted to Managing Board (9 June 1955). OEEC MBC(55)56.

Van de Kieft, statement to Council of Ministers (11 June 1955). OEEC C/M(55)20 (Prov.) (1st Revision).

he agreed at the ministerial meeting that the Dutch proposal deserved detailed consideration. The Managing Board was asked to convene a meeting of experts from central banks and to report back to the ministers if they could not agree by mid-July.

The Board appointed Calvet to chair the experts group; Hay and Posthuma also participated. Bolton warned Governor Cobbold that the Bank of England representatives (Bridge and Maurice Parsons) would have to agree that the UK would announce, at the time of convertibility, an exchange rate spread that would 'limit sterling fluctuations until further notice'.[53] For all practical purposes, the UK had yielded to Continental demands for fixed, though adjustable, exchange rates. Rates could fluctuate only within a narrow spread, announced in advance. Advance notice would also be required before the rates or the spreads could be changed.

The Calvet Groups

Under Calvet's adroit guidance, contentiousness among the central bank experts was carefully controlled. Within a week, on 20 June, he could report to the Managing Board that he had defined about a dozen technical issues, obtained some agreement, and ascertained the nature of the remaining disagreements.[54] Ten days later, he reported more agreement— but also new discord.[55] The Board thereupon appointed a five-person drafting group under Calvet to prepare a report on the projected multilateral system of settlements.[56] By the next meeting of the Managing Board, on 11 July, the drafting group had reduced the points of disagreement to three.

The Board promptly resolved all three issues. It decided that margins would be declared and settlements would be made in US dollars; interim finance would be limited to 10 per cent of the amount of credit in current EPU quotas; and the European Fund would guarantee up to $50 million of interim finance against any default by a member.[57] With Owen concurring, the Board also agreed that it would be desirable for margins to be as narrow as possible. Further concluding that bilateral agreements with inconvertible countries would not be compatible with the system,

[53] Bolton, 'European Exchange Arrangements'. Internal memo (15 June 1955). Bank of England OV 46/67.

[54] Calvet, statement to Managing Board on First Session of Group of Banking Experts (20 June 1955). OEEC TFD/PC/129.

[55] Calvet, statement to Managing Board on Second Session of Group of Banking Experts (29 June 1955). OEEC TFD/PC/137.

[56] Drafting Group members were Calvet, Bridge (UK), Emminger (Germany), Rinaldo Ossola (Italy), and Macdonald (BIS).

[57] EPU Board Minutes, 61st Session (11–16 July 1955). OEEC MBC/M(55)8.

Also UK del., 'Record of Discussion', 61st Session of the Managing Board (19 July 1955). Bank of England OV 46/47/42.

the Board stipulated that the terms and conditions of any such agreements should be reported and be subject to its review.

All that remained was to complete the Board's report and draft the legal texts. It was then decided that the new agreement should be called the European Monetary Agreement and that it should include both the European Fund and the settlements system.[58]

The basis for the post-convertibility settlements system was the ingenious compromise engineered by Posthuma. At an early meeting, the Calvet group had agreed that neither interim finance nor the settlements system would be used very much for payments among convertible countries under normal conditions. Countries would ordinarily obtain interim finance through central bank swaps and would settle before the end of the month by purchasing the borrowed currency on the foreign exchange market.

The principal function of the system would be its availability in the event that the exchange rate of a convertible currency moved beyond declared margins. A convertible currency would, in effect, carry an exchange rate guarantee, if its authorities decided to devalue. The principal ordinary use of the settlements system would be for payments between convertible currencies and those that might remain inconvertible.

THE OUTCOME AND ITS SIGNIFICANCE

The Managing Board report was a long and complicated document that recorded agreements on all the mandates with which it had been entrusted since January 1955. The OEEC Council adopted all the Board's recommendations on 29 July 1955.[59]

The European Monetary Agreement (EMA) charted a smooth course to convertibility. The agreement was a marriage of the British and Continental approaches: the move would be undertaken collectively, but cautiously. The EMA had been negotiated under the pressure of fears about a premature UK move to convertibility. In Continental eyes, the economies of several major trading partners, and the UK itself, did not seem strong enough to assure a successful move yet. The UK had agreed to significant restraints, which would inhibit a rash dash.

The United Kingdom would take the lead, and most other OEEC

---

[58] EPU Board Report, 'The Renewal of the EPU and A European Monetary Agreement for the Establishment of a European Fund and of a Multilateral System to Facilitate Settlements Between Member Countries' (25 July 1955). OEEC C(55)189 (1st revision).

[59] OEEC press release, 'Decisions of the Council'. Summarizes preceding events, beginning with Butler's presentation of Collective Approach to OEEC in March 1953 (5 Aug. 1955). OEEC Press/A(55)40.

countries were likely to join in a truly collective approach at a time of the UK's choosing. The European Fund would provide a safety net in the form of credit for weaker countries. The multilateral settlements system would provide a safety net for other members of the system if any country found it necessary to change its exchange rate. However, if the move to convertibility were smooth and successful, and if it included all but a few smaller trading countries, the safety nets would probably atrophy for lack of use.

The Continentals had yielded on the desirability of a metamorphosis: a strong European financial institution would no longer exist, once the British made their decision. The OEEC as an institution for European integration would be diminished for want of effective authority over its members' trade, payments relations, or internal fiscal and monetary policies. In these matters, the IMF and the GATT should be the successors to the EPU Managing Board and the Steering Board for Trade. Countries that attached great importance to the economic integration of Europe would pursue it thereafter through the Common Market negotiations.

The United Kingdom yielded much of the freedom and flexibility it originally sought, once it recognized the value of agreement and compromise with its European trading partners. In a conversation with Rowan after Butler had agreed to consider the Dutch proposal, Bolton noted, 'We are faced with a dilemma of incompatibility between an economic policy of exchange flexibility and a political policy of co-operation with Europe which demands more or less fixed rates and consultation.'[60] Under these circumstances, the UK successfully resisted intense pressure to accept a predetermined limit on the spread it might announce for its post-convertibility exchange rate, but it accepted a system that required a narrow spread. It was therefore unlikely to declare convertibility before it was strong enough to sustain it. Its internal economy, foreign exchange reserves, and balance of payments would have to be adequate to support both non-discriminatory trade practices and a stable exchange rate. When the European Monetary Agreement was signed, that was not the case.

POSTPONING THE RIDE

Anxiety about sterling had been mounting steadily in the market-place during the spring and summer of 1955. In June, the Bank of England had again unsuccessfully sought permission to unify the exchange rates

---

[60] Bolton, 'Paris Discussions and Exchange Policy'. Internal memo (20 June 1955). Bank of England OV 46/67.

for sterling within a spread of 3 per cent on either side of parity, and incidentally thus to terminate the EPU.[61] Cobbold persisted with this advice until Chancellor Butler put his foot down, first on 21 July 1955 and finally on 10 August 1955. He did so after the Bank's views had appeared in the press and after President Eisenhower had cautioned Eden in Geneva against floating the pound.[62] In response to the Governor's latest urgings, Butler said in July that 'the best course to follow was to get the internal economy right and then to move to convertibility from strength'.[63] That statement indeed reflected the views of the Cabinet, as well as Butler himself.

Butler now began to wonder 'whether it was possible for the UK to run a policy of convertibility allied to free trade'.[64] In September, Board of Trade officials 'were reacting violently against convertibility being adopted in any foreseeable future'. Any action that might force the UK 'to adopt a trade policy of non-discrimination forthwith must, at any cost, be avoided'.[65]

By September 1955, Butler had come a long way from ROBOT. In Istanbul, at the IMF Annual Meetings, he announced that the 'pound was not to float but would remain within fixed margins and be steadily defended'.[66] Bolton had persistently promoted an early move to sterling convertibility, first with a floating rate and later with a 3 per cent spread. Now he sat at Butler's elbow to make sure the proper incantation was pronounced to reassure the nervous foreign exchange markets.

The route to convertibility had been charted, but the lead rider would not be ready to proceed for some years. By then, the environment was very different from the one for which the EMA had been conceived.

---

[61] 'Exchange Rate Policy'. Note of meeting in Chancellor's Room (24 June 1955). Economic Sec., Governor and Deputy Governor, Bank of England, and several key advisers were present.

Also Gilbert letter to Governor replying to letter of 21 June 1955 to Sir Edward Bridges (24 June 1955). Bank of England OV 44/65.

[62] 'Economic Situation'. Record of discussion at Treasury (21 July 1955). Only the Chancellor, Bridges, Rowan, and Governor and Deputy Governor of Bank of England were present. Bank of England G1/99.

[63] 'Economic Situation'. Record of discussion at Treasury (21 July 1955). Bank of England G1/99.

[64] 'Meeting in the Chancellor's Room' (10 Aug. 1955). Chancellor, Governor, and senior officials of Treasury and Bank of England were present. Chancellor informed Governor of position he proposed to take at Sept. meetings of the IMF in Istanbul. Bank of England G1/99.

[65] Collective Approach Com., report of a meeting chaired by Rowan (5 Sept. 1955). Bank of England OV 44/65.

[66] Butler (1971).

Part Four

Anticipating 'C-Day'
1955-1958

13 Last Years of the EPU: An Overview

The conclusion of the European Monetary Agreement and the further hardening of the EPU in mid-1955 marked a milestone for the Union. Its first five years had been tempestuous; the Board was under constant pressure. Rearmament crises, disagreements about the terms for renewing the EPU, and the convertibility controversies had created one turmoil after another. Now the Board looked forward to a calmer period during which trade and payments restrictions would be lifted, one by one, until a meaningful convertibility could be consummated. That, in fact, is what happened during the last three and a half years of the Union, though not without important problems and crises along the way.

THE LATTER FIFTIES

The Political Environment

During the second half of the 1950s, major political developments elbowed economic recovery issues out of the limelight. British and French political and financial difficulties delayed a general European move toward convertibility, although most other OEEC countries continued to progress toward the goal. While the EPU became a broader and freer system, 'C-Day' itself awaited a British initiative. Several years would elapse before responsible British authorities felt that conditions were ripe. Once the UK Cabinet began to ponder a move, it became increasingly concerned about French participation, as were many Continentals.

Having earlier withdrawn its armed forces from Indo-China, France was determined to hold on in North Africa, especially in Algeria, where a large French population had long been settled. The Algerian population was equally determined to achieve independence, and a revolt broke out late in 1954. The resulting hostilities intensified France's economic problems over the succeeding years.

In July 1956, the Egyptian government of Abdul Nasser nationalized the Suez Canal after the US blocked financing of his favourite Aswan dam project. Britain and France decided to use force if negotiations failed and, in October, they landed troops in Egypt. Nasser promptly scuttled ships in the Canal, blocking its further use for a protracted period. Still seeking a negotiated outcome, the US had received no prior notice of the landing. Eisenhower, Dulles, and Humphrey were outraged. A run on sterling ensued, and the Americans refused financial support unless the troops were withdrawn.

The closing of the Canal caused petroleum shortages and higher energy costs throughout the EPU area. For some months, a renewed atmosphere of European solidarity and co-operation blossomed in the meeting rooms and corridors of the OEEC, though many members were troubled by the use of troops. Controversies about convertibility, exchange rates, trade and tariff restrictions, and the Common Market were submerged in a common concern about the immediate economic outlook.[1] As the crisis atmosphere eased, disagreements broke out into the open again.

The foreign ministers of the six countries that had tried to establish a European Defence Community met in Messina in June 1955 to salvage the European idea. They agreed to study the creation of a customs union and, in May 1956, began negotiations for a Common Market. Still unwilling to consider a political commitment to Europe themselves, the British were dismayed. At first sceptical that anything would come of the Messina ideas, they rejected proposals for tariff reduction within the entire OEEC area in mid-1956, as they had in 1955. In December 1956, the UK belatedly initiated negotiations for an industrial Free Trade Area to include all OEEC countries. Two years later, France vetoed Common Market participation in it, prompting widespread fears about a 'divided Europe'. The French veto occurred in the wake of another major political event. In mid-1958, the Fourth French Republic ended dramatically, and General Charles de Gaulle returned to power.

Other, less dramatic, political developments improved the economic environment. The insecurity that had hung over western Europe almost since the end of the war diminished markedly. NATO's conventional military capabilities improved steadily behind the US nuclear shield, and the Soviet Union seemed much less threatening. Unrest in Poland and Hungary made eastern Europe seem like a less reliable base for a Russian military move against the West. In addition, most western European countries enjoyed greater internal political stability. Except in France and Italy, the constant cabinet turnovers of the early postwar years became less frequent.

The Economic Environment[2]

In the latter 1950s, western Europe began to experience both the benefits and the strains of a new era of industrialization. Investment to expand

---

[1] OEEC Secretariat, 'Action by the Organisation Concerning the Economic and Financial Repercussions of the Suez Crisis'. Information memo for the Managing Board (14 Dec. 1956). OEEC MBC(56)112.

[2] Data from various *Annual Reports* of OEEC, BIS, and EPU Board.

and modernize factories continued at an impressive rate, and the first signs of a flow of private capital from North America appeared. European exports to the dollar area, and to the rest of the world, finally began to grow, rising impressively over the last half of the decade. Europe was regaining its competitiveness in world markets and rebuilding confidence in its economic outlook and the value of most of its currencies. Apart from the political disturbances, the foundations for a bright economic future seemed more solid than at any time since the outbreak of the First World War.

Indeed, by mid-1955, Europe was beginning to enjoy the fruits of a decade of hard work, careful savings and investment, and substantial foreign aid. OEEC-wide industrial production in 1955 was 37 per cent higher than in 1950; in 1957, it was 47 per cent higher. The population at large now saw within its grasp the more comfortable lifestyles that a growing proportion of the middle class had begun to enjoy. A 'revolution of rising expectations' spread throughout Europe as it produced and marketed to its citizens a rising stream of automobiles, washing machines, radios, and other consumer goods. Housing was becoming less crowded and better equipped; widespread television loomed on the horizon.

As expectations rose, they carried prices up with them. Once again, inflation began to escape its cage. Heavy demand pushed up prices of raw materials needed to produce equipment and consumer goods. Popular aspirations for more material comforts combined with low levels of unemployment and high levels of investment to trigger increasingly insistent wage demands. As a result, after two years of stability, both wholesale and retail prices resumed their increase in mid-1955. Inflation rates did not approach the annual double-digit levels of the 1950-2 rearmament period, and they were modest compared with those following the oil shocks of the 1970s. Nevertheless, by 1957, prices were 10-15 per cent higher than in 1954 in the UK, France, Italy, the Netherlands, and Scandinavia. They increased much less than that in Germany, Belgium, Switzerland, and Portugal; and more, only in Turkey.

The different rates of inflation had prompt, as well as damaging, effects on balances of payments. The shortage of foreign exchange reserves made deficits unacceptable, and most European countries introduced anti-inflationary measures in 1956. Unfortunately, these proved inadequate in many countries. By the late summer of 1957, it was widely believed that exchange rates would have to be adjusted, especially with respect to the pound, French franc, and German mark. Heavy speculative movements of capital followed, and drastic corrective measures had to be taken. By 1958, European prices were again generally stable, central bank discount rates could be reduced, and short term interest rates fell.

Whereas western Europe's foreign exchange reserves had increased sharply from mid-1952 to mid-1954, the rate slowed markedly thereafter. Taken individually, European countries fared very differently. Apart from France, Germany, and the UK, most OEEC countries continued to add steadily but modestly to their foreign exchange reserves. After peaking at over $3 billion in mid-1954, UK reserves fell almost continuously until 1958. By the autumn of 1957, only $1.8 billion remained, despite large drawings at the turn of that year from the IMF and credits from the US. France also experienced heavy losses of reserves in 1956 and 1957. German reserves, on the other hand, increased dramatically in every year after 1951, exceeding $4 billion by September 1957.

WIDENING THE SYSTEM

Freer Trade and Payments

To some extent, reserves increased more slowly after mid-1954 because trade and payments restrictions of every variety were being lifted. EPU member countries were taking steps toward convertibility as rapidly as conditions would permit. The Managing Board reached out in every direction to find new ways to make progress.

By the end of 1956, 89 per cent of intra-European trade had been liberalized; eleven of the sixteen countries were above the 90 per cent level. About a year later, 64 per cent of imports from the US had been liberalized, with six countries above 85 per cent.[3] Governments were also granting licences more freely for those goods that remained under the umbrella of import quotas. Nevertheless, European agriculture was still protected assiduously, and the United Kingdom was adamant about limiting imports of manufactures from North America.

As trade became increasingly free of restrictions, attention turned to services. In June 1955, the OEEC decided that they should be liberalized within Europe as of November, though individual countries could lodge reservations about specific types of transactions. A Committee on Invisible Transactions, parallel to the Steering Board for Trade, was created to oversee the new rules. Some 47 types of service transactions were identified, covering such diverse economic sectors as tourism, advertising, interest, dividends, rents, profits, and emigrant remittances. A year later, reservations reported to the OEEC were pretty well confined to seven out of the 47 categories. Films, insurance, and transportation services were the sectors most resistant to OEEC pressures for liberalization.

---

[3] Intra-European and dollar liberalization percentages calculated with reference to actual imports in 1948 and 1953 respectively. Therefore, not strictly comparable. All percentages apply only to imports on private account, excluding state trading.

Tourist allowances were still controlled as well, differing widely among member countries.

International transactions could not be liberalized fully without addressing the highly sensitive matter of transfers of capital. Destabilizing capital flows during the interwar period had made most countries hesitant about removing controls. Indeed, the IMF Articles of Agreement permitted the regulation of capital movements and even prohibited the use of IMF resources to meet a large and sustained outflow of capital.

Nevertheless, very early in its life, the Managing Board had urged countries in a stronger position to ease restrictions on capital movements. During its first discussions about the meaning of full convertibility, Rossy and Ansiaux had insisted that capital movements must be included, not just the proceeds of current transactions. The Board thereafter actively promoted the removal of restrictions on transfers of capital within the EPU area. In December 1954, members were encouraged to report to the Board such measures to free capital flows as they felt able to introduce.[4] Subsequently, scarcely a Board meeting passed without one of the stronger economies announcing some new liberalization.

In 1955, the OEEC urged all members to remove restrictions on direct investments, blocked accounts, the repatriation of sums realized from asset sales, and the transfer of common stock certificates. In 1957, members formally agreed to free such transactions. Germany had stopped limiting the export of capital to other OEEC countries in 1956, and Switzerland had opened its market to some borrowing by both OEEC governments and private business firms. The World Bank had also begun to borrow on the markets of a few EPU members.

Expanding Transferability

While many EPU countries were still hesitant about convertibility with the dollar area, they had fewer reservations about freeing transactions with the rest of the world. Many countries outside the EPU currency area soon recognized the advantages of replacing bilateral agreements with currency transferability, and EPU members welcomed the opportunity to make freer arrangements with them. The pound sterling had become fully transferable outside the dollar area in 1953; first Germany and then Italy followed suit with their currencies. The Benelux countries, Denmark, and Sweden also adopted such transferability, though they excepted eastern Europe and a few other countries.

The only European countries outside both the OEEC and the Soviet bloc were Spain, Finland, and Yugoslavia. As early as May 1953, the

---

[4] EPU Board Report, 'Liberalisation of Capital Movements' (13 Dec. 1954). OEEC C(54)327.

Managing Board began to consider whether they could be associated with the EPU. Major political and economic difficulties were soon uncovered, but the Board redoubled its efforts after concluding the European Monetary Agreement in mid-1955.

In 1956, Finland's relations with most EPU members were put on a multilateral basis, its earnings becoming freely transferable within the EPU area. In exchange, Finland liberalized 82 per cent of its imports from OEEC countries. After a session with the Governor of the Finnish central bank in 1958, the Board was ready to welcome full Finnish participation in the EPU, but Soviet objections prevailed.

Although at odds with the Soviet Union, Yugoslavia was a Communist country and hesitant about freeing its economic system. Nonetheless, EPU members agreed in 1956 to permit at least 10 per cent of Yugoslavia's earnings in their currencies to be transferable into any EPU currency.

Still ruled by General Francisco Franco, Spain was a political anathema to some OEEC governments, and Franco was reluctant to relax his system of tight economic controls and highly subsidized state monopolies. However, an association agreement with the OEEC was signed early in 1958. Spain then undertook its first small steps toward liberalization in the hope of later joining the OEEC trade and payments arrangements.

In 1955 and 1956, most EPU members had joined a Hague Club with Brazil and a Paris Club with Argentina. Both these clubs provided for terminating bilateral payments arrangements, for non-discrimination in trade and payments among participants, and for transferability of their currencies at official exchange rates. (Both Brazil and Argentina maintained multiple exchange rates.) In July 1956, Brazilian representatives met with the Managing Board in an informal session to discuss the principles on which the Hague Club operated.[5]

All such arrangements for extending the EPU multilateral system to other countries were based on bilateral negotiations, and the Managing Board played no role in their administration. However, it studied each case and fostered all of them. Although EPU accounts could be distorted by allowing non-members of the system to exchange EPU currencies, the Board was interested primarily in reducing its members' bilateral arrangements with other countries. It did not lose sight of its commitment to move Europe continuously and prudently toward a free, worldwide, trade and payments system.

Welcome 'Hanky-Panky'

After the mid-1955 agreements, the EPU clearing and settlements system operated very smoothly on the whole. With all monthly surpluses and

---

[5] EPU Board Report, 'Exchange of Views Between the Members of the Managing Board and Two Brazilian Experts' (19-21 July 1956). OEEC MBC(56)83.

deficits settled 75 per cent in gold, the Union was nearly twice as convertible as at its inception. EPU quotas had been increased commensurately with higher gold settlement ratios, to retain the same absolute amount of credit in the system. This reduced the likelihood of quota exhaustion, and only a handful of countries were in crisis within the system over its last three and a half years.

From the very beginning of the system, the monthly positions of countries were reported to the public and were carefully scrutinized by currency traders in Zurich and New York, as well as by operators on European black or grey markets. In the early years, they reflected rather accurately the current account position of each member with the rest of the system, although speculative activity tended to exaggerate surpluses and deficits that became large and persistent.

In 1954, some central banks began to smooth their net positions through operations in the dollar market. Germany drew sterling under the EPU interim finance provision and sold it for dollars to reduce its EPU surpluses.[6] The Bank of France purchased EPU currencies for dollars to run surpluses in the EPU.[7] At the time, France received 100 per cent in gold for its monthly surpluses, recovering gold it had paid to settle earlier post-quota deficits. Later it bought EPU currencies to reduce its EPU deficits. Eased restrictions on the transferability of sterling facilitated such operations.

After the market rate for 'cheap sterling' was brought close to the official rate, early in 1955, these transactions proliferated. Ansiaux promptly called the attention of the Board of the National Bank of Belgium to the possibility of selling such sterling for dollars to reduce Belgium's EPU surpluses.[8] At its January 1956 meeting, the Managing Board was told that Austria had bought EPU currencies for dollars to reduce its deficits and that Greece and France had earlier done the same.[9] In the spring of 1956, the Bank of England told the Chancellor that the transferable sterling/EPU arrangements 'have become a clearing for sterling outside the dollar area: incidentally they give rise to a lot of hanky-panky in each monthly settlement, with everybody trying to make a turn out of the difference between the transferable rate and the EPU rate'.[10]

Neither British nor Continental members of the Board objected to

---

[6] R. P. F. (Fenton), 'Effect of 75% gold ratio'. Internal memo (17 Mar. 1955). Bank of England OV 46/48.

[7] R. H. Turner, 'France—Move to Convertibility'. Internal memo (16 May 1955). Bank of England OV 46/48.

[8] Minutes of the Board (1 Mar. 1955). National Bank of Belgium PV 1273/3.

[9] Travers notes. OECD EPU Archive Box 52.

[10] Governor's private and personal memo for Chancellor of Exchequer (12 Apr. 1956). Bank of England OV 44/65.

these practices. Calvet argued that such transactions were the logical outcome of establishing free markets for foreign exchange and a movement toward convertibility, and the Board decided against any action.[11] The transactions usually served to reduce the size of the monthly deficits and surpluses reported to the EPU Agent and thus helped reduce reported imbalances.

RENEWING THE EPU

Largely because of British opposition to longer extensions, the EPU was renewed for only one year at a time. These annual renewals were pivotal in reconciling conflicting interests and improving the system. The need to agree on terms for renewal each year focused the Board's energies on resolving disagreements among the members. They were constrained to find acceptable compromises on issues that hindered extending the Union.

In 1955, three mainstays of the early years stepped down from the Managing Board. Having been promoted to Vice-Governor of the National Bank of Belgium, Ansiaux had to yield his responsibilities as Chairman of the OEEC Payments Committee, and Posthuma declined reappointment. Posthuma's longtime Alternate, Eric Liefrinck, assumed Ansiaux's post, and Cecil de Strycker, chief of the foreign department of the National Bank of Belgium, replaced Posthuma. Health forced Rossy's resignation, and Hay succeeded him as a full member of the Board.

In January 1956, the Board turned to its yearly rites of renewing the EPU, this time for a seventh year. The new creditor representatives attempted to revive the proposals of their predecessors. De Strycker suggested moving to 100 per cent gold or dollar settlements and starting up the European Fund, but he encountered strong resistance from Calvet, Owen, and Getz Wold. In vain, Liefrinck and Hay pleaded for at least a symbolic increase from 75 to 80 per cent in the gold/credit settlements ratio. In January and again in May 1956, von Mangoldt proposed automatic repayment of credits, but found little support.[12] The balance-of-payments difficulties of France and the UK precluded any agreement about further progress toward a more convertible system. The controversy ended when Italy, Norway, and Great Britain concluded bilateral agreements with the creditors to amortize $200 million more of their debts.[13] The Union was renewed without change for the 1956/7 financial year.

The next renewal appeared on the Board's agenda in January 1957, in

---

[11] EPU Board Minutes, 67th Session (16–19 Jan. 1956). OEEC MBC/M(56)1, Part I.

[12] Von Mangoldt, 'Proposals' (18 Jan. and 9 May 1956). OEEC TFD/PC 218 and TFD/PC 289.

[13] EPU Board Report, 'Renewal of the European Payments Union' (30 June 1956). OEEC C(56)118.

the immediate aftermath of the Suez crisis. All concerned promptly agreed that a speedy agreement was desirable to avoid further disturbances in the already unstable foreign exchange markets. The Board completed its report at its March 1957 session, recommending renewal with no change in the general operating rules.[14] Even so, the Norwegian delegation to the OEEC reserved its position, objecting to continuing settlement of large German surpluses with gold payments equal to 75 per cent. A month later, it withdrew its reserve. It had found much sympathy for its position but little support, given prevailing instability in the currency markets.

When EPU renewal for still another year was first discussed in February 1958, the Free Trade Area negotiations were uppermost in the minds of OEEC members. Geoffrey Wilson, who had succeeded Owen as the UK nominee, announced that his government would have a payments proposal to make to the Ministerial Committee on a Free Trade Area.[15] If the negotiations in that forum were successful, the UK would offer to renew the EPU with provision for automatic repayment of credit that had been outstanding for two years. In addition, a fund would be created alongside the automatic credit system to offer *ad hoc* credits, based on member subscriptions or loans from persistent creditors and borrowings on the money market. De Strycker asked that the proposal be made formally to the Managing Board, which could report its views to the Ministerial Committee. Wilson obtained London consent to this procedure, thus avoiding another unhappy episode such as had arisen over the Collective Approach in 1953.

Unfortunately, the tense atmosphere of the Free Trade Area negotiations carried over into the EPU renewal discussions. Countries that were outside the Common Market all asked for a renewal of only six months, pending the outcome of the negotiations. With the Common Market scheduled to take effect at the beginning of 1959, the Swiss were particularly adamant. Hay contended that trade discrimination against other OEEC countries would result, unless provisions were made for a European free trade area.[16] His government hoped that a threat to dissolve the EPU would put pressure on the Six to accept the free trade area, and Getz Wold endorsed his position.

Von Mangoldt, de Strycker, and Liefrinck offered a counterproposal to the British that would end EPU automatic credits and replace them with quasi-automatic credits. Members could request an *ad hoc* credit up

[14] EPU Board Report, 'Renewal of the European Payments Union after 30 June 1957' (22 Mar. 1957). OEEC C(57)45.

[15] US del. tel. and airgram to Washington. POLTO 2595 (22 Feb. 1958) and POLTO A-479 (28 Feb. 1958).

[16] S. W. P. (Payton), UK Alternate, 'Renewal of the Union from 30th June 1958'. Report on Managing Board meeting (24 Feb. 1958). Bank of England OV 46/23.

to a limited amount and use it to settle deficits without regard to the fixed gold/credit ratio. Wilson could not accept such an end to automatic credit since it would mean *de facto* convertibility of sterling and provoke unwelcome pressures. Countries holding sterling balances would ask to convert them into dollars, and North America would demand an end to trade discrimination.[17]

The British soon began to back away from the idea of limiting the renewal of the EPU to six months. Realizing that an end to the EPU would mean either that sterling would become convertible or that Britain would have to retreat to bilateralism, they preferred to renew the EPU for a full year.[18] Otherwise, the date for convertibility might be fixed by the outcome of the Free Trade Area negotiations. De Strycker and Kaplan had both warned about 'the danger of a renewed wave of speculation if the Union were renewed for as short a period as six months'.[19] The warning was duly reported and noted.

The Common Market creditors were far from trying to force a premature British move. They offered their proposal primarily to obstruct British efforts to add an *ad hoc* credit system to EPU automatic credits. Calvet saw no reason to change the EPU simply because a free trade area might be formed.

Nevertheless, the Board did not agree until June 1958 to renew the EPU unchanged for another year. Even then, Getz Wold insisted on registering a dissenting view. He wanted the gold payments ratio to be reduced to 60 per cent, and to 50 per cent for extreme creditors, namely Germany. Only at the last minute—the OEEC Council meeting on 27 June 1958—did Norway agree not to press this point further.[20]

COUNTRY PROBLEMS

Throughout its last years, the Managing Board continued to hold quarterly reviews of the economic situation of each member. Although few countries posed problems, the three with the largest quotas in the system were a continuing concern. For most other members, the reviews revealed steady progress toward sounder and more prosperous economies.

In October 1955, a delegation from Vienna proudly presented a picture of Austrian economic growth, success in bringing its foreign accounts

[17] US del. tel. and airgram to Washington. POLTO 2872 (4 Mar. 1958) and POLTO A-543 (21 Mar. 1958).

[18] S. W. P. (Payton), 'Future of the EPU' (24 Mar. 1958) and G. W. Wilson, 'Renewal of the EPU' (24 Apr. 1958). Bank of England OV 46/23.

[19] S. W. P. (Payton), 'Future of the EPU' (24 Mar. 1958). Bank of England OV 46/23.

[20] US del. tel. to Washington. POLTO 4385 (27 June 1958).

into balance, and determination to maintain a tight fiscal and credit policy. A structural debtor at the beginning of the EPU and an economic weak sister since World War I, Austria had brought its EPU position into balance and expected to keep it there.[21] Greece, another initial structural debtor, had been settling entirely in gold because its debtor quota was blocked.[22] In July 1957, the block was removed because Greece had achieved sufficient stability in both its internal and external economic relations. Italy managed to maintain a prospering economy while reducing its EPU deficits in 1956. It reported surpluses in 1957, and Carli then agreed to terminate the 1955 special credit that had been granted to Italy but never used. Norway continued to run EPU deficits and to claim justification for not reaching the 90 per cent trade liberalization level. However, it was able to finance its deficits, amortize older EPU debts, and add somewhat to its rather small foreign exchange reserves.[23]

The Board asked pointed questions of country representatives at each of these quarterly reviews. It also offered advice from time to time, usually in an effort to support country officials who were trying to improve their government's fiscal and monetary institutions and policies. Strong recommendations did not seem appropriate for countries that were, on the whole, progressing satisfactorily toward the objectives of the Union.

Most of the large creditors of the EPU's earlier years moved toward greater balance with their EPU partners. After July 1955, Switzerland ran deficits for three years, the Netherlands for two. In mid-decade, Belgium finally began to expand production at as high a rate as other EPU members, while still avoiding much inflationary pressure.[24] After running a surplus of $222 million in EPU financial year 1955/6, it reduced its surplus to only $14 million in the next.

In its last months, the Board was able to address a problem that had long hung over its operations. From the inception of the EPU system, Turkey had been little more than a nominal member. After its debtor quota was exhausted, it had been denied further credit and had deliberalized its trade with the other members. Finally, in 1958, this situation came to a head, and the Board helped the IMF organize a drastic stabilization programme for Turkey. Chapter 16 provides an account of what happened.

The most serious country problems confronting the Board concerned Germany, France, and the United Kingdom. France and the UK had persistent balance-of-payments problems, including large EPU deficits,

---

[21] EPU Board Minutes, 64th Session (17–20 Oct. 1955). OEEC MBC/M(55)11, Part II.

[22] EPU Board, *Second Annual Report* (1952), 38, and *Seventh Annual Report* (1957), 62.

[23] EPU Board Minutes, 66th Session (13–16 Dec. 1955). OEEC MBC/M(55)13, Part II.
Also EPU Board Minutes, 72nd Session (28 May–1 June 1956). OEEC MBC/M(56)6, Part III.

[24] EPU Board Minutes, 69th Session (13–14 Mar. 1956). OEEC MBC/M(56)3, Part II.

over the last three and a half years of the Union. Germany ran large surpluses that almost matched the combined deficits of France and the UK.[25] Totalling more than $2 billion, the French deficits were almost twice the size of the UK's. They were by far the most troublesome for the Managing Board.

The German surpluses and the French deficits commanded most of the Board's attention during its last years, as reported in the next two chapters. Concerns about the situation of the United Kingdom in 1956 and 1957 were expressed in Board reports, but it could do little more than watch and comment cautiously.

United Kingdom Crises

For three years, from 1955 to 1957, the British economy floundered from crisis to crisis. Butler's September 1955 statement in Istanbul was followed by a more restrictive Autumn Budget. Thereafter, the draining of UK foreign exchange reserves stopped, and they began to increase slowly. However, wage pressures kept British inflation going, despite a sharp decline in the rate of increase in production. The new Chancellor, Harold Macmillan, reinforced the restrictive measures in February 1956, including an increase in the discount rate to 5.5 per cent.

Although sterling troubles were brewing once again, Governor Cobbold sought the Chancellor's permission in April 1956 to unify the rates for transferable and dollar sterling, making sterling fully convertible *de facto* and replacing the EPU with the EMA.[26] Macmillan firmly rejected this proposal, as his predecessor had done, refusing to risk pressure for removing discrimination against the dollar area. Two months later, Macmillan sent Eden a gloomy 'Half-time' paper on the economic situation and proposed drastic steps.[27] They included sharp cuts in defence and controls over non-essential construction to forestall a possible devaluation of sterling and break-up of the sterling area. Pressures for wage increases seemed to be beyond control at the time.

After Nasser seized the Canal, a small cabinet Suez Committee began to plan a military action. Macmillan supported the decision to proceed, despite Treasury and Bank of England warnings. His subordinates felt that without US support for the action, 'the strain might be so great that, whatever precautionary measures were taken, we should be unable

---

[25] EPU Board, *Final Report* (1959), 36.

[26] Governor's private and personal memo for Chancellor of Exchequer (12 Apr. 1956). Bank of England OV 44/65.

[27] Chancellor of Exchequer, 'Half-time'. Draft paper on economic situation. Sent to Prime Min. and later to Foreign Sec. and Min. of Defence (4 June 1956). PRO PREM 11/1325.

to maintain the value of the currency'.[28] Britain had lost a further $318 million in reserves by the end of October 1956, and the Chancellor was desperately considering a lower support rate for transferable sterling and a return to bilateral payments arrangements.[29] Macmillan told Eden that 'without the oil, both the United Kingdom and Western Europe are lost.'[30] His accompanying paper estimated the heavy costs of an interruption in traffic through the Canal, including higher prices for oil and much larger costs of transportation.

As predicted, speculation against sterling accelerated after the troops landed. Macmillan quickly counselled acquiescence to the US demand for withdrawal. In response, the US supported IMF assistance totalling $1.3 billion, part in a drawing and part in a standby credit. In addition, it provided a $500 million credit from the Export-Import Bank, and waived $110 million in interest due on its 1945 loan. Britain drew $561 million from the IMF and also added $250 million from the Export-Import Bank to its reserves.

Such sums were obviously of a magnitude well beyond the resources of the EPU. Furthermore, they were provided in response to the post-Suez crisis of confidence in sterling, without the economic policy conditions that the Managing Board attached to its special credits. The United Kingdom reported large EPU deficits between mid-1955 and the end of 1957, but it was able to settle 75 per cent of them in dollars and also repay some of its older debts. Still concerned about the deficits, the Managing Board would have liked to suggest remedial action but lacked the leverage to do so effectively. Nor was it asked to join the operation to support sterling, though it was a very interested bystander. While further speculation against sterling ended soon after the large credits were announced, very little reversal of the previous speculation occurred.[31] The higher cost of oil and tankers still bore heavily on the UK economy and its balance of payments.

Soon afterwards, Macmillan succeeded Eden as Prime Minister and Thorneycroft became Chancellor of the Exchequer. Thorneycroft's Spring 1957 Budget was tighter than his predecessor's, but the UK economic situation remained precarious. By September, Britain's foreign exchange

---

[28] E. E. B. (Sir Edward Bridges). Memo to Chancellor of Exchequer. Reports meeting in Treasury attended by Deputy Governor, Bank of England (H. C. B. Mynors) and Bolton (12 Sept. 1956). Bank of England G1/124.

[29] D. H. F. Rickett, 'Possible Action if the Drain Continued'. Memo to Bridges (29 Sept. 1956). Bank of England G1/124.

[30] UK Treasury, 'The Economic Consequences of Colonel Nasser'. Paper sent to Prime Min. by H. M. (Macmillan) with accompanying memo. Eden immediately approved circulation to Suez Com. (26 Aug. 1956). PRO PREM 11/1135.

[31] OEEC Secretariat, 'Supplementary Report on the Current Situation in France, Germany and the United Kingdom' (6 June 1957). OEEC C(57)103.

reserves had dropped to $1.25 billion, excluding the sums drawn from the IMF. Finally, the government took the draconian restrictive measures that had been needed for so long to stabilize the economy and generate real confidence in the pound sterling. Severe additional cuts were made in the government budget, the discount rate was raised to the then incredibly high rate of 7 per cent, and the private banks agreed not to increase their loan levels above the average level of the previous twelve months.

At the September 1957 Annual Meetings of the IMF, both the German and British Governors declared that existing parities would be maintained. This time, speculation was not only contained but reversed. UK production subsequently ceased to expand for a year, prices stabilized, and reserves rose steadily, reaching $3.1 billion at the end of 1958. Great Britain could finally contemplate a move to convertibility from strength. For those who had been waiting on the other side of the Channel, the long-anticipated 'C-Day' was about to dawn.

14 How Germany's Surpluses Began

Germany's surpluses started early in the life of the EPU and still preoccupy the international agenda in the 1980s. They began shortly after the resolution of the 1950/1 payments crisis, leaving the Managing Board little time to savour its first success. The Board's elation and relief faded as Germany's cumulative EPU deficit was soon transformed into a rapidly growing creditor position. Over the next 35 years, the broad picture of international payments showed the Federal Republic running a current account surplus in all but five years and rapidly accumulating foreign exchange reserves. The origins can be traced in Table 5. Except in 1955, German payments surpluses surged throughout the life of the EPU.

TABLE 5. *Evolution of Principal Components of the German Balance of Payments, 1950–1958 (in billions of Deutsche Mark)[a]*

	Net Merchandise Trade (f.o.b.)	Balance on Current Account	Net Capital Movements	Increase in Gold and Foreign Exchange Reserves
1950	−2.31	−0.32	+0.64	−0.56
1951	+1.49	+2.48	−0.54	2.04
1952	+2.16	+2.73	+0.01	2.90
1953	+3.65	+4.15	−0.70	3.64
1954	+3.92	+4.01	−0.71	2.97
1955	+3.23	+2.68	−0.64	1.85
1956	+5.62	+4.99	−0.16	5.01
1957	+7.32	+6.54	−1.65	5.12
1958	+7.36	+6.63	−2.73	3.44

[a] $1 US = 4.20 Deutsche Mark.

Source: Deutsche Bundesbank (1988), 254–5.

A FRAGILE CONVALESCENT?

Export-mindedness

From his earliest days at ECA, Hoffman had preached about Europe's need for exports to close the dollar gap. Nowhere was his message better heeded than in German industry and government. Over the succeeding decades, 'export-mindedness' would become a hallmark of German thinking about its economy. However, in the early 1950s, no one imagined Germany would be able to export enough to earn persistent surpluses of foreign exchange.

At the time, the German economy was regarded at home and abroad as a fragile convalescent, not an international economic locomotive. Germany reluctantly agreed to assume the latter role much later, at the Bonn Economic Summit in 1978. It soon regretted acquiescing, as its current account dipped into the red for one of the few times since the fifties.

When the surpluses first appeared in 1951, the Managing Board welcomed them as a sign that Germany would be able to repay quickly both its special credit and the debts within its EPU quota. Yet the Board remained sceptical about how long the turnaround would last. Germany's deficits might well reappear once its inventories were depleted and trade liberalization resumed.

Debts and Restitution

Within Germany, and to some extent in foreign circles, current account surpluses seemed necessary and desirable. Under Chancellor Adenauer's forceful leadership, the Federal Republic was determined to gain international acceptance and respectability. An important element in this policy was settling all Germany's outstanding debts and paying indemnities for the damages of the Nazi past—insofar as they could be compensated with money. Moreover, the occupying powers made their recognition of German sovereignty dependent on an agreement to repay prewar and postwar debts, both public and private.

In the ensuing debt negotiations and arrangements, all parties were mindful of the 'transfer problem' that had plagued the interwar period. Protectionist policies of trading partners had then prevented Germany from earning current account surpluses. As a result, Germany could not acquire adequate supplies of the currencies needed to pay reparations to designated recipients. In the 1950s, the EPU and OEEC Code of Trade Liberalisation made it possible for Germany to meet its transfer obligations. However, it still had to earn the surpluses.

By the time the London Debt Agreement was concluded in February 1953, Germany had already accumulated a substantial cushion of foreign exchange reserves. Nevertheless, the terms for repayment were generous, since all participants were anxious to avoid repeating past mistakes. A few months earlier, in September 1952, the Federal Republic had also concluded a restitution agreement with the State of Israel, under which it would provide DM 3.45 billion in goods over a twelve-year period. Thereafter, Germany passed legislation to indemnify persons who had suffered from Nazi persecution. Because a preponderant majority were living abroad, large foreign exchange payments would be required for decades.

While the Federal Republic freely assumed all these obligations, substantial doubts remained about whether it could continue to earn sufficient current account surpluses to meet them.[1] Net payments for indemnities and donations first began to bulk large in the German balance-of-payments accounts for 1955. By that time, their annual rate exceeded DM 800 million, nearly $200 million. That sum doubled over the next two years and continued to grow, but Germany's payments surpluses with the EPU area and the rest of the world also grew. Its foreign exchange reserves totalled some $3 billion by the end of 1955— the equivalent of more than six months of imports—and the increase persisted.[2]

Mild Concern, 1952-4

At first, the OEEC felt encouraged by Germany's economic progress and success in stimulating exports. 'Germany's share in world exports . . . remains well below pre-war,' it wrote in January 1954, but 'recovery and expansion are taking place at an adequate pace.'[3] A year later, the OEEC noted that 'the increase in exports had to be regarded as a normal development bound to continue if Germany was to regain its pre-war position as a supplier of Member countries, the EPU area and the whole world.' Nevertheless, it concluded that it is 'clearly desirable that the [German] government should continue and intensify its action to reduce it [its EPU surplus]'.[4]

The Managing Board was only somewhat less indulgent as Germany's EPU surpluses mounted. For the financial year beginning in July 1952, it agreed to increase Germany's EPU quota. In September 1952, it proposed a $100 million *rallonge*—an extension of the quota that would be settled half in gold and half in credit. In fact, Germany did not exhaust its quota until May 1953, and the *rallonge* was extended by another $50 million for the year beginning in July 1953. Von Mangoldt readily agreed to these settlement terms.

At about this time, von Mangoldt joined the EPU creditors' club, a group that urged a hardening of the EPU as the appropriate path to convertibility (explained in Chapter 11). During subsequent negotiations on refurbishing the EPU, vehement debates arose. As the Union's largest and most persistent creditor, the Federal Republic became a special target for criticism and recommendations from deficit countries. In October 1953, Germany agreed to a further $200 million *rallonge*, and in December another $300 million was added. For surpluses above 40 per cent of

[1] Bank deutscher Länder, *Geschäftsbericht* (1952), 80. Stolper, Häuser, Borchardt (1967), 253.
[2] See Table 7.
[3] OEEC, *Progress and Problems of the European Economy: Fifth Annual Report* (1954), 111–13.
[4] OEEC, *Sixth Report: From Recovery towards Economic Strength* (1955), ii. 60, 72.

Germany's quota, von Mangoldt asked for 65 per cent gold in settlements, but agreed to 50 per cent, pending resolution of the debt repayment issue. After mid-1955, all EPU settlements, including the German *rallonges*, changed to 75 per cent gold.

THE 'GOOD CREDITOR'

Advice and Response

At each decision about a further *rallonge*, the Board pressed the German authorities to take additional measures consistent with 'good creditor policies'. But pressures from the Board as a whole (and the OEEC itself) were confined to measures that would increase German imports, reduce export promotion, and augment the export of capital. Recommendations concerning imports went well beyond further liberalization to unilateral tariff reduction, reduced agricultural protection, and the removal of restrictions on purchasing foreign transportation services. To promote the export of capital, the Federal Republic was urged to lift exchange restrictions and to broaden its capital market.

The German government did not respond as fully and as rapidly to all this advice as the Board would have liked, but it did enough to demonstrate a sincere desire to co-operate and be a responsible partner. Von Mangoldt was remarkably successful in convincing German policy-makers to open up the German economy to foreign imports and to become attuned to its future role as a major exporter of capital. The free market orientation of the Bonn government provided a generally receptive climate for his representations.

Most invisible transactions were gradually liberalized, and the export of capital to the rest of the EPU area was permitted and encouraged. Germany was one of the first EPU members to lift restrictions on the transfer of interest and dividends to other members.[5] Blocked D-Mark accounts were liberalized in 1954, and the regulation of capital transfers to other EPU countries was substantially relaxed.[6] In 1954, some $18 million worth of goods were purchased in the EPU area for delivery to Israel under the restitution agreement.[7] By 1964, three-quarters of all German foreign debts had been repaid, in advance of previously agreed schedules.

[5] OEEC, 'Transfer of Capital Earnings'. Notification from Federal Republic of Germany (4 Oct. 1953). OEEC Council C(53)231.
[6] EPU Board, 'Further Relaxation of German Foreign Exchange Regulations'. Statement by von Mangoldt, 51st Session (26 Oct. 1954). OEEC MBC(54)64.
[7] EPU Board, *Fourth Annual Report* (1954), 14.

Germany resumed its liberal import policy, freeing 90 per cent of its trade with other EPU members by 1953. Customs tariffs for industrial products were reduced, in five unilateral steps, from 16 per cent to 9.6 per cent between 1955 and 1957.[8] Agricultural imports were a more difficult political issue in Germany, as in most other countries, and their effective tariff rates remained at 7.5 per cent. The lower import barriers did not restrain German surpluses for very long. Instead, they led to lower costs and prices and thus made Germany even more competitive on world markets. Despite von Mangoldt's specific request, the Managing Board refused to offer special praise for German liberalization of imports from the dollar area.[9] That, too, would improve competitiveness.

Until 1955, von Mangoldt was able to persuade his authorities to yield gracefully on their demand for higher gold payments in settling German *rallonges*. Germany had little negotiating leverage unless it was prepared to restrict exports or withdraw from the EPU altogether. Neither step was consistent with its economic, commercial, or financial interests. Its EPU partners valued the important and expanding German market, as well as the imports available for D-Marks instead of dollars. These considerations limited the scope for bargaining, as both sides realized. They accepted a reasonable compromise for settlements: Germany would receive 50 per cent in gold for further surpluses and lend the other half to the EPU.

More Expansionary Policies

Attracting imports through faster growth was another standard feature in the conventional bag of good creditor policies, but it was difficult to apply to Germany. During the years 1952-4, the German economy was growing at an annual rate of between 7 and 9 per cent and absorbing the stream of refugees from eastern Germany into the labour force (see Table 6). To sustain that growth, the central bank's discount rate was reduced progressively from 6 per cent during the payments crisis to 3 per cent in 1954-5.

---

[8] Schmieding (1988).
[9] US del. tel. to Washington. ECOTO 1206 (25 Feb. 1954).

TABLE 6.   *Annual Growth in German GNP and Inflation, 1951–1958*
(*in percentages*)

	Real GNP Growth (in 1980 prices)	Inflation Rate (Cost of Living)
1951	+ 9.4	7.8
1952	+ 9.0	2.0
1953	+ 8.5	− 1.7
1954	+ 7.1	0.1
1955	+11.8	1.7
1956	+ 7.5	2.6
1957	+ 5.9	2.0
1958	+ 4.1	2.2

Source: Deutsche Bundesbank, *Monthly Report* (May 1988), 17.

Getz Wold recommended even more expansionary policies and less preoccupation with price stability. Responding to Scandinavian concerns, the British conditioned their 1954 debt repayment offer on internal, as well as external, German measures to increase imports. At about the same time, the OEEC Economic Committee concluded that it would be desirable for Germany to intensify its economic expansion by reducing taxation, lowering interest rates, and other appropriate steps.[10] None the less, the majority of Managing Board members were hesitant about urging measures that might stimulate inflation. Germany's success in restraining price increases was something von Mangoldt's colleagues wanted their own countries to emulate. They were reluctant to follow Getz Wold or the Economic Committee on this matter.

Nor did they heed Getz Wold's suggestion in 1954 that Germany might revalue the D-Mark. Committed to the virtues of exchange rate stability, the Continentals preferred to urge other countries to restrain their inflationary pressures as successfully as Germany had done. Thereafter, deficit countries could devalue their currencies, if necessary, to correct damage from previous inflation. A German revaluation would only ease the pressures on other countries to look seriously at adopting anti-inflationary policies. On this matter, the Board also supported the conclusion of the Economic Committee that 'an appreciation of the deutschemark . . . might worsen the German dollar position, and thus retard convertibility.' Managing Board recommendations did not mention exchange rate adjustment.

[10] OEEC Economic Com. Report, 'Causes of Disequilibrium in the EPU which have led to Germany's Extreme Creditor Position' (24 Mar. 1954). OEEC Council C(54)82.

During the three years preceding the European Monetary Agreement, the Managing Board was preoccupied primarily with convertibility and probably paid less attention to the German surpluses than it might have otherwise. German willingness to agree to the *rallonges* limited the Board's sense of urgency about resolving problems posed by the surpluses; the 1954 refurbishing placated German authorities. The rising tide of foreign exchange reserves in most EPU countries diverted concern from the fact that German reserves were accumulating much faster than those of any other member.

ON THE HORNS OF A DILEMMA: 1955-1956

For the German economy, 1955 was in many ways a watershed. The country reached full employment, while the rate of GNP growth surged to 11.8 per cent in real terms. The cost of living, which had not risen since 1952, increased by 1.7 per cent. For the first time since the Korean crisis, the current account surplus decreased, from $955 million in 1954 to $638 million in 1955 (see Table 5). German leaders found themselves impaled on the horns of a major policy dilemma. They saw signs of an overheating economy, but the external surpluses seemed to warrant economic expansion.

'The Julius Tower'

In the view of the Bank deutscher Länder (then Germany's central bank), monetary policy could no longer rely merely on 'the braking effect of the public authorities' cash surplus'.[11] Hitherto, the government had planned for budget surpluses, anticipating large defence expenditures once the European Defence Community was established. The prolonged and failed EDC negotiations had produced a pile of sterile funds, amounting to more than DM 7 billion by 1956. The accumulation was nicknamed the 'Julius tower', after the Berlin fortress tower where Frederick the Great had kept his war treasure.

The 'tower' was built out of tax revenues set aside for later use. It thus sterilized money, reducing liquidity and exercising a contractionary influence on the German economy. 'Unintentionally the Federal budget assumed in part a task of the central bank,' Emminger later commented.[12] None the less, the German economy boomed through the first half of the

[11] Bank deutscher Länder Report (1956), 17.
[12] Emminger (1986), 76.

1950s, with high growth rates and without much inflation. Not unexpectedly, the tower's very existence later led to a parliamentary spending spree.

Whatever the anti-inflationary effect of the tower, it also tended to increase German foreign exchange surpluses and reserves (see Table 7). That relationship hardly entered into the thinking of the Finance Ministry, which thought simply in terms of accumulating funds for a rapid defence build-up. Foreign criticism was muted because other countries expected much of the tower to be spent on imported supplies and equipment. During the second half of 1955 and thereafter, the Bank deutscher Länder felt that monetary policy could no longer be based on the anti-inflationary influences implicit in constructing this tower of cash. Nevertheless, it was still growing when the Bank acted.

TABLE 7. *German Net Foreign Reserves: End of Year, 1951–1958 (in billions of Deutsche Mark)[a]*

	Total	of which		
		Gold	US & Canada dollars	Claims on EPU[b]
1951	1.5	0.1	1.4	0.0
1952	4.6	0.6	2.1	1.1
1953	8.2	1.4	3.5	1.8
1954	10.9	2.6	5.5	2.1
1955	12.8	3.9	5.8	2.2
1956	17.9	6.3	7.3	2.9
1957	23.0	10.7	6.1	4.2
1958	26.2	11.1	7.4	4.6

[a] $1 US = 4.20 Deutsche Mark.
[b] not taking account of last EPU settlement in year.

Source: Bank deutscher Länder and Deutsche Bundesbank, *Monthly Reports* (1954–8).

Discount Rate Increases

On 3 August 1955, the Bank deutscher Länder increased the discount rate from 3 to 3.5 per cent, raised minimum reserve requirements for the commercial banks, and introduced quotas for the amounts the banks could rediscount. It wanted to give a clear signal that 'a turning point' had been reached in its hitherto 'liberal' credit policy.[13] With growing labour

[13] Bank deutscher Länder Report (1955), 1.

shortages, wage increases had accelerated and the ratio of investment to GNP had reached 23 per cent. As prices began to rise, the Bank believed that the German economy was overheating.

Judging that its August measures had not been effective, the Bank pulled the reins in further during the following spring. In each of two steps, it raised the discount rate by a full percentage point, to 5.5 per cent by mid-May. 'The rising trend in demand during the first months of 1956 continued almost as strongly as before', while capital investment 'if anything actually rose further'.[14] These actions were taken despite the fact that German EPU surpluses had risen sharply to $144 million in the first quarter of the calendar year 1956.

Storms of Criticism

As might have been expected, the Managing Board's reactions bordered on the violent, and von Mangoldt found it difficult to justify the central bank's behaviour. The Board expressed concern after the first increase in the discount rate, fearing it would accentuate the tendency for German EPU surpluses to increase.[15] It attacked 'the extreme domestic orientation of German policies and its neglect of external considerations in policy making . . .'.[16] Von Mangoldt admitted that defence expenditures in 1956 would be insignificant and unlikely to reduce German EPU surpluses. His promise that Germany would permit exporters to use their foreign exchange earnings to purchase foreign stocks and shares offered little consolation to his colleagues. High German interest rates were likely to be more attractive to the exporters.

Six weeks later, after the second discount rate increase, he tried to explain to the Board the evidence of Germany's 'booming economic situation' and the need for anti-inflationary measures.[17] His announcement of further dollar liberalization as an anti-inflationary measure produced more dismay about the prospective trend of German EPU surpluses. More imports from the dollar area might well mean less from Europe.

At a late July 1956 Board meeting, von Mangoldt emphasized that 'speculative elements were largely responsible for the size of the recent German surpluses.'[18] The Board responded by recording its considered view that 'one of the reasons for the present flow of short-term capital

[14] Bank deutscher Länder Report (1956), 6.

[15] US del. tel. to Washington. ECOTO 933 (20 Apr. 1956).

[16] Reports by von Mangoldt (24 July 1956) P/143/56, (8 Sept. 1956) P/145/56, (12 Oct. 1956) P/146/56, (17 Nov. 1956) P/148/56, (22 Feb. 1957) P/157/57.
EPU Board Minutes, 70th Session (17–18 Apr. 1956). OEEC MBC/M(56)4, Part II.

[17] EPU Board Minutes, statement by von Mangoldt, 72nd Session (28 May–1 June 1956). OEEC MBC/M(56)5, Annex I.

[18] EPU Board Minutes, 74th Session (19–21 July 1956). OEEC MBC/M(56)8, Annex III.

to Germany . . . was the differences between interest rates in Germany
and abroad.'

Tempest in Germany

The tightening of monetary policy also caused a storm within Germany.
Chancellor Adenauer was incensed. The latest decisions to increase the
discount rate had been taken by the central bank council in the presence,
and with the approval, of the Ministers of Economics and of Finance.
Both had failed to co-ordinate their stance with the Chancellor, and he
rebuked them publicly in a speech before the Federation of German
Industry. He accused the Bank deutscher Länder of trying to 'guillotine'
German small industry, which he thought would be hit the hardest. This
was one of the most serious conflicts in the history of German postwar
central banking.

By autumn, the Bank started to ease monetary policy again. It offered
many reasons for its course correction, insisting particularly that its
intention was 'not to stimulate activity'.[19] The growth in German GNP
had slowed only to 7.5 per cent, but the cost of living increased by 2.6 per
cent in 1956. Soothing the Chancellor's ruffled feathers was undoubtedly a
factor in the Bank council's decision. A more important factor, however,
was that its measures had turned out to be self-defeating. Larger foreign
surpluses and imports of capital had offset the restrictive effect of monetary
policy. Von Mangoldt had reported the warnings of the Managing Board
that this would happen, but the Bank apparently had to learn from its
own experience. With an undervalued currency and liberalized capital
movements, it found little room for manoeuvre. Limited in its ability to
use monetary policy to control inflation, it watched the cost of living rise
at annual rates of more than 2 per cent for the rest of the EPU period.

Over the ensuing years, the lesson of this early experience would have
to be relearned on many occasions. With fewer exchange restrictions,
short term capital was freer to move from country to country to take
advantage of interest rate differentials. As a result, monetary authorities
responsible for major currencies could no longer alter their policies
without regard for their effect on other currencies. Surplus countries
with strong currencies had to be especially cautious about using monetary
measures to restrain internal inflationary pressures. Not only might they
put unreasonable pressure on the managers of weaker currencies, but
their own purposes could be thwarted by an inflow of speculative funds.

---

[19] Bank deutscher Länder Report (1956), 19.

REVALUING THE D-MARK: CONFLICT AT HOME, SILENCE ABROAD

While German authorities were stymied by their monetary policy dilemma, the exchange rate of the D-Mark became the object of another heated debate and bitter controversy. That argument, however, was largely confined to Germany.

The occupation powers had fixed the exchange rate of the D-Mark rather arbitrarily at 3.33 to the dollar when the German currency was reformed in 1948. A year later, Britain devalued the pound sterling by 30.5 per cent. The new German Parliament followed suit, but it devalued the D-Mark by only 20.6 per cent, to 4.20 to the dollar. That decision also was somewhat arbitrary and political: the new rate was identical with the parity of the Reichsmark before 1933. When the Federal Republic joined the International Monetary Fund in 1952, it certified the 4.20 rate as the official par value of the D-Mark.

Rumours and Denials

Revaluation of the Deutsche Mark became an intense political issue in Germany after the Bank deutscher Länder began to tighten credit in 1955. Foreign currency traders thought that the German authorities would have to choose between revaluing the currency and inflating it. They bet on revaluation, increasing their credit balances with German banks even after the banks were forbidden to pay interest on such accounts. The 'leads and lags' also developed heavily in favour of the German currency.

By June 1956, the market-place was buzzing with rumours of both a German revaluation and a British devaluation to deal with the sterling crisis (see Chapter 13). At the Managing Board, von Mangoldt dismissed this public speculation, recording his regret that German official denials had been 'treated lightly'.[20] The German government neither intended to change the present parity of the mark, nor had it ever proposed the introduction of varying exchange rates, as had been rumoured. Nor had Germany ever recommended that other countries change the parity of their currencies.

The Board acknowledged von Mangoldt's statement with little comment. To the extent that they were aware of a controversy within Germany, members thought a firm decision had been taken against revaluation. A Managing Board attempt to reopen the matter might only heighten currency speculation and exacerbate the problems of the then weaker currencies, especially the pound sterling. 'Talking up' a strong currency

[20] EPU Board Minutes, 74th Session (19–21 July 1956). OEEC MBC/M(56)8, Annex III.

also meant 'talking down' a weaker one, as currency managers would learn many times in later years, to their regret.

Von Mangoldt's written statement noted that the rumours had been fanned by a 'misinterpretation' of a public utterance by Minister Erhard. In fact, Erhard was giving voice to his own losing position in a major dispute with other German authorities. His main arguments, and those of other supporters of revaluation, were: 'the inflationary impact of persistent balance-of-payments surpluses, the lopsided structural evolution of the German economy arising from overdependence on exports, the disturbing impact of the balance-of-payments disequilibrium on international trade and payments, and the dislike of the mistaken impression of "wealth" conveyed by Germany's mounting foreign-exchange reserves'.[21]

In the 1980s, it is difficult to understand the strength of the resistance to such reasoning within Germany. The German public itself would later recognize that revaluation was in its own interest and a contribution to the prestige of its currency. But fixed exchange rates were accepted doctrine in 1956. Exchange rate adjustments were a measure of last resort, permissible only in case of a 'fundamental disequilibrium' under IMF statutes and subject to IMF prior consent. No major European currency rate had been adjusted since 1949.

'Curing the Quick Instead of the Sick'

In the mid-1950s, revaluation was staunchly opposed by a majority of the German administration as well as the business and banking community. Their reasons were manifold. They argued that the German payments surpluses were a temporary phenomenon, not the manifestation of a fundamental disequilibrium. Once defence expenditures began in earnest, German exports would be restrained, as would its payments surpluses.

They also believed the onus for remedial action should be put on inflation-prone countries, such as France and the UK. They—not Germany—needed to alter fiscal and monetary policies and adjust exchange rates. A moralistic metaphor became popular in German circles. Was it not absurd 'to operate on a healthy economy in order to cure sick economies'?[22] The weaker currencies were in deficit with the dollar area as well as the EPU. Germany, on the other hand, was still running deficits in its dollar trade, though its EPU surpluses were larger. This made it natural, so the argument went, that Germany 'stayed with the dollar'.

---

[21] Erhard before press in Dortmund (9 Aug. 1957), quoted by Emminger (1977), 9.
[22] Emminger (1977), 10.

Antagonists further questioned whether currency revaluation had ever been successful. Precedents were hard to find, but the alleged failure of a Swedish revaluation in 1916-18 was frequently used to deny the appropriateness of German action.

The general public was easily frightened by warnings, such as 'don't tinker with the value (and par value) of money' and 'Is revaluation another kind of currency reform?' Having experienced two runaway inflations and traumatic currency reforms in one generation, the populace readily responded to such alarms.

The hard core of the opposition to a revaluation of the D-Mark came from the export lobby. Hermann Abs and Robert Pferdmenges headed major German commercial banks with substantial stakes in the export industry, both as sources of financing and as shareholders. Chancellor Adenauer relied heavily on their financial expertise, and recognized that Abs had negotiated the London Debt Agreement for him with great skill. Elections were scheduled for 1957 and the government counted on the support of export interests. German success in penetrating export markets had become a source of national pride; much of the improvement in economic conditions was ascribed to it. Revaluation might endanger that achievement, it was argued, and the Chancellor sided with these sentiments. So did President Vocke of the Bank deutscher Länder.

The Erhard-Macmillan Contretemps

Erhard had reopened the issue on an international level, prompting von Mangoldt's denials. Shortly before the OEEC ministerial meeting scheduled for 17-19 July 1956, he wrote to British Chancellor Macmillan, proposing an international monetary conference. Its purpose would be to discuss exchange rate relationships and to consider a general move to devalue deficit currencies against both the dollar and the D-Mark. He wrote, 'Theoretically, it is just as possible for currencies with a stable price level to revalue their currencies . . . It would, however, appear more appropriate that in those countries where the exchange rates and prices have remained in proper economic relation, no change should be made and that these rates . . . should be adopted as reference units for the general adjustment of exchange relations.'[23]

Only a month before, Macmillan had sent Prime Minister Eden his 'Half-time' memorandum, proposing drastic steps to forestall a possible devaluation of sterling and break-up of the sterling area. His commitment to the $2.80 par value never faltered. Erhard's proposal thus had no chance of being considered seriously. To make matters worse, Erhard

[23] Quoted in Travers notes on UK Treasury Files. OEEC EPU Archive Box 57.

disclosed his letter's existence to a British newspaper, the *Financial Times*, in an interview. He told the reporter that if countries did not wish to devalue, he would accept their using wider margins of 5 per cent on either side of parity. '[Germany] would be prepared to enter into serious negotiations about the setting up of a long-term credit fund to alleviate structural weaknesses in the balance of payments of such OEEC countries as would be ready to readjust their exchange practices.'[24]

Erhard was probably trying to reopen an issue on which he had been defeated within his own government. Undoubtedly, his proposal for a multilateral currency realignment expressed sincere conviction about what would serve the interests of all countries concerned. Macmillan's reply was brusque and hostile. He considered Erhard's interview to be 'most unfortunate'. Quoting Butler's September 1955 statement at Istanbul, he added that 'my Government do not see any useful purpose, and would not be prepared to take part in any international discussion of the exchange value of sterling.'

Nor were other Europeans pleased by the newspaper report of Erhard's proposal. Ansiaux noted that the strong D-Mark had attracted short term capital from Belgium and produced a rather welcome EPU deficit.[25] If Erhard formally presented his proposal to the OEEC, Belgium would insist that the OEEC had no jurisdiction for discussing exchange rates. That was a matter for the International Monetary Fund.

In private conversations with Macmillan during the ministerial meeting, Erhard apologized for his newspaper interview, saying he had no desire to discuss publicly the question of flexible exchange rates. He supported the OEEC Secretary General's idea of setting up a Ministerial Working Group on Internal Financial Stability, recognizing that it would consider the German surplus problem, among others. The Managing Board was asked, of course, to prepare a report for a meeting of the Working Group Deputies toward the end of the year.

Utopian Idea, Unmentionable Remedy

Late in July 1956, Nasser seized the Suez Canal, and an uprising in Hungary followed shortly. These events temporarily diverted attention from payments imbalances and exchange rates. Meanwhile, the German surpluses in the EPU continued to mount.

Within the Bank deutscher Länder, Emminger used his position to advocate revaluation. In the autumn of 1956, he presented Vocke with an eleven-page confidential memorandum that proposed widening the

---

[24] *Financial Times* (11 July 1956).
[25] Minutes of the Board (13 July 1956). National Bank of Belgium PV 1414/1. Also Deliberations of the Governing Council of the National Bank of Belgium (18 July 1956).

margins of fluctuation of the D-Mark to 6 to 8 per cent on either side of parity.[26] He later wrote that he had put his hands into a hornets' nest. When Vocke finally called a secret meeting of the Bank Directorate on 12 December 1956, Emminger found himself completely isolated.

In the spring of 1957, a confidential report of the Advisory Council of the German Federal Ministry for Economic Affairs endorsed a co-ordinated realignment of exchange rates.[27] Thereupon, Erhard paid a private visit to Vocke to seek his support for realignment, which would, of course, involve revaluation of the D-Mark. Erhard was worried about 'imported inflation' prior to the forthcoming autumn elections, but the central bank president's attitude was uncompromising. Per Jacobsson, the newly appointed Managing Director of the IMF, had recently sent him a letter that opposed an upward valuation of the D-Mark. Jacobsson never ceased his opposition to that measure. When Germany finally decided to revalue in March 1961, Emminger presented the official German request. Jacobsson received him in his office with the words, 'What have you done, you scoundrel?'[28]

Emminger later commented, 'In the then existing circumstances, however, concerted action by all the countries concerned was a Utopian idea. The process of multilateral exchange rate adjustment, which would indeed have been appropriate as early as 1957, dragged on over a period of ten years and a number of currency crises.'[29]

When the Managing Board assembled in September 1956 to tackle its report for the Working Group Deputies, it reviewed the economic situation of some eight OEEC countries. The report was limited to four— France, Germany, the United Kingdom, and Belgium. Its recommendations focused on the first two, and Germany soon became the centre of the debate.[30]

Virtually all the other Board members were sceptical about von Mangoldt's optimistic prognosis that German surpluses would soon diminish. However, they were equally hesitant about addressing the exchange rate issue that preoccupied Erhard, Emminger, and other German officials. When the Board finally approved a report on 29 October, its recommendations concerning Germany were hardly earth-shaking. It warned that high German interest rates were an obstacle to exporting private capital and called upon other countries to remove restrictions impeding the inflow of such capital. A new idea was to urge Germany to

[26] Emminger (1986), 80.
[27] Wissenschaftlicher Beirat (1957).
[28] Emminger (1986), 126.
[29] Emminger (1977), 9.
[30] OEEC Secretariat, 'Summary of Discussions on the Economic Situation of Germany' (6 Sept. 1956). OEEC TFD/PC/339 (1st Revision).

increase its export of government capital, for example, to pay the balance of the 18 per cent portion of its subscription to the World Bank. It also suggested prepayment of Germany's foreign indebtedness. The Federal Republic responded to these recommendations, as it had to earlier ones about lifting import barriers, but its surpluses were scarcely affected.

At the April 1957 Managing Board meeting, von Mangoldt had to cope with a particularly vehement attack on German measures to restrict credit and check inflationary tendencies.[31] Erik ib Schmidt, the economic adviser to the Danish Parliament, had joined the Board as the Scandinavian nominee for that year. He thought the new measures would lead to still higher exports, the opposite of what was needed to moderate the foreign payments imbalance. De Strycker agreed that the real problem was insufficient internal demand; more serious measures were needed to attack the fundamental problems. Hay criticized the maintenance of high interest rates despite the excessive liquidity of the banks. Kaplan could only say that none of the measures taken to date sufficiently addressed the damaging impact of the German surpluses on other European countries. Washington colleagues had shrugged off his suggestion that the US advocate a revaluation of the D-Mark.

De Strycker alone sought to introduce the obvious but unspoken remedy—revaluation. He said that 'fundamental steps' were necessary to moderate the German position.[32] There was no mistaking the meaning of the word 'fundamental' to the international financial community. IMF jargon had made it synonymous with exchange rate adjustment. No one else picked up on his idea. British officials recognized that revaluation of the D-Mark was warranted, but they hesitated to speak out after the Erhard–Macmillan contretemps.[33] Wedded to the current par value of the pound, they feared new calls for multilateral realignment and increased speculation against sterling.

At the June Managing Board meeting, von Mangoldt had a private discussion with Wilson about the immediately preceding meeting of the Deputies. Wilson said that he understood they had enjoined German authorities 'to take steps that would effectively cut their surpluses—the

[31] F. G. Conolly, 'Unofficial Note', 84th Session of the Managing Board (24–5 Apr. 1957). BIS EPU Archive.

[32] R. P. F. (Roy Fenton), UK Alternate, 'European Economic Situation' (29 Apr. 1957). Bank of England OV 46/22.

[33] R. P. F. (Fenton), 'European Economic Situation' (29 Apr. and 28 May 1957). Bank of England OV 46/22.

J. R. (Rootham), 'Future of European Payments Arrangements'. Internal note recording views of Thompson-McCausland, Raw, and Rootham (16 May 1957). Bank of England OV 46/22.

Also J. R. (Rootham), 'Meeting of the Ministerial Deputies in Paris' (17–18 June 1957). Bank of England OV 46/22.

nature of the steps was up to them to decide'.[34] And that is how the matter remained.

More German EPU Credit: A Sanction?

More German credit within the EPU offered another practical palliative, if not a remedy. Immediately after the July 1956 ministerial meeting, Owen warned von Mangoldt privately that the UK might insist on reducing the EPU gold settlement ratio for Germany from 75 to 50 per cent. Since 1955, the 75 per cent rate had applied to settlements within the quotas as well as the *rallonges*. Von Mangoldt responded that applying such a measure only to Germany would be 'a clear case of sanctions', and his authorities would reject the notion.

At the September 1956 Board meeting, Calvet offered his own suggestion for a general decrease in gold settlements. It would take some of the drama out of the tense currency situation in Europe and could hardly be called 'a decline in civilization'. The other creditors joined Germany in opposing any such back-pedalling on the institutional approach to convertibility. A month later, Owen added his voice to theirs, after Whitehall recalled its initial reason for supporting 75 per cent gold payments. A reduction would make British support of the transferable sterling rate more costly. Nor was it consistent with continued momentum for the Collective Approach to convertibility. Thereafter, the idea of a general softening of EPU settlement terms was dropped.

A less controversial proposal was that the EPU should borrow funds from surplus countries to provide special credits to deficit members. The OEEC Secretariat introduced the idea in September 1956, and even the other creditors warmed to the suggestion. At the time, Germany held 80 per cent of all claims against the EPU. Posthuma had once remarked sardonically that Germany had become 'the only remaining legitimate member of the creditors' club'. At the autumn 1956 meeting of the Deputies, Switzerland proposed that Germany make such a loan to the Union. Hay pursued the idea within the Managing Board.

At the Deputies' meeting, Germany rejected such 'untied' German lending to the EPU. It would not abstain from joining a co-operative action to assist deficit countries, but only in relation to its share of the EPU quotas and with suitable guarantees of repayment.[35] Nevertheless,

---

[34] R. P. F. (Fenton), 'European Economic Situation' (21 June 1957). Bank of England OV 46/22.

[35] J. R. (Rootham), 'Meeting of the Ministerial Deputies in Paris' (17-18 June 1957). Bank of England OV 46/22.

once the Board decided on 'co-operative actions', Germany did provide the lion's share of European bilateral funds. Both France and Turkey were beneficiaries in 1958, as reported in Chapters 15 and 16. The Federal Republic also agreed to permit EPU countries to draw Deutsche Marks from the IMF and to use them in EPU settlements. The Kreditanstalt für Wiederaufbau, a government bank that originally financed German reconstruction projects, began to fund projects in developing countries. None of these measures had more than marginal effects on the German surpluses. Indeed, they may have increased them over time by promoting German exports.

Calming the Markets

After the British landing in Egypt, speculative flows out of sterling and into D-Marks accelerated. The credits to Great Britain checked flows out of sterling, but money continued to move toward Germany, despite reductions in the central bank's discount rate. In the first half of 1957, such flows amounted to about DM 1 billion ($238 million). Germany's net surplus in EPU financial year 1956/7 exceeded $1.3 billion, two and a half times its peak in the previous year.

Revaluation rumours were hard to stifle under these circumstances. On 10 July 1957, the Bank deutscher Länder published a strongly worded denial of any intention to revalue the D-Mark. Erhard also had switched to a more guarded public position by this time, acknowledging that neither Chancellor Adenauer nor the Bank would budge from opposition to revaluation. A month later, France devalued the franc *de facto* (see Chapter 15), and speculation about further exchange rate adjustments intensified once again. The German government thereupon issued a categorical statement that 'all rumors regarding an impending revaluation of the D-Mark are unfounded.'[36] Even that failed to change market sentiment. In the third calendar quarter of 1957, speculative inflows into Germany were of the order of DM 2.2 billion ($524 million). It was a stupendous sum in those days.

Authorities in both London and Bonn concluded that only a synchronized and convincing action would halt the speculation. They decided to use the 1957 Annual Meetings of the IMF and the World Bank for co-ordinated announcements. But first each government took financial action to support its forthcoming statement. In August, the Deutsche Bundesbank, which had just succeeded the Bank deutscher Länder as the German central bank, lowered its discount rate further, from 4.5 to 4 per cent. The UK announced drastic fiscal and monetary restrictions

---

[36] Emminger (1977), 8.

just before the Meetings, including an increase in its Bank Rate from 5 to 7 per cent. The formal statements by Thorneycroft and by von Mangoldt (representing Germany) were closely co-ordinated. Their firm message was that no exchange rate action should be expected on the part of either country.

These co-ordinated moves were strikingly successful for a while. Currency speculation abated and was reversed for both currencies. British reserves increased, and German reserves fell slightly over the following nine months. The Federal Republic's foreign exchange position was close to basic balance, thanks both to adjustment measures in Britain and France and a slackening in worldwide economic activity and demand for imports. 'The German economy experienced a period of complete harmony between internal and external equilibrium.'[37] German discount rates were reduced further during 1958, to a record low of 2.75 per cent by January 1959. The opponents of revaluation felt justified in having argued that the extreme German surpluses were a temporary phenomenon and not a manifestation of a 'fundamental disequilibrium'. Their self-satisfaction did not long survive; reserves rose sharply again in 1960.

Did the Managing Board Fail?

Despite German responsiveness to its recommendations, the Managing Board had little impact on German EPU surpluses or on its accumulation of foreign exchange reserves. Extreme German EPU surpluses continued to the very end of the Union—$826 million in the financial year 1957/8 and $350 million in the last six months of the EPU. German gold and dollar reserves increased by over $400 million in 1958. On overall current account, the Federal Republic ran a larger surplus in 1958 than in 1957; that surplus declined in 1959 but remained at over $1 billion.[38]

In September 1959, the Bundesbank perceived another overheating of the economy. This time it slammed on the brakes with no illusions about the impact on Germany's foreign exchange position. By the spring of 1961, pressures for revaluation had built up again, culminating in the first increase in any exchange rate against the dollar. Many more would follow in the years to come, long after the EPU had been liquidated.

In the clear light of hindsight, a revaluation of the D-Mark would have been appropriate as early as 1956, to the benefit of Germany and all its trading partners, both within and outside the EPU. The exchange rate of 3.33 to the dollar, first fixed by the Allied Powers in 1948, would have better fitted the development of the German balance of payments in

[37] Emminger (1977), 10.
[38] BIS, *Thirtieth Annual Report* (June 1960), 125.

the 1950s and beyond. Such a rate might have avoided the extreme export orientation of German industry and allowed faster domestic growth without inflation safely into the 1960s. Indeed, the D-Mark reached that level again in 1971, at the time of the currency realignment under the Smithsonian Agreement. In the meantime, some of the foreign exchange difficulties experienced by other countries in the 1960s might have been mitigated.

However, the roof of the OEEC provided poor shelter for dealing with currency realignments. Its members recognized that exchange rates were the domain of the International Monetary Fund, and they had no penchant for a jurisdictional conflict. The IMF, on the other hand, had no power to initiate changes. It was further inhibited by animosities lingering since 1949, when a committee of its Executive Board actively espoused European devaluation. Currency values involved the national pride and political sensitivities of the authorities responsible for managing them. Governments dedicated to international co-operation on other matters stopped short at the very suggestion of interference with their exchange rates.

Perhaps the OEEC and the Managing Board were over-attentive to these sensitivities, though the Managing Board did discreetly and successfully promote a devaluation of the French franc and the Turkish lira. Those initiatives seemed less presumptuous because both the IMF and the EPU were working together and providing funds jointly to support stabilization programmes. In the German case, the leadership of the IMF at the time resisted any suggestion of currency revaluation.

Both the Managing Board and the major European governments thus were hesitant to press for a revaluation of the D-Mark. With his characteristically open demeanour, von Mangoldt did not hesitate to ask his colleagues in private for advice about what Germany should do to restrain its surpluses and reserve increases. They tended to list all the policy options, including exchange rate adjustment, but insisted that Germany itself must select the measures that suited it. Pressures for revaluation would only worsen the situation of the deficit countries unless Germany itself would respond and act. All the indications were that Germany would not, and other countries were reluctant to reopen the Pandora's box that followed Erhard's letter to Macmillan.

On the other hand, Chancellor Adenauer's policy was to co-operate with his fellow Europeans. Advisers such as Erhard and Emminger might have been more persuasive if they could have reported that their recommendations were supported by the IMF, other European governments, or by the United States. They were not able to do so during the life of the EPU.

Popular attitudes in Germany would change. Twelve years later, in

1969, the Social Democrats under Willi Brandt and Karl Schiller turned their support of a D-Mark revaluation into a principal election issue. Explaining its favourable effect on German consumers, they won sufficient support to form a coalition government with the Liberals that remained in power for more than twelve years. However, in the mid-1950s, such reasoning was premature. German economic recovery was still too new, and public confidence in the country's economic strength was not yet firmly established. Adequate remedial measures were not taken during the life of the EPU, and the problem of German surpluses long outlived the Union.

15   French Crisis of 1957-1958

In the 1950s, journalists referred to France as 'the sick man of Europe'. One diagnosis—by a Swiss writer, Herbert Lüthy—appeared in a widely read book, whose German title translates as 'French Clocks Are Set Differently'.[1] Lüthy felt that, under the Fourth Republic, France was no longer governed, but simply administered, albeit by highly competent senior civil servants. Neither the political nor the economic results of such a system were acceptable to France or to its allies.

Many years later, Calvet vividly recalled 1957 as the year he spent 'begging for my country'. His memory contained a kernel of literal truth. However, none of his colleagues on the Managing Board would have so described his behaviour or their own reactions. To be sure, France had run its foreign exchange reserves down to a dangerously low level and desperately needed foreign financing. But that was only a surface manifestation of what basically preoccupied both Calvet and his Managing Board colleagues.

ASSAINISSEMENT

In complete co-operation with Calvet, the Board directed its energies in 1957 to bringing about a fundamental *assainissement* of the French economy. Its goals were identical with those of senior French officials. They sought to persuade French ministers to introduce a thoroughgoing revision of economic, fiscal, and monetary policies in order to open up the French economy and restore its competitiveness on international markets. Only then could France play a major constructive role in moving Europe toward a freer and wider system of trade and payments. Only then would France be able to meet its obligations to the OEEC and to the Common Market, scheduled to take effect at the beginning of 1959.

The recalcitrance of ministers in a succession of weak and unstable coalition cabinets during the 1950s had frustrated key French civil servants as much as it had the Managing Board. The need for foreign financing provided both a carrot and a stick to induce ministers to adopt policy measures that were politically unpopular. An excruciating year was required before a programme of major reforms was in place, and even that programme had to be reinforced during 1958.

The two-year process of redressing the French economy was wearying

---

[1] Lüthy (1954).

for the Board and painfully enervating for Calvet. Caught between the pressures of his Managing Board colleagues and his authorities, Calvet seldom permitted the tensions of his personal situation to interfere with his professional responsibilities. Von Mangoldt managed the whole affair with consummate tact and sensitivity. In Calvet's words, 'He tried to be very helpful, though he never forgot his responsibilities to the EPU and to his own country.'[2]

The French Restrictive System[3]

In 1952, the remarkable speed of the French recovery had prompted Ellis-Rees to wonder what could produce such quick results. The explanation was simple: the government had tightened all the screws on a restrictive system of economic subsidies and controls. Some of these dated back to the First World War and had become entrenched by the early fifties.

As applied to foreign trade, the system reinforced traditionally high tariff levels. For a brief period after the advent of the EPU, France had lifted some foreign exchange controls and eliminated much of its quantitative limitation of imports from other EPU members. However, in February 1952, that trade liberalization was completely suspended, and France reverted to the quantitative restrictions that it had been employing since the beginning of the Depression. An elaborate collection of aids supported French exporters. It included rebates of indirect taxes and social security contributions, direct subsidies for exporting certain foodstuffs, special credit and insurance facilities, and export price guarantees.

These devices for managing foreign economic relations derived from endemic inflationary pressures. After World War II, Monnet's well-advertised plans for modernizing and re-equipping the French economy led to high rates of growth in both investment and production, though the percentage of GNP devoted to investment remained well below that of several other OEEC members. However, as in Great Britain, the long-deprived populace would not wait long for the economic benefits of victory. A quarter to a third of the electorate voted regularly for a Communist party that promised all sorts of material beneficence. The other political parties of the Fourth Republic had to combine in an endless succession of short-lived cabinets, each unable or unwilling to emphasize anti-inflationary policies. Entitlement programmes and housing

---

[2] Interview with Pierre Calvet (6 Apr. 1987). BIS EPU Archive.

[3] Detailed account of the French restrictive system in IMF *Eighth Annual Report on Exchange Restrictions* (Washington, 1957), 127–38. Monetary system described by Koch (1983).

Also various reports by EPU Board cited in this chapter.

subsidies soon became exceedingly generous, and concessions were made repeatedly to the unremitting demands for higher wages.

France's inflationary pressures stemmed from its public finances and its monetary system, as well as from rising labour costs. The governments' attempts to retain former colonial territories added major costs to an already strained economy. Nor could weak governments readily enact and collect tax increases.

Half of the banking system was nationalized, and a group of government institutions joined the banks in providing credit generously to both the private sector and the government itself. A number of important nationalized industries constantly sought and received large loans at below market interest rates.

The Bank of France's rediscount facilities were open to the various financial institutions, and it could not refrain from financing government deficits directly. The Bank was poorly placed to enforce the usual central bank responsibility for defending the currency. Not until 1973 was it charged by law with supervising money and credit and the functioning of the banking system.[4] Newly nationalized at the end of 1945, it had become an instrument of the Finance Ministry. Lacking a fixed term of office, its Governor served at the pleasure of the government and could readily be replaced. His power rested wholly on his ability to persuade the Finance Minister to accept his advice.

French ministries also presided over a labyrinth of internal economic controls and subsidies. In the mid-1950s, France still maintained an elaborate system of fixed prices and subsidies to producers of both agricultural and industrial goods, though its principal European trading partners had pretty well dismantled most of these vestiges of their wartime economies. With large government budget deficits and generous credit facilities, inflationary pressures on French prices were suppressed, rather than diminished, by these controls.

French Co-operation within the OEEC

Both the Managing Board and other OEEC bodies constantly prodded France to abandon this restrictive system as soon as possible, in the interest of France as well as its trading partners. For example, in the OEEC's *Sixth Report*, drafted in November 1954, the chapter on France concluded:

Some steps to soften the immediate impact of competition on the economy may be appropriate; but its restoration must be regarded as one of the most effective means to ensure France's economic recovery, and not as some far-off and uncertain

[4] Koch (1983), 54.

objective to be achieved when that recovery is complete . . . The progress to be achieved is extensive, varied and difficult. The disparity between French and foreign prices, a legacy from past inflation, has not yet been overcome and the elimination of the structural defects of the economy is difficult because protection of established positions at the expense of efficiency has become part of the accepted order.[5]

The preceding *Fifth Annual Report* had observed, 'The basic source of France's difficulties is undoubtedly protection which surpasses that of any other Member country.'[6] It was significant that the French delegation to the OEEC approved the publication of these reports, in keeping with normal OEEC practice.

Members of the justly famed French corps of *inspecteurs des finances* held the key positions in the various economic administrations. As administrators, they struggled valiantly to manage the country's economic affairs with a degree of responsibility and efficiency. On the whole, they made every effort to co-operate with their OEEC partners, within the limitations imposed by economic realities and by the reluctance of political leaders to take unpopular measures.

Thus they persuaded the government to use American aid to repay promptly the special EPU credit received in March 1952. When France exhausted its EPU quota in October 1952, it settled its subsequent deficits entirely in gold and dollars without seeking more credit. During the third EPU financial year (1952/3), France paid the Union $380 million, including $89 million in special resources provided by the US. During the succeeding year, France continued to settle 100 per cent in gold. By the fourth quarter of 1954, it was again reporting surpluses in the EPU, established in part through market purchases of transferable sterling for dollars. In mid-1954, it also began repaying the credits it had received within its EPU quota. As a result, by the end of 1955, France had reduced its cumulative deficit in the EPU to $369 million from a peak of $890 million in mid-1954, 70 per cent in excess of its quota. It then owed the EPU only $87 million.

Beginning in April 1954, France gradually resumed liberalizing its intra-European trade, after a two-year hiatus in honouring its OEEC commitments. At the same time, however, it introduced a 7-15 per cent compensations tax on the products that were liberalized. By April 1956, this selective *de facto* devaluation had permitted liberalization to reach 82 per cent, still short of the OEEC 90 per cent agreement but evidence of a serious desire to co-operate. French officials also selectively lowered or

[5] Final draft distributed to Managing Board (15 Nov. 1954). OEEC MBC(54)75. Printed in OEEC, *Sixth Report: From Recovery towards Economic Strength* (1955), ii, ch. 8.
[6] OEEC, *Progress and Problems of the European Economy: Fifth Annual Report* (1954).

eliminated the compensation taxes as rapidly as politically feasible; in mid-1956, some aids to exports were also reduced.

France and the US

These measures of French co-operation with Europe were made possible by a generous flow of US government funds. Appreciation of France's strategic position in Europe, as well as traditional friendship with its oldest ally, played a major role in US postwar generosity. For its own peace and security, the US wanted to see an end to Franco-German animosities. Moreover, France was the linchpin of further European political and economic integration, and NATO's defences were crucially dependent on supply lines through France.

When hostilities broke out in Indo-China, the US at first provided France with equipment and financing. When France decided to withdraw, the US provided substantial compensation for its previous military effort there. It also took over French responsibilities in that unhappy peninsula, and its expenditures in Indo-China permitted a substantial withdrawal of French capital from the area. When revolt erupted in Algeria late in 1954, however, the US was much less enthusiastic about France's effort at 'pacification' and far less forthcoming with support for it. Nevertheless, the flow of US government expenditures provided France with $763 million in 1953 and about $1 billion a year in 1954 and 1955.[7]

Generous financing was not accompanied by much pressure on France to liberalize its dollar imports. Only in January 1956 did France begin to remove restrictions on some goods imported from North America. It was a token measure, bringing dollar liberalization, as reported to the OEEC, to 11 per cent.

Throughout the postwar years, the US aid mission to France sought reforms in French economic policies. It hoped to replace recurrent inflationary pressures with stable growth and a more efficient and competitive economic structure. The US argued that a stronger French economy was essential to permit it to lead Europe in directions sought by French leaders themselves. However, US political interests precluded much pressure on the French cabinets, so that the assistance flowed without much effect on French economic policies.

THE CRISIS

Problems Escalate

By the beginning of 1956, the financial requirements of the war in Algeria, combined with a bad harvest and the demands of French wage earners,

[7] Koch (1983), 197.

were about to reignite the flames of inflation. The government fell, and a socialist-led government took office. Though wages were rising by some 8 per cent per year, the new government added to the inflationary pressures. It introduced an old age pension scheme, increased the military budget by 25 per cent, and permitted other current expenditures to increase by 17 per cent. The annual budget deficit, called the *impasse*, rose from 650 billion to over a trillion francs.[8] Anti-inflation efforts were focused on controlling prices and increasing subsidies on items in the cost-of-living index.

In the course of staff consultations with the IMF in June and July 1956, French officials saw little scope for early corrective action. They hoped to be better able to judge to what extent the set-backs had been temporary and to adjust their policy accordingly by the beginning of 1957. They expected to lose $450 to $500 million in foreign exchange reserves in 1956 and were willing to part with them, given the situation.

The French authorities, nevertheless, took some corrective action. Shortly after the meetings with the IMF staff, Calvet reported to the Managing Board that the government had introduced some credit restrictions and intended to finance its deficits without further expansion of credit in the economy as a whole.[9] Several months later, in October, he reported that a public loan had greatly exceeded expectations, providing substantial budgetary relief and reducing the availability of credit.[10] Even so, France's EPU deficits had averaged $73 million per month in the third quarter of 1956, twice the rate in the first half of the year. It lost $230 million in foreign exchange reserves in that same quarter.[11]

During the September 1956 Annual IMF Meetings, Per Jacobsson was designated to be Managing Director.[12] He had long been a critic of French monetary policy. Nevertheless, on a visit to Paris in October, prior to his arrival in Washington, he agreed to a French standby credit of $262.5 million.[13] Agreement could hardly have been related to a finding of 'reasonable efforts to solve their problems', the Fund's criterion at the time for so large a drawing.[14] But Jacobsson's appointment had been sponsored by the US Treasury, and it was reluctant to oppose his first act. The IMF Executive Board approved the credit on 17 October 1956.

[8] Koch (1983), 278.

[9] EPU Board Minutes, 'Statement by M. Calvet on Measures taken in France to Control Inflationary Tendencies', 74th Session (19–21 July 1956). OEEC MBC/M(56)8, Part I.

[10] EPU Board Minutes, 76th Session (8–10 Oct. 1956). OEEC MBC/M(56)10.

[11] EPU Board Report, 'The Current Economic Situation in Member Countries' (29 Oct. 1956). OEEC Council C(56)234.

[12] EPU Board Minutes, 'Statement by Mr. Sallé on Latest Developments in the IMF', 76th Session (8 Oct. 1956). OEEC MBC/M(56)10.

[13] Horsefield (1969), 428. Calvet informed Managing Board about IMF standby credit at 77th Session (26–7 Oct. 1956). OEEC MBC/M(56)11.

[14] Horsefield (1969), 404.

Twelve days later, France participated in the landing of troops in Egypt. Though the franc did not suffer as much as the pound sterling from the ensuing speculation, France's foreign exchange reserves fell by another quarter of a billion dollars during the last three months of the year. All told, French reserves declined by over $850 million in 1956, much more than the pessimistic mid-year forecast to the IMF staff.

First Call for Help

When the members of the Managing Board arrived in Paris for their December 1956 meeting, they found messages awaiting them from the Chairman. The opening session had been cancelled. Would the Board members please come instead, without their Alternates, to the office of the German delegation for a private meeting. Other than Cahan and Kaplan, only elected members of the Board had been asked to attend. Von Mangoldt opened the meeting by saying that he wanted to report a very confidential conversation with Calvet, who preferred to be absent from the meeting. Would members please neither take notes nor report the meeting to their governments.

Calvet had told von Mangoldt that the French payments deficit in 1957 could reach $1 billion; its EPU quota would soon be exhausted. France would obviously need help before long, and he wanted to be sure that he could correctly describe to his government the attitudes of Managing Board members toward providing assistance. None of the Board members had instructions, of course. But, one by one, they voiced both their sympathy for the French plight and their personal criticisms of French economic policies. Without a major and thoroughgoing reform of those policies, they could not responsibly recommend commitment of the EPU's limited resources. Credits would simply be spent with little prospect of repayment.

After this display of unanimity by the members of the Board, the Chairman called on the US Representative. Kaplan pointed to past US aid to France and the failed efforts to obtain policy changes. US government expenditures for France had declined sharply in 1956 and would fall further in 1957. An increase above what was already contemplated was unlikely. To date, the bulk of US aid to France had been used to pay for imports from Europe. If he correctly understood the attitude of his authorities, the time had come for Europe to accept responsibility both for influencing French policies and for providing assistance, as and when appropriate. Von Mangoldt closed the meeting by summarizing his understanding of US attitudes. 'You mean you have had enough.'

The Chairman promptly reported the essence of the Board's discussion to Calvet. France's difficulties were no secret in Europe, and speculation about what its government would do was widespread. Ansiaux, who was no longer on the Managing Board, told the Board of the National Bank of Belgium he understood that France would not ask for an EPU special credit; it would turn first to the IMF for more help and, if necessary, to the US.[15]

Early Credits and Stabilization Efforts

France's early attempts to address its economic difficulties appeared to consist of resorting once again to reinforcing restrictions. In January 1957, however, the Managing Board was eager to announce an early agreement about EPU renewal to calm down the jittery post-Suez markets. To that same end, some reopening of French credit lines in the EPU seemed warranted. At its February meeting, the Board agreed that France should have a $200 million extension of its quota, as part of the EPU renewal agreement. At 75 per cent gold settlements, that would offer France a $50 million credit for the year beginning in July, but using the credit would entail $150 million in gold payments to the Union.

Even that token gesture of solidarity drew a reservation from Hay, with some support from de Strycker.[16] French authorities should first be asked to propose what steps they intended to take to deal with their present economic difficulties. A month later, the French government finally began 'to undertake a study of the possibility of a change in policy'.[17] Calvet agreed that the Board should thoroughly examine the French situation in March.

At the March meeting, Calvet announced some corrective measures.[18] To stop the loss of foreign exchange, the special import tax would be applied at its highest rate, 15 per cent, to all liberalized goods. Importers would be required to deposit 25 per cent of the value of any import licence. New budgetary economies would prevent the *impasse* from rising above the current trillion francs a year rate. And the Bank of France was being asked to restrain credit.

Sceptical questioning over the next three days followed Calvet's statement. His explanations put the French measures in the best possible light, but he was careful neither to exaggerate their effectiveness nor to sound a note of optimism. Reserves at the end of February were down to $179 million, apart from the gold held by the Bank of France and a

[15] Minutes of the Board (8 Jan. 1957). National Bank of Belgium PV 1466/3.
[16] R. P. F. (Roy Fenton), 'EPU Renewal' (22 Feb. 1957). Bank of England OV 46/22.
[17] Koch (1983), 280.
[18] EPU Board Minutes, 'Comments by Mr. Calvet', 82nd Session (13-15 Mar. 1957). OEEC MBC/M(57)3, Annex II.

$40 million drawing from the IMF. France had recently arranged a $100 million credit from US private banks to pay for dollar oil. It also understood that 'it would not be expedient' to seek more IMF credit than its existing standby provided. For the moment, France had no intention of asking for more foreign loans.

In keeping with its usual procedure, the Board wanted to prepare a report on the French situation, with recommendations to the OEEC Council. Calvet at first argued that such a report would only damage an already precarious situation, but he finally yielded. A special meeting was called for 3 April 1957 to consider a Secretariat draft, to be prepared in the interim with Calvet's assistance.

With an eye on both the recently concluded Common Market negotiations and the anti-inflation measures introduced by Great Britain in February, Owen was instructed to press for strong French action. At the April meeting, he called for steps toward restricting internal demand, reducing the budget deficit, cutting investments for economic expansion, and restricting credit.[19] To Calvet's annoyance, other members permitted Owen to carry the brunt of the attack on French policies. Though softened within a long document with many mitigating clauses, the report pressed the French government to take new measures to increase taxes and restrict credit.[20] It called particular attention to the fact that medium term credit was being rediscounted too generously at the Bank of France.

Calvet and his colleagues in the French ministries used that report, the Board's repeated follow-ups, and the urgent need for foreign credits to persuade French ministers to become increasingly responsive. Measures were formulated by a group of senior French officials, headed by Pierre Paul Schweitzer, then Director of the Treasury. A few years later, Schweitzer would succeed Jacobsson as Managing Director of the IMF and establish a remarkable record in elevating the prestige and influence of that institution. To say the least, his 1957 assignment was equally challenging.

For nearly two more years, until the EPU itself was liquidated at the end of 1958, Calvet patiently presented a precise and detailed statement about the French economy at every Board meeting. His early presentations helped the Board understand the intricacies of the French economic system and its management. Later he helped prepare a succession of descriptive and prescriptive reports. Scarcely a meeting passed without his announcing new French measures. Members endorsed each constructive step, registered criticism and scepticism about the adequacy of steps taken hitherto, and encouraged Calvet and his colleagues to consider

---

[19] J. M. S. (Stevens), 'EPU-France'. Memo to the Governor (4 Apr. 1957). Bank of England OV 46/22.

[20] EPU Board Report, 'The Position of France' (4 Apr. 1957). OEEC Council C(57)65.

what else was feasible. Calvet was completely forthright with his Managing Board colleagues. He concealed neither the seriousness of France's problems nor the political and economic obstacles that limited the government's freedom of action.

Unfortunately, the early measures chipped away at the edges of France's problems, rather than attacking their root causes. The Algerian rebellion was to extend into the 1960s, so that France's economic stabilization efforts had to provide for financing continually heavy military expenditures.

With France's foreign exchange resources dwindling, Cahan startled the Board in May 1957 by proposing, in a note to all Board members, that Germany offer a gold loan of $100 million to the EPU, which the Union would then lend to France. The Cabinet that had presided over a deteriorating economy for a year and a half was on the verge of resigning. Calvet was as embarrassed by the timing of the proposal as von Mangoldt was, and the Board gave it no formal consideration.[21]

Coming to Grips with Fundamentals

Not until the summer of 1957 could Calvet announce more fundamental measures, introduced by a new Cabinet in which Felix Gaillard was the Minister of Finance. Himself an *inspecteur des finances* and a former aide to Monnet, Gaillard had a better grasp of the economic issues than his predecessor. Later in the year, he became the Prime Minister and introduced a stabilization programme that held some promise of real *assainissement*.

The Board had agreed to meet early in June in an extraordinary session at the BIS. To persuade the new Cabinet to implement 'an adequate program for the redressment of the economic situation', it offered a friendly gesture and an important promise. The quota extension it had earlier proposed for the year beginning in July might be used to settle France's June 1957 EPU deficit. More significantly, the Board also offered to consider what action it could recommend to support an adequate programme.[22] Calvet's report to that meeting had been exceedingly gloomy. Part of the Bank of France gold reserve might have to be called upon soon to meet debt maturities and current payments.[23] About $285 million worth of such gold was soon borrowed by the government and quickly spent.

---

[21] R. P. F. (Fenton) memos (13, 20 May 1957). Bank of England OV 46/22.
Also Minutes of the Board (10 May 1947). National Bank of Belgium PV 1500/3.
[22] EPU Board Report, 'The Further Development of the Situation in France' (6 June 1957). OEEC Council C(57)105.
[23] EPU Board Minutes, 'Situation of France', statement by Mr. Calvet, 85th Session (4 June 1957). OEEC MBC/M(57)6, Part II, Annex.

The Board was discomfited when, at its regular June meeting later in the month, Calvet announced that the new government had suspended all trade liberalization promptly after taking office. Calvet did his best to appease the members. Deliberalization, he said, was an unavoidable emergency measure. He expected it to be followed by rigorous restriction of the credit-granting capacity of the banks and by substantial tax increases.

The French government confirmed this promise on 12 July 1957, in a notice to the OEEC.[24] However, the measures were disappointingly mild. Taxes would be increased and expenditures reduced, but the budgetary *impasse* for 1957 was still projected at 863 billion francs, only 132 billion francs less than in 1956. The penalty rate for rediscounting commercial bank paper at the Bank of France was raised to 10 per cent.

At the July meeting, Calvet again had to try to assuage the Board's displeasure. The new measures were not a definitive expression of the government's policy; further measures were being studied. Nevertheless, he also conceded that social unrest was continuing; a succession of strikes had erupted in recent months.

In a report to the Council, the Board emphasized 'once more the importance it attaches to the implementation by France of an adequate programme for the restoration of the internal and external balance of the French economy . . . certain aspects of these measures [those recently notified to the OEEC] are still being defined and new measures are being examined. In these circumstances, the Board considers it premature to express an opinion on those measures which have already been taken.'[25]

Thereafter, the French government began to attack fundamentals rather than mere symptoms. In mid-August, it introduced a further *de facto* devaluation. The previous 15 per cent compensation tax on imports was replaced by a levy of 20 per cent, and the previous tax rebates to exporters were replaced by a uniform 20 per cent payment on the price of all exported goods.[26] About 41 per cent of French imports were exempted, however. The discount rate of the Bank of France was also raised again. In October, the Board gave a mild welcome to the new regime as a simplification and improvement of the previous system.[27] But it stressed its disquiet about the state of France's public finances. The deficit should be reduced to the point where it could be financed without recourse to

[24] French del., note accompanied by letter to Sec. General. Circulated to all OEEC dels. (15 July 1957). OEEC Council C(57)162.

[25] EPU Board Report, 'Opinion on France's Invocation of Article 3(c) of the Code of Liberalisation' (24 July 1957). France suspended liberalization under the escape clause of this provision. OEEC TFD/PC/524.

[26] French del., comments concerning trade system of franc area, in force from 12 Aug. 1957. Transmitted to OEEC Council (20 Aug. 1957). OEEC C(57)187.

[27] EPU Board Report, 'The Situation of France' (10 Oct. 1957). OEEC C(57)210.

inflationary means. Reducing public spending and increasing fiscal receipts should be pursued further.[28]

At the beginning of November, the *de facto* devaluation was extended a bit further. In response to criticism from both the Managing Board and the IMF, officials eliminated the exemptions from the 20 per cent import tax levy and export grant scheme.[29] When the Gaillard government took office on 6 November, it immediately proposed reducing the budget deficit to 700 billion francs.

Second Call for Help

By the time the Managing Board met in mid-November 1957, few doubted that France would have to receive some foreign credits in 1958. Deliberalizing imports and the *de facto* devaluations had reduced its EPU deficits, but 75 per cent gold payments were necessary to settle them. French officials were nearing the end of the ingenious devices they had concocted to find sufficient funds.

At the November Board meeting, Calvet announced that France would have to borrow $500 million from foreign sources in 1958.[30] Germany was the first to offer help. Its interests in reconciliation with France, in the Common Market, and in convertibility came to the forefront, reinforced by OEEC pressure for action to control its own burgeoning EPU surpluses. Accordingly, von Mangoldt picked up the idea he had rejected six months earlier, when Cahan had proposed it prematurely. Germany would lend the EPU $100 million as backing for a similar special credit to France. The EPU itself should offer France another quota extension of $400 million, yielding a total credit of $200 million to be matched by a similar amount in gold.

The other Board members greeted this idea with little enthusiasm. They thought that the *impasse* was still too large and that more inflationary financing by the Bank of France was embedded in the programme. Then, in December, the government submitted a budget to the Chamber of Deputies that reduced the 1958 deficit further, to 600 billion francs.[31] This deficit was less than the *impasse* financed without rising prices from 1952 to 1955. The Board recognized that this was as much as was politically feasible on the budget side. It turned to how the budget deficit would be financed and to the liberal credit available to the private sector.

---

[28] 'Supplementary Measures Taken by the French Government in Regard to Financial Policy and Foreign Trade'. Memo circulated to OEEC (22 Oct. 1957). OEEC C(57)224.

[29] French del., 'General Extension of the System of Trade and Payments Introduced by France on 10 August 1957'. Transmitted by letter (29 Oct. 1957) and circulated to Council (5 Nov. 1957). OEEC C(57)229.

[30] Minutes of the Board (14 Nov. 1957). National Bank of Belgium PV 1564/3.

[31] Deliberations of the Governing Council (11 Dec. 1957). National Bank of Belgium.

On the government side, it sought assurance that the *impasse* would be financed without recourse to the Bank of France and without using any of the counterpart of such foreign aid as France might receive. As for private credit, the Bank of France had been rediscounting large sums of medium and short term credit to finance agriculture, housing, and the nationalized industrial firms. The sums of such credit on the Bank's books had more than doubled between the end of 1955 and October 1957, reaching over 1.3 trillion francs. The Board felt that these credits needed to be curtailed.

THE RESOLUTION

Credits for a Stabilization Programme

Before the Managing Board meeting on 10 December 1957, von Mangoldt and Cahan were invited to meet with French ministers and senior officials for an oral presentation of their programme of redressment. After hearing their report, the Board decided to adjourn the session until 19 December. That day was devoted to a presentation and interrogation of a group of senior French officials, headed by Schweitzer. The subject matter included the 1958 budget, the situation of the Treasury, the financing of the housing programme, other government investments, internal credit policy, and the balance of payments.[32]

On the following day, Calvet made a formal request for $250 million of credit from the EPU. Part of that sum would be in the form of a *rallonge* that would be settled half in credit and half in gold; part would be in the form of a special credit that could be used in lieu of the gold payments. France would seek a total of $650 million in foreign credits, the remainder to be provided both by drawing the rest of its quota in the IMF and by the US government. France expected to reduce its overall balance-of-payments deficit from $1.5 billion in 1957 to $415 million in 1958. Some of the credits it sought would be used to rebuild reserves. The Board discussed the request without Calvet present and instructed Cahan to inform him of the results.

The Board still was not satisfied that the programme would enable France to restore internal and external equilibrium within a reasonable period. It wanted assurance that the Bank of France would not increase its financing of medium term credit in 1958, and it felt that the French monetary system was still too liquid. Furthermore, it doubted that France would be able to honour its commitments under the OEEC Code of Trade Liberalisation. France was obligated to liberalize 60 per cent of

---

[32] EPU Board Minutes, 90th Session (10-13, 19-21 Dec. 1957). OEEC MBC/M(57)11.

its intra-European trade by mid-1958 and 75 per cent by the end of that year.[33] Despite expressed French intentions to comply, few believed it would be able to do so without a further devaluation of the franc. Board members felt that a devaluation should provide the capstone, once inflationary pressures had been squeezed out of the French economy. The present programme did not yet seem sufficient for that purpose.

On instruction, Kaplan informed Board members privately that the US could not support a further French drawing from the IMF in excess of $131 million, the third quarter of its IMF quota. Moreover, that drawing should be in European currencies, presumably D-Marks, for use in settling France's EPU deficits. Since the US had no more bilateral aid funds that could be committed to France, Europe should be thinking about providing France with at least $300 million.

On 8 January, the Board met to prepare a report to the OEEC Council concerning the French request for credit.[34] Calvet announced that the French government was preparing a memorandum of commitment concerning its stabilization programme for presentation to the IMF and the US government, as well as the EPU. Monnet and Schweitzer would proceed to Washington, there to seek credits.

The government memorandum would provide a flat assurance that the impasse would be financed without recourse either to the Bank of France or to counterpart funds. However, Calvet was not very reassuring about medium term credit for housing and the nationalized industries. It might increase by 200 to 250 billion francs on the basis of authorizations already issued; further cuts were not feasible. Calvet felt, nonetheless, that the turning-point of the French crisis had been passed. France had been in current account surplus with both the EPU and the dollar area in December.

Despite its concern about further expansion of liquidity in the French monetary system, the Board was not prepared to reject the French request. Reluctantly, it agreed to a $400 million *rallonge*, involving $100 million in credit plus a special credit of $150 million.[35] The special credit could be used in lieu of the 75 per cent gold payments. France could draw D-Marks under an IMF standby and use them to settle its EPU deficits in any month for which Germany reported a surplus in the Union. The Board postponed completing its report pending the outcome of the talks in Washington. With the Managing Board finally willing to underwrite so large a credit for France, Washington could scarcely turn its back.

Kaplan was called to Washington to brief US officials. Before his

---

[33] Steering Board for Trade Report (7 Feb. 1958). OEEC C(58)55.

[34] EPU Board Report, 'The Situation of France and the French Government's Programme' (27 Jan. 1958). OEEC C(58)31.

[35] US del. tel. to Washington. POLTO 2016 (11 Jan. 1958).

departure, von Mangoldt impressed on him the importance of significant US participation in the loan package. He had encountered strong resistance to requests that other European countries supplement Germany's $100 million loan to the EPU. Much of the remaining $50 million in special credit would be financed out of the EPU's own resources. Politically, it would be embarrassing for both France and Germany if the latter were the only important bilateral contributor to the French aid package.

Jean Saltes was added to the French delegation leaving for Washington. Like Calvet, he was a Vice-Governor of the Bank of France, but primarily responsible for domestic credit and banking. Upon arrival, the group heard criticisms about French monetary policies and the medium term credit problem from virtually every official it encountered. Previously resistant to further measures, Saltes returned to explore what could be done. If the Bank of France was legally obliged to rediscount outstanding authorizations, perhaps a gentlemen's agreement could be reached with the commercial banks about a ceiling on the amounts they would present.[36]

The US did find a way to contribute. It put together a sum of $275 million, consisting of new Export-Import Bank credits and postponement of sums due for interest and amortization on previous loans. Thereafter, Switzerland agreed to supplement the German loan to the EPU with $7 million, and Belgium and Italy each added $5.5 million. The Board approved its $250 million credit to France as part of a package of international assistance provided by the IMF, the US, and the EPU. The package offered France credits totalling $656 million, announced simultaneously to the public by each of the three contributors on 30 January 1958.

If confidence were the last missing ingredient for the *assainissement* of the French economy, that sum should have sufficed. 'In a voice choked with emotion and tears, Calvet thanked the Managing Board on behalf of the French government for its considerable effort . . . Every French official connected with the loan negotiations considers himself personally committed to do everything within his power to see that the stabilization program is applied with great scrupulousness.'[37]

Consolidating the Stabilization Programme

The Managing Board's report recommending a credit to France was a 75-page document, prepared by the Secretariat with Calvet's collaboration. It included a detailed description of the situation of the French economy

---

[36] US del. tel. to Washington. POLTO 2217 (25 Jan. 1958).
[37] US del. tel. to Washington. POLTO 2217 (25 Jan. 1958).

and a critical evaluation of the French government's programme of redressment and the government's memorandum.[38] While approving the credit, the Board also insisted on recording reservations about the adequacy of the French programme. It divided the $150 million special credit into two instalments; $70 million would be available only after 1 July 1958 and after a full-scale review of the French stabilization programme in June.

The Board noted that additional credit in 1959 would not be possible. It hoped that the French budget *impasse* for that year would be less than 600 billion francs and would be financed without borrowing from the Bank of France. Calvet agreed to continue to report to the Board each month on the progress of the French economy. With his continued co-operation, the Board submitted a report on the situation of France to the OEEC Council after the end of each calendar quarter.

For some weeks after the international assistance package was announced, the French situation seemed to stabilize. Yet economic activity continued to be buoyant for a while, and the demand for imports remained strong. In March, France's EPU deficit again reached the $50 million a month level, a 'rude shock' to the French ministers.[39] The Board's first quarterly report recognized that the French government had implemented the programme to the letter.[40] Nevertheless, it was disturbed by the inadequate economic effects thus far. It suggested that French authorities seek out measures 'even beyond the programme elaborated at the end of 1957'.[41] Calvet reported in April a further increase in the Bank of France's penalty rediscount rate, but the Board's concerns were not allayed.[42]

The Algerian situation had continued to deteriorate, and another series of strikes broke out in France during the spring. Workers complained that they were being forced to bear the costs of the Algerian struggle. Meanwhile, the French military and the French population in Algeria demanded more support. The ensuing political crisis proved to be more deep-seated than others that had punctuated the life of the Fourth Republic. A cabinet crisis at the end of April lasted for several weeks before a new government was installed. Shortly after it took office, insurrection broke out in the ranks of the French military in Algeria.

[38] EPU Board Report, 'The Situation of France and the French Government's Programme' (27 Jan. 1958). OEEC C(58)31.

[39] Described by Director for External Finance, French Ministry of Finance. US Embassy France airgram to Washington 231 (4 Apr. 1958).

[40] EPU Board Report, 'Development of the Situation of France in the First Quarter of 1958' (22 Apr. 1958). OEEC C(58)98.

[41] EPU Board Report, 'Development of the Situation of France in the First Quarter of 1958' (22 Apr. 1958). OEEC C(58)98.

[42] US del. tel. to Washington. POLTO 3323 (15 Apr. 1958).

Finally, early in June, General de Gaulle returned to power. He obtained full legislative and executive powers for a six-month period, while a new constitution was drafted and submitted to the electorate.

The new Cabinet brought Antoine Pinay back into office as Finance Minister, the post he had held at the height of the 1952 economic crisis. The government promised to use its powers to introduce new economic measures, while honouring France's January commitments to the EPU and the IMF. One of its early steps was to devalue the franc officially to 420 to the dollar, thus regularizing the *de facto* devaluations of the previous year.[43] Confidence in a strong executive permitted a successful public bond sale, though indexation to gold contributed significantly to the public response. Pinay was also able to purchase substantial quantities of privately held gold on the French internal market.

Nonetheless, the new government was wracked for some months by internal debates about budget and economic policies. In keeping with the January agreement, the Board should have prepared a recommendation in June to release the second half of the EPU credit, but could not do so. Its recommendation had to be based on a finding that the French authorities were carrying out 'with satisfactory results the application of their programme'.[44] Such a finding could hardly be defended during the June turmoil, nor was the situation much more stable in July. The only certainty was that France had been unable to fulfil its OEEC commitment to liberalize 60 per cent of its intra-European trade by the month of June. The Board was still of the opinion it had expressed in April, namely that the programme needed additional measures.

Calvet agreed in June to postpone the Board's recommendation about releasing the second instalment of the EPU credit. A month later, the Board decided to risk approving the credit on the basis of a political judgement. It did so in the hope of inducing responsible economic decisions on the part of the new French authorities, 'in the firm expectation that the Government of France will continue to work out and to apply all measures necessary for the redressment of the situation'.[45] It called for the continuation of 'strict measures of credit control' and for resistance to 'demands for increases in social expenditures, for new investments of all kinds, and for further protection from foreign competition'. The Board thus registered its understanding and its opinion about the disagreements within the new Cabinet. Pinay was struggling to restrain proposed expenditure increases in the 1959 budget.

[43] French del., letter to Sec. General (17 June 1958). OEEC C(58)150.

[44] EPU Board Report, 'Prolongation of Settlement Facilities and Special Credits Granted to France in the EPU' (10 July 1958). OEEC C(58)185.

[45] EPU Board Report, 'Prolongation of Settlement Facilities and Special Credits Granted to France in the EPU' (10 July 1958). OEEC C(58)185.

The Board's strategy proved to be correct. A French commission was appointed in September, under the chairmanship of Professor Jacques Rueff, to prepare economic policy recommendations for the new government. Rueff was a member of the group of OEEC academic experts who, in 1952, had recommended strict fiscal and monetary policies to control inflation and permit an early return to convertibility. His recommendations were predictably consistent with the Managing Board's objectives. He urged a fully balanced budget, a return to trade liberalization, and a devaluation of the franc.

Meanwhile, the de Gaulle government had indeed honoured French commitments to the EPU and the IMF. The 600 billion franc ceiling agreed for 1958 had been respected; the final budget deficit for 1958 was only 550 billion.[46] Medium term credit for construction and the nationalized industries had been kept within the agreed limits. As a result, prices had finally stabilized, and economic activity had slackened. Inflationary pressure was being squeezed out of the internal economy.

However, the balance of payments was still in substantial deficit. At the Managing Board's October 1958 session, von Mangoldt and several other members discussed with Calvet in private the need for a further exchange rate adjustment.[47] With inflationary pressures easing, they thought that devaluation might be effective without stimulating a rise in internal prices. Calvet resisted, but did not reject the arguments for devaluation out of hand. Indeed, he initiated inclusion in the Board's report of a clear exposition of the need for a much better trade balance. Everyone understood that was unlikely at the current exchange rate. Pinay and Governor Baumgartner of the Bank of France would have agreed to devalue, but they were awaiting de Gaulle's resolution of differences among his ministers and advisers.

Not long after that Board meeting, rumours about devaluation stimulated speculation against the franc. Early in December, the United Kingdom initiated discussions about its decision to unify the rates for transferable and dollar sterling. Rumours about that decision appeared in the press and further fanned the flames of speculation against the franc. But as late as 14 December, Baumgartner told the Bank of England that 'the chances of an imminent devaluation were 50/50'.[48] A day later, Erhard told de Gaulle that the German government was willing to provide $300 million if France would devalue and join the move to currency convertibility.[49]

[46] BIS, *Twenty-Ninth Annual Report* (1959), 47.

[47] US del. tel. to Washington. POLTO 1191 (31 Oct. 1958).

[48] J. M. S. (Stevens), memo of conversation with Governor Baumgartner (14 Dec. 1958). Bank of England OV 44/23.

[49] 'Record of a Conversation between Erhard and Chancellor of Exchequer' (14 Dec. 1958). Bank of England OV 44/23.

The following day, de Gaulle reached his decisions about the French budget for 1959 and about devaluation. Though unwilling to accept all of the expenditure cuts proposed by Pinay and Rueff, he agreed to keep the 1959 budget deficit within 610 billion francs and to raise taxes. He further agreed to devalue the franc by about 15 per cent and to liberalize 90 per cent of France's trade with Europe. A symbolic measure was added to make the devaluation politically acceptable and effective. A new franc would be issued, a 'heavy' franc, equal to 100 old francs. Thus the new par value of the franc would be 4.94 to the dollar; the projected 1959 *impasse* would be 6.1 billion francs. With these decisions, France was ready to join the European move to convertibility, and did so.

Outcome of the French Crisis

With the devaluation of the franc and the move to convertibility, Calvet's two-year ordeal came to an end. The French economy had finally been stabilized, internally and externally, with a much less regulated economic system and without further foreign assistance. Indeed, in 1959 France ran a substantial balance-of-payments surplus, began to repay its international credits, and added to its foreign exchange reserves.[50] It liberalized 90 per cent of its intra-European trade and 88 per cent of its dollar trade as well.

Calvet was subjected, nevertheless, to sharp personal criticism by right wing Gaullists. They claimed that the EPU operation was offensive to the dignity of France and represented interference in French internal affairs. Calvet's replies were unfailingly prompt and firm. 'What the Managing Board did and recommended was good for France.'[51]

His critics understandably preferred to credit the *assainissement* of the French economy to their own Rueff programme and to the actions approved by de Gaulle in December 1958. The importance of those final measures is indisputable. But they were the culmination of a process begun a year and a half earlier under Gaillard, based on a programme devised by Schweitzer, Calvet, and their colleagues within the French administration. Relaying insistent pressures from the Managing Board, they were able to persuade politically weak cabinet ministers that unpopular anti-inflationary policies should no longer be delayed. To de Gaulle's credit, his decisions carried that programme to its logical conclusion.

Even in the midst of the spring 1958 political crisis, the effects of the 1957 policies had begun to appear. With a much smaller budget deficit,

---

[50] BIS, *Thirtieth Annual Report* (1960), 122-4.
[51] Interview with Pierre Calvet (6 Apr. 1987). BIS EPU Archive.

French money supply and bank credit had stopped growing at the beginning of 1958.[52] Price and wage increases had moderated considerably. Thereafter, political uncertainty led both to the accumulation of inventories and to wage increases; France's trade deficit had not yet shown much improvement by mid-year.

Once the political crisis was resolved and a strong central government had taken office, anti-inflationary pressures from the earlier stabilization programme began to affect the foreign accounts. France's trade deficit fell sharply in June, and the decline continued for the rest of the year. Price increases came to a complete halt in September.

The decisions in December 1958 were consistent with the Rueff commission's recommendations, except for a fully balanced budget. The Gaullists preferred not to acknowledge that their decisions also responded to pressures exerted by the Managing Board over the preceding two years. When they came to power, the foundations had already been laid for what remained to be done. They adopted the final measures— devaluation and liberalization. Both were timely and effective because of the stabilization programme introduced at the beginning of the year and continued by de Gaulle's government after it took office. Both measures provided an essential capstone to the structure of reforms.

The approaching end to US economic aid obliged France to dismantle its highly regulated economic system and bring its policies into harmony with those of its EPU partners. One might say that the generosity of US aid had enabled the French to reinforce that system earlier in the 1950s. However, US aid had also permitted the expansion and modernization of the economy and an easing of social tensions through rapidly rising living standards. Better living conditions eventually made it easier for the public to accept measures to control inflation.

As France began to exhaust its foreign exchange resources, it had to accommodate European partners who wanted an end to the regulated system. Once France had taken sufficient measures and its partners were prepared to offer substantial credit, the US set aside its own disillusionment and joined in supporting the stabilization effort. The results were as salutary for France as they were for other participants in the free world economy.

Given the long history of direct controls and the continuing political instability in France, the Managing Board remained sceptical and apprehensive even as the first results of the stabilization programme began to appear. Its willingness to release the second segment of financial

[52] 'France—Financial and Economic Indicators', presented exclusively for use of Managing Board (9 June 1958). OEEC MBC(58)27. Calvet submitted a 7-10 page update of indicators to Board at each 1958 meeting, as part of presentation on French economic situation.

assistance lent force and credibility to its advice and pleas for reinforcing the programme.

The use of conditional international credits to persuade a country in difficulties to stabilize and deregulate its economic system has since been repeated many times in the case of developing countries. The measures demanded in return for assistance and the accompanying critical surveillance of stabilization programmes were comparable to the treatment France encountered and accepted, to its own eventual benefit.

16 Returning Turkey to the Fold

Historians had called Turkey the sick man of Europe more than half a century before that characterization was applied to France. The last decades of the Ottoman Empire were years of progressive disintegration. When Kemal Ataturk created a new Turkish state in 1922, he inherited 'an extremely underdeveloped country, saddled with inherited debts and the destructive effects of ten years of war'.[1] It was essentially an agricultural and pastoral country; such industry as it possessed was largely state-supported. Ataturk set out to develop the economy and create a Western secular state. By the 1930s, he had embarked on a five-year industrialization plan anchored to new state enterprises, quantitative restrictions on imports, and bilateral trade and payments agreements. The Turkish restrictive system became at least as extensive as the French, and more pernicious, since it was fastened on a much poorer economy.

As World War II approached, the Turkish government found it could borrow once again. Foreign governments offered credits to prevent its entrance into the war on the side of Germany and Italy. Thereafter, its appetite for foreign financing grew, as it avidly tried to build a modern military establishment and a twentieth-century economy. By the end of 1946, its stock of gold and foreign exchange was estimated at $300 million. However, in subsequent years it repeatedly ran into balance-of-payments difficulties, despite a steady flow of foreign financing. By 1958, its foreign exchange crisis was much more dire than Germany's at the end of 1950, or France's at the end of 1957.

EARLY EPU PROBLEMS

The Marshall Plan Years

As World War II ended, Turkey was threatened by Soviet Premier Stalin's territorial demands. The United States responded with both military aid and government credits for development projects. Turkey also became a beneficiary of the Marshall Plan and a founding member of the OEEC. Before the war, Germany had been the principal market for Turkey's limited variety of exports—tobacco, raisins, and hazelnuts — as well as the main supplier of imported goods and equipment. In the early postwar years, Germany had no goods to spare for Turkey, nor

---

[1] Hale (1981), 35.

could it use its limited supply of foreign exchange to buy 'non-essentials'. The United States became Turkey's major trading partner.

Turkey's large defence budget and expanding state enterprises were heavily financed by central bank credit, as well as foreign aid. The consequential inflationary pressures were suppressed by price controls. Though the balance of payments was very strained, US aid covered the deficits in the 1940s and beyond. As the initial EPU negotiations neared an end, Adnan Menderes was elected Prime Minister, promising a freer economic system and greater emphasis on developing the country's agricultural base. Menderes was proud of the military establishment he had inherited and staunchly anti-Communist. His government was one of the few members of NATO to provide fighting men to serve alongside US troops in defending South Korea.

Turkey entered the EPU as a structural debtor, with a $25 million initial credit position, intended for the purchase of capital equipment in Europe. It promptly removed quantitative restrictions from some 63 per cent of imports from its EPU partners, satisfying the obligations of the initial OEEC trade liberalization programme. Unfortunately, by August 1951, it had exhausted both its initial credit position and its $50 million regular EPU quota. During the second year of the Union, the US provided an additional $47.5 million in special resources, and Turkey paid the Union some $60 million in gold to settle the rest of its $163 million cumulative deficit.[2] By the time the EPU was two years old, the Marshall Plan had ended, and US economic aid to Europe was shrinking. Turkey found itself in severe financial straits.

Living Beyond its Means

Beginning in April 1951, the Turkish government repeatedly asked the Managing Board for more credit, either in the form of a special credit or a larger EPU quota. For the next two years, Turkey was on the Board's agenda at almost every session. A succession of missions of economic officials came from Ankara to lay their plight before the Board. Each was headed by Fatim Rustu Zorlu, then in charge of economic questions in the Ministry of Foreign Affairs. On each occasion, the Board refused to recommend approval of the Turkish request.

The members felt that Turkey's EPU deficits resulted from attempts to live beyond its means. State economic enterprises and the agricultural sector were ordering imported capital equipment without providing for payment. Though sympathetic to the Turkish yearning for speedy economic development, the Board felt it inappropriate to use EPU credit

[2] EPU Board, *Second Annual Report* (1952), 39.

to finance long term investment programmes. Unable to attend a special meeting called for August 1952, Rossy sent a note to his Managing Board colleagues that recorded his views and theirs in characteristically direct language. The EPU 'cannot tie up its resources, which are already insufficient, to grant credits which are by nature long term credits'.[3]

Meanwhile, the Turkish government was in constant negotiations with the US for more aid. The US had little success in counselling a more deliberate investment programme and stricter control over the extension of internal credit. By May 1952, Turkey's gold reserves were reduced to $145 million, of which $55 million were pledged against short term loans from the Federal Reserve Bank and the Chase Bank of New York. By September, it was unable to settle its EPU deficit.

The Managing Board thereupon came under heavy political pressure to help Turkey. From its earliest days, it had been sensitive to political considerations in the case of countries whose officials were making efforts in good faith to correct their EPU payments imbalances. But Zorlu and his associates seemed interested only in credit; they appeared unresponsive to the Board's economic advice. Their government 'contended that all Turkey needed to rectify the situation was the provision of more foreign exchange in order to widen some of the bottlenecks'.[4] The Board offered some short term credit, if Turkey would agree to limit imports of capital goods to the amount of financing available. Furthermore, it asked that part of Turkey's gold reserves be pledged as collateral for the credit. In response, Turkey applied political pressure. Both the OEEC Council and the Secretariat were willing to capitulate if the Managing Board would yield.

In October 1952, the Chairmen of the OEEC Council and Executive Committee, as well as the Secretary General, attended a special meeting of the Board for the first—and last—time. The Board agreed only to a short term $20.3 million special credit, to cover gold payments to the Union for Turkey's September and October deficits. The credit was to be repaid in equal instalments during the following December, January, and February. Turkey thereafter yielded to the Board's insistence that it sell an excellent grain crop at world market prices. It was thus able to repay the credit in full, prior to the final maturity.

Payments Arrears and Backtracking

Nevertheless, Turkey began to deliberalize its EPU imports and revert to bilateral trading, without formally notifying the OEEC.[5] Calvet, Carli,

[3] EPU Board Minutes, 26th Session (26-7 Aug. 1952). OEEC MBC/M (52)8.
[4] Sturc (1968), 208.
[5] US del. tel. to Washington, 'Turkish Trade Deliberalisation' (29 Apr. 1953).

and several other Board members also reported that companies in their countries had shipped goods to Turkey without receiving payment. During a heated session with Zorlu in April 1953, members complained about a Turkish decree, issued the previous January. It seemed to subject the release of funds to pay for imports to Turkey's bilateral payments situation with the exporting country.[6] That sounded like a discriminatory trade practice. At the formal meeting, Posthuma dramatically confronted Zorlu with a copy of an official Turkish letter instructing a bank to delay paying bills for imports, a clear violation of the EPU Agreement.

Pieter Lieftinck was asked to attend the Board's next session.[7] A former Dutch Finance Minister, Lieftinck was then head of a resident group of World Bank officials in Ankara. Though his report was restrained and sympathetic about Turkish aspirations, the economic situation he depicted reinforced the Board's concerns. Turkey had greatly increased investments in inventories, as well as in capital goods, helped by liberal internal credit. Lieftinck felt that a 'drastic revision of Turkey's credit policy was required'. Later in the same session, the Chairman of the Steering Board for Trade discussed the Turkish position. His Board was concerned about Turkey's de facto deliberalization and its relapse into trade discrimination.[8]

Lieftinck observed that trading partners were contributing to the return to bilateralism. They were trying to re-establish their traditional Turkish market as their own production and exportable supplies grew. In exchange for exports, they were purchasing Turkish agricultural and mineral products and providing short term credit. As a result, Turkish imports from other OEEC countries tripled between 1950 and 1952. That could hardly be sustained, since credits could not be repaid as they became due.[9] In the calendar year 1953, imports from OEEC countries fell once again, and Turkey's payments deficit with the EPU dropped to $33 million, from $119 million the previous year.

In mid-1953, the Managing Board once again rejected a Turkish request for a large increase in its EPU quota.[10] Cahan protested, terming the Board's report 'nasty' and responsive principally to British and American views.[11] Shortly afterwards Turkey obtained a $20 million drawing from the IMF, which hoped the funds would be used partly to reduce the payments arrears. The Board formally recorded its displeasure that the IMF decision had been taken without consulting it.[12]

[6] EPU Board Minutes, 36th Session (20-5 Apr. 1953). OEEC MBC/M(53)4, Part II.
[7] EPU Board Minutes, 'Interview with Mr. Lieftinck', 37th Session (19 May 1953). OEEC MBC/M (53)5, Part II, Annex.
[8] US del. airgram to Washington. REPTO A-1388 (4 June 1953).
[9] Steering Board for Trade Report (12 Mar. 1953). OEEC C(53)74.
[10] EPU Board Report, 'Prolongation of the Union' (1 June 1953). OEEC C(53)134.
[11] Cahan memo to Marjolin (3 June 1953). OEEC JFC-324.
[12] EPU Board Minutes, 40th Session (24-30 Sept. 1953). OEEC MBC/M(53)8, Part I.

Turkey's payments arrears continued to accumulate as European suppliers competed for orders on the basis of generous credits, guaranteed almost automatically by government export credit insurance agencies. The insurance agencies at that time were reluctant to exchange information with each other. Nor would they put limits on the amounts they would insure for a particular country, lest their own businesses be placed at a competitive disadvantage. OEEC countries tried to negotiate bilateral agreements for repaying old credits, offering in return to open up new credit lines. At the Board's November 1953 meeting, members reported such data on arrears as they could compile.[13] For all OEEC countries, their estimate came to $100 million, with Germany reporting $40 million, the United Kingdom $20 million, and Italy $16 to $17 million. In this atmosphere, the Board watched helplessly while Turkey was saddled with an excessive debt burden. Board members saw no way to exert control from within their own countries, unless Turkey itself became a more cautious borrower.

In January 1954, the OEEC Council established a liaison group (later called a co-ordinating group) to work on Turkish trade and payments problems. Immersed in negotiations about refurbishing the EPU, the Managing Board was relieved to have the Turkish problem removed from its agenda. Later in the year, however, the Council asked for a report on Turkey's return to bilateralism, and the Board responded very sternly. Under its bilateral agreements, any Turkish credit balance on a bilateral account could be used automatically by creditors against their arrears. Hence a clearing through the EPU would not occur.[14] Turkey was thus violating its EPU obligations and could be suspended from the Union. Alternatively, the EPU Agreement could be suspended in relations with Turkey, allowing other members to negotiate and operate bilateral agreements with more freedom.[15] At the time, only four members had such bilateral agreements in effect. Once again Turkey responded with diplomatic representations in the capitals of several EPU Board members, asking that the Board adopt a softer attitude. The Board stood firm, but the OEEC Council took no action on its report.

Thereafter, France, Germany, Italy, and several other countries concluded bilateral agreements, but they were not very satisfactory.[16] While Turkish monthly EPU deficits declined, they still totalled $101 million during the three financial years beginning in July 1954. Turkey

[13] US del. circular airgram. ECOTO A-167 (4 Dec. 1953).
Also EPU Board Minutes, 42nd Session (23-8 Nov. 1953). OEEC MBC/M (53)10, Part I.
[14] W. Bruppacher, BIS Alternate, 'Unofficial Note', 52nd Session of EPU Board (16-19 Nov. 1954). BIS EPU Archive.
[15] EPU Board Minutes, 51st Session (11-15 Oct. 1954). OEEC MBC/M(54)8, Part II.
[16] Bruppacher, 'Unofficial Note', 55th Session of EPU Board (15-19 Feb. 1955). BIS EPU Archive.

settled entirely in dollars, adding to the $166 million it had paid the Union previously.

THE CRISIS

A headlong, uncontrolled investment programme proceeded on the basis of bilateral credit and US aid. The Turkish government was unwilling to change course and, for a while, it managed to cope. Its trading partners were disgruntled but resigned to the situation.

In February 1956, the Board scheduled a review of the Turkish economy, its first for more than two years. An OEEC Secretariat statement conveyed only a sense of helpless dismay. By the end of 1955, Turkey's long term foreign indebtedness exceeded $300 million. Its short term debts were over $400 million, including $150 million in supplier credits and $150 million in trade arrears. Inflationary credit was fuelling rising prices, and a poor harvest in 1954 had converted Turkey into a net importer of grain. Without eliminating the budget deficit and limiting new credits to the amounts needed to complete projects, the prospects for correction were bleak. Turkish prices were far out of line with foreign prices, and that, too, needed corrective action.

For the next two years, the Board's occasional review of the Turkish situation was rather perfunctory, based entirely on OEEC Secretariat information. No improvement was visible. From time to time, members exchanged information about their difficulties with arrears and bilateral agreements, but the Board took no action.

Climax in 1958

As 1958 dawned, Turkey could look back on a decade of foreign aid, credits, and unpaid bills, altogether totalling some $2 billion. Most of that money had been spent to import capital equipment. Had it been put to good use, growing domestic production should have been replacing imports or significantly increasing exports. Unfortunately, that did not seem to be happening. In 1956 and 1957, the volume of Turkish exports was the same as in 1949 and 1950, and the volume of imports was 10 per cent higher. GNP grew by less than 4 per cent per year between 1953 and 1957, while inflation ran at 15 per cent per year despite price controls.[17]

The state enterprises were a serious drain on the economy, having again become the dominant investors after 1954. They were managed by

[17] Hale (1981), 109.

government officials, proud of their roots in a venerable civil service. However, neither entrepreneurial talent nor ability to manage cost-and-profit-sensitive businesses were very evident. The defects of the state enterprises were thus summarized by one author: 'first, a system of pricing which bore little relation to costs and a consequent resort to inflationary deficit financing; secondly, a tendency to establish new plants for purely political reasons, with little regard to locational advantages or the needs of the market; and thirdly, continued political interference and stifling red tape in day-to-day administration'.[18] New plants were started with foreign credits and remained unfinished for lack of domestic financing and foreign exchange.

By the beginning of 1958, Turkey's foreign exchange situation was also in shambles. Foreign debt exceeded a billion dollars, three times yearly export earnings. Debt repayments had absorbed a quarter of export earnings in 1957, arrears were still accumulating, and additional suppliers' credits were increasingly difficult to obtain.[19] Sight liabilities falling due in 1958 amounted to $371 million, more than the total value of 1957 exports.[20]

Not long after the French assistance package was announced on the last day of January 1958, the Turkish government approached the US Embassy in Ankara about a similar package of credit. Upon seeing the report, Kaplan telegraphed Washington and Ankara, reminding them of the 'procedural duration and course of the French negotiations. . . . Particularly in view of the arrears problem, believe desirable United States not become committed re participation in financial assistance until Turkish stabilization programme has been thoroughly considered by international bodies.'[21] Early in the year, the Turkish government sent a mission to Moscow to seek Soviet aid, though the visit was probably intended largely to jog the Americans into a rescue programme.

A skilled and tactful member of the IMF staff, Ernest Sturc, had led a 1953 mission to Turkey. He developed good relations with the conservative officials of the Finance Ministry and hoped they might persuade their cabinet officers to adopt a sensible stabilization programme. Though the IMF agreed to a drawing intended to buttress these advisers, the Turkish government was no more receptive to IMF advice in 1953 than it had been to the Managing Board. By 1958, however, it had begun to appreciate that international help was needed and would require more co-operative behaviour. At home, the government was losing the support

[18] Hale (1981), 92.
[19] Hale (1981), 103-5.
[20] US del. circular airgram. POLTO A-731 (28 May 1958).
[21] US del. tel. to Washington. Repeated to Ankara, Bonn, and London. POLTO 2658 (28 Feb. 1958).

of both the intelligentsia and the army, who felt that inflation was steadily reducing their standard of living.[22] Inflation was reaching runaway proportions, industrial consumer goods based on imported raw materials had disappeared from the Turkish market, and black market quotations of the Turkish lira were five times the official parity.

Pressure for Help

By April 1958, the Turkish government had re-established contact with Sturc and prepared the outline of a stabilization programme, including a realignment of its exchange rate system. However, Turkey had only modest possibilities for drawing more IMF funds. The Turkish Ambassador to the OEEC, Mehmet Ali Tiney, approached von Mangoldt about putting Turkey on the agenda for the Managing Board's April session, but von Mangoldt discouraged him. By this time, Zorlu had become Vice-Premier and Minister for Foreign Affairs, and Hassan Isik had responsibility for economic matters in that ministry. Zorlu came to Paris in mid-April for a NATO meeting, requested $100 million in OEEC assistance, and brought along ten economic experts to begin negotiations with the Managing Board.[23] Sturc also had come to Paris, at Turkey's request, to prepare for formal IMF consultations in Ankara in June.

The Board felt it was being stampeded and refused to hear Isik and his economic experts without a mandate from the OEEC Council. After receiving one limited to advising on procedure for handling the Turkish request, the Board listened to a presentation of a programme of economic reforms. Replying on behalf of the Board, von Mangoldt observed that the Turkish problem appeared to be largely structural, requiring long term measures and long term loans. The EPU could only offer credits to help countries overcome temporary difficulties. The Board concluded that independent experts should be sent to Ankara at the time of the IMF consultations, to serve as a buffer between it and the Turkish government. Wilson (UK) made the first in a series of statements emphasizing the need for close co-operation with the IMF, particularly because of the importance of the exchange rate problem, an IMF responsibility.[24]

By the time of the May meeting, von Mangoldt had told Isik that his government had thus far presented only 'chapter headings' of a programme. His colleagues were equally sceptical of Turkish intentions. Both the Swedish and British delegations to the OEEC opposed any further consideration of the Turkish request, even the sending of a mission to Ankara. Von Mangoldt, on the other hand, contended that the Board

---

[22] Sturc (1968), 206.
[23] Conolly, 'Unofficial Note', 95th Session of EPU Board (16-19 Apr. 1958). BIS EPU Archive.
[24] US del. circular airgram. POLTO A-654 (30 Apr. 1958).

could not refuse the request of any OEEC member to have its economic and financial situation examined. Furthermore, the EPU must protect its existing credits to Turkey. Calvet and Getz Wold also felt that it would be an error to discourage the Turkish government, if it was having a change of heart and seeking a *rapprochement* with the OEEC after years of remaining apart.

The OEEC decided to send a mission to Turkey in June, and von Mangoldt reluctantly agreed to participate if the Secretariat members felt that preliminary discussions were promising. The Secretariat group joined Sturc in Turkey on 16 June, and von Mangoldt proceeded to Ankara a month later. The negotiations had not been easy, but the veteran civil servants in the Turkish Finance Ministry, led by Memduh Aytür, were heartened to see political superiors listening to their advice, at the urging of the multilateral agencies.

THE RESOLUTION

Finally, a Stabilization Programme

To everyone's surprise, the IMF/OEEC missions and the Turkish government were able to agree on a promising stabilization programme. Merle Cochran, Deputy Managing Director of the IMF, joined von Mangoldt in Ankara for the final stages. At a meeting with Cochran and von Mangoldt, Prime Minister Menderes said, in the presence of the Cabinet, that the Turkish government would accept a memorandum prepared by the OEEC/IMF experts *in toto*.[25]

The programme included an array of measures. The government would: lift price controls except for three basic commodities (wheat, coal, and electric power); forbid state economic enterprises to borrow from the central bank, with some exceptions; take over the debt to the central bank accumulated by these enterprises and repay it in annual instalments over a 100-year period; reduce government expenditures and introduce new tax measures; add a surcharge of 6.2 liras per US dollar to the par value of 2.8 liras for all payments to foreign claimants; pay a similar premium on all non-traditional exports (largely agricultural); license raw materials, spare parts, and assorted consumer goods on the basis of global quotas; pay for all imports by letter of credit; and prohibit external borrowing except by the government.[26]

The Turkish government wanted to introduce that programme by the

[25] US del. tel. to Washington, repeated to Ankara, Bonn, and London. POLTO 207 (15 July 1958).
[26] Sturc (1968), 208-9.

end of July, before the new harvest. To do so and to persuade the Turkish public of its efficacy, the government would need substantial foreign assistance, at least $250 million over and above the ongoing US aid programme. In addition, Turkey wanted all OEEC governments to accept a standstill on further servicing of existing Turkish debts, while a debt conference was organized and agreement reached on an appropriate repayment schedule.

Lunch at Chiberta

The IMF mission returned to Washington and enthusiastically reported its results, but the IMF could add only $25 million to the Turkish drawing right. C. Douglas Dillon, the US Under Secretary of State for Economic Affairs, sent Kaplan telephone instructions to seek a $100 million credit through EPU channels—and to arrange it before the end of the month. Aware of the Board's long-standing scepticism toward Turkey and uninformed about the details of what had transpired in Ankara, he promised to do his best. Though far from optimistic, he was heartened that Frank Southard had endorsed the Turkish programme. Southard's international reputation for resisting inadequate promises about stabilization policies might reduce the scepticism. Nevertheless, $100 million was a large sum to raise from Europeans, who had yet to begin providing aid to independent developing countries other than their own former colonies.

Von Mangoldt had returned to Paris to advise the OEEC Council about his mission, and Kaplan hesitantly invited him to lunch at one of the Chairman's favourite Paris restaurants. Von Mangoldt's report about the Ankara results was very positive, but he did not believe an aid package could be assembled before the end of September.[27] Fearing that might diminish the momentum in Turkey, he was delighted by the US desire to complete arrangements before the end of July. Ellis-Rees and Cahan had already gone to London to put the mission findings before the UK Chancellor, who was also Chairman of the OEEC Council.

Von Mangoldt planned to report to the OEEC Council on 17 July and ask for authority to call an immediate special meeting of the Managing Board. The next question was where the money would come from. Some hurried scribbling of numbers over the luncheon table produced a possible financial package. The OEEC Council would be asked to agree to a 90-day standstill on servicing Turkish debts. The EPU could offer Turkey a *rallonge* of $100 million. That would provide $25 million in credit, the

---

[27] US del. tel. to Washington, repeated to Ankara, Bonn, and London. POLTO 207 (15 July 1958).

standard terms. At the most, the EPU might add a $25 million special credit to be used as part of the required matching gold payments. That left $50 million to be contributed by EPU creditor countries. Recalling his difficulties in raising funds for the French assistance package, von Mangoldt reluctantly conceded that only Germany might respond by the end of the month. If the US would match $100 million in European assistance, he would try to persuade his government to provide the missing $50 million. Both men agreed to recommend this package to their respective governments. Not too optimistically, von Mangoldt noted that he had already informed German Finance Minister Franz Etzel that a debt standstill would require him to find $75 million to cover government guarantees.

The Final Assistance Package

London was reserved about the Ellis-Rees/Cahan report, and von Mangoldt's proposal was initially resisted in Bonn. Neither capital thought a debt service standstill was advisable. German authorities asked why other OEEC members should not contribute to the Turkish package. The Federal Republic might offer some assistance, but it would all be tied to German exports. In that event, it could not be used, as von Mangoldt had contemplated, for gold payments within the EPU *rallonge*. The OEEC Council meeting was delayed while von Mangoldt discussed the issues privately with heads of other delegations.

These discussions reinvigorated among OEEC members a spirit of co-operation to solve a significant problem. Turkey was the only member not observing the very basic obligations of membership. The bilateral agreements and arrears negotiations were not only contrary to OEEC rules. They had also proved demeaning and self-defeating, as each government sought to negotiate a better deal for itself with Turkish authorities, who then played one off against the other. In 1953 and 1954, the Council had not shared the harsh views of the Managing Board about Turkey's lack of co-operation; it had little to show for its own softer approach. If von Mangoldt was now convinced that Turkish intentions were serious, member governments should support a new effort to bring Turkey back into the OEEC fold.

The discussion moved toward a consensus that everyone should join in helping Turkey, though without reducing the proposed German contribution. At the Council meeting on 22 July, Roger Ockrent (Belgium) made a strong plea for aid by all OEEC members.[28] Rather than burden the EPU with a special credit, other OEEC members might contribute

---

[28] US del. tel. to Washington. POLTO 308 (22 July 1958).

$25 million to the Turkish package. The Council also appointed an expert committee to examine the technical problems raised by the proposed standstill on servicing Turkish debts. Some government experts had objected to stopping payments due for contracts signed under existing bilateral agreements. In addition, the Council agreed to warn the OEEC ministers that the Turkish issue would be addressed at their next meeting, scheduled for the end of July.

The Managing Board met a few days later.[29] Despite misgivings about the reliability of Turkish commitments, the Board agreed to the $100 million *rallonge*. The US Representative was authorized to make a firm offer of $100 million in additional US assistance to Turkey if Europe would match it. Von Mangoldt was able to promise a $50 million German contribution, but he indicated privately that only $12.5 million would be in cash. Menderes would meet with Adenauer, however, after which more details about the German contribution would be available. Wilson offered $10 million in transferable sterling, and de Strycker said that Belgium would contribute toward the remaining $15 million. Despite France's need for the second part of its EPU credit, Calvet was willing to offer a token French contribution, if his Board colleagues would not object.

The Turkish authorities were dissatisfied with the terms of the US, as well as the British and German, offer.[30] Only one-quarter of the matching US aid would finance current imports. The remainder would consist of loans for new development projects, half of them tied to US exports. Zorlu and Hassan Polatkan, the Finance Minister, came to Paris to register concern about how they could finance the filling of their depleted pipeline of imported goods. The US delegation thereupon urged Washington to consider using its development loans to complete projects already underway.

When the OEEC ministers met during the last days of July, they agreed on a financing package that satisfied the Turkish authorities. Under the aegis of the OEEC, they would match the US offer of $100 million. They urged all members to supplement the EPU *rallonge* credit, to the greatest extent possible in a form that could be used to purchase any goods anywhere within the EPU monetary area. The ministers accepted a 'substantially complete' standstill for six months on servicing Turkish debts and agreed to convene a conference to arrange for the repayment of those debts. They agreed that debt repayment should take into account Turkey's ability to pay, as well as equitable treatment for all member countries.[31] Eventually, ten other OEEC members joined

  29 US del. circular tel. to Washington. Highlights of special meeting of EPU Board. POLTO 369 (26 July 1958).

  30 US del. tel. to Washington. POLTO 372 (27 July 1958).

  31 US del. tel. to Washington. Contains text of resolution to be adopted by Mins. in the next day or two. POLTO 402 (29 July 1958).

Germany and the United Kingdom in contributing; only the other developing countries in the OEEC abstained. The final US contribution came to $114 million of additional assistance, plus the postponement of $44 million due for servicing debts to the US government.

The Turkish government signed its letters of commitment to the OEEC and the IMF a week later, and both the stabilization programme and the assistance package were announced to the press.

Conference on Financial Aid to Turkey and on Turkish Debts

The OEEC ministers had reached a decision quickly, leaving the details to be ironed out later. To deal with them, the Managing Board agreed in September to call a conference, and designated Eric Liefrinck as its chairman. All OEEC members were invited to participate. Turkey sent Ambassador Oguz Gökmen to Paris to head a large Turkish delegation. He established himself in residence for a lengthy negotiation. In fact, it took eight months.

The Conference on Financial Aid to Turkey and on Turkish Debts first had to define an equitable procedure for releasing the bilateral credits. It drafted a model assistance agreement for the bilateral negotiations. Half of each country's assistance would be released promptly; the remainder in two equal instalments after the OEEC was satisfied that the Turkish programme was being implemented. After some wrangling, all bilateral donors agreed that their credits would carry a uniform rate of interest, 5.75 per cent.[32] These arrangements were not completed until the EPU itself had been liquidated and responsibility for the Conference transferred to the European Monetary Agreement and its Board of Management.

As January 1959 came to an end, the Conference was still trying to establish how much debt needed rescheduling. Though virtually all the European credits were insured by government agencies, their status was obscure. Agreement had to be reached about the amounts still outstanding; records of the Turkish government and of the European creditors about individual debts were not always comparable.

Since the US wished to accommodate European concern that US creditors might obtain more favourable treatment, it agreed to participate in the debt conference. However, the US had no legal authority to negotiate on behalf of its private creditors. At that time, it had no government facility for insuring exporter credits, nor did it have much information about Turkish debts to US citizens. An advertisement in a US government publication yielded a flood of affidavits concerning claims,

---

[32] 'Report of the Conference to Board of Management of the European Monetary Agreement'. Submitted by the Board to the OEEC Council (29 Jan. 1959). OEEC C(39)28.

some for very small amounts. (A Philadelphia bookseller reported an unpaid bill for $5.00.) A US creditors' committee was organized, informed about the progress of the Conference, and told that the US government would not ask for more favourable treatment than European creditors received. By a stroke of good fortune, one of the largest US creditors was represented by retired General J. Lawton Collins. A former Chairman of the Joint Chiefs of Staff, he remembered the qualities of Turkey's fighting men in Korea with great fondness. As the elected chairman of the US creditors' committee, the General was very effective in counselling reason. The US claimants had financed their credits themselves, fully recognizing the risks they were taking. Their banks had repeatedly refused to underwrite such loans.

During the Conference, claims totalling $422.7 million were identified and agreed as requiring settlement. Expecting to be the principal source of continuing aid for Turkish development, the US government was reluctant to see much of its aid diverted to servicing these debts. Moreover, it felt that the competitive offers of commercial credit to Turkey had been imprudent and unseemly. Were they rewarded by favourable repayment provisions, the process might start all over again. Hence it supported the efforts of the Turkish negotiators to limit debt service to a reasonable share of Turkey's probable ability to pay, and the eventual agreement so decided.

The agreement provided for repayment over eleven years, beginning in 1959, at an interest rate of 3 per cent. At such unfavourable terms, some creditors preferred to accept Turkish liras for reinvestment in Turkey, and $97.4 million were thus paid off.[33] At $21.6 million the first year, rising to a peak of $45.2 million in 1964, service on old commercial debts could be expected to absorb about 10 per cent of Turkish export earnings.[34] Adding payments on new and old bilateral and multilateral official credits, Turkish debt service might reach 20 per cent. That seemed manageable, given the financial assistance package and the expectation of vigorous export growth once the stabilization programme had taken effect. Creditor governments had agreed to a subsidized interest rate in exchange for a reasonable prospect of full payment for goods that had been sold, in many cases, at inflated prices.

THE OUTCOME

Despite the financial assistance and the stabilization programme, Turkish GNP only grew by 3 to 4 per cent over the following two years.

[33] IBRD (World Bank) (1975), 130.
[34] IBRD (World Bank) (1975), 346, table 4.6.

Menderes's political opposition became more strident; he declared martial law in April 1960 and was deposed by a military *coup* a month later. A series of new governments each fully embraced the commitments entered into by their predecessor in 1958. Sturc could assert in 1968 that, after 1958, all the Turkish governments 'were and are committed to pursuing the economic development of their country in conditions of reasonable stability. This firm adherence to a single policy reflects the lesson the nation learned during the period 1954-58.'[35]

In 1962, the OEEC organized a Turkish aid consortium and invited von Mangoldt to serve as its chairman. Its members disbursed $2.5 billion on behalf of Turkey over the next decade.[36] By the middle 1960s, remittances from Turkish workers employed in OEEC countries began to supplement export earnings by substantial amounts. The additional foreign exchange helped balance the foreign accounts, and GNP grew by 67 per cent over the course of the 1960s. Inflation fell to an average rate of 5 per cent a year between 1963 and 1969. When it reached double-digit proportions again in 1970, another substantial devaluation became necessary. By mid-1961, Turkey had liberalized 52 per cent of its 1959 imports from other OEEC members.

Turkey faithfully serviced the debts as agreed in 1959, though another consolidation exercise was necessary in mid-decade. Its overall debt service ratio peaked at 24 per cent in 1964 and fell to about 10 per cent in 1972.[37] In 1969, foreign exchange reserves increased by over $120 million, the first significant increase in many years; reserve growth continued thereafter until the 1973 oil crisis.

Turkey was the Managing Board's only experience with stabilizing the economy of a developing country. Co-ordinating efforts with the IMF provided more expertise and more pressure for policy reforms than either organization could have exerted alone. Nevertheless, obtaining results proved much more difficult and time-consuming than in the case of the EPU's industrialized members. For many years, a substantial flow of aid, over and above debt service, was essential to support a continuing development process.

Turkey's OEEC colleagues learned from the experience, as did Turkey itself. Turkey co-operated out of necessity, accepting outside interference by well-wishers—to its own benefit and that of its trading partners. Europeans were able to re-establish their traditional market in Turkey, while Turkey was able to meet its import requirements at competitive prices. Although inflation continued to be a persistent problem, it did not get so far out of hand as to threaten a high rate of economic expansion.

[35] Sturc (1968), 209.
[36] IBRD (World Bank) (1975), 21.
[37] IBRD (World Bank) (1975), 132.

A reasonable programme for rescheduling all debts, adjusting total debt service requirements to the country's ability to pay, proved successful. The stabilization programme, associated with assistance, thus brought the country back into the OEEC fold.

17   Operation Unicorn: End of the EPU

The European Monetary Agreement placed squarely in British hands the initiative for the final moves to terminate the EPU and establish convertibility. By the end of 1957, the latter step would be largely symbolic for Belgium, Germany, the Netherlands, Norway, and Switzerland. They had virtually achieved resident convertibility with respect to most trade and current payments. Except for Ludwig Erhard, however, few Continental cabinet members were thirsting for an early UK decision. For him, the move would crown the free market philosophy with which he had guided the German economy. Yet even in Germany, the final move was scarcely an overriding priority. Chancellor Adenauer was much more preoccupied with the successful inauguration of the Common Market. The timing of the move would thus depend on British economic and financial considerations, without much pressure from other EPU members. As the calendar year 1957 came to a close, the United Kingdom appeared to be nearly ready.

CONVERTIBILITY RESURFACES IN BRITAIN

The stabilization programme introduced by Chancellor Thorneycroft in September 1957 reflected a major change in the economic priorities of the British government. For the first time since the end of the war, fiscal and monetary policies were directed more at short-term correction of imbalances in British foreign exchange accounts than at economic expansion and increased employment. Thorneycroft had insisted on these measures against the advice of Treasury civil servants, led by Sir Roger Makins, then Permanent Secretary.[1] When the Cabinet proposed a modest increase in government spending toward the end of the year, the Chancellor objected as a matter of principle and resigned, with his two junior ministers, in January 1958. He was succeeded by Derrick Heathcoat Amory, the Minister of Agriculture.

Despite his reservations about the September stabilization measures, Makins began to consider their possible ramifications, even as the cabinet controversy reached its peak. Early in January 1958, he asked Governor

[1] Brittan (1964), 190.

Cobbold to 'look again at the structure of our sterling exchange system'.[2] After repeated rejections of his previous proposals to unify the sterling exchange rates, the Governor now had a Treasury invitation to resubmit his views. He did so a month later, predictably proposing that the official and transferable rates be amalgamated 'in the fairly near future'.

Rowan's instinctive reaction to Cobbold's latest sally was as negative as it had been ever since the Bank had abandoned its espousal of freely floating rates late in 1954. He noted that the 'pre-conditions' of the old Collective Approach had not yet been fulfilled and that Parliament was pressing 'for further discrimination against dollar goods rather than relaxation'.[3]

After a meeting with Chancellor Amory, a small group of senior Bank and Treasury officials was asked to review the implications of Cobbold's proposal. Rowan's memoranda to this group included, without attribution, virtually all the negative arguments advanced by Continental members of the Managing Board in 1953.[4] He added a few more timely points—an ongoing US recession, Germany's payments surpluses, low prices for commodities exported by the rest of the sterling area, internal pressure for higher wages, and the effect on Britain's allies in the Free Trade Area negotiations. He preferred to maintain momentum by 'a vigorous programme in this field [removing dollar discrimination]'.

Sir George Bolton had left the Bank of England in 1956 to head a private bank, and most of his former responsibilities now fell to Maurice Parsons. The latter's reply argued that the problems raised by Rowan would remain, whether or not sterling rates were unified. On the other hand, the United Kingdom was currently being deprived of benefits because the transferable sterling market 'lies mainly in Zurich and New York'.[5] The Bank's long-standing priority was thus again made clear and explicit.

By early April, the Bank and the Treasury had reached full agreement, except on the matter of timing. On exchange rate policy, the Bank and the Treasury had both concluded that the UK should adopt neither a floating rate nor a wider spread. Either move would 'call seriously into

---

[2] Cobbold letter to Makins (4 Feb. 1958). Response to Sir Roger's suggestion of a month or so ago. Bank of England OV 44/21.

[3] Parsons, memo to Governor about a meeting with Rowan and Rickett (7 Feb. 1958). Bank of England OV 44/21.

[4] Rowan, 'Bringing the Rates Together: Arguments against action in the immediate future' (Mar. 1958). Supplemented by 'The Arguments against a Move Now', attachment to letter to Parsons (24 Mar. 1958).

Also Rickett, 'Exchange Rate Policy'. Draft memo to Rowan sent to Parsons (24 Mar. 1958). Rickett concluded, '. . . arguments for maintaining our present policy of a sterling rate fluctuating only within narrow margins are overriding.' Bank of England OV 44/21.

[5] Parsons, ' "Pros" for Early Amalgamation of Official and Transferable Sterling'. Enclosure to note to Rowan (27 Mar. 1958). Bank of England OV 44/21.

question the future of sterling as a trading and still more as a reserve currency. It would be regarded as a major move away from the objective behind the International Monetary Fund and the OEEC. It would threaten the destruction of sterling as a form of international liquidity, and thus accentuate the present tendencies towards a world recession.'[6] An annex spelled out UK commitments to the IMF, to the Commonwealth, and to Europe via the EPU and EMA agreements. Changes in these obligations might be negotiated, but the results would not be worth the time required. From then on, all these views were treated as settled UK policy.

Rowan submitted the group's agreements and disagreements to the Chancellor and to Makins, with a covering note that quoted Churchill on the subject of timing: '. . . while historians may easily mark what would have been the best possible moment for any great undertaking, the good moment must content the Administrator.'[7] The new Chancellor proved to be as reticent about accepting the Bank's advice on timing as his predecessors had been. For the next few months, the government's international economic priority continued to be the Free Trade Area negotiations. But the French political crisis in June and July made those negotiations seem much less promising.

Operation Unicorn

By midsummer 1958, the stabilization measures seemed to have taken effect; the British economy had improved in many respects. With economic expansion at a standstill, Britain's reserves had risen, and prices had stabilized. For the first six months of 1958, the sterling area reported a small EPU surplus, the first over so long a period for many years. Moreover, the US recession appeared to be nearing an end. Then, early in September, the US proposed to increase all IMF quotas.[8] In this more propitious environment, careful preparations were launched for making sterling a convertible currency, at least to the extent of rate unification.

At first dubbed Operation Moonshine, the effort was quickly renamed Operation Unicorn. In name and nature, it was very different from its impetuous predecessor, ROBOT. The name reveals no link with individuals. Apparently, it derived only from a fabulous, mythical horse with a single straight horn. Perhaps the author had in mind the unicorn in

---

[6] 'Exchange Rate Policy: Paper II, Flexible Exchange Rates'. Sent to Sir Roger Makins and the Chancellor. Agreed among Rowan, Hall, Rickett, Arnold France of Treasury, and Parsons and W. Hamilton of Bank of England (2 Apr. 1958). Bank of England OV 44/21.

[7] W. S. Churchill, *The River War*. Quoted in Rowan, 'Exchange Rate Policy'. Memo to Makins and the Chancellor (2 Apr. 1958). Bank of England OV 44/21.

[8] Horsefield (1969), i, 446-8.

Great Britain's coat of arms—or the unicorn tapestry in the Cluny museum in Paris, with its motto, 'À mon seul desir'. A more important contrast with ROBOT was Unicorn's thorough analysis of the implications of the proposed move. Detailed plans and procedures would be formulated to meet a variety of problems that might arise.

A significant step was taken first to placate the Americans. At the Commonwealth Trade and Economic Conference, held in Montreal in mid-September 1958, the United Kingdom announced an end to discriminatory restrictions on imports from the dollar area for certain manufactured goods, including machinery and newsprint.

After that conference, Chancellor Amory proceeded to New York for a private meeting with the US Secretary of the Treasury, Robert Anderson, and his Assistant Secretary.[9] Anderson, who had succeeded Humphrey a year earlier, had little more experience with international finance than had his predecessor on taking office. With the Prime Minister's prior approval, Amory told Anderson that convertibility of sterling might take place in a few months—perhaps within six months. The US Secretary warmly 'welcomed the prospect'. He did not raise any of the issues that had preoccupied the previous generation of high US officials—exchange rate policy, non-discrimination, Article VIII of the IMF, EPU, European integration, trade liberalization, or France and other weaker European economies. Within the US administration at the time, primary responsibility for most of these matters was lodged with the State Department.

All these issues would be addressed by the Unicorn group on its own, at the initiative of other UK cabinet officers or in response to Continental reactions. Anderson honoured Amory's request that he tell no one but President Eisenhower. Ten days later, at the IMF Annual Meetings in New Delhi, the US Secretary, on reflection, asked for a hint when the move was firmly in prospect, so that he could talk it over with his advisers.[10]

At the same IMF meetings, the Chancellor made a similar statement of UK intentions to Jacobsson and to Karl Blessing, President of the German Bundesbank.[11] Both encouraged him to act soon, but expressed concern about French reactions and advised speaking to the French government in advance. The Chancellor had been briefed about the consent needed from countries holding 50 per cent of the EPU quotas. But he refrained

---

[9] Note of talk between Chancellor and Sec. of US Treasury (27 Sept. 1958). Bank of England OV 44/21.

[10] Operation Unicorn, 'Record of Conversation with Anderson' (6 Oct. 1958). NDC(58)8. Bank of England OV 44/24.

[11] 'Record of Conversation with Jacobsson' (5, 8 Oct. 1958). NDC(58)12 and 17. Bank of England OV 44/24.

'Record of Conversation with Blessing' (6 Oct. 1958). NDC(58)9. Bank of England OV 44/24.

in New Delhi from taking any country other than Germany into his confidence. The British and German quotas totalled 37.5 per cent. Concurrence from several more countries would be required, but presumably would not be difficult to obtain.

The preconditions for sterling convertibility, which earlier had seemed out of reach, were now pretty much in place. As long ago as 1950, Cripps had defined them as larger UK reserves and a US foreign exchange position in balance or in deficit. Butler's 1953 Collective Approach had incorporated both of these preconditions. With a 50 per cent increase in IMF resources, the UK could contemplate at least $4.5 to $5.0 billion in reserves to support a convertible pound. The US had run a balance-of-payments deficit in every calendar year since 1952, even during brief recessions. Moreover, the essential precondition Butler had enunciated to Cobbold in August 1955 had been realized: the internal British economy now seemed to be 'sound'. The Bank of England's single-minded aspiration for opening up foreign exchange markets in London for all types of sterling might finally be satisfied.

In New Delhi, the Chancellor's public announcement suggested his intentions in veiled language.

This strengthening of sterling has enabled us to make substantial further progress in the removal of discrimination in trade and has brought us still nearer to the convertibility of the pound which is our objective. When we judge that the necessary conditions have been achieved and we can do so without risk we shall move forward.

Unicorn in Action: October 1958

The formal work of Operation Unicorn could begin in earnest without awaiting the Chancellor's return to London. The announcements in Montreal and New Delhi were all the press needed to pry and to print speculative stories. Pressures from journalists and from officials of other countries for more information suggested to British officials a certain urgency about their preparations. So did a flow of speculative capital into sterling, totalling perhaps $150 to $350 million. While that money was welcome, it could prove a mixed blessing if it flowed out again immediately after a move. Its loss would put pressure on the sterling exchange rate at the very moment of unification.

At an initial meeting of ten Treasury and Bank officials, the Unicorn group considered about twenty different problems and discussed four carefully prepared major papers.[12] The most important decision taken

[12] Operation Unicorn, minutes and memos, 1st meeting (8 Oct. 1958). MS(58)1 dealt with minor points, MS(58)2 with IMF Articles VIII and XIV, MS(58)3 with Unification and EMA, MS(58)4 with Exchange Control and Exchange Dealing Matters. Bank of England OV 44/24.

was not to accept the Article VIII obligations of the IMF at the moment the rates were amalgamated. (Article VIII forbade payments restrictions and discriminatory currency arrangements.) If all went well, that step might be taken at the next Annual Meeting of the IMF, preferably in conjunction with all other currencies that became convertible. The Bank of England would begin consultations by first talking to its German and French counterparts. Next, similar conversations would be conducted with six other prospective European participants in the move to convertibility. These consultations would be followed by an announcement, then market intervention, and finally unification. The optimistic author of a paper on the EMA thought it might be operational on the fifth working day after consultations began.

After this meeting, the flow of Unicorn papers proliferated. The Treasury was asked to open discussions with the Board of Trade about a programme of dollar liberalization to begin in 1959.[13] But the advisability of devaluing the pound sterling before moving to convertibility apparently was not considered. A resumption of economic growth, an end to dollar discrimination, and the relaxation of other foreign exchange restrictions might put pressure on the pound after the move. The assumption seemed to be that sterling, which was strong at the moment, could remain so.

By 17 October 1958, plans were sufficiently advanced for the Cabinet to be informed, and a paper was circulated to its members.[14] Rowan advised a move before the French general elections, scheduled to begin on 23 November. The ministers proved more circumspect, and Prime Minister Macmillan supported their stance. Led by Selwyn Lloyd, the Foreign Minister, the Cabinet stipulated that more consideration be given to the reactions of other countries. It specifically suggested that the Chancellor seek 'the willing acquiescence' of the French.

The Unicorn group reassembled on 24 October to consider papers on the attitudes of France and other countries.[15] The papers were upbeat and optimistic. The French might wish to take advantage of the British move to initiate a further devaluation at the same time, a notion that proved critical for French co-operation. On other matters of probable concern to the French, the Unicorn group had conciliatory suggestions. The UK itself would offer an extended period for the repayment of France's EPU liquidation debt and would urge the Germans, who would hold much the largest claim on France, to do likewise. The UK would

---

[13] Operation Unicorn, 'Trade and Exchange Steps Connected with Unification' (15 Oct. 1958). MS(58)12. Bank of England OV 44/24.

[14] T. L. R. (Rowan), 'Exchange Rate Policy'. Memo to the Chancellor (17 Oct. 1958). Bank of England OV 44/22.

[15] Operation Unicorn, 'The Transition from EPU to EMA', MS(58)16, revised (27 Oct. 1958) and 'France', MS(58)17, revised (27 Oct. 1958). Bank of England OV 44/24.

also support an early French drawing, equal to France's remaining EPU credit line, on the European Fund. Since the British did not intend to accept the obligations of IMF Article VIII for a period, the French need not be concerned about having to do so immediately either. No other major country was expected to present unmanageable difficulties; the concerns of some smaller EPU members could be satisfied.

FINDING 'THE GOOD MOMENT'

The Hesitations of November

A few days later, a meeting with officials of other ministries uncovered more hesitations. The Foreign Office, the Commonwealth Relations Office, and the Colonial Office all wanted earlier consultation with their principal clients. More distressingly, the President of the Board of Trade emphatically opposed the whole operation on internal political grounds. He would have preferred to widen the spread between transferable and dollar account sterling, rather than to unify the rates.[16] That view did not prevail.

By this time, speculation in the press had led other European governments to discuss among themselves the implications of an imminent British move. Reports of these discussions flowed into London and gave reason for pause. The Six were determined to maintain their unity and would not move to convertibility and the EMA without the French.[17] On 3 November, von Mangoldt told Ellis-Rees that he hoped the UK was not thinking about an immediate move. The Free Trade Area negotiations should be got out of the way first.[18] Blessing also felt any action was best postponed until after the French elections.[19] These German views were reported on the very day that telegrams of notification about a proposed move had been sent to members of the Commonwealth.[20]

The Treasury promptly asked the Bank of England whether it would be possible to put Unicorn into effect while continuing the EPU more or less indefinitely. Startled by this unwelcome suggestion at the very moment its long-standing goal seemed within reach, the Bank counselled a brief delay. A move before the French elections 'might damage the Free

[16] J. M. S. (Stevens), Report of Unicorn meeting (27 Oct. 1958). Bank of England OV 44/24.

[17] S. W. P. (Payton), conversations at meeting of Managing Board (28-30 Oct. 1958). Bank of England OV 44/24.

[18] Bank of England, internal memo quoting Ellis-Rees letter to Arnold France (3 Nov. 1958). Bank of England OV 44/24.

[19] Bank of England, internal memo quoting Ellis-Rees letter to Arnold France (3 Nov. 1958). Bank of England OV 44/24.

[20] Governor's tel. to Australia, Canada, India, New Zealand, Pakistan, Rhodesia, and South Africa (3 Nov. 1958). Bank of England OV 44/24.

Trade Area negotiations'. Perhaps the initial approach to European governments might be postponed until, say, 8 December. In the meantime, Cobbold might meet with Baumgartner and Blessing.[21] It was so decided.

During the November meetings of the BIS in Basle, Cobbold suggested the possibility of a move between the French elections and the end of the year.[22] Both Baumgartner and Blessing indicated they would personally welcome one. Blessing was sure that Erhard could resist pressure for delay from other Common Market countries, but Baumgartner was less sanguine about his government's attitude. Convertibility might get tied into Free Trade Area politics. A few days later, von Mangoldt firmly informed Ellis-Rees that the Germans would stand by the French if the British moved against French wishes.[23]

On that very day, the Free Trade Area negotiations resumed, and Jacques Soustelle announced that France was unable to accept a Free Trade Area such as the British envisaged. As chairman of the Inter-Governmental Committee charged with reaching an agreement, Maudling promptly suspended the negotiations. Upon returning to London, where he held the cabinet post of Paymaster General, he advised his fellow ministers that a move on the currency front would only exacerbate relations with the French and would be resented by them as a movement out of spite on the part of the British.[24] Macmillan and Amory agreed to defer Unicorn for a short time, until the dust had settled.

The dust settled over Europe very unevenly. Erhard, the Free Trade Area's principal supporter within the German Cabinet, had reacted sharply at the Inter-Governmental Committee to this latest display of French recalcitrance. The Common Market Commission subsequently developed a conciliatory offer, with French agreement. It proposed that the first reduction in quantitative restrictions among the Six, scheduled for the beginning of 1959, should be extended to all OEEC members. That would avoid any trade discrimination between OEEC members for at least the first year of the Common Market. During the November meetings of the Managing Board, von Mangoldt changed his advice to the British, encouraging David Pitblado (the new UK nominee to the Managing Board) to proceed with convertibility. He did not believe that the French would block the move.[25] The Benelux representatives were

---

[21] J. M. S. (Stevens) letter to Rickett (4 Nov. 1958). Bank of England OV 44/24.

[22] C. F. C. (Cobbold), 'Note of Conversations in Basle'. Sent to Makins (11 Nov. 1958). Bank of England OV 44/24.

[23] S. W. P. (Payton), Unicorn memo noting recent tels. and reports from Paris (13 Nov. 1958). Bank of England OV 44/24.

[24] 'Note of a Conversation with Sir Denis Rickett'. Internal Bank memo (19 Nov. 1958). Bank of England OV 44/24.

[25] S. W. P. (Payton), 'Conversations in Paris this Week' (21 Nov. 1958). Bank of England OV 46/68.

less sanguine. De Strycker gingerly suggested a delay in order to amend the EMA by incorporating fixed limits on the exchange spreads. The Dutch wondered about first revising the European Fund to increase the German share of the contributions.

Prodded by the Bank of England, the Chancellor approached the Prime Minister once again early in December.[26] He urged that consultations with other governments should begin on 8 December and that the move to convertibility should be announced to the House of Commons a week later. His justification featured the Bank's long-standing priority— permitting British banks to deal in all kinds of sterling. He further argued that it was no longer in Britain's interest to restrict imports on dollar goods that would only substitute for non-dollar goods; further delay in eliminating discrimination made sense only in the case of goods that would otherwise be imported in larger quantities. He tried to present the unification of sterling rates as only 'a technical move in the exchange field'.[27]

Delay for de Gaulle

Chancellor Amory's cabinet colleagues were not impressed by this reasoning. They remained reluctant to authorize a move until Continental support was assured.[28] The imperturbable Chancellor offered to await a more favourable moment, possibly in mid-January. He also sent Cobbold to Washington to solicit Secretary Anderson's support for a renewal of the UK's IMF standby and to inform him of the delay. While agreeing to support renewal of the standby, Anderson expressed mild disappointment at the postponement of convertibility. He hoped that a positive decision might be taken 'sooner rather than later'.[29]

The early December meetings of the BIS buzzed with anticipation of a British move. John M. Stevens had succeeded Bolton as an Alternate UK Director of the BIS. With Cobbold in Washington, Stevens represented the Bank of England in Basle. Baumgartner openly discussed his problems with his fellow governors and expressed to Stevens his appreciation of British willingness to take his timing problems into account. He expected de Gaulle to accept Rueff's recommendations, but the General was still against devaluation, and Pinay's endorsement was

[26] Chancellor of Exchequer, 'Unicorn'. Draft minute to Prime Min. (2 Dec. 1958). Bank of England OV 44/23.

[27] Chancellor of Exchequer, 'Exchange Rate Policy'. Draft memo (28 Nov. 1958). Bank of England OV 44/22.

[28] M. H. P. (Parsons), memo to the Governor (4 Dec. 1958). Bank of England OV 44/23.

[29] Governor, tel. from Washington for Chancellor of Exchequer. UK Embassy tels. to Foreign Office 3330 and 3331 (9 Dec. 1958). Bank of England OV 44/23.

uncertain.[30] Governor Frère left the meetings with the mistaken impression that the UK wanted to harden the EPU settlements to 100 per cent in gold for a period of three months, during which time the EMA would be revised, and he so informed the Belgian Minister of Finance.[31] The President of the Swiss National Bank, Walter Schwegler, got the impression that the French government had informed the British that it would regard a UK initiative to end the EPU and inaugurate the EMA as 'unfriendly'.[32]

On returning to Paris, Baumgartner apparently won Finance Minister Pinay over to devaluation. On 10 December, he telephoned the Bank of England to say that 'France was ready to follow our lead on unification.'[33] After Christmas would be suitable timing. He would call again in a few days to confirm the conversation.

The Chancellor immediately asked the Prime Minister for permission to move at the same time as the French. He needed a decision by the morning of 12 December, when he would be leaving for a NATO ministerial meeting in Paris. The British Cabinet met on the twelfth and decided to 'unify the rates provided that it occurred simultaneously or after a French move'.[34] Fearing a trap, the Foreign Minister insisted that the French be told that the UK had made no decision on timing.

Von Mangoldt's Dinner Party

Despite the secrecy of these private conversations, speculation in the press heightened. Much of it suggested that a British move was planned in reprisal for the failure of the Free Trade negotiations. European officials who had not been involved in the discussions became more insistent about being informed. Managing Board members who had attended the BIS meetings came directly to Paris for a Board meeting on 10 December. They claimed that Stevens had told them that the Cabinet had decided to unify the rates.[35] Getz Wold began the official meeting by pointedly criticizing the Board for discussing minor matters while

---

[30] J. M. S. (Stevens), 'Basle Meeting' (6-8 Dec. 1958). Bank of England OV 44/23.

Also Bank of England memo to Makins, 'Exchange Rate Policy' (10 Dec. 1958). Bank of England OV 44/23.

[31] Minutes of the Board (9 Dec. 1958). National Bank of Belgium PV 1683/16.

Also Minutes of the Board, 'Conversation with the Minister of Finance' (12 Dec. 1958). National Bank of Belgium PV 1684/1.

[32] Schwegler, 'Problems Raised and Measures Taken following the Replacement of the EPU by the EMA'. Statement to Board of Swiss National Bank (13 Feb. 1959). Minutes of the Board 701, Annex 26.

[33] J. M. S. (Stevens), 'Note for the Record' (10 Dec. 1958). Bank of England OV 44/24.

[34] J. M. S. (Stevens), 'Note for the Record'. Meeting in Makins's room on 12 Dec. 1958, memo (16 Dec. 1958). Bank of England OV 44/23.

[35] US del. tel. to Washington. POLTO 1660 (12 Dec. 1958).

major ones were on everybody's mind. Thereupon, von Mangoldt halted further open discussion and invited the elected members of the Board to a private dinner.[36]

His dinner guests spoke as if the British decision had been made and as if the British would readily amass 50 per cent of the quotas for the liquidation of the EPU. Calvet said that France would join the move, also making the franc convertible. Von Mangoldt was noncommittal about British timing, but all the other Continentals said their countries were very reluctant to move immediately to the EMA. They preferred to maintain the EPU, at least for an interim period, perhaps until 30 June 1959.

Their arguments for doing so were more political than economic. Calvet and Carli were particularly vocal about the timing of the British move. Within their own governments, they were ardent supporters of co-operation on an OEEC-wide basis; both felt the move would strengthen the tendency to divide Europe into the Common Market and the rest. The EPU was a well known symbol of intra-European co-operation, and its liquidation would be widely interpreted as 'a conscious act against European monetary cooperation'. Not only was the EMA a much less satisfactory instrument, it was unknown both to cabinet ministers and to the public. Hay strongly endorsed this point of view. In the back of everyone's mind was the uncertainty about whether France would devalue. If not, its move to convertibility might well be accompanied by stringent controls over trade and payments. Currency convertibility could then become a caricature of the real thing, as Carli had described it in 1952.

Except for Getz Wold, all the Continentals preferred to continue the EPU for a while with 100 per cent gold settlements. Pitblado countered with the reasons the UK had long advanced for considering such an arrangement incompatible with a convertible pound sterling. Rather than pursue a doctrinal disputation, the Continentals responded by raising technical questions. Carli and de Strycker wanted to negotiate improvements in the EMA before it was brought into being. Calvet did not fancy France's having both to pay off its debts to the EPU and to finance a contribution to the European Fund at a difficult moment. De Strycker wanted to revise the Posthuma formula for liquidating the EPU; the allocation of EPU debts to member countries for amortization was disadvantageous to some of the creditors. Getz Wold wondered whether the UK would be willing to finance the Scandinavian countries' deficits with the Common Market countries. Hay was reluctant to contribute to

[36] Pitblado reports about the dinner. UK del. tel. to Foreign Office No. 158 (12 Dec. 1958). Letter to Rickett (12 Dec. 1958). Payton report to Bank of England (13 Dec. 1958). Bank of England OV 44/23.

the European Fund so long as a possibility still existed of trade discrimination between the Six and the other OEEC countries.

Since the British were determined to confine discussion with the US to the Secretary of the Treasury, the US Representative to the Managing Board was not invited to von Mangoldt's dinner. However, Board members talked to him rather freely during the intervals between these early December meetings. Pitblado and the others told him that unification of the rates would not be associated with convertibility in the sense of moving to IMF Article VIII, and he so notified the Department of State and other Washington officials.[37]

THE DECISION

During the NATO ministerial meetings, Erhard urged Amory to make an early move.[38] The Chancellor responded that if it were helpful to the French, rather than being interpreted as aggravating their difficulties, that could make a difference to the British government. He himself was not inclined to open the subject with Pinay at their scheduled meeting. Erhard promised to offer de Gaulle $300 million in assistance when they met the next day.

At a dinner on 17 December, Pinay told the Chancellor that the franc would be devalued and that a UK move on the exchange front would be a good thing. It would help progress on European co-operation if the move occurred after Christmas but before New Year's Day, the date set for the Common Market to take effect. At the same dinner party, the Chancellor, Pinay, and Etzel (German Finance Minister) agreed that their central bank governors should be asked to work out the technical steps.[39] On his return to London, the Chancellor asked for immediate authority to unify the rates, and the Prime Minister approved.

Final Arrangements

The Unicorn group promptly reassembled on a note of triumph.[40] Once France decided to devalue, everything else would fall into place. Sensitivity to other major European trading partners had paid off; the move could take place without major political recrimination.

All that remained was to arrange the final steps. Central banks had to

---

[37] US del. tel. to Washington. POLTO 1660 (12 Dec. 1958).

[38] Unicorn, 'Record of a Conversation' (14 Dec. 1958). Bank of England OV 44/23.

[39] Chancellor of Exchequer, 'Unicorn'. Draft memo to Prime Min. Encloses a 'Record of Conversation' (17 Dec. 1958). Bank of England OV 44/23.

[40] Note of meeting on Unicorn in Rickett's room (18 Dec. 1958). Bank of England OV 44/23.

be informed so that they could prepare the necessary changes in their regulations. The EPU had to be terminated, and a transition to the EMA initiated. The Unicorn group prepared a detailed schedule. Notifications would be sent to Jacobsson, UK Embassies, Secretary Anderson, Uniscan, other OEEC countries, members of the Commonwealth, the Colonial Governors, and the Secretary General of the OEEC. The notifications would begin on 18 December and end with an announcement to the IMF Executive Board and the press on the evening of 31 December. The rates would be unified on 1 January 1959.

A single omission, apparently unpremeditated, marred the generally co-operative and sensitive attitude. No provision was made for a formal notification to the EPU Managing Board. The Board was thus excluded from direct participation in arranging for the interment of the EPU system. Its first official word of the move would come after the Secretary General of the OEEC had been notified that countries holding a majority of the EPU quotas had decided to end their participation. Arrangements with EPU member countries would be made through bilateral talks with the principal central banks. As a result of this oversight, some difficulties arose, and some ill feeling was generated. Had von Mangoldt been notified and asked to arrange the transition from the EPU to the European Fund with his colleagues, much of this would have been avoided.

The first steps in the British schedule were to talk to the Bundesbank and then to the Bank of France. Jasper Rootham, like Stevens an Alternate UK Director of the BIS, travelled to Frankfurt. There he met with Bundesbank Directors Johannes Tüngeler and Emminger. Schleiminger (one of the authors of this book) also participated. Then an official of the Bundesbank, he had chaired the meetings of the EPU's Group of Alternates since 1955.

The Bundesbank Directors quickly accepted a 'formula' for an agreement between the British, French, and German governments.[41] It would bring the EMA into force on 1 January and unify existing foreign exchange rates on external current accounts. Responding to French reluctance to inaugurate the European Fund at the same time, the 'formula' provided for a delay in calling up European contributions. At first only $113 million out of the EPU residual capital would be transferred to the European Fund. In case of urgent need resulting from the cessation of EPU credit, sympathetic consideration would be given to short term *ad hoc* assistance on a bilateral basis. Schleiminger hoped the OEEC Council would set a reasonable time limit for the bilateral debt negotiations required under the EPU liquidation rules. Of course, von Mangoldt was promptly informed about the 'formula', and the Germans quickly regretted

41 Rootham, letter to Parsons from Frankfurt (20 Dec. 1958). Bank of England OV 44/23.

their hasty acquiescence in the provision concerning the European Fund.

On the day after the Bundesbank meeting, Stevens and Pitblado met with Baumgartner, Calvet, and Julien Koszul of the Bank of France.[42] Before the meeting, Calvet had reported that the Monetary Committee of the Common Market had just come down in favour of postponing unification of the rates. Baumgartner brushed that aside with a statement to Stevens that France preferred 29 December as the date for unification and the move to EMA. He also accepted the 'formula', though his Cabinet had yet to decide formally to devalue the franc. Calvet wondered whether the US would agree to the transfer of the $113 million, if the rest of the European Fund agreement was kept in suspense. The UK officials confidently undertook to arrange an approach to the US government at the highest level to assure US co-operation with the 'formula'. The French said they intended to proceed with an early re-negotiation of the European Fund, and the British also would have welcomed an opportunity to reduce their contribution and increase Germany's. The British agreed to provide a £20 million swap facility to help tide France over the beginning of the EMA.

Calvet's concern about the US reaction did not stem only from his memory of the 1955 European Fund negotiations. He had received Kaplan in his office a few days before, saying he believed it only right that senior US government officials should be informed about the status of discussions on the UK unification proposal.[43]

Kaplan's report was the first official word to the State Department and the first word to the Secretary of the Treasury since Cobbold had informed him of the delay. Washington promptly instructed its representative to make it clear that US consent to the transfer of the EPU capital depended on full execution of the 1955 agreements. First, the European Fund provisions should be retained intact. Second, the US assumed that unification would mean convertibility and an end to dollar discrimination, in keeping with its letter of agreement to the transfer of the EPU capital. Calvet had expressed the hope that the US would understand that some countries were joining the British move reluctantly, for political reasons. They could not be expected to change their trade system in the near future. Despite UK representations in Washington, the US position held firm.

Stevens went on to Rome to meet with Governor Donato Menichella, Carli, and Professor Paolo Baffi of the Italian central bank. They were fully supportive after being told that the French were happy about the move. Another Bank of England official found a similarly favourable

[42] UK del. tel. to Foreign Office No. 122 (21 Dec. 1958). Bank of England OV 44/23.
[43] US del. tels. to Washington. POLTO 1749 (18 Dec. 1958) and POLTO 1769 (19 Dec. 1958). Also Washington tel. to US del. TOPOL 2074 (18 Dec. 1958).

reception in Brussels and the Hague. Ansiaux told him that the French had arranged for about $240 million in short term credit from the Belgian, Netherlands, and German central banks and the BIS.[44]

A similar visitor to Stockholm was received no less amicably, but Oslo was a different story. Erik Brofoss (Governor of the Norwegian central bank) was critical, and Arne Skaug (Minister of Commerce) was incensed. Given his own stalwart support of the British Free Trade Area proposal, the Minister regarded the lack of prior consultation as a personal betrayal. The elimination of Norway's EPU credit and the need to repay its EPU debt (largely to Germany under the Posthuma formula) would hurt Norway's economic programme.[45]

A Swiss central bank delegation was invited to come to London. Although it exhibited less anger, it was hardly enthralled by the prospective move. The Swiss thought it was premature; the British economy was not yet strong enough to support a convertible pound sterling. They would not want their quota counted among those who would notify the Secretary General of a desire to terminate the EPU. Accepting the inevitable, they returned home to make the necessary technical adjustments in their regulations and operations.[46]

Terminal Meeting of the Managing Board

On 23 December, the British government formally notified the German government that the 'formula' had been agreed. Von Mangoldt immediately called a special meeting of the Managing Board for 29 December. Everyone understood that its business was the termination of the EPU and transition to the EMA. On 27 December, all the Common Market countries and the United Kingdom notified the Secretary General of the OEEC that they wished to invoke the termination clause of the Agreement. Together, they represented 72.1 per cent of EPU quotas. The Scandinavian countries and Portugal submitted their notifications immediately afterwards, and Switzerland followed. Austria, Iceland, Greece, and Turkey abstained.

A day before, the US had sent a letter to the OEEC Secretary General reaffirming its 1955 agreement to the establishment of the European Fund and the transfer of the residual assets of the EPU to that Fund, in accordance with the 1955 provisions.[47] The letter went on to record US

[44] Leslie Crick, 'Visit to Belgium and Holland' (23–4 Dec. 1958). Unicorn memo (29 Dec. 1958). Bank of England OV 44/23.

[45] R. C. R. (Rupert Raw), 'Visit to Oslo and Stockholm', Unicorn memo (29 Dec. 1958). Bank of England OV 44/23.

[46] Schwegler, 'Problems Raised and Measures Taken following the Replacement of the EPU by the EMA'. Statement to Board of Swiss National Bank (13 Feb. 1959). Minutes of the Board 701, Annex 26.

[47] Burgess letter to Sergent (OEEC Sec. General) (26 Dec. 1958). Enclosure to OEEC C(58)280.

understanding that the transition was associated with a 'desirable move toward full convertibility' and that OEEC member countries 'intend to make all feasible further progress toward the elimination of discriminatory restrictions on trade and other current transactions with non-Member countries'. A request for confirmation of that 'understanding' produced some turmoil and distress on the part of both the British and the French, as well as the Danes. Nevertheless, the OEEC Council authorized the Secretary General to satisfy the US.

The provision in the 'formula' for suspending European contributions to the European Fund was thus in limbo. The US Representative to the Managing Board had neither been informed of the formula's existence nor asked to concur. Von Mangoldt developed an answer to this problem, as he had done with so many problems during the life of the Union. Realizing that re-negotiation of the European Fund would involve pressure for a larger German contribution, he had earlier persuaded Emminger to register second-thought reservations with his Bank of England colleague. Prior to the Board meeting, von Mangoldt repeated these reservations to Pitblado, noting that Turkey would lodge an immediate claim on the Fund that would have to be honoured. He suggested replacing the 1955 agreement to defer calling up the Italian and Austrian contributions with a similar deferment for France. While at first that appeared to satisfy Calvet, he soon decided against requesting a deferment. The French contribution toward the first $100 million of European Fund loan disbursements would be small.[48] As a result, the European Fund was activated promptly upon the termination of the EPU.

At the meeting, Getz Wold initiated a discussion that permitted the smaller countries to vent their dissatisfaction with the absence of serious prior consultation.[49] In private, he had made no secret of his pessimism concerning the economic soundness of the move. However, he moderated his statement to the Board, emphasizing his hopes as well as his fears. Hay was at least as pessimistic about Britain's ability to sustain meaningful convertibility. He feared the reintroduction of quantitative restrictions in the event of a set-back and doubted whether the UK had adequate foreign exchange reserves. Switzerland also worried that the UK henceforth would be less interested in pursuing the Free Trade negotiations. Calvet and Pitblado calmed the atmosphere a little by explaining that the need for secrecy had made prior consultations impracticable. They expressed their faith that governments would adopt proper economic policies to make a worldwide payments system work, a statement that de Strycker supported as well.

[48] US del. tel. to Washington. POLTO 1841 (31 Dec. 1958).
Also Pitblado, 'The European Fund'. Letter to Rickett (30 Dec. 1958). Bank of England OV 46/24.
[49] US del. airgram to Washington. POLTO A-443 (9 Jan. 1959).

Liquidation of the EPU

After this discussion, the Board took the series of technical decisions needed to liquidate the EPU and transfer its assets to the EMA.[50] It set the date for the final operations on 15 January 1959 and charged the Agent, as usual, with carrying them out. It authorized the Alternates to take any decisions on technical and administrative matters that might be required. Board members could be contacted if any important questions of substance arose, though most of them scattered for an abbreviated Christmas holiday. As far back as 1956, the Agent had completed careful preparation for the liquidation whenever it should arise. It had drafted telegrams of instruction to each central bank in the EPU system; only dates and amounts had to be inserted. The final operations were thus executed on time without a hitch.

The major problem of the liquidation was settling outstanding credits and debts on the books of the Union, totalling $1,571,757,000. To distribute the risk of default as broadly as possible, these were allocated among all the members of the Union, under the Posthuma formula. Every country except Germany had to pay some of the Union's debts and every country except France received some payment on account of the credits.[51] Some 105 payments arrangements were to be negotiated bilaterally under the supervision of the Board. Agreements were soon completed that provided for full repayment within a maximum of seven years.

At the same meeting, the Managing Board was reconstituted, with identical membership, as the Board of Management of the European Monetary Agreement. It continued to meet under both hats until the business of the EPU was concluded. All that remained was arranging for the final accounts and audit and preparing a final report and press release on the liquidation of the Union. In September 1959, the EPU Managing Board approved the auditor's report and thus completed its work.[52]

MIXED EMOTIONS AND EXPECTATIONS

The termination of the European Payments Union at the end of 1958 marked the final triumph of the system negotiated and inaugurated in 1950. A prominent purpose was to facilitate European progress from a stultifying system of bilateralism to a freer system of trade and payments based on convertible currencies. At its termination, all but a handful of members made their currencies convertible on a global basis, although

---

[50] EPU Board Minutes, 104th Session (29-30 Dec. 1958). OEEC MBC/M(58)13.
[51] EPU Board, *Final Report* (1959).
[52] EPU Board, 'Action Memo', 110th Session (9 Sept. 1959). OEEC MBC(59)11.

only for current account transactions by non-residents. Though trade discrimination against the dollar area continued, everyone realized that that could not last long. Many said, 'Mission accomplished.'

The occasion, nevertheless, was marked by mixed emotions and expectations. Terminating the EPU denoted the end of one era and the simultaneous launching of a new one. Europe was losing a system that had worked. An institution that had raised European co-operation on economic and financial issues to a level of unprecedented intensity was being dissolved. The EMA had not been designed as a successor system, but only to offer safety nets in case of need.

The Bank of England and the City of London were jubilant about the unification of rates for dollar and transferable sterling. They were joined by most other European central bankers in greeting enthusiastically the decision to let markets clear and settle most payments affecting their currencies. The Bundesbank celebrated the move 'as a milestone in post-war monetary history', qualifying its pleasure only by regret that it did not go further.[53] As of 1 May 1959, Germany removed 'all such remnants as still existed of restrictions, for residents and for non-residents, on payments in connection with goods, services and capital . . .'.[54] Erhard was not alone in thinking that with the achievement of convertibility, most problems of international finance had been solved.

Yet some of those who had long yearned for European convertibility muted their expressions of satisfaction. The British Treasury's press announcement on 'C-Day' was flat and technical: '. . . the Government has decided that the time has come to merge transferable and official sterling.'[55] Opposition in Britain to convertibility, and especially to non-discrimination, was still strong. Sir Denis Rickett (the government spokesman at the press conference) took pains to emphasize that the move was not much of a change from the previous 1 per cent difference between the rates for the two types of sterling.

When the European executive directors of the IMF notified their Board officially of the move to non-resident convertibility and the EMA, Southard 'welcomed this important step towards full convertibility'. He was joined by his Canadian colleague in hoping that EMA members 'would be prepared to reaffirm their intention to move towards the elimination of all discriminatory restrictions as soon as possible'.[56] Some two years later, in February 1961, nine former EPU members notified the IMF that they would henceforth accept the obligations of Article VIII.

[53] Deutsche Bundesbank Report for 1958 (Frankfurt, 1959), 43.

[54] Deutsche Bundesbank Report for 1958 (Frankfurt, 1959), 44-5.

[55] HM Treasury Press Office, 'Press Announcement' (27 Dec. 1958). Bank of England OV 44/23.

[56] UK Embassy in Washington to Foreign Office, Inward Saving tel. 249 (28 Dec. 1958). Bank of England OV 44/23.

Most members of the Managing Board were optimistic at the moment the EPU was terminated, although some had grave doubts about the wisdom of the timing. Both Hay and Getz Wold felt that the British economic situation had not yet improved enough to sustain a convertible pound sterling. They also feared that a divided Europe would follow termination of the EPU so soon after the breakdown of the Free Trade Area negotiations. Calvet worried about substantial tension in European economic relations with the US and Canada, since trade discrimination was being continued.[57] Others joined these Board members in regretting that the EPU was not being continued for a while on a 100 per cent gold settlements basis. That would permit a considered review of the 1955 EMA arrangements; perhaps they could be revised to suit better the conditions of 1959.

Whether the history of the subsequent decade would have been much different had the EPU been modified and maintained or the EMA reviewed and transformed remains an open question. Answers would involve both hindsight and probing into the history of the 1960s and later, an endeavour beyond the scope of this book. A number of participants in and observers of international financial diplomacy during that period have recorded their experiences and views about what happened.[58] Their accounts offer different perspectives; readers must render their own judgements.

---

[57] US del. tel. to Washington. POLTO 1769 (19 Dec. 1958). Summarizes passages from Calvet memo to his government written two weeks previously.

[58] Roosa (1967), Coombs (1967), Guindey (1973), Southard (1979), Gilbert (1980), Solomon (1982), Emminger (1986), de Vries (1987).

Part Five

A System that Worked

18 Managing the System

The EPU acquired all the ingredients of an international monetary system—a 'complex amalgam of arrangements involving institutions, policies, procedures and practices', to borrow the definition offered by the current Managing Director of the IMF.[1] The EPU system began with a binding inter-governmental Agreement that established basic rules, policy constraints, and procedures; an Agent to operate the automatic mechanism; and a formal institutional structure for managing the system.

The operating rules of the clearing and settlements mechanism were laid out from the beginning in the EPU Agreement and Directives.[2] The initial rules provided only one major constraint: the system compelled both member governments and its managers to focus on policy adjustments needed to control extreme imbalances. Other policies, procedures, and practices evolved as the system matured, as did the locus of managerial authority.

The OEEC created the EPU and provided it with a full organizational framework. The Council was the forum for final decision-making by member governments. The Steering Board and Invisibles Committee were responsible for liberalization measures, and the Secretariat provided supporting services. The OEEC retained the BIS to carry out the operations of the automatic mechanism. And it established the Managing Board, which became the keystone of the EPU's institutional structure.

EPU MANAGING BOARD

The EPU Managing Board was an unusual organism, composed of nominally independent financial experts. It was neither the executive arm of an international organization nor a body with independent juridical status. It was only empowered to make rather routine decisions, and even they could be reviewed and reversed by the OEEC Council. A component of the OEEC, the Board also acquired a life of its own in the public eye. Though its meetings were tightly closed, coverage of the EPU in the press at times seemed to eclipse its parent.[3]

---

[1] Camdessus (1988).

[2] OEEC (1950*b* and *c*).

[3] The OEEC published a 77-page bibliography of books and articles about the EPU and convertibility of European currencies. Economic and financial periodicals of every member country are cited. OEEC (1955*b*).

Designed as another committee within the OEEC structure, the Board became much more than that. It turned into a focal point around which European co-operation and major activities of the OEEC revolved. Perforce and without premeditation, it soon evolved into the main multilateral forum in Europe for diplomacy about financial and economic policies, as well as multilateral payments arrangements.

What accounted for the Board's early prominence and accomplishments? One explanation is that its responsibilities corresponded to the urgent necessities and aspirations of its time. But more than that was required. From the beginning, the Board had to deal with an unremitting stream of difficult problems; it could have been overwhelmed had it not faced and resolved them. Moreover, it encountered stern and powerful opposition.

Through its success in solving serious problems, the Board was transformed *de facto* into a powerful body and thus was able to produce results. The ingredients that made its achievements possible defined it as an authentic institution, though it neither received nor sought legal status as such.

Its Authority and Mandate

A brief clause in the EPU Agreement assigned the Managing Board responsibility for supervising what many hoped would be a largely automatic mechanism. That mechanism became the key to the Board's authority, and the key to the system's success proved to be the authority of the Board.

When extreme imbalances threatened the existence of the mechanism, its managers reacted promptly with funds and advice, and member governments responded. In country after country, an adjustment process was set in motion. Success fed on itself, enhancing the Board's prestige and influence and broadening the scope of responsibilities that governments conferred on it.

Before the system had adjusted to the aftermath of the war in Korea, the mechanism was again threatened. The member with much the largest quota proposed a dash to convertibility that the others considered premature. They rallied to support the Managing Board's blueprint for a more deliberate institutional approach. By the time the European Monetary Agreement was signed in 1955, the Board's authority had been firmly established on the foundation of member government support.

The US had at first proposed an independent board with supra-national authority to require member governments to adjust their economic policies, if necessary. That concept was endorsed by Ansiaux's Experts Committee and embodied in the OEEC's *Second Report*. According to the report,

'Whenever the position of a Member, whether a net creditor or a net debtor, was, in the opinion of the Management, the consequence of an undesirable monetary, financial, or general economic policy being followed by him, it would be their duty to place conditions on access to the facilities of the EPU.'[4]

Although British authorities approved publication of that report, they recorded reservations about any such mandate, and they soon found widespread support. Governments were reluctant to cede such power over their sensitive affairs. The IMF expressed its fears that such a body would diminish the Fund's authority over stabilization and liberalization policies. The European central bank governors added their own reservations about another powerful international financial institution.

Yet even these opponents of a strong managing board recognized that the proposed system could founder unless imbalances were corrected and that, therefore, it could not leave members to their own devices. To forestall unwelcome recommendations, governments kept final authority to issue them in the OEEC Council, whose decisions had to be unanimous. The *Directives for the Application of the Agreement* also tried to wall off the Council from the Board with an elaborate cobweb of committees. They assigned to the OEEC Economic Committee primary responsibility for reviewing the economic and financial situation of member countries and submitting proposals to the Council. Various other committees could submit comments, as could the Managing Board.

The initial 'Mandate of the Managing Board' did not explicitly mention authority to initiate proposals about economic and financial policies.[5] It only directed the Board to submit 'appropriate proposals' and limited them to proposals about creditors that had exhausted three-quarters of their EPU quotas or others that might be unable to fulfil their obligations under the OEEC trade rules. The Board was given no explicit instruction to initiate proposals about countries that incurred extreme EPU deficits. It could take decisions by majority vote, but its recommendations would go to the Council, via the Joint Trade and Payments Committee and the OEEC Executive Committee.

This elaborate machinery was bound to break down when most needed, and it was short-circuited repeatedly from the very beginning. Fortunately, the OEEC lived more by realities than by its forms and prescribed procedures. When its Legal Counsel was asked to interpret the Board's mandate, he pointed to its ambiguity. It seemed to authorize examining and making appropriate proposals to the Council about any matter involving the Board's responsibility to supervise the execution of the

---

[4] OEEC, *European Recovery Program: Second Report* (1950), 234.

[5] OEEC Council, 'Resolution Concerning the Mandate of the Managing Board of the European Payments Union'. Adopted on 18 Aug. 1950. OEEC C(50)255.

Agreement.[6] At each critical moment, the Board used this ambiguous mandate as a basis for acting. It formulated recommendations that were expedited through the OEEC committees and received timely Council approval.

Early in 1952, the Joint Trade and Payments Committee recommended that the requirement for Board recommendations be extended to situations where debtors, as well as creditors, had exhausted only 50 per cent of their quotas. The Board resisted, firmly and successfully. Too many recommendations might diminish their force when a truly threatening situation arose. Sensitive to government resistance to outside interference in internal policy-making, the Board preferred to confine itself to major problems. It did not want to become an indiscriminate and tiresome preacher. The matter was resolved by modifying the Board's mandate to permit it to report on the position of a country when, in its opinion, 'a critical situation may develop'.[7] The Board used this authority with restraint, challenging the authority of member governments only when mismanagement threatened the system.

Composition of the Board

The controversies that erupted in arriving at an EPU Agreement eliminated any of the negotiators from consideration as the first Chairman of the Managing Board. The disagreements had been too intense for the key protagonist countries to offer an acceptable candidate. Both Britain and France sought the controlling position on the Board, to no avail. A consensus formed around a nominee proposed by Italy, a country with a relatively small quota and a low profile in the preceding negotiations. Guido Carli was, at the time, senior adviser of the Ufficio Italiano dei Cambi and Italy's first Executive Director of the International Monetary Fund. His appointment was joined to an agreement that Great Britain and France, which together held over two-fifths of all EPU quotas, would each nominate a Vice-Chairman.

Including the Chairman of the OEEC Payments Committee as a non-voting observer, eight seats were available on the Board to represent the fifteen currencies in the Union. In addition to the officers, seats were allocated to countries with relatively large quotas. The initial Board included nominees representing 82 per cent of the quotas. Members were elected by the OEEC Council for a single financial year, but they could be reappointed.

[6] Pierre Huet, OEEC Legal Counsel, letter to Figgures (24 Jan. 1951). OECD EPU Archive Box 68, SJ 1719.

[7] OEEC Council, 'Resolution Amending the Resolution of 18 August 1950 on the Mandate of the Managing Board'. Adopted on 9 May 1952. OEEC C(52)121.

After two years, Carli asked to be relieved of the responsibilities of Chairman. The obvious and uncontested choice to succeed him was Hans Karl von Mangoldt, who chaired the Board for the rest of the EPU's life. A private banker in Berlin when Hitler took power, he had thereupon retreated to a Bavarian farm until Adenauer called him to head Germany's first postwar delegation—to the OEEC. Upon appointment to the Board, von Mangoldt had resigned as head of his country's delegation, and thus held no official government position, unlike the other members of the Board.

During the early German deficit crisis, he gained the deep respect of his colleagues through his concern for the integrity of the EPU system and all its members, as well as for his own country. His election as Chairman of the Board came less than seven years after the end of the war, while the German government was still subject to the authority of the Allied High Commission. He was the first German selected to head an international body during the years when his country was striving to re-establish its acceptability in the international community.

The Board was intended to be a body of financial experts of high standing. Among the first members, three were central bank directors (Ansiaux, Hartogsohn, and Rossy), while two were senior finance ministry officials (Ellis-Rees and Keesing). Like Carli, Calvet was an exchange control official, Director of the French Office des changes. Four members were among the Financial Experts who had negotiated the EPU Agreement—Ansiaux (Belgium), Ellis-Rees (UK), Hartogsohn (Denmark), and Keesing (Netherlands).

Membership of the Board was extraordinarily stable over its eight and a half years of existence. Von Mangoldt and Calvet served throughout, while Carli stepped down for only one year. Ansiaux and Rossy served for the first five years, after which de Strycker and Hay succeeded to the Belgian and Swiss seats. After Keesing's initial year, the Netherlands nationals on the Board were Posthuma and Liefrinck in succession. Getz Wold was the Scandinavian nominee for five and a half years, with Hartogsohn serving for two. The US government was represented by Havlik for the first four years and thereafter by Kaplan. Great Britain changed its nominee more frequently, designating five different Treasury officials. Owen served the longest, for three and a half years.

Members from central banks usually designated a finance ministry official as their Alternate, and vice versa, so that each government had representatives of both agencies at Board meetings. Most Alternates were rotated every year or two, though Mario Cardinali was the Alternate to the Italian member throughout. Schleiminger (Germany) served from mid-1954 to the end and also chaired the meetings of the Alternates. Hay and Liefrinck were Alternates for four years, and Baron Mackay (Netherlands) for three and a half.

The subsequent careers of the Board members and Alternates attest further to the credentials of participants in the work of the EPU. Ansiaux, Hartogsohn, Posthuma, and Rossy were members of central bank boards at the time of their appointment. Ansiaux, Calvet, Getz Wold, and Rossy were appointed to be central bank vice-governors while serving on the Managing Board, and Hay became one shortly afterwards. Ansiaux, Carli, de Strycker, and Getz Wold subsequently served as central bank governors. Ellis-Rees resigned from the Board to head the UK delegation to the OEEC and to chair the OEEC Council of permanent delegates. Geoffrey Wilson was later a Vice-President of the World Bank, and another British member, David Pitblado, was subsequently the UK Economic Minister in Washington and Executive Director of both the IMF and the World Bank. After his career at the Swiss National Bank, Hay became president of the International Committee of the Red Cross.

Among the Alternates, Getz Wold, Hay, and Liefrinck became full members of the Board. Renaud de la Genière was later appointed Governor of the Bank of France; another French Alternate, Michel Poniatowski, served as Minister of the Interior. Richard Mikkelsen became a member of the Board of Governors of the National Bank of Denmark, and Jean-Maxime Lévèque headed Credit Commercial and Credit Lyonnais, two of France's largest commercial banks. Gabriel Ferras (France) and Schleiminger (Germany) were, at different times, General Manager of the Bank for International Settlements. Roy Bridge (UK) was Deputy Chief Cashier and Assistant to the Governor of the Bank of England. Three Alternates—Hans Lundström (Sweden), Otto Pfleiderer (Germany), and Schleiminger—served on the IMF Executive Board after their terms at the EPU.

Methods of Work

The Managing Board went to work with little clear authority and not much precedent for dealing with member countries whose extreme deficits or surpluses endangered the system. The urgency of the problems and the crowded agenda required methods of work that would produce practical decisions with minimum delay. The Board had to blaze its own trail. Many of the procedures and practices it employed were later adopted by one international body or another in addressing the payments imbalances of participants.

To establish both its independence and its authority, the Board held very formal sessions. Attendance was limited to those whose presence was absolutely essential, a practice that facilitated decisive action. Meetings were normally held in a small room in the Château de la Muette, next door to the OEEC Council chamber. Members, observers, the Agent, and a designated representative of the OEEC Secretary General sat behind long tables, covered in the traditional green baize and arranged so that everyone faced each other. Alternates and supporting members of the Secretariat sat behind their principals, in chairs lining the walls. When guests were invited, they were excused after the purpose of their visit had been fulfilled. Otherwise, the meetings were strictly closed.

The Secretariat fixed the Board's agenda, after consulting the Chairman. Minutes were circulated to all OEEC delegations. As independent experts, members seldom felt it necessary to establish a record of official government positions before tackling the issues. Thus the minutes were usually confined to the Board's conclusions and decisions, though presentations about difficult country situations and discussion of general topics, such as convertibility, were reported at some length. At times, the Secretariat circulated—but only to Board members—a full account of a complicated discussion of a particularly controversial matter.

When the Board forwarded its disagreements to the Council, differing views were presented as those of one member, several members, or a majority—without identifying individuals or their nationality. Of course, members usually identified the proponents of particular views in reports to their own governments. Board members tried to avoid press probings about these disagreements, but inevitably the stories leaked.

Given a full agenda, members quickly learned to minimize debate at the formal meetings. They could work out solutions more efficiently in small groups, meeting informally to seek accord or reduce the areas of disagreement. After being briefed before each meeting by the Secretariat and the Chairman of the Alternates, von Mangoldt tried to explore difficult issues with the most concerned members before or between sessions. Presiding patiently and attentively during the discussion, he would usually identify the emerging consensus or the manner in which a disagreement might be treated to the satisfaction of the contending members. More often than not, compromises were arranged in private meetings, in the corridors or at lunch or dinner. The Board seldom took a formal vote before unanimity had been achieved.

Continuity of membership produced a strong sense of collegiality among the Board members, reinforced by the Board's early achievements and public recognition of its authority. Continually involved in negotiating with each other and committed to co-operation, they did not lose sight of their purpose—constructive action to solve problems. Members developed confidence in each other's judgement and ability to persuade their governments to co-operate. Disagreements were inevitable, but mutual respect never abated, and personal acrimony was notably absent, despite serious and prolonged conflicts. Trust proved to be the essence of fruitful co-operation, as the Board became an institution for helping, rather than preaching and standing aside.

A constant procession of issues and negotiations made the workload of the Board very demanding. Extreme imbalances, special credits, convertibility, debt repayment, hardening settlement terms, and renewing the Union were issues that appeared and reappeared on the agenda.

The negotiators of the EPU Agreement thought that the Managing Board might meet about once a month, for several days at a time. Between March 1951 and June 1952, as extreme imbalances plagued the Union, the Board met for 156 days. Several sessions continued for two to three weeks at a time; night sessions were common. Ansiaux insisted that meetings be scheduled over weekends, so that he could have some time for his work in Brussels.

For the next three years, convertibility and the future of the Union became the dominant topics before the Board. The new agenda was more intellectually demanding, but less time-consuming. The number of days the Board was in session per year fell into the sixties.

Although the agenda continued to be full after this, the problems were less novel and less contentious. The Board had acquired a body of experience and precedents that permitted further problems to be handled more expeditiously. After mid-1955, it continued to meet monthly, but three to four days at a time usually sufficed. During financial year 1957/8, it was able to cope with both the French and Turkish crises, among other issues, though it met for only 44 days.

Inviting National Delegations

In dealing with its first crisis (described in Chapter 6), the Board discovered the usefulness of inviting senior government officials to come to Paris to explain their situation and their plans for dealing with it. As extreme imbalances spread from country to country in the wake of the Korean War, the Board found it advisable to continue that procedure. At first only officials from countries not represented on the Board were invited. During the first half of 1951, delegations came from Greece, Austria, Portugal, Norway, and Turkey. The Board sought to ascertain from its visitors not only facts but policy options that might be practicable and acceptable to their cabinets.

By the beginning of its second year, the Board realized that visits by officials of countries represented on the Board would also be fruitful. They might enhance the Board members' effectiveness in persuading their own governments to follow the Board's recommendations. Accordingly, delegations were received from Belgium, the United Kingdom, Italy,

Sweden, France, and Switzerland. Visiting delegations varied in their composition, but they usually included central bank presidents or directors, sub-cabinet officials, and heads of relevant government departments. The Board questioned its visitors diplomatically and professionally, and the delegations responded with a wealth of insights, as well as data.

By the end of its first two years, the Board had acquired a unique and profound understanding of the economic situation and the policy options of most of its member countries. Both the volume of factual information and the frankness of the policy discussions were without precedent at the time. The acceptability and successful implementation of the recommendations owed much to these procedures and to the forthright explanations provided by visiting delegations. That helped create a precedent not only for the Managing Board, but also for other OEEC bodies and for other international organizations.

More secure in its understanding of the policies and problems of member countries, the Board invited delegations from capitals only in special cases in succeeding years. Usually, it limited its quarterly country reviews to presentations by OEEC Secretariat experts and by the Board member from the country under discussion.

The Group of Alternates

Each member designated an Alternate, subject to the approval of the OEEC Council. As originally conceived, the Alternates were to participate in Board meetings, replacing regular members when they were unable to attend. However, the members were rarely absent.

As the tempo of the Board's work accelerated, the Secretariat suggested that the Alternates hold separate formal meetings to prepare the way for the regular Board sessions.[8] As this practice developed, the Group of Alternates was able to settle many agenda items, subject to a quick approval by the Board at its next meeting. In the minutes of its November 1952 meeting, the Board noted that it 'was referring an increasing number of questions as well as the preparation of many Reports to the Group of Alternates'.[9]

A major responsibility of the Alternates was to review and reformulate reports before their submission to the OEEC Council. Many disagreements were thus resolved and the remaining ones clarified. Before Board meetings, each Alternate briefed his principal on contentious issues and the views individual colleagues would probably express. In addition, each

---

[8] Cahan letter to Chairman Carli (8 Oct. 1951). OEEC TFD-325.
  Also Secretariat note, 'Methods of Work of the Managing Board' (26 May 1952). OEEC MBC(52)34.
[9] EPU Board Minutes, 30th Session (17-22 Nov. 1952). OEEC MBC/M(52)12.

Alternate bore the major responsibility for drafting private reports for circulation within his government.

The published annual reports of the Managing Board were largely prepared on the responsibility of the Alternates. The Board itself seldom offered more than minor comments or amendments before forwarding them to the Council, which then approved their publication.

OEEC FRAMEWORK

The Council

The Board offered recommendations, but decisions about important matters were reserved for the OEEC Council, where all member governments were formally represented. It met at least once a week at the level of permanent delegates and several times a year, as necessary, at ministerial level.

The requirement for Council approval of all Board recommendations proved to be a help, not a hindrance. The Council was an effective forum for organizing the co-operation of member governments. Its rule of unanimity was, at that time, a constructive force for inter-governmental agreement. Governments were reluctant to veto advice from a body whose recommendations were effective and whose help was beneficial.

The need for unanimous approval at the Council also exerted an important disciplinary effect on Board members. They had to strive for agreements that would not be overruled. Governments, on the other hand, were reluctant to exercise their veto power in the Council, given the climate of co-operation that existed at the time and the widespread attachment to the integrity of the EPU system. The Board never was overruled. When members reached full agreement, it was generally ratified by the permanent delegates. Ratification transformed the Board's recommendations into formal agreements between all member governments.

Experts and Cabinet Ministers

The most contentious issues required the attention of cabinet officers, meeting in the OEEC Council at ministerial level. Cabinet ministers also cleared most of the decisions about major matters that were taken by the permanent OEEC Council. Their consent was thus needed for Managing Board recommendations to become binding.

For that purpose, the constitution of the Board as a body of independent experts proved to be a very useful myth. Appointed to serve in that capacity, most members were high-level permanent officials in their countries as well. Their home duties were closely related to the work of the Board. In almost every case, they were advisers to cabinet officers and had direct access to ministers, including those who represented their governments at OEEC ministerial meetings. They could thus negotiate authoritatively on behalf of their governments within the Board. Yet their collective decisions and recommendations had the status of emanating from an expert body. The acceptability of the Board's many proposals owed much to the dual capacities in which most members served.

The Board gained recognition for views that reflected the interests of the EPU system and the OEEC community, rather than the parochial concerns of individual governments. That increased both the force of its proposals to the OEEC Council and the ability of individual members to persuade colleagues and ministers within their own governments. In a public presentation concerning the EPU after its first year, Calvet observed that 'the dominant characteristic is that each of the members of the Board continues to exercise, in his own country, active functions that keep him in constant contact with the realities, give him precious experience for the deliberations of the Board, and permit him at the same time to oversee the application of its recommendations.'[10]

As a body of experts, the Board drafted its reports and justified its recommendations in technical economic language. But as senior policy advisers to their governments, the members were well aware that political considerations underlay virtually all the major issues they encountered. The Board was unabashedly political when appropriate and necessary, despite its technical mandate and the preference of its members for sound economic policies. The Board's determinations had to be politically sensitive, as well as economically viable, if ministers were to ratify them.

When members expressed personal views, at Board meetings or in private, their suggestions were apt to be acceptable to their governments, if the Board as a whole would agree. If not, they could advise their own ministers about what was unlikely to be acceptable and about how to address such matters in the least objectionable way. Rarely, if ever, did a member voice views that were superseded by a contrary position taken later by his minister at an OEEC Council meeting. Dual responsibility thus helped to minimize misunderstanding and controversy at ministerial meetings. Seldom were there surprises when disputes broke out among cabinet-level representatives.

On the relatively few occasions when all its members could not agree, the Board's reports carefully narrowed the scope of the disagreements. Ministers were asked to resolve only a limited number of politically charged issues. Usually, von Mangoldt and his colleagues were able to develop the lines of a possible compromise and reconciliation before the

---

[10] Calvet (1951).

ministers actually met. The issues were invariably connected to the periodic renewal of the Union, and the Board was fully aware that no minister was willing to veto a renewal. Yet it also had to keep in mind that no minister wanted to be faced with a decision he could not accept. The ministers usually adopted the proposed compromise and referred the matter back to the Board to work out the details and formulate an agreement that could be translated into legal language.

The ministers were thus able to exercise their responsibility for final decisions on issues that were most important to them. They were exposed at first hand to the views of their colleagues from other countries, though they came to the meetings well briefed by their own members on the Board. They were able personally to make important political concessions in the interest of the OEEC community and thereby enhance their own status at home. In the political environment of the 1950s, the premium placed on co-operative behaviour made this arrangement remarkably fruitful.

OEEC Support

The OEEC Secretariat and other constituent organs of the OEEC provided further indispensable support. Within the Secretariat, the Trade and Payments Directorate had been responsible for stimulating and servicing the negotiations of the EPU Agreement. It continued to perform such functions for the Managing Board. Frank Figgures had led the early work, but he returned to Great Britain after the EPU's first financial year. Thereafter, J. Flint Cahan continued to provide creative and indefatigable leadership for the work of the Secretariat. Recruited by Marjolin from the British Board of Trade, Cahan continued the tradition of impartial international service set by Figgures.

Under their supervision, members of the OEEC Secretariat drafted agendas, minutes, and reports for Board consideration. They also kept the Board informed about relevant activities in other parts of the OEEC. The Secretariat often initiated recommendations and suggestions about how problems might be resolved. Though the Board did not accept all their proposals, it considered them carefully as the products of competent and responsible officials whose first loyalty was to the OEEC community as a whole. Usually, the Secretariat was asked to amend its drafts in accordance with the formal discussions. The staff often did so between the Board's adjournment in the early evening and its reassembly the next morning. The OEEC legal advisers later converted the Board's various decisions and recommendations into legal documents that bound all member governments.

Reports and recommendations about individual member countries drew heavily on the Secretariat's country experts and on the work of the OEEC Economic Committee. In the early years, that Committee (at first called the Programme Committee) reviewed member country recovery programmes and requests for Marshall Plan aid, and it continued to be responsible for the annual reports of the OEEC. Composed of resident members of national delegations, it reported annually on each member country's economic situation and its prospects. Its documents were based on materials submitted by governments, but the Economic Committee also heard presentations by delegations of senior officials from capitals and critically questioned the visitors. The quarterly presentations to the Managing Board by Secretariat country experts derived largely from that work.

The Steering Board for Trade reviewed country trade restrictions and recommended further liberalization, subject to the Managing Board's opinion on whether the balance of payments justified continuing restrictions. The Invisibles Committee assumed comparable responsibility for restrictions on payments for services, and it took over from the Managing Board responsibility for liberalization of capital transactions.

THE AGENT: THE BIS

Very early in the negotiations, the OEEC Financial Experts recognized that a financial agent would be needed to carry out 'the operations of the EPU under the direction of their managers'.[11] The Bank for International Settlements was an easy choice for this role, and its Board of Directors quickly agreed to serve an EPU, well before its precise character had been defined.

Rarely have partnerships between international organizations been as advantageous to both sides as the one between the OEEC/EPU and the Basle-based BIS. The BIS worked with the OEEC at a critical moment, when the Bank was struggling to re-establish its role in the postwar financial world. It had been established in 1930 to promote central bank co-operation and to provide facilities for international financial operations.[12] After a promising start, its activities were reduced to a minimum during World War II.

When the first Intra-European Payments Scheme was arranged in 1947, the BIS became its agent. The Bank continued in that capacity for the next two IEPS agreements, thus demonstrating its usefulness as a European operating institution.

[11] OEEC, *European Recovery Program: Second Report* (1950), 236.
[12] BIS (1930).

The OEEC benefited from the services of a skilled institution with a highly qualified staff and experience in working directly with European central banks. The OEEC could delegate to the BIS all the operational duties for its payments agreements, while retaining full policy control. Switzerland was a founding member of the OEEC, and Basle was only a few hours away from Paris by train. Lines of communication between the BIS and the central banks were well established.

The choice of the BIS as financial agent for the EPU was obvious and straightforward. It had performed its functions under the IEPS efficiently and well. Under its guidance, central banks in each OEEC member country had reported their payments balances with each other for more than two years. Thus when the Financial Experts developed their proposal for a fully transferable clearing union, one of their first decisions was to invite the BIS to serve as agent. At the time, both the top management of the BIS and the central bank governors on its Board had reservations about the concepts formulated by Bissell and the Financial Experts.[13] However, they wanted the BIS to continue as the agent for whatever new system might eventually be concocted. They immediately accepted the invitation, which was formally extended by the OEEC Council at the recommendation of the Experts.

The EPU Agreement itself specifically designated the BIS as the Agent for EPU operations. In accordance with Article 21 of the Agreement, the BIS reported each month on 'the execution of the operations and the management of the fund' (the Union's assets). These reports were first examined and approved by the Alternates and the Managing Board, before being adopted by the OEEC Council. Data from the reports became the basis for the OEEC's widely read monthly press releases concerning the state of the Union's accounts. The Statutes of the BIS explicitly permitted it to act as 'Trustee or Agent in connection with international settlements'.[14] As Agent, the Bank 'carried out duties of a purely technical nature and without political obligations of any kind'.[15] A small staff, distinct from the Bank's departmental structure, was responsible for these activities.

The Agent was charged 'with carrying out the administrative and the banking operations of the Union'.[16] 'Administrative' referred to all operations related to the clearing and settlement of bilateral balances reported by the central banks. The OEEC *Directives for the Application of the EPU Agreement* spelled out how these operations were to be

---

[13] See Chapter 2.

[14] BIS (1930), Articles 21, 24.

[15] BIS, *Twenty-First Annual Report* (1951), 247.

[16] OEEC Council, 'A European Payments Union and the Rules of Commercial Policy to be followed by Member Countries'. Approved on 7 July 1950. OEEC C(50)190.

conducted, including the responsibilities of the central banks. In the initial stages, the Agent undertook an intensive educational effort to instruct the central banks about their bookkeeping and reporting responsibilities. It supplemented its discussions with detailed *aides-mémoire* about the EPU. Thus the BIS became the centre for technical operational instructions to the central banks and for the Union's accounting; actual transactions were decentralized and performed by the central banks themselves.

An immense number of calculations were necessary every month to establish each country's net position in the Union, the amounts of gold or dollars it would pay or receive, and the size of the automatic credit it would obtain or grant. Today an elaborate computer system would be used. In the 1950s, half a dozen BIS officers did it all within days— with the help only of the mechanical calculating machines available at the time.

The 'banking' function of the Agent consisted primarily of managing the Union's liquid assets. Deficit countries had the option of paying in gold or dollars, and surplus countries were required to accept payment in whichever the Union received. If payments to the Union were insufficient to meet obligations to surplus countries, the Agent drew the necessary additional funds from the Union's US Treasury account, through the Federal Reserve Bank of New York. If payments received exceeded the sums to be paid to creditors, the Agent invested the surplus, on instruction from the Managing Board. Liquid assets of the Union received in dollars were invested in US Treasury bonds or bills, or kept on sight account at the BIS. Gold assets were deposited in London, New York, or Paris, earmarked for the account of the EPU. After 1955, gold was also held at the BIS, on either fixed term or sight account. The BIS also offered central banks the opportunity to open gold sight accounts to smooth the payments traffic connected with EPU settlements.

Frederick Conolly represented the Agent at Board meetings throughout the EPU's existence. Willy Bruppacher served as his Alternate for the first six years, Karl Schmid for the remaining time. They were particularly helpful advisers concerning the investment of the Union's liquid assets and the technical problems implicit in the many proposals for changing the Union's operating rules. The Agent performed its functions proficiently from the earliest days of the EPU to the intricate liquidation procedures. The latter functioned like clockwork, thanks to its detailed advance preparation. Neither the OEEC nor the BIS ever had reason to regret the relationship they had formed for the operation of the EPU mechanism.

THE INTERNATIONAL MONETARY FUND

Unlike its harmonious relationship with the BIS, the EPU's initial relations with the International Monetary Fund were discordant. After a stormy beginning, marked by mutual hostility, the relationship was gradually transformed into one in which working together benefited both institutions.

Camille Gutt, the first Managing Director of the IMF, was indignant that the US should sponsor a European monetary institution without the IMF participating in its design, management, and financing.[17] His US Deputy, Andrew Overby, shared Gutt's jurisdictional concern. In addition, Overby opposed any regional arrangement, believing it would hinder convertibility, rather than advance it. Both men travelled to Europe to encourage officials who disagreed with the concepts being developed at the OEEC. In March 1950, when the IMF Executive Board recorded views about how the EPU should operate, Europeans resented its attempt to intrude gratuitously in their delicate and difficult negotiations. The substantive EPU Agreement coldly provided for the Managing Board 'to examine and report to the Council what shall be the appropriate relationship'.[18]

Despite IMF insistence and some US urging, the Managing Board refused to admit an IMF observer to its meetings until 1953. Beset by a succession of immediate practical problems, the Board paid little attention to the IMF's jurisdictional concerns. It felt that the IMF would be better advised to consider how its resources might be more readily available to European members with payments problems. At US insistence, the IMF had decided, in April 1948, that recipients of Marshall Plan aid might draw US dollars from · the IMF only in exceptional or unforeseen circumstances. The decision was unpopular with the Europeans and they tested it, to no avail. After the IMF eased its attitude toward drawings, relations did improve.

The ice began to thaw, though very slowly, after August 1951, when Ivar Rooth succeeded Gutt; Overby also left the IMF the following January. With Southard's support, Rooth persuaded the US Treasury to agree that IMF members should have the benefit of any doubt if they wished to draw the equivalent of their initial gold payments to the IMF.[19] The Fund's approval of the Belgian standby agreement in June 1952 was much appreciated by the Managing Board and acknowledged with satisfaction in the OEEC Council minutes. An October 1952 decision by the IMF Executive Board to approve the principle of standby credit arrangements, if only for six months, further improved the atmosphere.[20]

A more important turning-point in the Managing Board's attitude

---

[17] Deshormes (1986).

[18] OEEC (1950a), 14.

[19] IMF, *Annual Report* (1952), 42.

[20] 'Standby Credit Arrangements'. Memo transmitting Decision No. 155-(52/57) of IMF Exec. Board (1 Oct. 1952) to Managing Board (20 Nov. 1952). OEEC MBC(52)81.

toward the IMF was reached early in 1953. The United Kingdom had decided to bring its Collective Approach to convertibility to Washington, while the Managing Board was developing its own institutional approach. European governments soon realized that after convertibility, the IMF would become their principal source of short term credit, and the Managing Board began to seek better relations. At the beginning of 1953, Jan Mladek was appointed to head the IMF's Paris office, after devoting considerable effort over the previous year to improving his institution's ties with the EPU. His pragmatic and low-key approach was reassuring and effective, and he was invited to attend the February 1953 meeting of the Board as an observer. In April, that invitation was changed to a permanent one. Rooth himself met with the Managing Board during a special meeting held in Basle in June 1953, and he also chaired an informal meeting between the Board and the European executive directors of the IMF during its Annual Meetings in September 1953.

The completion of the EMA negotiations in 1955 added impetus to steadily improving relations. It became apparent that once the EMA was activated, the IMF Executive Board was likely to assume functions affecting its European members that had been performed previously by the Managing Board. The EMA would offer safety nets, but its board appeared unlikely to be a competitive body. After this, the IMF also became more flexible about permitting member countries to draw on its resources.

The 1958 packages of assistance for France and Turkey capped the process of building co-operation. In the French case, the Managing Board bore the brunt of the burden of arranging a stabilization programme; in the Turkish case, the IMF staff did so, building on considerable experience in working harmoniously with Turkish officials. In each case, both organizations contributed as much as their own resources would permit to a joint effort that was ultimately successful. With the liquidation of the EPU at the end of 1958, the IMF soon came into its own as the international monetary centre of a world in which all the major currencies were convertible for most practical purposes.

19 Aims and Accomplishments

The European Payments Union was a system that worked. Its contribution to unparalleled economic progress throughout western Europe in the 1950s was material and significant. Organized under the framework of the OEEC, it was the first institutionalized system for integrating the economies of western Europe. It was also an unprecedented experiment in purposeful monetary co-operation. In these two roles, it made its most enduring contribution. Member governments and central banks experienced working together on a broad range of specific policy problems, and they learned as they laboured and profited from their successes. While operating a functioning payments system, they came to understand much better the benefits and methods, as well as the difficulties, of co-operating on international financial matters. Nothing so intense and systematic had been attempted up to that time, and the effort bore fruit.

EPU CONTRIBUTIONS TO EUROPEAN PROSPERITY

Preambles to the legal instruments that establish multilateral organizations typically contain a rather ambitious statement of purposes and objectives, frequently using lofty and general language. The *Agreement for the Establishment of a European Payments Union* was no exception, although its language was somewhat restrained. Many goals were stated specifically enough to be verified. The system was to foster among its members (1) liberalization, on a non-discriminatory basis, of trade and invisible transactions; (2) independence of extraordinary outside assistance; and (3) a high and stable level of trade and employment, bearing in mind the need for their internal financial stability. The EPU itself was supposed to provide members with (4) resources to play the role of gold and foreign currency reserves, and (5) incentives to strengthen their gold and foreign currency reserves. And it was to facilitate (6) a return to full multilateral trade and to the general convertibility of currencies.

Factual records demonstrate the extraordinary extent to which each of these goals was attained by 1959, the year after the EPU was liquidated (see Table 8). Individual countries progressed unevenly, to be sure, but each contributed to the results for the OEEC area as a whole. Surely

TABLE 8.   *The Economy of Western Europe Before and After the EPU*[a]

Economic Indicator	Unit of Measurement	Before EPU	After EPU
Intra-European Trade Liberalization	per cent of private trade	56	89
Trade Liberalization with the Dollar Area	per cent of private trade	11	72
Intra-European Trade	Imports, c.i.f. monthly average in millions of dollars	845	1,943
OEEC Exports to N. America	f.o.b. monthly average in millions of dollars	144	441
OEEC Imports from N. America	c.i.f. monthly average in millions of dollars	324	508
OEEC Exports, Worldwide	volume index, 1950 = 100	100	185
OEEC Imports, Worldwide	volume index, 1950 = 100	100	175
Employment[b]	monthly average in thousands of persons employed	100,564	110,915
Gross National Product	volume index, 1950 = 100	100	148
Industrial Production	volume index, 1950 = 100	100	165
Prices	GNP price index, 1950 = 100	100	145
Gold and Foreign Exchange Reserves	billions of US dollars	9.9	20.5

[a] Most *before EPU* measures are for calendar year 1950 or end of 1950, as appropriate. Most *after EPU* measures are for calendar year 1959 or end of 1958, as appropriate. Intra-European trade liberalization *before EPU* is as of 30 June 1950. Dollar trade liberalization is measured from 1 Jan. 1953 to 1 Jan. 1959. Employment data are for mid-years 1950 and 1960.

[b] Excluding Greece, Iceland, Ireland, Portugal, and Turkey.

Sources: OEEC *Twelfth Annual Economic Report*, Statistical Annex (1961); IMF *International Financial Statistical Yearbook* (1979); Maddison (1982).

neither the OEEC nor the system can claim sole credit for the remarkable performance of western European economies during the EPU's lifetime. Government policies, US assistance, and the efforts of management and workers in each member country were essential and deserve full recognition. Yet, just as surely, the EPU served as a catalyst, a role explained throughout this book. Moreover, its catalytic role was probably indispensable, given the circumstances of the era in which the EPU functioned. Sceptics are referred to the interwar record when independent policy-making, high tariff barriers, bilateralism, quantitative restrictions, and competitive depreciation of exchange rates stifled both trade and economic growth.[1]

Liberalizing Intra-European Trade

The EPU's most immediate and direct target was the existing network of bilateral agreements and quantitative restrictions that hampered and distorted trade relations within Europe. With one stroke, the EPU created a currency area in which bilateral balances no longer mattered. At the outset, it made all European currencies interchangeable, for the first time since the outbreak of World War II. These steps were indispensable for inducing countries to give up bilateralism, quantitative restrictions, and discrimination in trade with each other. They were supplemented by enough credit to encourage and support the process of freeing trade and payments.

TABLE 9.   *Intra-European Trade Liberalization, 30 June 1950 and 31 December 1958 (in percentages of private trade)*

	30 June 1950	31 December 1958
Austria	53	90
Belgium-Luxembourg	56	96[a]
Netherlands	55	
Denmark	53	86
France	58	90
Germany	47	91
Greece	—	96
Iceland	—	29
Ireland	64	90
Italy	54	98
Norway	39	81
Portugal	53	94
Sweden	53	93
Switzerland	81	91
Turkey	42	0
United Kingdom	57	95
All OEEC countries	56	89

[a] This figure applies to Belgium-Luxembourg and the Netherlands combined.

Sources: 1950 data from OEEC *Twelfth Annual Economic Report* (1961), 201; 1958 data from OEEC *Tenth Annual Economic Report* (1959), 126.

[1] Maddison (1982) provides annual measures of economic growth, cost of living, and volume of exports, 1870 to 1979. Pre-1950 data based on his calculations.

On the whole, the inducements were effective. Trade liberalization within Europe had reached 56 per cent before the EPU was instituted, but each country's percentage was much lower for goods that competed with domestic output. Under the EPU, liberalization rose to 89 per cent on average (see Table 9).

The excluded goods were essentially those that members wished, for domestic political reasons, to protect from any foreign competition. No member country completely eliminated its quantitative restrictions in intra-European trade, though Italy came very close. France retreated twice from its liberalization commitments, and the UK and Germany once each. Turkey did not resume liberalization after suspending it in 1953. Other members progressively lowered their barriers during the life of the Union.

Once trade liberalization was well underway, restrictions on service transactions began to be lifted. By the time the EPU came to an end, all countries except Iceland, Greece, and Turkey had freed 47 categories of service transactions, excepting only tourism, transportation services, insurance, and films. Many countries had also removed restrictions on capital movements within the EPU area, and the OEEC adopted a formal Code for such liberalization within a year of the liquidation of the EPU.

The growth in intra-European commerce under the EPU was startling. Its value multiplied 2.3 times, and its volume probably doubled.[2] During the preceding interwar period, none of the larger European countries had been able to raise its export volume even to 1913 levels. Only the Netherlands and the Scandinavian countries had increased their exports by as much as 50 per cent between 1913 and 1938.[3]

Independence of Extraordinary External Assistance

The freeing of intra-European trade spurred production increases and unleashed a competitive drive for markets. European export prices rose little, if at all, once the inflation arising from the Korean War was under control.[4] With growing production, Europeans were thus able to penetrate the North American market in the later 1950s. By 1959, such exports earned three times as much as in 1950, and their volume was at least two and a half times larger.

As countries found competitive suppliers elsewhere in Europe, their need for imports from the US fell. In the later 1950s, such imports grew much less than exports to North America. Indeed, they dropped sharply in value between 1957 and 1959.

As a result, the once fearsome 'dollar gap' vanished. Though the US

[2] Estimating about a 15 per cent increase in foreign trade prices over the 1950-9 period.
[3] Maddison (1982), 250-1.
[4] IMF, *International Financial Statistics* (July 1962), 32.

continued to earn a large trade and current account surplus in worldwide exchanges, it had fallen into payments deficit with western Europe. This was largely because of the continuing cost of maintaining a substantial military establishment there and a rising flow of long term private capital. The US had terminated economic aid to Europe, except for France, Greece, Iceland, and Turkey, although it continued to provide many of its NATO allies with military equipment.

Production, Employment, and Prices

With international markets opening ever wider, European investors responded by expanding and modernizing their production facilities. The result was a rapid increase in production. In the OEEC area as a whole, gross national product grew, in real terms, by 48 per cent and industrial output by 65 per cent during the EPU period. This corresponded to annual compound rates of growth of about 5 and 7 per cent respectively. No precedent exists in the records of market economies for such intense growth in so many countries over so long a period of years. The United States did not quite reach that rate even in the years from 1940 to 1949, when it mobilized a depressed economy for war and postwar reconstruction.

The momentum thus generated throughout western Europe continued at about the same rate until 1973. Angus Maddison characterizes the 1950s and 1960s as the 'Golden Age', when 'economic growth in the advanced capitalist countries surpassed virtually all historical records'.[5] From 1913 to 1950, gross output in most western European countries had increased at rates averaging less than 1 per cent per year. Wartime destruction accounted for only a fraction of the disparity between European economic performance before and after 1950.

Of course, employment also grew, especially in Germany and Italy. The former absorbed into its labour force a large number of émigrés from eastern Germany, and the latter reduced its high unemployment rate from 16.5 per cent in 1954 to 12.2 per cent in 1959. In other countries, unemployment rates in 1959 were 3 per cent or less.

During the EPU years, inflation was a constant concern, but prices in the area as a whole were fairly stable after their surge following the outbreak of hostilities in Korea. From 1953 to 1959, wholesale prices of goods rose only 5 per cent or less in most OEEC industrialized countries. France did much less well, and the increases in Austria, Norway, and the UK reached 11 per cent. As expanding industrial production attracted workers from lower-paid service jobs, however, the price of services rose rather steeply. All told, the price index for all European goods and

[5] Maddison (1982), 126.

services increased by 24 per cent over those six years, and consumer prices in most countries rose 10 to 20 per cent (roughly 1.5 to 3 per cent per year). That degree of price stability during years of sharply increasing production and low unemployment was a significant achievement, fulfilling another explicit purpose of the EPU.

Strengthening Gold and Dollar Reserves

In 1950, the total gold and dollar reserves of all OEEC members did not quite reach $10 billion. More than a third of that sum belonged to Great Britain, which had sterling liabilities several times the size of its reserves. Belgium, Portugal, and Switzerland accounted for another 30 per cent, relatively adequate sums for their economies. All other countries had to nurse their meagre reserves with extreme care. By the end of 1958, total reserves had doubled, and most countries found themselves in a much easier situation. However, British reserves were smaller than in 1950. French reserves also were still inadequate, but they quadrupled in the following four years.

As reserves rose, so did the liberalization of imports from the dollar area. Until 1953, every European country except Switzerland and Belgium strictly controlled all imports from the dollar area. Licences were issued parsimoniously to assure that dollars were spent only on 'essentials'. By the autumn of 1954, seven countries had begun to eliminate such licensing for a range of products, primarily raw materials. By the beginning of 1959, OEEC members as a group had freed 73 per cent of their dollar imports. Only Turkey still licensed all such imports.

EFFICIENCY OF THE MECHANISM

The Preamble to the EPU Agreement referred only once to the clearing and settlements mechanism itself. It mentioned a desire to provide member countries with resources 'to play in part the role of gold and foreign currency reserves'. The automatic mechanism described in Chapter 5 bore the burden of fulfilling that purpose. How well it performed was crucial to the Union's other goals. Unless the mechanism afforded substantial economies in the use of reserves and could supplement them with credit, countries were unlikely to risk freeing their transactions with one another. Member countries wanted the advantages of lifting restrictions but feared for their scarce hard currency reserves.

From the very outset, the mechanism proved to be extremely effective in reducing the need for reserves to settle intra-European payments imbalances. This was especially important in the initial stages of the

Union. Trade liberalization increased during the Korean War period, even though imbalances became particularly severe and foreign exchange reserves were still sorely lacking. Thereafter, the need for economies in the use of reserves lessened progressively as imbalances were reduced and reserves increased. The mechanism continued to be just as efficient. It operated like a seventeen-jewel Swiss watch.

Compensations

During its first two years, the compensations mechanism of the Union cleared and cancelled out 70 per cent of all bilateral monthly deficits and surpluses. That proportion persisted over the eight and a half year period (see Table 10). Of the $46 billion in bilateral positions reported to the Agent, $20 billion were offset multilaterally against net positions reported in the same month by other members. A further $12 billion were compensated over time, as countries reversed from surplus to deficit or vice versa.

In fact, an even larger volume of multilateral compensations occurred outside the EPU system, though under its aegis. The gradual introduction of multilateral arbitrage after 1953 enabled the exchange markets to reclaim from the central banks much of their own clearing function. The bilateral positions offset in the market place were never reported, as was normal and intended. The EPU increasingly became a 'clearer of last resort'.

Automatic Credit and Gold Settlements

Only the balances remaining after compensations had to be settled by paying gold to the Agent or by using the credit facilities of the system. These net monthly surpluses and deficits totalled $13.4 billion over the life of the EPU. A summary statement of the balances, by year, for each currency is shown in Table 11.

In the first two years, net country positions after the compensations were highly volatile, and EPU credits allowed further economies in the need for foreign exchange reserves. In the following two years, credit played a lesser role, as deficit countries moved into the upper *tranches* of their quotas. After the 1954 refurbishing of the EPU, more old credit was repaid than new credit extended for several years. With reserves also rising, the four middle years of the EPU saw trade liberalization increase from 66 per cent to 89 per cent, even with a net decrease in outstanding credit. The mere availability of credit facilities sufficed.

The picture changed again over the last two and a half years, as France and Great Britain ran large deficits and Germany experienced large

TABLE 10. *The EPU Clearing and Settlements: Cover for the Total Bilateral Positions, July 1950–December 1958*

	Financial Years								July–Dec. 1958	Total: July 1950–Dec. 1958
	1950/1	1951/2	1952/3	1953/4	1954/5	1955/6	1956/7	1957/8		
A. In billions of dollars										
1. Total bilateral positions (deficits plus surpluses)	6.3	8.7	5.3	3.9	3.5	3.9	5.7	6.5	2.6	46.4
2. Multilateral compensations	3.0	3.5	2.9	1.9	1.7	1.4	2.0	2.6	1.0	20.0
3. Compensations through time	1.0	3.0	2.0	0.9	1.4	1.1	0.9	2.1	0.3	12.6
4. Effect of special settlements and adjustments	0.7	0.0	0.0	+0.0	+0.0	+0.0	+0.0	+0.0	+0.0	0.4
5. Balance (= (1) minus (2), (3), and (4))	1.6	2.2	0.4	1.2	0.5	1.4	2.8	1.9	1.3	13.4
6. Balance settled in gold	0.4	1.3	0.3	1.3	0.6	1.5	2.3	1.8	1.0	10.7
7. Balance settled in credit	1.2	0.9	0.1	−0.1	−0.1	−0.1	0.4	0.1	0.3	2.7
B. As percentages of the total bilateral deficits plus surpluses										
2. Multilateral compensations	47	40	54	49	47	37	35	39	40	43
3. Compensation over time	16	34	37	22	39	28	16	32	12	27
TOTAL compensations ((2) plus (3))	64	74	92	71	86	65	51	71	52	70
4. Effect of special settlements and adjustments	10	0	0	+1	+1	+1	+0	+0	+2	1
5. Balance	26	26	8	30	14	36	49	29	50	29
6. Balance settled in gold	7	16	7	33	17	39	41	27	38	23
7. Balance settled in credit	19	10	2	−4	−3	−3	8	2	12	6

Source: EPU Board, *Final Report* (1959), 39.

TABLE II. *Annual Net Deficits or Surpluses: 1 July 1950–27 December 1958*
(in millions of dollars)

Country	Financial Years								1 July–27 Dec. 1958
	1950/1	1951/2	1952/3	1953/4	1954/5	1955/6	1956/7	1957/8	
Austria	− 104	− 38	+ 42	+106	− 103	− 6	+ 23	− 4	+ 24
Belgium–Luxembourg	+ 236	+ 509	− 33	− 55	+ 80	+ 222	+ 14	+ 153	+ 66
Denmark	− 68	+ 46	− 17	− 92	− 94	+ 4	− 43	+ 10	− 1
France	+ 194	− 602	− 417	− 149	+ 115	− 180	− 969	− 576	− 317
Germany	− 281	+ 584	+ 260	+ 518	+ 296	+ 584	+ 1,336	+ 826	+ 350
Greece	− 140	− 83	− 28	− 40	− 27	+ 40	+ 5	+ 7	+ 49
Iceland	− 7	− 6	− 4	− 5	− 2	− 4	− 3	+ 3	− 9
Italy	− 30	+ 194	− 223	− 210	− 225	− 125	− 94	+ 219	+ 73
Netherlands	− 270	+ 477	+ 139	− 42	+ 84	− 62	− 36	+ 86	+181
Norway	− 80	+ 21	− 59	− 61	− 70	− 27	+ 41	− 78	− 30
Portugal	+ 59	+ 28	− 23	− 19	− 59	− 33	+ 38	− 54	− 37
Sweden	− 59	+ 284	− 44	− 37	− 104	+ 6	+ 111	− 30	+ 11
Switzerland	+ 11	+ 158	+ 85	+ 73	+ 10	− 66	+ 83	− 189	+ 20
Turkey	− 64	− 96	− 50	− 94	− 38	− 27	− 36	− 50	− 14
United Kingdom	+ 604	− 1,476	+ 371	+107	+136	− 327	− 225	− 317	−267
TOTAL	+/−1,104	+/−2,301	+/−897	+/−862	+/−722	+/−856	+/−1,529	+/−1,301	+/−725

Source: EPU Board, *Final Report* (1959), 36.

surpluses. Bilateral positions reported to the Agent rose sharply, compensations fell, and credit once again played a significant role. Nevertheless, net credit still accounted for only 15 per cent of all settlements, including the repayment of old debts under bilateral agreements.

During the 1950 negotiations, critics had feared the creation of a soft currency area, within which competitiveness with the outside world would take second place to exports on easy credit terms. That criticism was refuted by the significant role of gold in the settlements during the very first years of the Union, as described in Chapter 7. Afterwards, its role became even larger, accounting for 80 per cent of total settlements over the entire life of the Union. A higher settlement ratio combined with debt repayment in the later years had greatly enhanced the place of gold in the system.

On the whole, member countries used the credit facilities of the Union responsibly, conscious of an unquestioned obligation to repay debts in full. Indeed, they were not eager to borrow in the first place. The initial agreement provided for the repayment, through the EPU system, of $851 million in credits outstanding under the preceding bilateral payments arrangements. All but $10 million had been repaid by the time the EPU was terminated. Repayment of EPU debts did become an issue in 1954. Debtor countries objected to creditor proposals, primarily because they wanted the creditors to import more and thus reverse their positions within the Union. Nonetheless, repayment agreements on reasonable terms were concluded. After 1954, older debts were repeatedly consolidated in bilateral repayment agreements with creditors. After the EPU was liquidated, repayment arrangements on credits still outstanding were concluded promptly, and the debts were fully repaid without a single default as payments became due.

The shortage of reserves made credit important to the system initially, and the availability of credit as needed made the risks of liberalization acceptable. There was little evidence of a desire to buy or sell on easy credit and let the lenders take the consequences.

CONVERTIBILITY

By 1958, the stage had thus been set for convertibility. European competitiveness was generally well established, reserves were at a more comfortable level, and experience with extensive liberalization of imports from the dollar area had proved successful. At the end of 1958, the transferability between European currencies was extended to other areas, including the dollar area. From then on, residents outside the EPU area could freely exchange any European currency they acquired on current account for other European currencies or dollars.

At that moment, only a few countries—Benelux, Germany, and Switzerland—had currencies that were convertible for their own residents as well. However, after a few years, residents of other European countries were relieved of the major restrictions on doing business in dollars. OEEC members as a group liberalized 83 per cent of their dollar imports by the end of 1959 and 89 per cent by May 1961. Some months earlier, the major European countries had accepted the obligations of Article VIII of the IMF. After this, discrimination against importing from the dollar area came to an end. 'Full convertibility' as the Managing Board had defined it in 1953 was nearly a reality.

Liberalization of capital movements followed at a more uneven pace. Again, Germany followed the Swiss lead in mid-1959, permitting residents to export capital to any other country in the world at the official exchange rate. Other countries' efforts and progress differed widely.

OTHER REGIONAL CLEARING ARRANGEMENTS

The efficiency and success of the EPU mechanism led countries in other parts of the world to initiate clearing arrangements that would increase their intra-regional trade. Shortages of foreign exchange suggested using the EPU as a model for fostering their own economic and financial integration. The first payments union outside Europe was established soon after the liquidation of the EPU. A Central American Clearing House began operating in 1961, following a 1960 treaty whose objective was to create a common market in Central America. A group of South American countries soon followed in the Central American footsteps. By the 1980s, regional payments arrangements had been established in many parts of the developing world—the Caribbean, Southeast Asia, the Arab States, and both East and West Africa.

These other regions, however, found that their own situations precluded the adoption of the full EPU mechanism. Because their foreign trade is overwhelmingly with other parts of the world, their achievements have been less striking. Trade with each other remains modest, and resource limitations inhibit its ready expansion. A periodic clearing arrangement permits some compensation of intra-regional surpluses and deficits, thus promoting trade while minimizing the need for settlements in foreign exchange. However, achieving a balance in their intra-regional trade is still an impractical objective.

In the EPU area—including the currency areas of European countries— regional balance was a practical goal, at least for a limited period while economic reconstruction was in progress. Elsewhere, it would lead to uneconomic distortion of trade patterns, discouraging economic efficiency and competitiveness on global markets. Had the founders of the EPU failed to incorporate the sterling area fully in their system, they might well have encountered comparable difficulties.

Their limitations notwithstanding, regional clearing arrangements in the developing world have established closer contacts and promoted economic co-operation. As in the EPU, these clearing and credit agreements demonstrate the advantages of working together, both to the governments and to the citizens.

ADJUSTING PAYMENTS IMBALANCES

The Preamble stated that an indispensable condition for the proper operation of the payments system was the maintenance of internal and external financial equilibrium by each of the members. Particularly in its early stages, the freeing of trade and payments depended on members maintaining balance in their payments positions within the Union. If not, both surplus and deficit countries were supposed to adjust economic policies to correct imbalances. Otherwise, quotas would be exhausted, the strain on partner countries would become excessive, and the system would tend to break down. Thus the basic requirement for member co-operation within the EPU was a willingness to accept responsibility for constraining imbalances.

The initial design of the EPU included incentives for members to adjust policies appropriately. Deficit countries faced rising gold payments if their deficits persisted. Creditors had to extend credit for half of the surpluses within their quotas. Furthermore, they did not know how much more credit they might have to extend or whether their exporters would face discrimination after their quotas were exhausted. The Managing Board was empowered to ease the adjustment process by offering special credits to countries in difficulty. It soon assumed authority to recommend policy changes to member countries that were seriously remiss in attaining balance.

The monthly results were reported and discussed in the press and other forums. With the system in the public eye, member governments had to discharge their responsibilities toward it prudently and conscientiously. Public scrutiny added a critical disciplinary constraint.

The early imbalances largely reflected temporary maladjustments stemming from the Korean War and from ambitious rearmament programmes. For the most part, they could readily be corrected by adjusting fiscal and monetary policies. Deficit countries adjusted their policies either in response to Managing Board recommendations, as in the case of Germany and France, or in anticipation of what these would be, as in the case of the United Kingdom, the Netherlands, and Denmark. During this period, the Managing Board successfully supported the use of restrictive monetary policies to control inflationary pressures, an effective policy tool that had long been neglected. Surplus countries—Belgium, Italy, Portugal, Sweden, and Switzerland—also responded to Board recommendations, as France and the United Kingdom had done when they ran surpluses in the first year of the Union.

The universal shortage of foreign exchange forced attention to the views of the managers of a system that was helping to reduce the shortage. Only France failed to respond appropriately, maintaining trade restrictions for an extended period after 1952, despite an EPU special credit. A large flow of US government dollars enabled it to reduce indebtedness to the system and thus to resist, for some time, Board pressures for fiscal and monetary reform.

From mid-1952 to mid-1955, virtually all countries were in reasonable balance within the system, and the need for the Board to propose policy adjustments was sharply reduced. The Board's quarterly reviews of each member country kept it abreast of developments and enabled it to offer cautionary advice before imbalances became excessive. In 1955, imbalances once again became a major problem, but by then the value of automatic credit had been reduced through the hardening of the system. Moreover, relaxation of exchange controls tended to enlarge the magnitude of some imbalances, and global imbalances had become more important than those within the system. A special credit to Italy in 1955 was essentially a political gesture, designed to show support for policies already adopted— credit tightening and continued trade liberalization.

The major imbalances that Britain and Germany developed in the later years were more deep-seated, and the EPU could do little to require suitable adjustment. Lack of authority over exchange rates was a major handicap, as was the Board's limited capacity to offer special assistance. The United Kingdom escaped the authority of the EPU system by obtaining large credits from the US and the IMF. So did France, though only until 1957. Germany was spared more pressure because it further eased its trade and payments restrictions, agreed to repeated extensions of its quota, and provided additional loans to the system.

In 1957-8, the Managing Board was much more effective in dealing with France and Turkey because it was able to join hands with the IMF and also gain US government support in negotiating stabilization programmes linked to large credits. In these two cases, it supplemented its own limited resources for extending special credits with loans from Germany and other member governments. During its final period, the

Board was thus able to maintain as direct and strong a constructive influence over the adjustment policies of these two member countries as it had over Germany in 1950/1.

Germany and the United Kingdom took actions jointly late in 1957 that temporarily eased their global imbalances, but that occurred bilaterally, without Board participation. Their efforts created an economic environment for moving toward convertibility a year later and liquidating the Union. However, the fundamental problems of both countries continued beyond the end of the system, resurfacing only a year later.

THE INTANGIBLE LEGACY

Can the contribution of the EPU be measured only in quantitative and easily identifiable terms? In its *Final Report*, the Managing Board did not think so.[6] Since that report was written only months after the Union was terminated, a qualitative appraisal would have been premature. Wisely, the Board did not attempt one. Its report focused on a quantitative description of how the mechanism had functioned and noted briefly the role of 'practical methods of cooperation'—special assistance to debtor countries in difficulty, additional credit extended by creditors who had exhausted their quotas, repayment of old credits, and the various compromises reached about the periodic renewals of the Union. With appropriate modesty, an evaluation of the less tangible contributions was foregone.

Yet these very intangibles may constitute the EPU's most valuable legacy. The system demonstrated the benefits of economic integration to the governments and peoples of western Europe, as well as the virtues of a co-operative approach to international trade and payments problems. The 'practical methods of cooperation' were readily identifiable, but the more subtle forms were probably more important. The liberalization of trade and payments initiated the integration of the economies of western Europe. While that process has had to overcome periodic set-backs, it has persisted over the intervening decades. In 1985, the twelve Common Market countries revived Paul Hoffman's call in 1949 for a 'single market', agreeing to create one by the end of 1992.

The integration process could not have succeeded without the full co-operation of member governments and their central banks, centred and co-ordinated within the Managing Board and the OEEC. The Board generated a spirit of dedication, co-operation, and mutual concern that spread throughout the OEEC and, more significantly, through member

[6] EPU Board, *Final Report* (1959), 17–29.

governments. The meeting rooms and corridors of the Château de la Muette were dominated by concern about developments in all member countries. Solving problems, resolving disagreements, concession, and compromise were institutional watchwords.

Policy 'co-ordination' or 'convergence' had not yet permeated the international vocabulary. But adjusting national policies with consideration for their effect on trading partners acquired prominence on the international agenda. The ideas took ever firmer root as the pace of economic recovery, under the umbrella of a European multilateral trade and payments system, surpassed all expectations. Many veterans of the EPU experience went on to responsibilities in broader arenas, where they continued to exercise the habits and skills of co-operation. Co-operation seemed to benefit everyone, and no government was then willing to be the first to utter an important 'Nay'.

Functioning in such an atmosphere, the Managing Board became the instrument for defining a generally acceptable approach to problems. Much more important, its agreements and recommendations were effective in resolving most of the problems they addressed.

The major legacy of the EPU was thus the power of the two basic ideas that motivated its founders—European economic integration and financial co-operation. The phrases could not be defined precisely, and the legal draftsmen found no place for them in the formal language of the EPU Agreement. That did not diminish their force. Ideas were the fundamental instruments for accelerating Europe's remarkable economic recovery. They left imprints on European monetary co-operation, beyond the limits of 'European' and 'monetary'.

The EPU started the integration of the economies of western Europe by making their currencies transferable and by freeing their trade from quantitative restrictions and the need for bilateral balance. As these were achieved, another powerful idea—currency convertibility and multilateral trade on a global basis—was transformed from a distant and evanescent goal to an objective within the grasp of most members. Implementing that idea brought the EPU to a successful conclusion.

Epilogue

IS IT RELEVANT?

The relevance of the EPU experience to contemporary policy issues may be viewed from very different perspectives. The record of an effective system is interesting for its accomplishments, even though it was terminated thirty years ago. Yet it may be too divorced from current realities to be applicable under existing circumstances. On the other hand, some of the ingredients of distant successes, however dated, may still be useful.

The major problems resolved by the EPU no longer preoccupy the international agenda, at least, that of the more industrialized countries. Bilateralism, discriminatory quantitative restrictions, pervasive exchange controls, and inconvertible currencies on current account are no longer important, if prevalent. Moreover, the circumstances in which the EPU successfully attacked them were unusually favourable. In addition, the fixed, though adjustable, exchange rate system of the 1950s has been supplanted by floating rates, more or less managed. These propositions are beyond denial.

The political and economic environment in which the EPU was born begged for an effective address to the problems. The outbreak of a shooting war in Korea, almost at the moment the EPU Agreement was approved, gave rise to the kind of economic tensions that the EPU was designed to mitigate. It also strengthened common bonds in Europe. In this setting, success fed on itself, reinforcing the influence of the system and the responsiveness of member governments to its incentives and prescriptions. The managers of the system were then able to chart an acceptable course to currency convertibility as European economic recovery progressed in leaps and bounds. That course was pursued to a fruitful finish. All this occurred during a period of major constraints on national policy-making that no longer exist for the industrialized countries. Ingenious as was the EPU's automatic mechanism, it was obviously time-bound to an era of fixed exchange rates, as well as inconvertibility, foreign exchange controls, and lack of international liquidity.

A contrary view is that other problems addressed under the aegis of the EPU still persist—extreme payments imbalances, adjustment policies, quantitative restrictions and other non-tariff barriers, developing country debt, and European economic integration. Attachment to national sovereignty continues to hamper inter-governmental co-operation. The respective responsibilities of surplus and deficit countries for rectifying payments imbalances remain at issue.

These matters now manifest themselves very differently; they also appear in altered and less auspicious circumstances. On the other hand, in some respects the environment may be more favourable. Interdependence has grown considerably over the intervening decades, the economies of western Europe are significantly more integrated, and their governments are committed to further collective measures. Moreover, circumstances do change. Thus it is possible that some of the EPU institutional arrangements and some of its experience with policy adjustment measures may still be applicable, even after several decades. Readers of this book will draw their own conclusions about relevance.

OF ROOTS AND WINGS

Launched in an era of new beginnings in Europe, the EPU experience was intense, varied, and far-reaching. Constructive decisions were reached, difficulties were confronted and overcome, and the policies of sovereign governments were reconciled through a well-designed and innovative institutional arrangement. Controversies within and between governments abounded, but they led to practical and productive agreements, many of whose benefits stretched beyond the boundaries of western Europe.

The history of the EPU is also the story of financial diplomacy in the 1950s. Making western European currencies freely convertible into dollars was an essential preliminary step toward broader international financial relationships. The United States proposed and supported a system to help Europe move from bilateralism to convertibility and a single market. The Europeans responded with steps to make their currencies transferable and to end bilateral trade and payments arrangements with each other.

The EPU blazed new paths by raising economic co-operation among European governments to an unprecedented level. That spurred an equally unprecedented rate of modernization and industrialization of their economies. The Union helped free international trade and payments from a variety of hobbling restrictions that dated back to the early 1930s. It thereby launched the process of unifying the economies of western Europe. Its success depended on convincing member governments to adjust internal economic policies to accommodate the requirements of the system. The initial goal was a balanced payments position with each other. Achieving it helped in attaining balance on a global basis, as well.

These processes have continued to evolve, and some of the problems they engender continue to arise. Aspirations for further unifying European economic life remain. The problems created by payments imbalances in

Europe and elsewhere still confound international economic relations. Current generations must deal in their own way with the modern manifestations of these processes and problems. Reflecting on the beginnings may stimulate their imagination and creative energies. The past can give the present roots—and wings.

Appendix A

Where Did the Ideas Come From?

Where did the principles and concepts of the European Payments Union come from? One may as well ask for the source of the ideas that produced any other international agreement or new institution. The simplest answer is that all originated in problems, more or less widely perceived. Academic journals, intellectual magazines, and newspaper columns are full of international problems, carefully identified and dissected. More often than not, the analyses are accompanied by prescriptive remedies, but not many are adopted.

Our sense of the romantic leads us to look for some genius whose vision conceived and inspired the new institution. Secluded behind the ivy-covered walls of academe, or perhaps relieved of day-to-day responsibilities by assignment to a government planning office or a private research institute, genius laboured in quiet solitude until the 'right idea' was born and commended itself to the authorities by the very power of its inspiration.

Examples of such a process are very difficult to find, though not for lack of either claimants or authors easily seduced by the romantic ideal. Neither the United Nations, the International Monetary Fund, the Marshall Plan, nor the European Payments Union were so conceived. As first proposed and finally agreed, they reflected ideas collected from many sources, from a climate of ideas rather than from any one inspiration.

Widely perceived failings of predecessor institutions and arrangements stimulated creative policy-makers. Living daily with the urgencies of problems and the difficulties posed by suggested solutions, experienced officials were themselves able to identify arrangements that were adequate and capable of eliciting consent.

In the instances where perceptions of a problem and ideas about its resolution were transformed into an effective international institution, two elements were essential: intelligent leadership and a recognized centre of power. Both were needed to induce or compel essential compromises. A process of international negotiation had to take place, in the course of which the proponents of the new institution had to be as unflinching in purpose as they were flexible about details. The perceived interests of each sovereign government somehow had to be accommodated. Power had to be combined with the will to apply it in a way that would command the respect and concurrence of all parties to the nascent agreement.

All of these ingredients were present in the conception of the European Payments Union—a problem, a climate of ideas about its resolution, failed predecessor arrangements, innovative policy-makers with power, and authority used skilfully and flexibly in the course of purposeful negotiations. The true genius behind the EPU was the amalgamation of all these elements into a package that was agreed and that worked.

THE PROBLEM

Freeing international trade and payments from governmental restrictions was an objective common both to the universalists and the regionalists, as explained in Chapter 1. Bilateralism was an acknowledged evil, though many socialist leaders felt it essential to the maintenance of full employment in a world of trading partners with unstable economies. Yet few remembered with equanimity the history of European bilateralism between the two World Wars. Neither European productivity nor competitiveness on world markets nor living standards had flourished under this system. The use of bilateral agreements by the Nazis had left a particularly bitter taste. Hardly anyone contested the basic argument against bilateralism—that it fostered attempts to balance bilateral trade and economic inefficiency.

If bilateralism was eschewed in principle, it was, none the less, embraced in practice after World War II, *faute de mieux*. The alternative—eliminating restrictions—seemed too risky for European countries that were short of consumer goods, raw materials, and, above all, the foreign exchange to pay for importing them. The first attempts to wean countries from bilateralism were the IEPS arrangements. As explained in Chapter 1, they proved to be ineffectual.

THE IDEAS

A Multilateral Clearing System

As early as autumn 1941, John Maynard Keynes conceived of an International Clearing Union as the cornerstone of a free and multilateral postwar international economic system. Countries would settle through accounts that each held in the union. As he saw it, the union would create internationally acceptable assets needed to finance its operations by recording overdrafts on its books. Country quotas would define the maximum each could borrow, and access would be automatic, though the policies of persistent debtors would be subject to the scrutiny of the union. No limit would be placed on credit balances. Settlements would be based on a unit of account, which Keynes proposed to call Bancor. His formulation yielded to a much less automatic system, derived mainly from a US proposal and incorporated in the original Bretton Woods Agreement of 1944.

The subsequent European Payments Union was similar to Keynes's concept, but very different. It was a regional, rather than a universal, system. It created much less international credit and provided a much more important role for periodic settlements in gold or US dollars. However, it did provide for freely transferable currencies and for automatic clearing of payments between central banks for all current account transactions. The latter provisions were the essentials of Keynes's vision about how to move toward free multilateral trade and payments. That conception would permit large economies in the use of gold and equivalent foreign exchange reserves and thus provide a framework within which restrictions could be eliminated.

A European Clearing Union

The earliest recorded proposal for a European Clearing Union was framed in September 1946 by Theodore Geiger, then an official of the US Embassy in London.[1] There he met Harold Van Buren Cleveland and began a collaboration on ideas about how the US should promote a united Europe. Later, as ECA officials, both regarded the agency's day-to-day problems as manifestations of more fundamental phenomena that they analysed and sought to address in long memoranda. Both left government service after the end of the Marshall Plan but continued to write creatively about international economic issues.

Trained as an economic historian, Geiger foresaw in 1946 an even stronger repetition of the bilateralism that had dominated the European experience from 1918 to 1925. He therefore proposed that this time European trade should be renewed on a multilateral basis. A clearing union would balance off all bilateral surpluses and deficits on current account at the end of each quarter. Debtors could either pay off or convert their deficits into long term debts. Persistent net creditors would assume one-third of the debts as long term loans, and the World Bank would fund the rest on a long term basis. His proposal was sent to Washington but never left the State Department.

The idea of a European regional clearing union was first injected into an international forum at the very first meeting of the CEEC in July 1947. Felix LeNorcy, an official of the French Ministry of Finance, had earlier proposed to his government a system of currency transferability and compensations along the same lines as Geiger's.[2] His ideas were presented to the CEEC Financial Committee.

At the same meeting, Benelux officials proposed that the European countries should (*a*) multilateralize their bilateral payments arrangements; (*b*) make their currencies freely transferable into one another; and (*c*) free trade with one another from quota restrictions. Hubert Ansiaux and Cecil de Strycker, F. A. G. Keesing and Suardus Posthuma were the principal contributors.

Their memorandum involved a much less audacious departure from the then-existing system of bilateral trade and payments than Geiger and LeNorcy had proposed. The credit margins in each of the bilateral agreements would be maintained and continue to govern the relations between each of the countries. The transferability of currencies would require the consent of each involved country, at least at first.

The CEEC Financial Committee recommended that the technical details of the Benelux proposal for intra-European currency transferability should be worked out by experts. A meeting was held in London on 22 September 1947, under the chairmanship of Sir David Whaley of the United Kingdom. Guido Carli, an Italian participant, remembers vividly that the meeting was held in the underground War Cabinet rooms, now an important London tourist attraction.

For that meeting the Benelux delegations provided a technical description of

---

[1] 'Proposal for Renewal of Intra-European Trade on a Multilateral Basis'. Later attached to letter to W. Y. Elliott, Staff Director, House Foreign Affairs Committee (29 Sept. 1947). US Archives. ECA Geiger Files.

[2] Interview with Guindey, CEEC Financial Committee chairman (12 May 1987).

a scheme that was acceptable to Italy and France as well. It led to the voluntary Agreement on Multilateral Monetary Compensation described in Chapter 1. The Financial Committee proposed that part of US aid should be spent on procurement in Europe. This would finance the intra-European surpluses (and deficits) that would remain after the multilateral compensations were completed and after credit remaining under the bilateral payments agreements had been used.

The United Kingdom had a different vision of how European currencies might become freely transferable and thus serve as a vehicle for relaxing restrictions. Sterling could be used freely by countries within the extensive membership of the sterling area, but that membership included only two OEEC participants, Iceland and Ireland. Four other OEEC participants—Italy, the Netherlands, Norway, and Sweden—were in a sterling transferable account system that entitled them to pay transferable sterling freely to residents of other transferable account countries, as well as to any member of the sterling area. Bank of England officials would have welcomed all the other OEEC countries into the transferable account system.

As a Staff Consultant to the House Select Committee on Foreign Aid, Geiger again suggested a clearing house for European payments that would eliminate the necessity for bilateral barter and compensations agreements.[3] A report issued by that committee thought that net deficits should be financed 'individually or jointly by the creditor members . . . , the Bank for International Settlements, the International Monetary Fund, and even by the United States as part of the proposed European Recovery Program'. Geiger was still groping for a method of financing an intra-European free trading area with full transferability of currencies, yet minimal need for gold or dollars to finance imbalances.

On taking office as the ECA Assistant Administrator, Richard Bissell promptly invited Geiger to become his Special Assistant and encouraged him to continue the fray. By this time, Geiger saw a clearing union primarily as a first institutional step toward a United States of Europe. Bissell supported the clearing union idea on its own merits, though he was reserved about the feasibility of Geiger's more ambitious objective.

The ECA Proposal of May 1948

Geiger and Frank Lindsay, another Special Assistant, drafted an ECA staff paper on an Intra-European Payments Clearing System. Bissell presented the paper to the US National Advisory Council on International Monetary and Financial Problems (the NAC), where it was discussed on 29 May 1948.[4] This was less than two months after ECA issued its first authorization for procurement with Marshall Plan funds.

The ECA paper proposed that the OEEC organize an automatic multilateral clearing system for current transactions. OEEC countries would extend credits

---

[3] US House of Reps., Select Com. on Foreign Aid, *What Western Europe Can Do for Itself.* Preliminary report 14 (13 Feb. 1948).

[4] NAC analysis and recommendations with ECA draft as an Appendix. NAC Staff Document 698 (2 June 1948). US Archives. Treasury NAC Files.

on a multilateral basis. The amounts would be in proportion to anticipated net creditor positions *vis-à-vis* all participating countries. Each prospective debtor would be allowed to draw up to 120 per cent of its anticipated net deficit, with no discrimination as to where the drawings could be spent in the OEEC area. Existing accumulated intra-European balances would be funded. For a specified part of debtor drawings, the US would pay for procurement in creditor countries.

Though similar to the existing compensations agreement, what ECA proposed was more ambitious. The need for government consent to compensations and for bilateral payments agreements would have been eliminated, and the amount of credit would not be fixed bilaterally.

The initial NAC reaction was favourable. But, by the time of decision, only the Federal Reserve member would support the specific proposal. The decision of 2 June 1949 did not oppose the idea of a multilateral clearing mechanism, and it approved US procurement in Europe to finance a portion of the net credit balances. However, the NAC felt that the Europeans should be allowed to design their own institution. The International Monetary Fund should participate actively, but only in the form of administrative and technical assistance.

Excluding possible IMF financial assistance for such a scheme was a deliberate reiteration of the IMF's so-called 'ERP decision' of 5 April 1948. That decision effectively blocked Marshall Plan recipients from using IMF resources for the duration of the European Recovery Program. The NAC decision added a seemingly gratuitous thought that ECA should encourage the Europeans to work with the IMF, rather than the BIS, which then served as Agent for the existing European compensations scheme.

Thus, very early in the Marshall Plan period, some basic principles of the EPU had been conceived, had received important support, and were under active discussion both within the US government and among OEEC countries. First, the desirability of eliminating quantitative restrictions on intra-European trade and other current transactions. Second, the need for freely transferable currencies to make such freer trade possible. Third, the need for an automatic clearing mechanism with an agreed unit of account that would offset bilateral surpluses and deficits. This would make currency transferability possible, while minimizing payments in gold or dollars. Fourth, the need for periodic settlements of net deficits or surpluses. Fifth, the need for limits (quotas) to restrict the amounts that members could borrow or would have to lend to the system. Sixth, the need for some external financing in the form of gold or dollars. Finally, recognition of the problem posed by large debts contracted under the existing bilateral arrangements.

Financing Intra-European Surpluses and Deficits

Implementing any set of ambitious principles always raises serious practical problems, and these principles provided no exception. Many of the problems were recognized early, but the first solutions proved unacceptable.

The most obvious and thorniest problem was the financing of net surpluses and deficits among the participating countries. Even in the unlikely event that each OEEC member could bring its payments for current transactions into balance with the rest of the OEEC as a group, some financing for bilateral imbalances had to be provided. Obviously credit would be needed between the periodic settlement dates, but some would be required on the settlement dates as well. Otherwise, the prevalent shortage of gold and dollars would lead countries to try to avoid running any deficits. Inevitably, the effort to maintain a balanced position would involve restrictions on imports and other current payments, and the very purpose of the system would be defeated.

Furthermore, all members of the OEEC except Switzerland were receiving US and Canadian aid because they were unable to pay for all the goods and services they needed from the dollar area. That aid was to end in mid-1952. Meanwhile, each country would have liked to reduce its need for aid by earning dollars from other OEEC countries or by reducing its need to pay dollars for purchases within the OEEC area.

Geiger's early proposals suggested all the conceivable sources of financing in various combinations—the World Bank, the IMF, the BIS, the US, and the net creditors. The first three—the multilateral institutions—proved to be unrealistic alternatives.

The Benelux proposal to the CEEC in 1947 had also grappled unsuccessfully with the problem of financing net positions. It suggested that the parties to the existing bilateral agreements should agree on the maintenance or increase of the credit margins in those agreements, that the currencies of the deficit countries should be allocated between the surplus countries, and that any bilateral deficits in excess of the agreed credit margins should be settled in gold or dollars. The US would be asked to guarantee the required conversion into gold and dollars, setting aside a portion of the deficit country's aid allotment for that purpose. However, countries that expected to run deficits in their intra-European trade would not accept a proposal for so using scarce dollars.

At about the time ECA prepared its Clearing System proposal, the IMF staff sent to its Executive Board a plan for Fund participation in the IEPS. The IMF should offer $338 million to multilateralize the existing credit margins in the bilateral agreements between European members of the IMF.[5] Since Belgium was the major creditor, the sum would be made available to other countries primarily in Belgian francs. Then Belgium would be able to draw dollars from the IMF, if necessary. Led by the opposition of the US Executive Director, the Board refused to endorse the plan. Its statement of position was issued early in June 1948, only days after the NAC had refused to support the first ECA scheme.

Another approach was crafted by Robert Triffin in March 1949. Then the IMF Managing Director's representative in Paris, he proposed that one-third of the drawing rights under the IEPS should be financed in equal parts by the creditors, ECA, and the IMF, up to a limit of $600 million.[6] However, the IMF Executive Board also refused to endorse this scheme, though it authorized its transmittal to the OEEC as a 'personal and technical proposal'.

[5] Horsefield (1969), 220-1.

[6] Robert Triffin, IMF rep. to OEEC Intra-European Payments Com., 'Outline of Proposed Intra-European Payments Plan, 1949-50' (29 Mar. 1949). US Archives. ECA Geiger Files.

Dollar Discrimination

While it was thus apparent that a regional clearing system would require the use of some US aid and some intra-European credit, neither the amounts nor the terms had been defined in an acceptable fashion. Before substantial US aid could become available for a system, another issue had to be addressed— discrimination against exports from the dollar area.

To be sure, the US was passively accepting discrimination by Marshall Plan recipients; explicit acceptance was another matter. Would the US agree to provide government funds for a system that would inevitably involve discrimination against US goods and services for a time? Given the shortage of dollars throughout Europe, OEEC members could hardly be expected to relax quantitative restrictions on imports from the dollar area. A regional clearing system required such relaxation on imports from other participating countries without corresponding treatment of imports from the dollar area.

The NAC discussed intra-European payments arrangements inconclusively for a year after its cool reception of the Geiger–Lindsay paper. However, in August 1949 it explicitly accepted discrimination, in a paper entitled 'U.S. Position on the Liberalization of Intra-European Trade and Payments'.[7] That paper endorsed maximum relaxation of trade and payments barriers within the OEEC countries as an essential immediate objective. It further urged the abolition of quantitative restrictions and exchange controls on current transactions between the participating countries, their dependent overseas territories, and the sterling area.

> The United States does not believe that elimination of trade barriers inside Europe must be delayed until it can be accomplished simultaneously with elimination of trade barriers against other areas. The United States will therefore tolerate discrimination against United States exports which arise not from increased barriers to dollar trade but from decreased barriers to intra-European trade.

The paper recognized that ECA dollars would be needed for the rest of the Marshall Plan period to finance some intra-European payments, as had been true from the beginning of the European Recovery Program.

The August 1949 NAC language was precipitated by the need to prepare for a meeting of US, Canadian, and British cabinet officials, at which the dire foreign exchange position of the United Kingdom would be discussed. John Snyder, the US Secretary of the Treasury, expected his British counterpart, Sir Stafford Cripps, to ask for extraordinary assistance, including explicit relief from the United Kingdom's non-discrimination commitment under the 1945 Lend-Lease settlement. In the event, Cripps revealed to Snyder a decision to devalue the pound.[8] Willingness to accept the limited discrimination described in the NAC paper was as far as the Treasury and other US universalists would go to meet

---

[7] NAC Sec., memo with two attachments (24 Aug. 1949). Attachment A is the position paper. Attachment B expresses earlier NAC views (30 June 1949). NAC Document 876. US Archives. Treasury NAC Files.

[8] Southard (1979).

UK concerns and probably did little for the Chancellor. But the concession was critical for subsequent US support of a European payments system.

Co-ordination of National Economic Policies

The failure to find an acceptable formula for freeing intra-European trade and payments from bilateral restrictions lay behind Paul Hoffman's 'single market' speech. The speech had been preceded by a substantial effort within ECA/ Washington to devise a new approach. Cleveland and John C. L. Hulley joined Geiger as the chief contributors to this effort.

Hulley had come to ECA after completing his college degree. At Harvard, he had studied under John H. Williams, whose ideas about postwar international financial arrangements were noted in Chapter 1. Hulley tackled the problems of devising a workable clearing union with both enthusiasm and imagination.

All three men prepared and discussed their own memoranda and consolidated them into joint documents, after discussion with Bissell and other members of the ECA staff.[9] Though they devised proposals for freeing intra-European trade and payments arrangements, they soon concluded that such a system alone would falter before long. Only economic and political unification would succeed. Nevertheless, they pressed on with conceiving co-operative arrangements for liberalizing intra-European payments, while trying to incorporate provisions that would 'encourage further organic development'.

As a further step toward unification, they added to the earlier conception of a clearing union the notion of promoting a balanced intra-European payments position for each member of the system. Since that would be difficult on a strictly European basis, they proposed including the entire sterling area. They also tried to develop both automatic and administrative mechanisms to discourage excessive imbalances.

On this broader base, they thought that balance would require tighter co-ordination of national economic policies. Otherwise the system of free trade and payments within Europe would not be durable.[10] Accordingly, they proposed the creation of an OEEC Advisory Monetary Committee to review frequently and make recommendations on monetary policies and exchange rates by less than unanimous vote. Committee recommendations could be supported by ECA action on the use of dollar aid and its counterpart in local currencies. In Cleveland's thinking, such a monetary committee was crucial. Its supra-national authority would propel the unification of Europe that he saw as the ultimate objective of the scheme. Events were to disprove the need for a central monetary authority and a pooling of foreign exchange reserves for the EPU proposal to succeed. A

---

[9] e.g. Cleveland, 'The Problem of Convertibility and a Free Trade Area in Western Europe' (13 Apr. 1949). Geiger, 'First Draft of Long Range Proposals' (18 Mar. 1949). Geiger, Cleveland, and Hulley, 'The Problem of Western Europe's Competitive Position in the World Economy and its Remedies' (19 July 1949). Cleveland, 'United States Position on the Liberalization of Trade and Payments and its Consequences' (3 Aug. 1949). Geiger, Bissell, and Cleveland, 'The Economic Integration of Western Europe' (15 Oct. 1949). US Archives. ECA Bissell Files.

[10] Cleveland/Hulley tel. for Bissell, then in Paris. TOREP 8769 (25 Oct. 1949).

degree of policy co-ordination was necessary, but it was achieved without provoking issues of sovereignty so directly.

After the Hoffman speech, the two principal division chiefs under Averell Harriman in Paris returned to Washington. They worked with the Geiger-Cleveland-Hulley team to review and refine the clearing union proposal. Henry Tasca was an international finance expert. Lincoln Gordon, on leave from the Harvard Business School, was more reflective and scholarly. Both Tasca and Gordon, as well as Harriman, were much less concerned with supra-national authority and European political unification than with the more immediate and practical objective of freeing intra-European trade and payments.

A Gold-Free Swing Margin and a Gold/Credit Ratio

Two weeks after Hoffman's speech, Hulley submitted a paper that introduced the idea of a gold-free swing margin for each country.[11] At about the same time, Frank Figgures was developing an OEEC Secretariat proposal for a very wide range of gold-free settlements. Both Hulley and Figgures would have settled imbalances in excess of the swing partly or totally in gold. However, credit would be more limited in the Hulley conception; payments in gold or dollars would play an important role at an early stage. He viewed some gold payments as a method of providing incentives for policies conducive both to a balanced payments position within Europe and to easing countries toward a system of universal convertibility.

THE PACKAGE

The Bissell proposal, drafted primarily by the Geiger-Cleveland-Hulley team, sorted and packaged concepts from all the papers and discussions. At the time, all were part of the intellectual climate of the international financial community. IMF and OEEC Secretariat papers were available to ECA and to European officials. Some of the ECA papers were provided to the Secretariat.

The package began with the seven concepts (noted above) that were widely recognized at least a year and a half earlier. To these were added components and refinements, none of which was particularly novel in itself. However, they made the package more likely to work successfully, as well as more attractive to the variety of prospective members of the clearing union. These further ideas were:

1. Every member should strive for balance over time in its foreign exchange accounts within the system.
2. If such balance were to be a realistic objective, the settlements system would have to include the entire sterling area.

---

[11] Hulley, 'Proposed U.S. Position on Economic Institutions and Activities for European Integration' (11 Nov. 1949). US Archives. ECA Geiger Files.

3. The settlements mechanism should be structured so as to induce each member to balance its position.
4. The incentives for balance would derive from a progressively increasing role for gold in settling deficits and for credit in settling surpluses.
5. To reinforce these incentives, a supervisory body should be authorized to recommend needed changes in national economic policies.
6. The US would provide the necessary gold or dollar financing for the system, even though the Union would encourage discrimination against US exporters temporarily, while Europe became more competitive.

Few, if any, Europeans were in as good a position as ECA to absorb all the various concepts, analyse and dissect them in vigorous debate with critics, and judge the acceptability of the various notions to the critical decision-makers. Only ECA had aid to use as an incentive for inducing governments to compromise their perceptions of national interest. Moreover, the NAC decision to accept discrimination made it credible for ECA to disclaim any immediately self-serving national economic purpose. To be sure, the package did serve the ultimate purpose of the European Recovery Program that ECA was charged with administering. The first strong endorsement came from the source of ECA's funds, the US Congress. That was of no small importance to European governments, as well as to the rest of the US Executive Branch.

Calendar of Major EPU-Related Events

1947

5 June	Secretary of State Marshall proposes US aid for European recovery.
July	Soviet Union refuses to participate in a joint recovery programme. Britain and France call conference (CEEC) to formulate a programme.
July	UK makes sterling convertible but has to reverse a few weeks later.
October	CEEC delegation presents report to US administration.
November	The first Agreement on Multilateral Monetary Compensation is signed.

1948

January	Belgium, the Netherlands, and Luxembourg form customs union (Benelux).
16 April	OEEC Convention is signed by 16 European countries and the military governors in western Germany.
April	US Congress enacts European Recovery Program and ECA begins operations.
June	German currency reform.
June	Soviet Union blockades West Berlin.
October	All OEEC members sign Agreement for Intra-European Payments and Compensations for 1948-9.

1949

April	North Atlantic Treaty Organisation Agreement (NATO) is signed.
August	Council of Europe is established in Strasbourg.
September	Agreement is signed for Intra-European Payments and Compensations Scheme for 1949-50.
September	Devaluation of pound and other European currencies.
October	Federal Republic of Germany becomes an OEEC member. Hoffman's 'Single Market' address to OEEC ministers, preceded by similar address to heads of dels. in August.
December	Proposals for new European multilateral payments system. Financial Experts group is established to examine them.

1950

January	Financial Experts submit report.
February	UK elections.
March	Negotiations for an EPU begin.
June	Outbreak of hostilities in Korea.
7 July	OEEC ministers decide to establish EPU.
August	OEEC adopts Code of Trade Liberalisation.
August	UK announces first large increase in rearmament programme, followed by other European NATO members.
19 September	Seventeen OEEC members (including Germany) sign EPU Agreement, with retroactive effect from 1 July 1950.
October	First meeting of EPU Managing Board.
October	OEEC members accept 60 per cent trade liberalization commitment, to be raised to 75 per cent on 1 February 1951.
December	EPU special credit to Germany.

1951

February	Germany suspends liberalization.
April	France, Germany, Italy, and Benelux sign European Coal and Steel Community Treaty.
July	Negotiations begin for truce in Korea.
July	OEEC Council adopts Code of Liberalisation for Invisible Transactions (services).
August	OEEC countries announce intention to increase production by 25 per cent.
December	UK reduces trade liberalization. Further reduction the following February.
December	Marshall Plan aid ends. ECA is replaced by Mutual Security Administration (MSA).

1952

February	UK Cabinet considers and rejects ROBOT—convertibility with floating rate.
March	EPU short term credit to France.
March	Steering Board for Trade is established.
April	France suspends trade liberalization. Germany re-liberalizes to 75 per cent.
May	France, Germany, Italy, and Benelux sign European Defence Community Treaty.
June	Agreements with Belgium to repay its post-quota credits to EPU.

August	UK exceeds its EPU debtor quota.
October	France exceeds its EPU debtor quota.
October	EPU short term credit to Turkey.
December	First Managing Board report on convertibility.
December	Commonwealth Prime Ministers endorse UK Collective Approach to Convertibility.

1953

February	London Debt Agreement settles German debts.
March	Managing Board report on Future of the Union. Believes move to convertibility premature.
March	Eden and Butler discuss Collective Approach with new US administration. US is unwilling to provide support.
March	OEEC ministers order study of orderly transition from EPU to wider system. UK announces first re-liberalization measures.
March–May	Continental members of Managing Board develop institutional approach to convertibility.
May	Some EPU members reintroduce multilateral arbitrage for foreign exchange transactions.
May	Germany exceeds its EPU creditor quota.
June	EPU is renewed without change.
July	End of war in Korea.
October	Second Managing Board report for ministers on convertibility. Meeting is inconclusive. UK increases liberalization to 75 per cent.
December	Four major EPU creditors have exhausted their quotas and agreed to *rallonges*.

1954

March	UK widens transferability of sterling outside dollar area and reopens London gold market.
April	France resumes partial liberalization with some *de facto* devaluation.
May	Third Managing Board report on convertibility.
June	OEEC Council approves general refurbishing of EPU. Bilateral debt repayment agreements. EPU gold settlements ratio is raised to 50 per cent.
July	First meeting of Ministerial Examination Group on Convertibility. UK seeks acceptance of essential features of its Collective Approach.
July	France withdraws troops from Indo-China.

August	French National Assembly rejects European Defence Community.
September	During IMF annual meeting, UK indicates postponement of convertibility plans.

1955

January	OEEC Council accepts 90 per cent liberalization target. Ministerial Examination Group reviews UK Collective Approach.
February	UK begins to support exchange rate for transferable sterling.
April	EPU special credit to Italy.
April	Robert Marjolin, first OEEC Secretary General, leaves office, and is replaced by René Sergent.
January–July	Managing Board negotiates European Monetary Agreement (EMA).
June	Six Coal and Steel Community countries undertake study of a Common Market.
July	EPU gold settlements ratio is increased to 75 per cent.
August	EMA is signed, ending controversies between UK and Continentals about approach to convertibility.
September	At IMF/IBRD meetings in Istanbul, UK Chancellor denies any intention to let the pound float.

1956

January–February	French Army reinforces military action in Algeria.
June	Intra-European trade is now 89 per cent liberalized.
July	Egypt ends international status of Suez Canal.
October	Uprising begins in Hungary.
October	France receives IMF standby credit, equal to half its quota.
October	UK, France, and Israel land troops in Egypt.
December	UK obtains IMF drawing and standby credit of $1.3 billion and $500 million credit from US Export–Import Bank.

1957

February	OEEC Council decides to begin negotiations for a European Free Trade Area.
March	European Economic Community and Euratom Treaties are signed in Rome.
March	France extends *de facto* devaluation measures.
June	France again suspends all trade liberalization.

August	France further extends *de facto* devaluation.
September	At IMF annual meeting, UK and Germany announce synchronized internal measures and firm determination to take no action concerning their exchange rates.
November	France further extends *de facto* devaluation of franc to full 20 per cent from par value.

1958

1 January	European Economic Community and Euratom come into force.
January	French comprehensive stabilization programme, supported by financial assistance from EPU, OEEC members, IMF, and US.
June	General de Gaulle becomes French Prime Minister, with special powers.
July	EPU releases second half of credits to France.
July	Turkish stabilization programme, supported by credits from EPU, OEEC members, IMF, and US.
September	Managing Board organizes Turkish debt conference.
October	UK Chancellor tells US, Germany, and IMF Managing Director in confidence of possible early move to convertibility.
October	Operation Unicorn begins planning for move and UK Cabinet approves if France concurs.
November	France rejects Free Trade Area. Negotiations are suspended.
December	De Gaulle agrees to further 14.8 per cent devaluation of French franc and reliberalization of trade with Europe.
27 December	Countries representing 72.1 per cent of EPU quotas notify OEEC of intention to terminate participation in EPU.
29 December	Managing Board initiates liquidation of EPU.

1959

1 January	EMA comes into force. Most European currencies become convertible for non-residents.

Glossary of EPU Technical Terms

Accounting Period
: The calendar month, except for the first three months of the EPU and for cases of exchange rate changes.

Agent
: Bank for International Settlements in Basle.

Alternates
: Treasury or central bank officials, designated by EPU Board members with approval of OEEC Council. Exercised function of a Board member if the latter was unable to attend a meeting of the Managing Board. Also held separate meetings to prepare for meetings of the Board.

Automatic Mechanism
: EPU compensations and settlements system.

Compensations
: 1. Offsetting each month of a country's bilateral deficits against the sum of its bilateral surpluses (multilateral compensations).
2. Offsetting, through a reversal of positions, of an accounting surplus or deficit against deficits or surpluses accumulated in earlier accounting periods.

Conditional Aid
: US aid to an OEEC member, conditional on its making an equivalent amount of its own currency available to other OEEC members.

Cumulative Position
: Algebraic sum of all previous monthly accounting positions.

Debt Consolidation
: Bilateral agreements for repaying outstanding debts to and from the EPU, usually on easier terms than those laid down in the EPU liquidation rules.

Drawing Rights
: Under the pre-EPU compensations arrangements, funds made available to other OEEC countries in return for conditional aid.

EPU Quota
: Limits on the creditor and debtor side, within which the cumulative accounting positions of member countries were settled by a combination of credit granted or received and gold received or paid. The original quotas were generally equal to 15 per cent of member countries' payments and receipts for trade and invisible transactions with the OEEC area in 1949.

Existing Resources
: Holdings of other OEEC currencies by EPU members, acquired in pre-EPU years and not subject to repayment on a fixed amortization schedule. Usable in EPU settlements.

Initial Positions	Initial credit balances allotted to countries expected to have a persistent debtor position within the EPU. Initial debit balances allotted to countries expected to have persistent EPU surpluses.
Interim Finance	Unlimited credit granted by central banks to each other during an accounting period.
Invisible Transactions	Import and export of services, such as transport, insurance, and allowances of foreign exchange for tourists.
Liberalization	Elimination of quantitative restrictions (import quotas) on importing goods and services. For items liberalized under the OEEC Code, import licences had to be granted freely for the whole EPU area. Liberalization was also progressively introduced for imports from the dollar area.
Offshore Procurement	Purchases of goods and services from EPU member suppliers for delivery to an aid recipient under a US foreign assistance programme.
Operations	Compensations and settlement of monthly accounting positions.
Rallonges	Extensions of quotas, normally on the creditor side.
Settlements	Discharge of monthly accounting positions after compensations by a combination of credit granted or received and of gold or dollars received or paid, in proportions laid down in the EPU Agreement (and later amendments to the Agreement).
Tranche	A 20 per cent fraction of each country's EPU quota.

Bibliography

PUBLICATIONS

Following is a list of the published materials most consulted and cited. Extensive bibliographies of published materials may be found in many of the books listed below. See particularly OEEC Bibliographies, 1 (1955*b*), Kindleberger (1984), Milward (1984), Cairncross (1985), Hogan (1987).

Bank deutscher Länder (after 1 August 1957, Deutsche Bundesbank), *Monthly and Annual Reports* (1950-9)
Bank for International Settlements, *Statutes* (Basle, 1930)
—— *Annual Reports* for the financial years 1948-59 (Basle, 1949-60)
—— *The Bank for International Settlements and the Basle Meetings 1930-80* (Basle, 1980)
Blancpain, J. P., *Vom Bilateralismus zur Konvertibilität* (Zürich, 1962)
Brittan, S., *The Treasury under the Tories 1951-64* (Harmondsworth, 1964)
Butler, R. A., *The Art of the Possible: The Memoirs of Lord Butler* (London, 1971)
Cairncross, A., 'The First Year of EPU: The Handling of the German Case', unpublished paper (1951)
—— *Years of Recovery*, 1945-51 (London, 1985)
—— 'A Visit to Germany' (*a*) and 'The German Balance of Payments Crisis 1950-51' (*b*). German translations of both manuscripts in: Ludwig-Erhard-Stiftung (1986), listed below
—— 'The UK economic crisis of 1955', unpublished manuscript (1987)
Calvet, P., 'L'Union européenne de paiements', *Le Financement des investissements*, Conference held at the International Banking Summer School, September 1951 (Paris, 1951)
Camdessus, M., *The Evolving International Monetary System: Some Issues*, Deshmukh Memorial Lecture (Bombay, India, October 1988)
Coombs, C. A., *The Arena of International Finance* (New York, 1967)
Department of State, *Foreign Relations of the United States*, Series for each of the years 1949-51, for 1952-4, and for 1955-6. Several volumes in each series (Washington, 1974-86)
Deshormes, E., 'Camille Gutt—Premier Directeur Général du Fonds monétaire international 1946-51', Supplement to *Revue de la Banque* (Brussels, July 1986)
Deutsche Bundesbank, *Währung und Wirtschaft in Deutschland 1876-1975* (Frankfurt, 1976)
—— *40 Jahre Deutsche Mark: Monetäre Statistiken 1948-1987* (Frankfurt, 1988)
Diebold, W., *Trade and Payments in Western Europe* (New York, 1952)
Economic Commission for Europe, *A Survey of the Economic Situation and Prospects of Europe* (Geneva, 1948)

Economic Commission for Europe, *Economic Survey of Europe in 1948* (Geneva, 1949)

Economic Cooperation Administration (ECA), *A Report on Recovery Progress and United States Aid* (Washington, 1949)

Emminger, O., 'Die Europaeische Zahlungsunion als Etappe der europaeischen Waehrungs-Neuordnung', *Zeitschrift für die gesamte Staatswissenschaft*, 107. 4 (1951)

—— 'The D-Mark in the Conflict between Internal and External Equilibrium 1948-75', *Essays in International Finance*, 122 (Princeton, NJ, June 1977)

—— *D-Mark, Dollar, Währungskrisen* (Stuttgart, 1986)

—— 'Ordnungs und währungspolitische Probleme der Korea-Krise', in Ludwig-Erhard-Stiftung (1986), listed below

European Payments Union, *Annual Reports of the Managing Board* for each financial year (Paris, 1951-9)

Gilbert, M., *Quest for World Monetary Order* (New York, 1980)

Guindey, G., 'The International Monetary Tangle: Myths and Realities', *International Journal of Politics* (New York, Spring 1977). Also published as book (White Plains, NY, 1977). French edition (1973)

Hale, W., *The Political and Economic Development of Modern Turkey* (London, 1981)

Hansard, *Parliamentary Debates, House of Commons, Official Report* (London, 1953)

Hoffman, S. and Maier, C. (eds.), *The Marshall Plan: A Retrospective* (Boulder, Colorado, 1984)

Hogan, M. J., *The Marshall Plan: America, Britain and the Reconstruction of Western Europe, 1947-52* (Cambridge and New York, 1987)

Horsefield, J. K., *The International Monetary Fund 1945-1965*, i, *Chronicles* (Washington, 1969)

International Bank for Reconstruction and Development (World Bank), *Turkey: Prospects and Problems of an Expanding Economy* (Washington, 1975)

International Monetary Fund, *Annual Reports*, 1949-60 (Washington)

—— *International Financial Statistical Yearbooks* (Washington, annually)

Jacobsson, E. E., *A Life for Sound Money: Per Jacobsson, his Biography* (Oxford, 1979)

Jones, J. M., *The Fifteen Weeks* (New York, 1955)

Kahn, R. F., 'The European Payments Union', *Economica* (London, Aug. 1950), 17.5. 306-16

Kindleberger, C. P., *A Financial History of Western Europe* (London, 1984)

Koch, H., *Histoire de la Banque de France et de la Monnaie sous la IVᵉ République* (Paris, 1983)

Ludwig-Erhard-Stiftung, *Die Korea Krise als ordnungspolitische Herausforderung der deutschen Wirtschaftspolitik: Texte und Dokumente* (Stuttgart and New York, 1986)

Lüthy, H., *Frankreichs Uhren gehen anders* (Zurich, 1954). English edition: *The State of France* (London, 1955)

MacDougall, D., *The World Dollar Problem* (London, 1957)

Maddison, A., *Phases of Capitalist Development* (Oxford and New York, 1982)

Marjolin, R., *Le Travail d'une vie* (Paris, 1986)

Matthews, R. C. O., Feinstein, C. H., and Odling-Smee, J. *British Economic Growth 1865-1973* (Oxford, 1982)

Mayne, R., *The Recovery of Europe: From Devastation to Unity* (New York, 1970)

Milward, A. S., *The Reconstruction of Western Europe, 1945-51* (London, 1984)

Möller, H., 'The Reconstruction of the International Economic Order and the Integration of the Federal Republic into the World Economy', *Zeitschrift für die gesamte Staatswissenschaft* (Tübingen, 1981), 137. 344-6

Organisation for Economic Co-operation and Development, *Main Economic Indicators, 1955-1971* (Paris, 1973)

—— *From Marshall Plan to Global Interdependence* (Paris, 1978)

Organisation for European Economic Co-operation, *Convention for European Economic Cooperation* (Paris, 1948)

—— *A European Payments Union and the Rules of Commercial Policy to be Followed by Member Countries* (Paris, 1950) (*a*)

—— *Agreement for the Establishment of a European Payments Union* (Paris, 1950) (*b*)

—— *Directives for the Application of the Agreement for the Establishment of a European Payments Union* (Paris, 1950) (*c*)

—— *Financial Stability and the Fight against Inflation* (Paris, 1951)

—— *Liberalisation of Europe's Dollar Trade* (Paris, 1955) (*a*)

—— *OEEC Bibliographies: European Payments Union, Convertibility of Currencies*, 1 (Paris, 1955) (*b*)

—— *Liberalisation of Europe's Dollar Trade: Second Report* (Paris, 1957)

—— *Annual Reports*, 1-12 (Paris, 1949-61)

Pollard, S., *The Integration of the European Economy Since 1815* (London, 1981)

Posthuma, S., *Analyses en Beschouwingen in Retrospect* (Leiden/Antwerpen, 1982)

Rees, G. L., *Britain and the Postwar European Payments System* (Cardiff, 1963)

Roll, E. (Lord), *Crowded Hours* (London, 1985)

Roosa, R. V., *The Dollar Problem and World Liquidity* (New York, 1967)

Rossy, M. P., *L'Union européenne de paiements . . . et après* (Basle, 1953)

Sayers, R. S., *Financial Policy 1939-45* (History of the Second World War, United Kingdom Civil Series; London, 1956)

Schelling, T. C., 'International Cost-Sharing Arrangements', *Essays in International Finance*, 24 (Princeton, NJ, 1955)

Schleiminger, G., 'Europäische Zahlungsunion', *Handwörterbuch der Wirtschaftswissenschaft* (Stuttgart and New York, 1979)

Schmieding, H., *Strategien zum Abbau von Handelschemmnissen* (Referat vor der Jahrestagung des Vereins für Sozialpolitik; Freiburg, 1988)

Solomon, R., *The International Monetary System, 1945-1981* (New York, 1982)

Southard, F., 'The Evolution of the International Monetary Fund', *Essays in International Finance*, 135 (Princeton, NJ, 1979)

Stolper, G., Häuser, K., Borchardt, K., *The German Economy 1870 to the Present*, translated by Toni Stolper (New York, Chicago, San Francisco, and Atlanta, 1967)

Sturc, E., 'Stabilisation Policies: Experience of Some European Countries in the 1950s', International Monetary Fund *Staff Papers*, 15. 2 (Washington, 1968), 197–217

Triffin, R., *Europe and the Money Muddle* (New Haven, 1957)

de Vries, M. G., *Balance of Payments Adjustment, 1945 to 1986: The IMF Experience* (Washington, 1987)

de Vries, M. G., Horsefield, J. K., *et al.*, *The International Monetary Fund 1945–1965*, ii, *Analysis* (Washington, 1969)

Wexler, I., *The Marshall Plan Revisited* (Westport, Connecticut, 1983)

Williams, J. H., *Post War Monetary Plans and other Essays* (New York, 1945)

—— *Economic Stability in the Modern World*, Stamp Memorial Lecture (London, 1952)

—— *Economic Stability in a Changing World* (New York, 1953)

Williams, P. M., *Hugh Gaitskell: A Political Biography* (London, 1979)

Wissenschaftlicher Beirat des Bundesministerium für Wirtschaft, *Wirtschaftliche Problematik der deutschen Exportüberschüsse: Gutachten* (Bonn, 1957)

OFFICIAL RECORDS AND DOCUMENTS

The principal sources for this book are original records and documents. A variety of primary source materials were reviewed and pertinent documents collected or copied as necessary. These documents have been deposited in two archival collections of EPU-related materials, one at the Organisation for Economic Co-operation and Development (OECD) and the other at the Bank for International Settlements (BIS).

Footnotes in the text use the indicated abbreviations for the primary source and reference numbers to the primary source file. Cited documents are in one or both of the EPU archives described below.

The OECD Archive

The OECD Archive on the EPU was assembled in chronological order by Harry Travers. It consists of 66 numbered binders and additional files and reports, including national documents and materials extracted from files of the Organisation for European Economic Co-operation (OEEC).

OEEC

Consultative Group of Ministers: Minutes (COM/M)

Council Documents: Decisions, Statements, and Reports to the Council (C)

Council Minutes (C/M)

European Payments Union: Managing Board Documents (MBC)

—— Managing Board Minutes (MBC/M)

Executive Committee Minutes (CE/M)

Financial Experts: subgroup of Executive Committee Working Party No. 3 (unnumbered)

Intra-European Payments Branch: Internal Secretariat Memoranda (SP/DI)
Intra-European Payments Committee: Documents (PC)
—— Minutes (PC/M)
Joint Trade and Intra-European Payments Committee: Documents (TP)
—— Minutes (TP/M)
Ministerial Group on Convertibility: Documents (GMC)
—— Minutes (GMC/M)
Steering Board for Trade: Reports (SB)
Trade and Finance Directorate: Draft Reports (TP/DI and TFD/DL)
—— Internal Secretariat Memoranda (TFD)
—— Memoranda to delegations, boards, and committees (TFD/TD)
Trade Committee: Reports (TC)

United Kingdom
  Cabinet Committees:
    Cabinet Minutes (CM)
    Cabinet Papers (CP)
    Economic Policy Committee (EPC)
    Minutes and Memoranda (CAB 130 and 134)
  Prime Minister's Office:
    1945-51 (PREM 8)
    1952-4 (PREM 11)
  Travers Notes based on official UK documents
  Treasury:
    European Economic Cooperation Committee (T 232)
    Marshall Aid Committee (MAC) (T 237)

Belgium
  Extracts from Minutes of the Board of the National Bank of Belgium,
  1950-1 (PV)

Switzerland
  Federal Archives: several reports by Mr Paul Rossy and Ambassador Gérard
  Bauer
  Swiss National Bank: Extracts from Minutes of the Council and the Bank
  Committee, 1947-59

United States
  Federal Reserve System: Central Files (1950-5)
  National Archives (1949 and 1950)

The BIS Archive

The BIS Archive on the EPU is in two parts. The first consists of files of
materials collected and maintained during the EPU era. The second contains

copies of documents from various primary sources, assembled and deposited by the authors.

The first part includes 51 numbered boxes of materials dating from the first meetings of the CEEC financial experts in 1947 through the IEPS agreements and the EPU itself. Also two bound volumes of *aides-mémoire* circulated by the Agent to central banks, four bound volumes of minutes of the 108 meetings of the Managing Board, and two boxes of the Agent's Unofficial Notes, taken during Board meetings.

The second part consists of nineteen boxes of selected documents from various official archives. One box contains interviews conducted by the authors.

Materials in each box are arranged chronologically. Access to documents from the files of the Bank of England, National Bank of Belgium, and the Federal Republic of Germany requires prior permission from their authorities.

United Kingdom
   Bank of England, 1949–58:
      Documents from numbered Bank files, arranged chronologically. Contains Cabinet and Treasury documents as well as Bank memoranda and reports
   Public Records Office, 1951–6 (PRO):
      Cabinet Committees (CAB 134)
      Cabinet Minutes and Conclusions (CAB 128)
      Prime Minister's Office (PREM 11)
      Treasury:
         Economic Section (T 230)
         European Economic Cooperation Committee (T 232)
         Marshall Aid Committee (T 237)
         Overseas Finance Division (T 236)

Belgium
   National Bank of Belgium, 1951–8:
      Extracts from Deliberations of the Regency Council (unnumbered)
      Extracts from Minutes of meetings of the Bank Board (PV)

Federal Republic of Germany
   Von Mangoldt Reports (G)

United States
   Federal Reserve System, Central Files, 1949–56
   Harry S. Truman Library, Independence, Missouri, Oral History Interviews with Lincoln Gordon, Hubert Havlik, and Milton Katz
   US National Archives (US Archives):
      Department of State Files, 1949–54 (840)
   ECA (includes files of successor agencies, MSA and FOA), 1949–55 (RG 286, 6/66)
      Sub-file designations and reference numbers:
         Administrator (Hoffman) (42/6 and 7)

Assistant Administrator for Program (Bissell) (44–50)
Special Assistant to Assistant Administrator (Geiger) (50/3–10)
US Delegation in Paris:
Finance and Trade Division (Havlik) (30/6 to 32/1)
Special Assistant for Staff Planning (Tasca) (26/5)
Special Representative (Harriman) (26/1)
Treasury NAC Files, 1945–8 (Lot 60 D 137)

The US Files listed above include:
Documents prior to 1955 from National Archives; messages after 1955 from Department of State in response Freedom of Information Act Request No. 8603577
ECA and US del. memoranda, communications with OEEC Secretariat and other national delegations
Telegrams and Airgrams from US del. to OEEC, sent to Washington and frequently to posts in OEEC capitals. Most report Managing Board meetings (REPTO, TOECO, and TOPOL)
Telegrams from Washington to US del. to OEEC (ECA, MSA, FOA, Department of State) (TOREP, ECOTO, and POLTO)

Index

Note: Abbreviations are used in the index as follows: CEEC = Committee for European Economic Cooperation; EDC = European Defence Community; EMA = European Monetary Agreement; EPU = European Payments Union; GATT = General Agreement on Tariffs and Trade; IEPS = Intra-European Payments and Compensations Scheme; IMF = International Monetary Fund; MSA = US Mutual Security Administration; OEEC = Organization for European Economic Cooperation

Index compiled by Meg Davies (Society of Indexers)